Taste of Home

Everyday

light
meals

Taste of Home
B O O K S

REIMAN MEDIA GROUP, INC. • GREENDALE, WISCONSIN

A TASTE OF HOME/READER'S DIGEST BOOK

Editor: Jennifer Olski

Art Director: Lori Arndt

Layout Designer: Nancy Novak

Proofreader: Linne Bruskewitz

Indexer: Jean Steiner

Editorial Assistant: Barb Czysz

Recipe Testing and Editing: Taste of Home Test Kitchen
Diane Werner, RD
Peggy Woodward, RD

Food Photography: Reiman Photo Studio

Cover Photography: Rob Hagen

Senior Editor, Retail Books: Jennifer Olski

Vice President/Executive Editor, Books: Heidi Reuter Lloyd

Creative Director: Ardyth Cope

Senior Vice President/Editor in Chief: Catherine Cassidy

President: Barbara Newton

Founder: Roy Reiman

International Standard Book Number (10): 0-89821-518-8
International Standard Book Number (13): 978-0-89821-518-2

Library of Congress Control Number: 2006926594

Printed in China.
1 3 5 7 9 10 8 6 4 2

Healthy choices for delicious, fuss-free family dishes.

With the dozens of preplanned menus inside *Everyday Light Meals,* you can enjoy the tantalizing flavors of classic comfort foods every night of the week without loading up on extra calories, fat, sodium or carbs...or spending hours getting dinner on the table.

These 489 tasty recipes have all been family-approved by health-conscious home cooks like you.

Every recipe has been double-tested by the home economists on the *Taste of Home* Test Kitchen staff and then reviewed by our team of Registered Dietitians. That means you're always guaranteed delicious, nutritious and reliable results every time.

93 Meals, Unlimited Possibilities
The first half of this cookbook includes 93 menus for family dinners and special occasions. Each one includes recipes for two courses, plus recommendations for appealing partners to round out your meal.

You'll find more than 300 additional recipes in the second half of the book to help you expand your menu and mix and match dishes to suit your family's tastes. With so many options, you'll have months of meal ideas ready to go.

Complete Nutrition Facts
All recipes in this book fit into a balanced diet for healthy adults. Every recipe also includes complete Nutrition Facts, calculated following these guidelines:

- When a choice of ingredients is given in a recipe (such as 1/3 cup of sour cream or plain yogurt), the first ingredient listed is always the one calculated in the Nutrition Facts.

- When a range is given for an ingredient (such as 2 to 3 teaspoons), we calculate the first amount given.

- Only the amount of marinade absorbed during preparation is calculated.

- Garnishes listed in recipes are typically included in calculations.

Helpful Health Categories
Some people may be watching specific foods and nutrients in their diet, so we've included four different at-a-glance icons to help you identify dishes best suited to your own nutritional needs. Refer to the health categories index on page 336 to find recipes that correspond to your specific needs.

Diabetic Exchanges are assigned to recipes in accordance with the guidelines from the American Diabetic and American Dietetic Associations. The majority of recipes in this book are suitable for diabetics.

At-a-Glance Icons

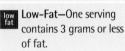

low fat **Low-Fat**—One serving contains 3 grams or less of fat.

low sodium **Low-Sodium**—One serving contains 140 milligrams or less of sodium.

low carb **Low-Carbohydrate**—One serving contains 15 grams or less of carbohydrates.

meat less **Meatless**—Appetizers, salads, breads, side dishes and entrees that contain no meat. In this book, meatless icons are assigned for breads only in the meal chapters. However, all recipes in the Breads chapter are meatless. Although the icon has been omitted on those recipes, they will still be categorized as meatless in the index.

page 136

Table of Contents

page 24

page 174

page 188

page 209

page 319

Use these simple strategies to lighten up your family meals and emphasize balanced nutrition.

Planning a delicious meal that satisfies everyone at the dinner table can be quite a challenge. Add in trying to balance different dietary needs or simply incorporating sound nutrition, and it all starts to feel impossible.

But don't toss in the towel and head for the drive-through just yet! The USDA's Dietary Guidelines for Americans help take some of the guesswork out of nutritionally balanced eating.

Gone are the days of the traditional, bottom-heavy food pyramid once used to illustrate USDA recommendations. Today's Food Pyramid emphasizes making smart choices from every food group, balancing the amount of calories consumed with increased physical activity and getting the most nutrition out of those calories.

The result is a lifestyle approach—not just a diet—focused on moderation, variety and personalization that can help you reduce your risk of heart disease, diabetes, osteoporosis or cancer and can increase your chances for a longer life.

Build on the Basics
Eating smart is the first step toward healthier living. According to the USDA guidelines, a healthy diet is one that emphasizes fruits, vegetables, whole grains and fat-free or low-fat milk and milk products. It also includes lean meats, poultry, fish, beans, eggs and nuts. Finally, a healthy diet is low in saturated fats, trans fats, cholesterol, sodium and added sugars.

Mix Up Your Choices
Strive for variety in your daily meals, and you'll see how easy it is to hit your nutritional recommendations. Consider these pointers:

Focus on fruit. Fruit provides essential vitamins, fiber and antioxidants which help head off heart disease and prevent strokes. Eat a variety of fresh, frozen, canned and dried fruits, avoiding juices, which often have added sugar.

Vary your veggies. Vegetables help lower the risk of type 2 diabetes and may prevent cancer, lower blood pressure or drop high cholesterol levels. The more veggies you eat, the better! So include plenty of colorful

MyPyramid.gov
STEPS TO A HEALTHIER YOU

Recommended Daily Intake by Pyramid Group *(based on a 2,000-calorie diet)*

Group	Daily Amount	# of Servings	Serving Size	Calories Per Serving
Grains	6 oz.	6	1 oz.	80-100
Veggies	2-1/2 cups	5	1/2 cup	25-40
Fruits	2 cups	2	1 cup	60-80
Fats	6 tbsp.	6	1 teaspoon	40
Milk	3 cups	3	1 cup	90-120
Protein	5-1/2 oz.	2	3 oz.	165-225

options such as broccoli, carrots, cauliflower and beans; and eat plenty of dark-green leafy foods like spinach, kale or leaf lettuces. But pass on the deep-fried varieties such as French fries and onion rings.

Get your calcium-rich foods. For stronger bones, rely on protein-rich, calcium-fortified foods such as milk, yogurt and cheese. Reach for the low-fat or fat-free varieties and take it easy on whole milk and full-fat yogurt and cheeses. If you don't or can't consume milk, you can still meet your daily requirements by choosing lactose-free milk products or other calcium-fortified foods.

Make half your grains whole. Look to whole grains as your primary source of carbohydrates. Cut back on refined grains like white bread, white rice or ready-to-eat cereals high in sugars or fats. Then focus on whole-grain breads, brown rice, oatmeal and whole-wheat pastas.

Go lean with protein. Bake, broil or grill lean meats and poultry, and add in more fish, beans, peas, nuts and seeds. The variety of protein sources will provide essential amino acids, minerals and vitamins necessary for building muscle and tissue.

Know your fats. Choose foods low in saturated fats. Good bets are ones that use olive, canola, peanut or walnut oils (monounsaturated) or corn, soybean or safflower oils (polyunsaturated). Aim for zero trans fats—a big culprit in commercial foods and restaurant foods.

Make the Most Out of Your Calories
In general, how much of these foods you eat should depend on your gender, age and level of physical activity. For a personalized approach to the Food Pyramid, visit *www.mypyramid.gov* for tools to help build a unique plan of your own.

Let's say you get 2,000 calories per day, according to the dietary guidelines. You could use up that entire amount on just a few calorie-packed choices. But chances are, you won't get all the vitamins and nutrients your body needs to be healthy.

When deciding which foods offer the most benefits for the calories, ask yourself these questions:

Is this food providing nutrients or empty calories? Try baked whole wheat pita chips with hummus instead of fat-laden potato chips and dip.

- **Fruit:** Keep servings to about the size of your fist.
- **Cheese:** Enjoy pieces that are about the size of your thumb.

By monitoring serving sizes, you might find that you can enjoy a variety of items normally "off-limits" when you're watching your weight. For example, the carbohydrates and fat in a cake may not be an issue if a sensibly sized slice is served as opposed to a large wedge. Simply balance a slight indulgence by skimming back on serving sizes later in the day.

Know the Nutrition Facts

At a glance, you'll be able to quickly make wise food choices when you rely on the Nutrition Facts included on food labels—and all the recipes in this book. To get started, familiarize yourself with the recommended daily allowances of nutrients, and then try these tips:

- **Check and compare.** Use the "% Daily Value" column when possible to see how a food stacks up. A 5% daily value or less is low, 20% daily value or more is high.
- **Aim high.** Look for options rich in potassium, fiber, vitamins A and C, calcium and iron.
- **Settle for less.** Limit saturated fats to less than 10% of your total calories and consume no more than 300 mg of cholesterol daily. Cap sodium at 1,500 mg daily.

If you're counting your carbohydrate choices or exchanges, you should know that 1 choice or exchange contains 15 grams of carbohydrates.

Pay attention to the serving size listed with the Nutrition Facts and notice how many servings you're actually

How can I increase the nutrients in my meal? Instead of tortillas or taco shells, wrap taco meat in leaves of romaine lettuce.

How does this food fit into the big picture? If you're craving a snack and you've yet to have a vegetable, munch on cucumber slices or carrot sticks.

Living in a world of super-sized fare, many people forget that the amount of food they eat is just as important as the types of food they choose. Keep these visual cues in mind when filling your plate or reaching for a snack:

- **Meat:** A reasonable serving should be the size of a deck of cards.

Portion Pointers

Try these tips to better control serving sizes:

- Ask for a to-go container at restaurants and pack the food you will take home before you start eating.

- Avoid serving meals "family style." Portion food onto a plate and bring it to the table.

- Use smaller dinner plates.

- Don't eat directly from bags or cartons. Set the food on a plate or napkin and put the rest away.

eating of a particular food. Your first inclination might be to scoop up a big spoonful, which could be twice the actual size of a serving.

Take time to read the ingredient list on packaged foods, too, to avoid sugar overload. Make sure that added sugars are not one of the first few ingredients. Some names for added sugars include sucrose, glucose, high fructose corn syrup, corn syrup and fructose. Sugar serves up lots of calories with few nutrients, so look for foods and beverages without these extras.

Get Physical
If all this information makes you want to run away, that's not such a bad idea! Combining savvy food choices with increased physical activity is the final part of creating a healthy lifestyle for yourself or your family.

Regular, moderate physical activity helps you manage body weight, improve fitness and lower the risk of heart disease, type 2 diabetes and high blood pressure. Before starting

an exercise program, consult your physician for recommendations tailored to your level of fitness and appropriate for your health. For better results, work toward these goals:

- Be physically active for at least 30 minutes most days of the week.
- Increasing the intensity or the amount of time that you are physically active can have even greater health benefits and may be needed to control body weight. About 60 minutes a day may be needed to prevent weight gain.
- Children and teens should be physically active for 60 minutes every day.

Taking the First Steps
Now that you're armed with the right information and a big batch of light-done-right recipes, you're ready to start planning nutritious meals the whole family will enjoy! Use the 93 meal ideas that begin on the next page as inspiration for a lifetime of good health.

Recommended Daily Nutrition Guide
(based on a 2,000-calorie diet)

Nutrient	Amount*
Total Fat	65 g
Saturated fat	20 g
Cholesterol	300 mg
Sodium	2400 mg
Potassium	3500 mg
Total carbohydrate	300 g
Fiber	25 g
Protein	50 g
Vitamin A	5000 IU
Vitamin C	60 mg
Calcium	1000 mg
Iron	18 mg
Vitamin D	400 IU
Vitamin E	30 IU
Vitamin K	80 mcg
Thiamin	1.5 mg
Riboflavin	1.7 mg
Niacin	20 mg
Vitamin B6	2 mg
Folate	400 mcg
Vitamin B12	6 mcg
Biotin	300 mcg
Pantothenic acid	10 mg
Phosphorus	1000 mg
Iodine	150 mcg
Magnesium	400 mg
Zinc	15 mg
Selenium	70 mcg
Copper	2 mg
Manganese	2 mg
Chromium	120 mcg
Molybdenum	75 mcg
Chloride	3400 mg

* grams (g)
milligrams (mg)
International Unit (IU)
micrograms (mcg)

Toss together a **tangy** salad for lunch or dinner.
It's **fast, filling** fare when partnered
with **piping-hot** bread.

You'll get plenty of greens with this beefy salad featuring both asparagus and broccoli. Serve it with a loaf of fresh-baked bread. The quick-rise yeast hurries along the preparation of these hearty loaves.

Beefy Broccoli Asparagus Salad

low carb

Betty Rassette, Salina, Kansas

PREP: 10 MIN. **BROIL:** 15 MIN. + CHILLING

3/4	pound boneless beef sirloin steak
8	cups water
4	cups cut fresh asparagus (1-inch pieces)
2	cups fresh broccoli florets
1/4	cup reduced-sodium soy sauce
2	tablespoons white wine vinegar
4-1/2	teaspoons sesame oil
1	teaspoon minced fresh gingerroot
2	teaspoons sugar

Dash pepper

Place steak on a broiler pan coated with nonstick cooking spray. Broil 3-4 in. from the heat for 6-10 minutes on each side or until meat reaches desired doneness (for medium-rare, a meat thermometer should read 145°; medium, 160°; well-done, 170°); cool completely.

In a large saucepan, bring water to a boil. Add asparagus and broccoli; cover and cook for 3 minutes. Drain and immediately place vegetables in ice water. Drain and pat dry; refrigerate.

For dressing, in a jar with a tight-fitting lid, combine the soy sauce, vinegar, oil, ginger, sugar and pepper; shake well. Thinly slice beef and place in a bowl; add dressing and toss to coat. Cover and refrigerate for 1 hour. Just before serving, add vegetables and toss to coat. **YIELD:** 4 SERVINGS.

Nutrition Facts: One serving (1-1/4 cups) equals:
229 calories
10 g fat (2 g saturated fat)
56 mg cholesterol
670 mg sodium
11 g carbohydrate
3 g fiber
24 g protein

Diabetic Exchanges: 2 lean meat, 2 vegetable, 1 fat.

Cheddar-Topped English Muffin Bread

low fat meat less

Anne Smithson, Cary, North Carolina

PREP: 15 MIN. + RISING **BAKE:** 25 MIN.

2	tablespoons cornmeal
5	cups all-purpose flour
2	packages (1/4 ounce *each*) quick-rise yeast
1	tablespoon sugar
2	teaspoons salt
1/4	teaspoon baking soda
2	cups warm fat-free milk (120° to 130°)
1/2	cup warm water (120° to 130°)
1/2	cup shredded reduced-fat cheddar cheese

Coat two 8-in. x 4-in. x 2-in. loaf pans with nonstick cooking spray; sprinkle with cornmeal and set aside.

In a mixing bowl, combine 3 cups flour, yeast, sugar, salt and baking soda. Add milk and water; beat until smooth. Stir in remaining flour (dough will be sticky). Transfer to prepared pans. Cover and let rise in a warm place for 30 minutes.

Sprinkle with cheese. Bake at 400° for 25-30 minutes or until golden brown. Remove from pans and cool on wire racks. **YIELD:** 2 LOAVES (12 SLICES EACH).

Nutrition Facts: One serving (1 slice) equals:
112 calories
trace fat (trace saturated fat)
2 mg cholesterol
235 mg sodium
22 g carbohydrate
1 g fiber
4 g protein

Diabetic Exchange: 1-1/2 starch.

Appealing Partners

- Iced herbal tea
- Fat-free pound cake with sliced strawberries

Practical Tips

In a pinch, you can use frozen vegetables in place of fresh ones in the salad. Buy bags of frozen broccoli florets and asparagus, and measure out the amounts listed. Once thawed, cook the veggies as directed in the recipe.

If you like your bread toasted, eliminate the cheese from the Cheddar-Topped English Muffin Bread before baking. Otherwise, the cheese may burn in the toaster.

Just a **few minutes** the night before **saves time** when making this **classic combo** for a weeknight dinner.

The tasty gravy on this tender pot roast is jazzed up with Dijon mustard and Worcestershire sauce. Take advantage of reduced-fat and fat-free dairy products to make the accompanying potatoes super creamy.

Sweet 'n' Tangy Pot Roast

Carol Mulligan, Honeoye Falls, New York

PREP: 10 MIN. **COOK:** 9 HOURS 30 MIN.

- 1 boneless beef chuck roast (3 pounds)
- 1/2 teaspoon salt
- 1/2 teaspoon pepper
- 1 cup water
- 1 cup ketchup
- 1/4 cup red wine *or* beef broth
- 1 envelope brown gravy mix
- 2 teaspoons Dijon mustard
- 1 teaspoon Worcestershire sauce
- 1/8 teaspoon garlic powder
- 3 tablespoons cornstarch
- 1/4 cup cold water

Cut meat in half and place in a 5-qt. slow cooker. Sprinkle with salt and pepper. In a bowl, combine the water, ketchup, wine or broth, gravy mix, mustard, Worcestershire sauce and garlic powder; pour over meat. Cover and cook on low for 9-10 hours or until meat is tender.

Combine cornstarch and cold water until smooth. Stir into slow cooker. Cover and cook on high for 30 minutes or until gravy is thickened. Remove meat from slow cooker. Slice and serve with gravy. **YIELD:** 8 SERVINGS.

Nutrition Facts: One serving (3 ounces cooked beef with 1/2 cup gravy) equals:
- 249 calories
- 8 g fat (3 g saturated fat)
- 89 mg cholesterol
- 748 mg sodium
- 13 g carbohydrate
- 1 g fiber
- 30 g protein

Diabetic Exchanges: 3 lean meat, 1 starch.

Appealing Partners

- Torn romaine with low-fat vinaigrette
- Sauteed broccoli florets

Practical Tips

If you don't get the entree into the slow cooker in the morning, assemble it at lunchtime. Then simmer it in the slow cooker on high for 4-6 hours.

Don't have time to cook the potatoes before baking the casserole? Substitute 2-1/2 to 3 cups frozen hash browns that have been thawed or use cooked sliced home fries available in packages in the dairy section of most grocery stores.

Supreme Potato Casserole

Joy Allen, Forsyth, Georgia

PREP: 45 MIN. **BAKE:** 45 MIN.

- 3 medium potatoes (about 1-1/2 pounds)
- 1 cup (8 ounces) fat-free cottage cheese
- 1/2 cup reduced-fat sour cream
- 1 tablespoon fat-free milk
- 1 teaspoon sugar
- 1/2 teaspoon salt
- 1/8 teaspoon garlic powder
- 2 tablespoons sliced green onion
- 1/2 cup shredded reduced-fat cheddar cheese

Place potatoes in a large saucepan; cover with water. Cover and bring to a boil. Reduce heat; cook for 10-15 minutes or until tender. Drain. Peel potatoes and cut into cubes.

In a blender or food processor, combine the cottage cheese, sour cream, milk, sugar, salt and garlic powder; cover and process until smooth. In a large bowl, combine potatoes, processed cottage cheese mixture and green onion.

Pour into a 1-qt. baking dish coated with nonstick cooking spray. Bake, uncovered, at 350° for 30 minutes; sprinkle with cheese. Bake 15 minutes longer or until the cheese is melted. **YIELD:** 6 SERVINGS.

Nutrition Facts: One serving (1/2 cup) equals:
- 158 calories
- 3 g fat (2 g saturated fat)
- 15 mg cholesterol
- 391 mg sodium
- 24 g carbohydrate
- 2 g fiber
- 12 g protein

Diabetic Exchanges: 1-1/2 starch, 1 lean meat.

For a satisfying **meal-in-one** dish, start with this oven-baked favorite. Then **surprise** your hungry bunch with a **chewy, chocolate** treat!

A layer of seasoned ground beef and carrots is the perfect base for freshly mashed potatoes. Since your family will fill up fast on this traditional casserole, offer them a light dessert. The powdered sugar makes these chocolate cookies look extra special.

Appealing Partners

- Steamed broccoli
- Low-fat milk

Practical Tips

If you have leftover mashed potatoes, use them instead of cooking the potatoes for Shepherd's Pie. Eliminate the milk and butter, too.

The batch of cookies makes 3-1/2 dozen. Set aside some for dessert, then store the rest in an airtight container to add to brown-bag lunches. These yummy treats are best eaten within 3-5 days.

Shepherd's Pie

Carolyn Wolbers, Loveland, Ohio

PREP: 30 MIN. **BAKE:** 40 MIN.

- 6 medium potatoes
- 1 pound carrots, cut into 1/4-inch slices
- 1-1/2 pounds lean ground beef
- 1 large onion, chopped
- 1 jar (12 ounces) fat-free beef gravy
- 1 teaspoon salt, *divided*
- 1/2 teaspoon rubbed sage
- 1/2 teaspoon dried thyme
- 1/4 teaspoon dried rosemary, crushed
- 1/4 teaspoon pepper
- 1/3 cup fat-free milk
- 1 tablespoon butter
- 2 tablespoons shredded Parmesan cheese

Peel and cube the potatoes; place in a large saucepan and cover with water. Bring to a boil over medium-high heat; cover and cook for 20 minutes or until tender. Add 1 in. of water to another saucepan; add carrots. Bring to a boil. Reduce heat; cover and simmer until crisp-tender, about 7-9 minutes. Drain.

In a large nonstick skillet, cook beef and onion over medium heat until meat is no longer pink; drain. Stir in the carrots, gravy, 1/2 teaspoon salt, sage, thyme, rosemary and pepper. Transfer to a shallow 3-qt. baking dish coated with nonstick cooking spray.

Drain the potatoes; mash with milk, butter and remaining salt. Spread over meat mixture. Sprinkle with Parmesan cheese. Bake, uncovered, at 375° for 40-45 minutes or until heated through. **YIELD:** 6 SERVINGS.

Nutrition Facts: One serving (1 cup) equals:
- 390 calories
- 13 g fat (6 g saturated fat)
- 53 mg cholesterol
- 859 mg sodium
- 43 g carbohydrate
- 6 g fiber
- 30 g protein

Diabetic Exchanges: 3 lean meat, 2 starch, 2 vegetable, 1/2 fat.

Crinkle-Top Chocolate Cookies

Maria Groff, Ephrata, Pennsylvania

PREP: 15 MIN. + CHILLING
BAKE: 10 MIN. PER BATCH

- 2 cups (12 ounces) semisweet chocolate chips, *divided*
- 2 tablespoons butter, softened
- 1 cup sugar
- 2 egg whites
- 1-1/2 teaspoons vanilla extract
- 1-1/2 cups all-purpose flour
- 1-1/2 teaspoons baking powder
- 1/4 teaspoon salt
- 1/4 cup water
- 1/2 cup confectioners' sugar

In a microwave, melt 1 cup chocolate chips. Stir until smooth; set aside. In a small mixing bowl, beat butter and sugar until crumbly, about 2 minutes. Add egg whites and vanilla; beat well. Stir in melted chocolate.

Combine the flour, baking powder and salt; gradually add to butter mixture alternately with water. Stir in remaining chocolate chips. Cover and refrigerate for 2 hours or until easy to handle.

Shape dough into 1-in. balls. Roll in confectioners' sugar. Place 2 in. apart on baking sheets coated with nonstick cooking spray. Bake at 350° for 10-12 minutes or until set. Remove to wire racks to cool. **YIELD:** 3-1/2 DOZEN.

Nutrition Facts: One serving (1 cookie) equals:
- 84 calories
- 3 g fat (2 g saturated fat)
- 1 mg cholesterol
- 31 mg sodium
- 15 g carbohydrate
- 1 g fiber
- 1 g protein

Diabetic Exchange: 1 starch.

Whip up a four-ingredient marinade and you're on your way to a **tasty meal** on the table pronto!

The citrus zing of this easy marinade turns a regular cut of meat into a mouth-watering meal. Round it out with a scoop of these vegetables whose quick start comes from a packet of onion soup mix.

Grilled Citrus Steak

`low carb`

Joan Whyte-Elliott, Fenelon Falls, Ontario

PREP: 5 MIN. + MARINATING   **GRILL:** 40 MIN.

- 2/3 cup reduced-sugar orange marmalade
- 1/3 cup reduced-sodium soy sauce
- 1/3 cup lemon juice
- 1 tablespoon canola oil
- 2 pounds boneless beef top round steak (2 inches thick)

In a bowl, combine the orange marmalade, soy sauce, lemon juice and oil; mix well. Pour 1 cup marinade into a large resealable plastic bag. Score the surface of the steak with shallow diagonal cuts, making diamond shapes. Add the steak to the marinade. Seal bag and turn to coat; refrigerate for 6-8 hours, turning occasionally. Cover and refrigerate remaining marinade.

Coat grill rack with nonstick cooking spray before starting the grill for indirect heat. Drain and discard marinade from beef. Grill beef, covered, over direct medium-hot heat for 6-8 minutes or until browned, turning once. Place beef over indirect heat and continue grilling for 25-30 minutes or until beef reaches desired doneness (for medium-rare, a meat thermometer should read 145°; medium, 160°; well-done, 170°), basting occasionally with reserved marinade. **YIELD:** 6 SERVINGS.

Nutrition Facts:
One serving (4 ounces cooked beef) equals:
- 243 calories
- 7 g fat (2 g saturated fat)
- 96 mg cholesterol
- 337 mg sodium
- 6 g carbohydrate
    - trace fiber
- 37 g protein

Diabetic Exchanges: 4 lean meat, 1/2 fruit.

Onion-Basil Grilled Vegetables

`meat less`

Jan Oeffler, Danbury, Wisconsin

PREP/TOTAL TIME: 30 MIN.

- 3 medium ears fresh corn, cut into 3 pieces
- 1 pound medium red potatoes, quartered
- 1 cup fresh baby carrots
- 1 large green pepper, cut into 1-inch pieces
- 1 large sweet red pepper, cut into 1-inch pieces
- 1 envelope onion soup mix
- 3 tablespoons minced fresh basil *or* 1 tablespoon dried basil
- 1 tablespoon olive oil
- 1/4 teaspoon pepper
- 1 tablespoon butter

In a large bowl, combine the first nine ingredients. Toss to coat. Place on a double thickness of heavy-duty foil (about 28 in. x 18 in.). Dot with butter. Fold foil around the vegetable mixture and seal tightly.

Grill, covered, over medium heat for 25-30 minutes or until potatoes are tender, turning once. **YIELD:** 6 SERVINGS.

Nutrition Facts:
One serving (1-1/2 cups) equals:
- 164 calories
- 5 g fat (2 g saturated fat)
- 5 mg cholesterol
- 453 mg sodium
- 28 g carbohydrate
- 4 g fiber
- 4 g protein

Diabetic Exchanges: 1-1/2 starch, 1 vegetable, 1 fat.

Appealing Partners

- Blackberry Frozen Yogurt, p. 336
- Herbal iced tea

Practical Tips

Do not overcook the steak. Try it done medium-rare to medium. For the most tender results, slice the meat thinly across the grain.

For potlucks, serve the sliced beef on Italian buns.

When assembling the Onion-Basil Grilled Vegetables, feel free to add any produce your family prefers, such as mushrooms, zucchini or parsnips.

Your family will be **all smiles** when you
rustle up this meal. Make sure they leave room
for the **extra yummy** dessert!

Chock-full of nutritious beans, tomatoes, corn and ground beef, every bowl of this stew is seasoned to please and satisfy. Same for the cookies… so make an extra batch and store them in an airtight container for later!

Appealing Partners

• Tossed salad
• Corn bread

Practical Tips

Add extra nutrition to Texas Ranch-Style Stew by stirring in leftover cooked veggies when you add the pasta. Cook and stir until the vegetables are heated through.

Baked beans will give the stew a slightly sweeter taste. Experiment with different canned varieties to find your family's favorites.

Vanilla extract can be substituted for the almond extract in the macaroon recipe.

Texas Ranch-Style Stew

Sue West, Alvord, Texas

PREP: 10 MIN. **COOK:** 25 MIN.

    1 cup small shell pasta
    1 pound lean ground beef
    1 medium onion, chopped
    1 medium green pepper, chopped
    2 garlic cloves, minced
    3 cans (5-1/2 ounces *each*) reduced-sodium
       V8 juice
    1 can (15 ounces) ranch-style beans *or*
       baked beans, undrained
    1 can (14-1/2 ounces) southwestern diced
       tomatoes, undrained
  1/2 cup frozen corn, thawed
    1 tablespoon chili powder
  1/2 teaspoon salt
  1/4 teaspoon pepper

Cook the pasta according to package directions. Meanwhile, in a large nonstick skillet, cook the beef, onion, green pepper and garlic over medium heat until meat is no longer pink; drain. Stir in the remaining ingredients. Bring to a boil. Reduce heat; simmer, uncovered, for 10 minutes, stirring occasionally. Drain the pasta. Stir into the stew. **YIELD:** 6 SERVINGS.

Nutrition Facts:
One serving (1-1/3 cups) equals:
        307 calories
          7 g fat (3 g saturated fat)
       37 mg cholesterol
      886 mg sodium
        37 g carbohydrate
          7 g fiber
        22 g protein

Diabetic Exchanges: 3 lean meat, 2 vegetable, 1-1/2 starch.

Chewy Coconut Macaroons

Peggy Key, Grant, Alabama

PREP: 10 MIN. **BAKE:** 20 MIN. + COOLING

  2-1/2 cups flaked coconut
    3/4 cup all-purpose flour
    1/8 teaspoon salt
      1 can (14 ounces) fat-free sweetened
         condensed milk
  1-1/2 teaspoons almond extract

In a bowl, toss together the coconut, flour and salt. Stir in sweetened condensed milk and almond extract until blended. (Mixture will be thick and sticky.)

Drop by rounded teaspoonfuls 3 in. apart on baking sheets lightly coated with nonstick cooking spray. Bake at 300° for 18-22 minutes or until edges are lightly browned. Cool for 2 minutes before removing to wire racks. **YIELD:** 32 COOKIES.

Nutrition Facts: One serving (1 cookie) equals:
        83 calories
          3 g fat (2 g saturated fat)
        1 mg cholesterol
       41 mg sodium
        13 g carbohydrate
              trace fiber
          2 g protein

Diabetic Exchange: 1 starch.

Feed a **hungry crowd** with this big-pan
Italian meal or save the leftovers for a
hearty lunch later in the week.

*Shell pasta gives traditional
lasagna a tantalizing twist.
Partner it with a tossed
salad and this creamy
dressing with less fat than
most bottled dressings.*

Cheesy Shell Lasagna

Mrs. Leo Merchant, Jackson, Mississippi

PREP: 25 MIN.   **BAKE:** 45 MIN. + STANDING

1-1/2	pounds lean ground beef
2	medium onions, chopped
1	garlic clove, minced
1	can (14-1/2 ounces) diced tomatoes
1	jar (14 ounces) meatless spaghetti sauce
1	can (4 ounces) mushroom stems and pieces, undrained
8	ounces uncooked small shell pasta
2	cups (16 ounces) reduced-fat sour cream
11	slices (8 ounces) reduced-fat provolone cheese
1	cup (4 ounces) shredded part-skim mozzarella cheese

In a nonstick skillet, cook the beef, onions
and garlic over medium heat until meat is no
longer pink; drain. Stir in the tomatoes,
spaghetti sauce and mushrooms. Bring to a
boil. Reduce heat; simmer, uncovered, for
20 minutes. Meanwhile, cook pasta
according to package directions; drain.

Place half of the pasta in an ungreased
13-in. x 9-in. x 2-in. baking dish. Top with
half of the meat sauce, sour cream and
provolone cheese. Repeat layers. Sprinkle
with mozzarella cheese.

Cover and bake at 350° for 35-40 minutes
longer or until the cheese begins to brown.
Let stand for 10 minutes before cutting.
YIELD: 12 SERVINGS.

Nutrition Facts: One serving (1 slice) equals:
```
346  calories
 15 g  fat (8 g saturated fat)
 50 mg  cholesterol
515 mg  sodium
 29 g  carbohydrate
  2 g  fiber
 27 g  protein
```

Diabetic Exchanges: 3 lean meat, 1-1/2 starch,
1 vegetable, 1 fat.

Buttermilk Basil Salad Dressing

Nancy Johnson, San Dimas, California

PREP: 5 MIN. + CHILLING

1	cup buttermilk
1	cup reduced-fat sour cream
1/4	cup plus 2 teaspoons grated Parmesan cheese
3	tablespoons minced fresh basil
1	teaspoon onion salt
2	garlic cloves, minced

Torn mixed salad greens

In a bowl, combine buttermilk and sour
cream. Stir in Parmesan cheese, basil, onion
salt and garlic. Cover and refrigerate for at
least 1 hour. Serve over salad greens. **YIELD:**
2 CUPS.

Nutrition Facts:
One serving (2 tablespoons) equals:
```
 35  calories
  2 g  fat (1 g saturated fat)
  7 mg  cholesterol
173 mg  sodium
  2 g  carbohydrate
         trace fiber
  2 g  protein
```

Diabetic Exchange: 1/2 fat.

Appealing Partners

- Sesame breadsticks
- Mixed melon cup

Practical Tips

When making the lasagna, feel
free to substitute other pasta
shapes, such as macaroni, bow
ties or spirals.

Pick up extra fixings for your
salad drizzled with Buttermilk
Basil Salad Dressing. In the photo
at right, we used a European
blend, but choose your family's
favorite. You may also want to jot
down other ingredients, such as
tomatoes, mushrooms, etc.

Turn on your slow cooker in the morning and let the flavorful fixings simmer all day long for these scoop-and-serve sandwiches.

Flavor a rump roast with everything from cayenne to cola for a sensational sandwich that's sure to please. Arrange a variety of cut veggies on a platter and serve with this dip that's so thick and creamy, no one will guess it's light!

Shredded Beef Sandwiches

Marie Basinger, Connellsville, Pennsylvania

PREP: 30 MIN. + COOLING
COOK: 8 HOURS 15 MIN.

3/4	cup cola
1/4	cup Worcestershire sauce
2	garlic cloves, minced
1	tablespoon white vinegar
1	teaspoon reduced-sodium beef bouillon granules
1/2	teaspoon chili powder
1/2	teaspoon ground mustard
1/4	teaspoon cayenne pepper
1	boneless beef rump roast (2 pounds)
2	teaspoons canola oil
2	medium onions, chopped
1/2	cup ketchup
8	kaiser rolls

In a 4-cup measuring cup, combine the cola, Worcestershire sauce, garlic, vinegar, bouillon and seasonings; set aside. Cut roast in half. In a nonstick skillet, brown meat in oil on all sides.

Place onions in a 3-qt. slow cooker. Top with meat. Pour half of cola mixture over meat. Cover and cook on low for 8-10 hours or until meat is tender. Cover and refrigerate remaining cola mixture.

Remove meat from cooking liquid and cool. Strain cooking liquid, reserving onions and discarding the liquid. When meat is cool enough to handle, shred with two forks. Return meat and onions to the slow cooker. In a small saucepan, combine ketchup and reserved cola mixture; heat through. Pour over meat mixture and heat through. Serve on rolls. **YIELD:** 8 SERVINGS.

Nutrition Facts: One serving (1/2 cup meat mixture with roll) equals:
354 calories
10 g fat (2 g saturated fat)
59 mg cholesterol
714 mg sodium
40 g carbohydrate
2 g fiber
26 g protein

Diabetic Exchanges: 3 lean meat, 2-1/2 starch.

Dill Dip

Judy Bartnik, Wausau, Wisconsin

PREP: 5 MIN. + CHILLING

1	cup (8 ounces) reduced-fat sour cream
1	cup fat-free mayonnaise
1	tablespoon chopped onion
1	tablespoon minced fresh parsley
1	tablespoon dill weed
3/4	teaspoon seasoned salt
	Assorted vegetables

In a bowl, combine the first six ingredients. Cover and refrigerate for 1 hour or until chilled. Serve with vegetables. **YIELD:** 2 CUPS.

Nutrition Facts:
One serving (2 tablespoons) equals:
32 calories
2 g fat (1 g saturated fat)
7 mg cholesterol
175 mg sodium
3 g carbohydrate
trace fiber
1g protein

Diabetic Exchange: 1/2 starch.

Appealing Partners

- Cherry Coconut Bars, p. 324
- Coleslaw

Practical Tips

If you'd like your beef sandwiches with more "kick", increase the cayenne pepper and chili powder.

Avoid buying and cutting up whole vegetables to serve with the dip by purchasing precut celery, broccoli and other veggies from your grocery store's salad bar as well as baby carrots and cherry tomatoes.

Set aside just **10 minutes** for prepping this **effortless** main dish. Then sit down and relax while it **simmers** on the stove.

While your kitchen fills with the tempting aroma of the tangy tomato sauce, you can pull together the tender rice side laced with rosemary, garlic and Parmesan cheese.

Swiss Steak

Betty Richardson, Springfield, Illinois

PREP: 10 MIN. **COOK:** 1 HOUR 35 MIN.

- 4 beef cube steaks (4 ounces *each*)
- 1 tablespoon canola oil
- 1 medium onion, chopped
- 1 celery rib with leaves, chopped
- 1 garlic clove, minced
- 1 can (14-1/2 ounces) stewed tomatoes, cut up
- 1 can (8 ounces) tomato sauce
- 1 teaspoon beef bouillon granules
- 1 tablespoon cornstarch
- 2 tablespoons cold water

In a large nonstick skillet, brown cube steaks on both sides in oil over medium-high heat; remove and set aside. In the same skillet, saute the onion, celery and garlic for 3-4 minutes or until tender. Add the tomatoes, tomato sauce and bouillon. Return steaks to the pan. Bring to a boil. Reduce heat; cover and simmer for 1-1/4 to 1-3/4 hours or until meat is tender.

Combine cornstarch and water until smooth; stir into tomato mixture. Bring to a boil; cook and stir for 2 minutes or until thickened. **YIELD:** 4 SERVINGS.

Nutrition Facts:
One serving (1 steak with 3/4 cup sauce) equals:
- 255 calories
- 8 g fat (2 g saturated fat)
- 65 mg cholesterol
- 746 mg sodium
- 18 g carbohydrate
- 3 g fiber
- 28 g protein

Diabetic Exchanges: 3 lean meat, 3 vegetable, 1/2 fat.

Rosemary Rice

meat less

Connie Regalado, El Paso, Texas

PREP/TOTAL TIME: 25 MIN.

- 1/4 cup chopped onion
- 1 garlic clove, minced
- 1 tablespoon olive oil
- 1 can (14-1/2 ounces) reduced-sodium chicken broth *or* vegetable broth
- 1/4 cup water
- 1 cup uncooked long grain rice
- 1 tablespoon minced fresh rosemary *or* 1 teaspoon dried rosemary, crushed
- 1/4 teaspoon pepper
- 1/4 cup shredded Parmesan cheese

In a saucepan, saute onion and garlic in oil until tender. Add broth and water. Stir in the rice, rosemary and pepper. Bring to a boil. Reduce heat; cover and simmer for 15-18 minutes or until rice is tender. Remove from the heat; stir in Parmesan cheese. **YIELD:** 4 SERVINGS.

Nutrition Facts: One serving (3/4 cup) equals:
- 250 calories
- 5 g fat (1 g saturated fat)
- 4 mg cholesterol
- 367 mg sodium
- 42 g carbohydrate
- 1 g fiber
- 7 g protein

Diabetic Exchange: 3 starch.

Appealing Partners

- Steamed sugar snap peas
- Canned minestrone soup

Practical Tips

Use kitchen shears to cut the stewed tomatoes for the Swiss Steak while they're still in the can and eliminate unnecessary cleanup.

To give the hearty main course a flavor boost, purchase seasoned tomato sauce.

To trim even more sodium from the rice dish, replace the broth with water.

Set your table with this **comforting classic** and you'll **win raves** for your family-pleasing choice.

The moist seasoned slices of this meat loaf are the perfect start to a hearty, homemade meal. For a light and lovely accompaniment, toss together a cool combination of fruits and drizzle with a cinnamony dressing.

Appealing Partners

- Mashed potatoes
- Steamed brussels sprouts

Practical Tips

To further reduce fat and calories in the meat loaf, use lean ground turkey instead of lean ground beef.

Refrigerate leftover meat loaf and slice it when it's cold to make delicious sandwiches.

When making the fruit salad, pull the apples and grapes out of the fridge right before assembling and serving. Then the yogurt dressing will chill the bananas to the perfect serving temperature.

Deluxe Meat Loaf

Patricia Zwerk, Tucson, Arizona

PREP: 15 MIN. **BAKE:** 70 MIN.

2	eggs, lightly beaten
1-1/2	cups ketchup, *divided*
1	can (16 ounces) kidney beans, rinsed, drained and mashed
1	cup seasoned bread crumbs
1	large onion, chopped
1	celery rib, chopped
2	teaspoons Worcestershire sauce
1	teaspoon salt-free lemon-pepper seasoning
1/2	teaspoon seasoned salt
2-1/2	pounds lean ground beef
1/2	cup water

In a large bowl, combine the eggs, 1 cup ketchup, beans, bread crumbs, onion, celery, Worcestershire sauce, lemon-pepper and seasoned salt; crumble beef over mixture and mix well.

Shape into two loaves. Place in a 13-in. x 9-in. x 2-in. baking dish coated with nonstick cooking spray.

In a bowl, combine water and remaining ketchup; pour over meat loaves. Bake, uncovered, at 325° for 70 minutes or until meat is no longer pink and a meat thermometer reads 160°. **YIELD:** 12 SERVINGS.

Nutrition Facts: One serving (1 slice) equals:
267 calories
10 g fat (4 g saturated fat)
70 mg cholesterol
853 mg sodium
21 g carbohydrate
2 g fiber
24 g protein

Diabetic Exchanges: 3 lean meat, 1-1/2 starch.

Spiced Fruit Salad

Lavonne Hartel, Williston, North Dakota

PREP/TOTAL TIME: 10 MIN.

1-1/2	cups fat-free plain yogurt
1/4	cup packed brown sugar
1/4	teaspoon ground cinnamon
1/8	teaspoon ground nutmeg
2	pounds ripe bananas (about 3 medium), sliced
1	pound apples (about 2 medium), cubed
1	tablespoon lemon juice
1	pound red *and/or* green seedless grapes

In a small bowl, combine the yogurt, brown sugar, cinnamon and nutmeg. Gently toss bananas and apples with lemon juice; add grapes. Divide among individual bowls. Drizzle with the yogurt mixture. Serve immediately. **YIELD:** 12 SERVINGS.

Nutrition Facts: One serving (3/4 cup) equals:
136 calories
1 g fat (trace saturated fat)
1 mg cholesterol
26 mg sodium
34 g carbohydrate
2 g fiber
3 g protein

Diabetic Exchange: 2 fruit.

Head **south of the border** with this
variation on a proven favorite to add
some **sizzle** to your next supper.

*Stuffed peppers turn
up the heat with salsa
and green chilies.
Afterward, enjoy this
sweet, golden-topped
dessert that tastes so
delicious folks will never
know it's lower in fat.*

Mexican-Style Stuffed Peppers

LaDonna Reed, Ponca City, Oklahoma

PREP: 15 MIN. **BAKE:** 50 MIN.

    6   medium green *or* sweet red peppers
    1   pound lean ground beef
  1/3   cup chopped onion
  1/3   cup chopped celery
    3   cups cooked rice
1-1/4   cups salsa, *divided*
    1   tablespoon chopped green chilies
    2   teaspoons chili powder
  1/4   teaspoon salt
    1   cup (4 ounces) shredded reduced-fat
        Mexican blend cheese

Cut tops off peppers and discard; remove
seeds. In a Dutch oven or large kettle, cook
peppers in boiling water for 3-5 minutes.
Drain and rinse in cold water; set aside.

In a nonstick skillet, cook the beef, onion
and celery over medium heat until meat is
no longer pink; drain. Stir in the rice, 1 cup
salsa, chilies, chili powder and salt. Spoon
into peppers.

Place in a 13-in. x 9-in. x 2-in. baking dish
coated with nonstick cooking spray. Add
1/4 cup water to dish. Cover and bake at
350° for 45-50 minutes or until heated
through. Uncover; sprinkle with cheese and
top with remaining salsa. Bake 2-3 minutes
longer or until cheese is melted. **YIELD:**
6 SERVINGS.

Nutrition Facts: One serving (1 pepper) equals:
     326   calories
      10 g fat (4 g saturated fat)
      51 mg cholesterol
     540 mg sodium
      34 g carbohydrate
       3 g fiber
      23 g protein

Diabetic Exchanges: 3 lean meat, 3 vegetable,
1-1/2 starch.

Cinnamon Peach Crisp

low sodium

Leona Luecking, West Burlington, Iowa

PREP: 15 MIN. **BAKE:** 40 MIN.

    4   cups sliced peeled fresh peaches
  1/2   cup orange juice
    2   tablespoons brown sugar
  1/2   teaspoon ground cinnamon
    1   cup all-purpose flour
  1/3   cup sugar
    1   teaspoon baking powder
    1   egg, lightly beaten
    2   tablespoons butter, melted

CINNAMON-SUGAR:

1-1/2   teaspoons sugar
  1/8   teaspoon ground cinnamon

In a bowl, combine the peaches, orange juice,
brown sugar and cinnamon. Transfer to an
8-in. square baking dish coated with nonstick
cooking spray. Combine the flour, sugar and
baking powder. Add egg and butter; mix until
crumbly. Sprinkle over peaches.

Combine sugar and cinnamon; sprinkle
over crumb mixture. Bake at 350° for
40-45 minutes or until filling is bubbly and
topping is golden brown. Serve warm. **YIELD:**
6 SERVINGS.

Nutrition Facts: One serving (1 cup) equals:
     245   calories
       5 g fat (3 g saturated fat)
      46 mg cholesterol
      90 mg sodium
      48 g carbohydrate
       3 g fiber
       4 g protein

Diabetic Exchanges: 2 starch, 1 fruit, 1 fat.

Appealing Partners

- Light Guacamole, p. 208,
  with vegetables or fat-free
  chips
- Fresh-squeezed lemonade

Practical Tips

You'll need 1 cup of uncooked
rice to make the 3 cups cooked
rice for the stuffed pepper recipe.
If you make a big batch of rice,
you can store the rest in the
fridge for 1 week or in the freezer
for 6-8 months.

It's easy to peel fresh peaches.
Dip them, one at a time, in
boiling water for 20-30 seconds,
then place in a container of ice
water. Use a paring knife to easily
peel off the skin.

Here's a **one-dish wonder** that will have everyone **clamoring** for seconds before they clean their plates!

Start off your workweek with tender sirloin and crisp beans sauteed in a simple sauce. A quick tossed salad tastes even better topped with this five-minute dressing.

Appealing Partners

- Steamed sliced carrots
- Dinner rolls

Practical Tips

We suggest serving the Saucy Steak Strips over rice, but it's just as delicious served on top of your favorite pasta.

To save time, chop a whole onion when preparing this meal. Store leftovers in the fridge to use later in the week or freeze for longer storage.

When you pick up fixings for the salad drizzled with Creamy Buttermilk Dressing, get salad greens as well as other vegetables like cucumbers and tomatoes.

Saucy Steak Strips

`low carb`

Lacy Cook, Nedrow, New York

PREP/TOTAL TIME: 25 MIN.

- 3/4 pound lean boneless beef sirloin steak, trimmed and cut into thin strips
- 1 tablespoon canola oil
- 1-1/2 cups sliced onions
- 1 can (8 ounces) tomato sauce
- 1/2 cup beef broth
- 1 tablespoon chili sauce
- 1 teaspoon sugar
- 1/4 teaspoon salt
- 1/4 teaspoon pepper
- 1 package (10 ounces) frozen cut green beans, thawed

Hot cooked rice *or* yolk-free noodles, optional

In a large nonstick skillet, brown steak in oil over medium heat. Remove and set aside. In the same skillet, saute onions in drippings until tender. Add the tomato sauce, broth, chili sauce, sugar, salt and pepper; cook and stir for 3 minutes.

Add beans and beef. Cook and stir over medium heat until meat and beans are tender and sauce is slightly thickened. Serve over rice or noodles if desired. **YIELD: 4 SERVINGS.**

Nutrition Facts:
One serving (1 cup steak mixture) equals:
- 230 calories
- 9 g fat (2 g saturated fat)
- 57 mg cholesterol
- 779 mg sodium
- 15 g carbohydrate
- 4 g fiber
- 22 g protein

Diabetic Exchanges: 3 lean meat, 3 vegetable.

Creamy Buttermilk Dressing

`low carb` `meat less`

Emily Hockett, Federal Way, Washington

PREP: 5 MIN. + CHILLING

- 1 cup reduced-fat mayonnaise
- 1/2 cup reduced-fat sour cream
- 1/2 cup buttermilk
- 1 teaspoon onion powder
- 1 teaspoon cider vinegar
- 1/2 teaspoon garlic powder
- 1/2 teaspoon salt
- 1/8 teaspoon pepper

Place all ingredients in a blender or food processor; cover and process until smooth. Cover and refrigerate for at least 1 hour before serving. **YIELD: 2 CUPS.**

Nutrition Facts:
One serving (2 tablespoons) equals:
- 64 calories
- 6 g fat (1 g saturated fat)
- 8 mg cholesterol
- 206 mg sodium
- 2 g carbohydrate
  - trace fiber
- 1 g protein

Diabetic Exchange: 1 fat.

For a **soul-satisfying** Sunday dinner or weeknight meal, serve up this pleasing pair of **traditional, down-home** tastes.

Slow-Cooked Coffee Beef Roast

low carb

Charles Trahan, San Dimas, California

PREP: 15 MIN.   **COOK:** 8 HOURS

Don't pour your extra coffee down the drain. It's the key to this tender roast. The flavorful skillet side dish complements the beef, or most any entree.

1	boneless beef sirloin tip roast (2-1/2 pounds), cut in half
2	teaspoons canola oil
1-1/2	cups sliced fresh mushrooms
1/3	cup sliced green onions
2	garlic cloves, minced
1-1/2	cups brewed coffee
1	teaspoon Liquid Smoke, optional
1/2	teaspoon salt
1/2	teaspoon chili powder
1/4	teaspoon pepper
1/4	cup cornstarch
1/3	cup cold water

Appealing Partners

• Sauteed sugar snap peas
• Low-fat ice cream with strawberry sauce

Practical Tips

If you don't have any leftover brewed coffee to make the roast, you can stir 2 rounded teaspoons of instant coffee granules into 1-1/2 cups hot water.

For a tasty substitute, use rosemary instead of oregano when fixing the Spanish Potatoes.

To make the side dish suitable for vegetarians, we've offered vegetable bouillon granules as an option to the chicken bouillon. Look for it alongside other bouillon products in the soup aisle of your grocery store.

In a large nonstick skillet, brown roast on all sides in oil over medium-high heat. Place in a 5-qt. slow cooker. In the same skillet, saute mushrooms, onions and garlic until tender; stir in the coffee, liquid smoke if desired, salt, chili powder and pepper. Pour over roast. Cover and cook on low for 8-10 hours or until meat is tender.

Remove roast and keep warm. Pour cooking juices into a 2-cup measuring cup; skim fat. In a saucepan, combine cornstarch and water until smooth. Gradually stir in 2 cups cooking juices. Bring to a boil; cook and stir for 2 minutes or until thickened. Serve with sliced beef. **YIELD:** 6 SERVINGS.

Nutrition Facts: One serving (3 ounces cooked beef with 1/3 cup gravy) equals:
- 209 calories
- 7 g fat (2 g saturated fat)
- 82 mg cholesterol
- 244 mg sodium
- 6 g carbohydrate
- trace fiber
- 28 g protein

Diabetic Exchanges: 3 lean meat, 1/2 starch.

Spanish Potatoes

Connie Thomas, Jensen, Utah

PREP/TOTAL TIME: 30 MIN.

1-1/4	pounds small red potatoes, quartered
1-1/2	cups chopped onions
1	cup sliced green pepper
1/2	cup water
1	tablespoon olive oil
1	teaspoon chicken *or* vegetable bouillon granules
1	cup chopped fresh tomatoes
1/2	teaspoon dried oregano

Place potatoes in a large saucepan and cover with water. Bring to a boil. Reduce heat; cover and cook for 15 minutes or until tender.

Meanwhile, in a small saucepan, combine the onions, green pepper, water, oil and bouillon. Bring to a boil. Reduce heat; cover and simmer for 8-10 minutes or until vegetables are tender. Drain potatoes; add onion mixture, tomatoes and oregano. Stir gently to coat. **YIELD:** 6 SERVINGS.

Nutrition Facts: One serving (1 cup) equals:
- 113 calories
- 3 g fat (trace saturated fat)
- trace cholesterol
- 199 mg sodium
- 21 g carbohydrate
- 2 g fiber
- 2 g protein

Diabetic Exchanges: 1 starch, 1 vegetable, 1/2 fat.

Now you and your family can enjoy a
home-style casserole loaded with
gooey cheese and none of the guilt.

You can assemble this satisfying casserole in mere minutes. When you sit down to sample its slightly spicy flavor, grab a refreshing glass of these mellow malts. You can whip them up in minutes, too!

Appealing Partners

- Tossed salad with vinaigrette
- Cinnamon-sugared peach slices

Practical Tips

If your family doesn't like dishes that are very spicy, omit the green chilies when making the Chili Mac Casserole. But if your family enjoys lots of spice, add a chopped and seeded jalapeno pepper to the mixture.

To give this main dish a different look, use 1 cup uncooked small pasta such as shells, ziti or wagon wheels in place of 1 cup uncooked elbow macaroni called for in the recipe.

Chili Mac Casserole

Marlene Wilson, Rolla, North Dakota

PREP: 15 MIN.   **BAKE:** 30 MIN.

1	cup uncooked elbow macaroni
2	pounds lean ground beef
1	medium onion, chopped
2	garlic cloves, minced
1	can (28 ounces) diced tomatoes, undrained
1	can (16 ounces) kidney beans, rinsed and drained
1	can (6 ounces) tomato paste
1	can (4 ounces) chopped green chilies
1-1/2	teaspoons salt
1	teaspoon chili powder
1/2	teaspoon ground cumin
1/2	teaspoon pepper
2	cups (8 ounces) shredded reduced-fat Mexican cheese blend

Cook macaroni according to package directions. Meanwhile, in a large nonstick skillet, cook the beef, onion and garlic over medium heat until meat is no longer pink; drain. Stir in the tomatoes, beans, tomato paste, chilies and seasonings. Drain macaroni; add to beef mixture.

Transfer to a 13-in. x 9-in. x 2-in. baking dish coated with nonstick cooking spray. Cover and bake at 375° for 25-30 minutes or until bubbly. Uncover; sprinkle with cheese. Bake 5-8 minutes longer or until cheese is melted. **YIELD:** 10 SERVINGS.

Nutrition Facts: One serving (1 cup) equals:
- 343 calories
- 13 g fat (3 g saturated fat)
- 45 mg cholesterol
- 812 mg sodium
- 25 g carbohydrate
- 6 g fiber
- 32 g protein

Diabetic Exchanges: 3 lean meat, 1-1/2 starch, 1 fat.

Frosty Chocolate Malted Shakes

low fat

Dora Dean, Hollywood, Florida

PREP/TOTAL TIME: 10 MIN.

6	cups reduced-fat frozen vanilla yogurt
3-1/2	cups fat-free milk
1/4	cup sugar-free instant chocolate drink mix
1/4	cup malted milk powder
1-1/2	teaspoons vanilla extract

In a blender or food processor, cover and process ingredients in batches until smooth. Pour into tall glasses. **YIELD:** 10 SERVINGS.

Nutrition Facts: One serving (1 cup) equals:
- 193 calories
- 1 g fat (1 g saturated fat)
- 2 mg cholesterol
- 172 mg sodium
- 37 g carbohydrate
- 1 g fiber
- 9 g protein

Diabetic Exchanges: 1-1/2 fat-free milk, 1/2 starch.

If you're **counting carbs**, keep them in check with this **classy combo** straight from the grill.

An easy marinade and quick rub give the flank steak its flavor boost, and grilling it outside makes cleanup a breeze. As long as the grill's lit, throw on the veggies! Use a handful of ingredients to season the fresh spears before tossing them with Parmesan cheese.

London Broil

`low carb`

Susan Wilkins, Los Olivos, California

PREP: 10 MIN. + MARINATING   **GRILL:** 15 MIN.

- 1/2   cup water
- 1/4   cup red wine vinegar
- 2   tablespoons canola oil
- 1   tablespoon tomato paste
- 1-1/2   teaspoons garlic salt, *divided*
- 1   teaspoon dried thyme, *divided*
- 1/2   teaspoon pepper, *divided*
- 1   bay leaf
- 1   beef flank steak (1-1/2 pounds)

In a small bowl, whisk the water, vinegar, oil, tomato paste, 1 teaspoon garlic salt, 1/2 teaspoon thyme, 1/4 teaspoon pepper and bay leaf. Pour into a resealable plastic bag.

Score the surface of the steak, making diamond shapes 1/4 in. deep; add the steak to the marinade. Seal the bag and turn to coat; refrigerate for 3 hours or overnight, turning occasionally.

Coat grill rack with nonstick cooking spray before starting the grill. Discard marinade. Pat steak dry with paper towels. Combine the remaining garlic salt, thyme and pepper; rub over both sides of steak.

Grill steak, covered, over medium-hot heat for 6-8 minutes on each side or until a meat thermometer reaches desired doneness (for medium-rare, a meat thermometer should read 145°; medium, 160°; well-done, 170°). To serve, thinly slice across the grain. **YIELD:** 6 SERVINGS.

Nutrition Facts:
One serving (3 ounces cooked steak) equals:
- 175   calories
- 9 g   fat (4 g saturated fat)
- 54 mg   cholesterol
- 294 mg   sodium
- 1 g   carbohydrate
      trace fiber
- 22 g   protein

Diabetic Exchange: 3 lean meat.

Grilled Broccoli

`low carb` `meat less`

Alice Nulle, Woodstock, Illinois

PREP: 5 MIN. + STANDING   **GRILL:** 10 MIN.

- 6   cups fresh broccoli spears
- 2   tablespoons plus 1-1/2 teaspoons lemon juice
- 2   tablespoons olive oil
- 1/4   teaspoon salt
- 1/4   teaspoon pepper
- 3/4   cup grated Parmesan cheese

Place broccoli in a large bowl. Combine the lemon juice, oil, salt and pepper; drizzle over broccoli and toss to coat. Let stand for 30 minutes.

Coat grill rack with nonstick cooking spray before starting the grill. Prepare grill for indirect heat. Toss broccoli, then drain marinade. Place Parmesan cheese in a large resealable plastic bag. Add broccoli, a few pieces at a time; shake to coat. Grill broccoli, covered, over indirect medium heat for 8-10 minutes on each side or until crisp-tender. **YIELD:** 6 SERVINGS.

Nutrition Facts: One serving (1 cup) equals:
- 107   calories
- 8 g   fat (3 g saturated fat)
- 8 mg   cholesterol
- 304 mg   sodium
- 5 g   carbohydrate
- 2 g   fiber
- 6 g   protein

Diabetic Exchanges: 1-1/2 fat, 1 vegetable.

Appealing Partners

- New potatoes
- Rhubarb Shortcake Dessert, p. 332

Practical Tips

You can substitute the red wine vinegar that's called for in the steak's marinade with an equal portion of cider vinegar.

You'll need about 2 pounds of fresh broccoli for the side dish. When buying broccoli, look for firm but tender spears with compact florets that are dark green or have a slightly purple tint.

A favorite Italian specialty shows a bit of Mexican flair in this convenient casserole.

You'll save time with this lasagna since the recipe comes together with uncooked noodles and salsa. Although the entree is filling, save room for a cookie or two!

Mexican Lasagna

Sheree Swistun, Winnipeg, Manitoba

PREP: 15 MIN. **BAKE:** 60 MIN.

1 pound lean ground beef
1 can (16 ounces) fat-free refried beans
2 teaspoons dried oregano
1 teaspoon ground cumin
3/4 teaspoon garlic powder
9 uncooked lasagna noodles
1 jar (16 ounces) salsa
2 cups water
2 cups (16 ounces) reduced-fat sour cream
1 can (2-1/4 ounces) sliced ripe olives, drained
1 cup (4 ounces) shredded reduced-fat Mexican cheese blend
1/2 cup thinly sliced green onions

In a nonstick skillet, cook beef over medium heat until no longer pink; drain. Add the refried beans, oregano, cumin and garlic powder; heat through.

Place three noodles in a 13-in. x 9-in. x 2-in. baking dish coated with nonstick cooking spray; cover with half of the meat mixture. Repeat layers. Top with remaining noodles. Combine salsa and water; pour over noodles.

Cover and bake at 350° for 60-70 minutes or until noodles are tender. Spread with sour cream. Sprinkle with olives, cheese and onions. **YIELD:** 9 SERVINGS.

Nutrition Facts: One serving (1 piece) equals:
355 calories
12 g fat (7 g saturated fat)
51 mg cholesterol
655 mg sodium
35 g carbohydrate
4 g fiber
24 g protein

Diabetic Exchanges: 2 starch, 2 lean meat, 1 vegetable, 1 fat.

Chocolate Chip Cookies

Linda Todd, Coldwater, Michigan

PREP: 15 MIN. **BAKE:** 10 MIN. PER BATCH

1/2 cup butter, softened
1 cup sugar
1 cup packed brown sugar
2 eggs
1/2 cup egg substitute
1/4 cup corn syrup
2 teaspoons vanilla extract
4 cups all-purpose flour
2 teaspoons baking soda
1 teaspoon salt
1-1/4 cups semisweet chocolate chips

In a mixing bowl, cream butter and sugars. Add eggs, one at a time, beating well after each addition. Beat in the egg substitute, corn syrup and vanilla. Combine the flour, baking soda and salt; gradually add to creamed mixture. Stir in chocolate chips.

Drop by rounded tablespoonfuls 2 in. apart onto ungreased baking sheets. Bake at 350° for 9-11 minutes or until lightly browned. Immediately remove to wire racks to cool. **YIELD:** 5-1/2 DOZEN.

Nutrition Facts: One serving (1 cookie) equals:
87 calories
3 g fat (2 g saturated fat)
10 mg cholesterol
97 mg sodium
15 g carbohydrate
1 g fiber
1 g protein

Diabetic Exchange: 1 starch.

Appealing Partners

• Tossed salad with low-fat vinaigrette
• Baked tortilla chips with salsa

Practical Tips

For a meatless entree, eliminate the ground beef and add a can of rinsed and drained black beans to the refried beans. This switch boosts fiber content.

If you don't have time to bake all of the cookies, freeze some of the dough. Then just thaw and bake fresh cookies whenever you want them.

For minty chocolate chip cookies, add 1/4 teaspoon mint extract to the batter and reduce the vanilla to 1 teaspoon.

Tender, juicy beef piled high on crusty rolls couldn't be easier for a casual lunch or **on-the-go** supper.

You'll need just five ingredients for this slow-cooked beef sandwich seasoned with broth. Try the sandwich alone or topped with the relish. The colorful combo of broiled vegetables can also be served as a side dish.

Appealing Partners

- Low-fat potato salad
- Sparkling water

Practical Tips

For milder sandwiches, use a can of green chilies in place of jalapenos or strain the broth after cooking to remove the peppers. To please tender palates, simply eliminate the peppers altogether.

For an authentic French dip, serve the warm cooking juices in a ramekin or custard cup alongside each sandwich for easy dipping.

When weather allows, roast the peppers and eggplant on an outdoor barbecue grill until peppers are blackened and eggplant is soft.

Spicy French Dip

Ginny Koeppen, Winnfield, Louisiana

PREP: 5 MIN. **COOK:** 8 HOURS

1	boneless beef sirloin tip roast (about 3 pounds), cut in half
1/2	cup water
1	can (4 ounces) diced jalapeno peppers, drained
1	envelope Italian salad dressing mix
12	crusty rolls (5 inches)

Place beef in a 5-qt. slow cooker. In a small bowl, combine the water, jalapenos and dressing mix; pour over beef. Cover and cook on low for 8-10 hours or until meat is tender. Remove beef and shred using two forks. Skim fat from cooking juices. Serve beef on buns with juice. **YIELD:** 12 SERVINGS.

Nutrition Facts: One serving (1 sandwich with 3 tablespoons juice) equals:

    357 calories
      9 g fat (4 g saturated fat)
     68 mg cholesterol
    877 mg sodium
     37 g carbohydrate
      2 g fiber
     31 g protein

Diabetic Exchanges: 3 lean meat, 2 starch.

Eggplant Pepper Relish

Jeanne Vitale, Leola, Pennsylvania

PREP: 10 MIN. **BROIL:** 10 MIN. + STANDING

3	medium sweet red peppers, cut in half lengthwise
3	medium sweet yellow peppers, cut in half lengthwise
1	medium eggplant, cut in half lengthwise
2	tablespoons olive oil
1	garlic clove, minced
1/4	cup minced fresh parsley
1	tablespoon minced fresh oregano *or* 1 teaspoon dried oregano
3/4	teaspoon salt
1/4	teaspoon pepper

Place peppers skin side up on a broiler pan. Broil for 10-15 minutes or until tender and skin is blistered. Place in a bowl; cover and let stand for 15-20 minutes. Peel off and discard charred skin.

Broil eggplant skin side up for 5-7 minutes or until tender and skin is blistered. Place in a bowl, cover and let stand for 15-20 minutes. Peel off and discard charred skin. Cut peppers into strips and eggplant into cubes.

In a large bowl, combine the oil and garlic. Add peppers, eggplant, parsley, oregano, salt and pepper. Toss to coat. Serve at room temperature. **YIELD:** 12 SERVINGS.

Nutrition Facts: One serving (1/3 cup) equals:

     55 calories
      3 g fat (trace saturated fat)
      0 cholesterol
    150 mg sodium
      8 g carbohydrate
      2 g fiber
      1 g protein

Diabetic Exchanges: 1 vegetable, 1/2 fat.

Toss together this tempting salad the next time
you want to mix up your dinnertime routine.

Fresh spinach leaves and easy stir-fried beef are topped off with a delightful sweet-and-sour dressing. The down-home muffins keep folks reaching for the breadbasket without feeling an ounce of guilt.

Spinach Beef Salad `low fat` `low carb`
Janet Dingler, Cedartown, Georgia

PREP/TOTAL TIME: 30 MIN.

1/2	pound boneless beef sirloin steak, cut into thin strips
1	jalapeno pepper, seeded and chopped
1	garlic clove, minced
1	large sweet red pepper, julienned
1/2	medium cucumber, peeled and julienned
1/4	cup lime juice
2	tablespoons brown sugar
2	tablespoons reduced-sodium soy sauce
1	teaspoon minced fresh mint *or* 1/2 teaspoon dried mint
1	teaspoon dried basil
1	teaspoon minced fresh gingerroot
6	cups torn fresh spinach

In a large nonstick skillet coated with nonstick cooking spray, saute the beef, jalapeno and garlic until the beef reaches desired doneness. Remove from the heat. Stir in the red pepper and cucumber.

In a small bowl, combine the lime juice, brown sugar, soy sauce, mint, basil and ginger. Place the spinach in a large bowl; add beef mixture and dressing. Toss to coat. **YIELD:** 4 SERVINGS.

Editor's Note: When cutting or seeding hot peppers, use rubber or plastic gloves to protect your hands. Avoid touching your face.

Nutrition Facts: One serving (2 cups) equals:
136 calories
3 g fat (1 g saturated fat)
31 mg cholesterol
367 mg sodium
15 g carbohydrate
2 g fiber
13 g protein

Diabetic Exchanges: 2 lean meat, 1 vegetable, 1/2 fruit.

Raisin Rye Muffins `meat less`
Edna Hoffman, Hebron, Indiana

PREP/TOTAL TIME: 30 MIN.

1	cup rye flour
2	teaspoons baking powder
1/2	teaspoon ground cinnamon
1/4	teaspoon salt
1/2	cup water
2	tablespoons honey
2	tablespoons canola oil
1/2	cup raisins

In a large bowl, combine the flour, baking powder, cinnamon and salt. Combine the water, honey and oil; stir into dry ingredients just until moistened. Fold in raisins. Fill six muffin cups coated with nonstick cooking spray two-thirds full.

Bake at 400° for 15-20 minutes or until a toothpick comes out clean. Cool for 5 minutes before removing from pan to a wire rack. Serve warm. **YIELD:** 6 MUFFINS.

Nutrition Facts: One serving (1 muffin) equals:
160 calories
5 g fat (trace saturated fat)
0 cholesterol
234 mg sodium
29 g carbohydrate
3 g fiber
2 g protein

Diabetic Exchanges: 1 starch, 1 fruit, 1 fat.

Appealing Partners

- Raspberry iced tea
- Frozen yogurt

Practical Tips

To shave a few minutes off the clock, replace the homemade salad dressing in the main course with a bottled sweet-sour or Asian-inspired variety. Check the nutrition label to make sure it's low-fat.

Instead of mixing raisins into the rye muffins, add an equal portion of dates, dried apricots or dried cranberries.

Celebrate good grades or a great job with this **skillet meal** sure to win you **rave reviews**!

Take advantage of a canned soup to prepare the special sauce for the Dijon Mushroom Beef. The fast-to-fix entree is both flavorful and filling. For a different way to serve veggies, ladle up this low-fat chilled soup.

Dijon Mushroom Beef
`low carb`

Judith McGhan, Perry Hall, Maryland

PREP/TOTAL TIME: 20 MIN.

- 1/2 pound fresh mushrooms, sliced
- 1 medium onion, sliced
- 2 teaspoons olive oil
- 1 pound boneless beef sirloin steak, thinly sliced
- 1 can (10-3/4 ounces) reduced-fat reduced-sodium condensed cream of mushroom soup, undiluted
- 3/4 cup fat-free milk
- 2 tablespoons Dijon mustard

Hot cooked yolk-free noodles, optional

In a large nonstick skillet, saute mushrooms and onion in oil until tender. Remove and set aside. In the same skillet, cook beef until no longer pink. Add the soup, milk, mustard and mushroom mixture. Bring to a boil. Reduce heat; cook and stir until thickened. Serve over hot cooked noodles if desired. **YIELD:** 4 SERVINGS.

Nutrition Facts:
One serving (1 cup beef mixture) equals:
- 281 calories
- 11 g fat (3 g saturated fat)
- 82 mg cholesterol
- 567 mg sodium
- 15 g carbohydrate
- 2 g fiber
- 30 g protein

Diabetic Exchanges: 3 lean meat, 1 vegetable, 1/2 starch, 1/2 fat.

Chilled Squash And Carrot Soup
`low fat`

Elaine Sabacky, Litchfield, Minnesota

PREP: 30 MIN. + CHILLING

- 1-1/2 pounds butternut squash, peeled, seeded and cubed (about 3 cups)
- 1 can (14-1/2 ounces) chicken broth
- 2 medium carrots, sliced
- 1 medium onion, chopped
- 1/4 teaspoon salt
- 1/2 cup fat-free evaporated milk
- 3 tablespoons reduced-fat sour cream

In a large saucepan, combine the squash, broth, carrots, onion and salt. Bring to a boil. Reduce heat; cover and simmer for 15-20 minutes or until vegetables are very tender. Remove from the heat; cool.

In a blender or food processor, puree squash mixture in batches. Transfer to a bowl, stir in milk. Cover and chill until serving. Garnish with sour cream. **YIELD:** 4 SERVINGS.

Nutrition Facts: One serving (1-1/4 cups) equals:
- 127 calories
- 1 g fat (1 g saturated fat)
- 5 mg cholesterol
- 637 mg sodium
- 25 g carbohydrate
- 5 g fiber
- 6 g protein

Diabetic Exchanges: 2 vegetable, 1 starch.

Appealing Partners

- Asparagus spears
- Angel food cake

Practical Tips

Before preparing Dijon Mushroom Beef, partially freeze the meat to make it easier to slice.

The leftover beef is tasty in other dishes, too. Try it in a homemade potpie. The mustard will add a little zest to the dish.

To give individual bowls of soup a special presentation, use a toothpick to swirl small dollops of reduced-fat sour cream into a pretty pattern.

Get a **head start** on supper prep with this **change-of-pace** dinner. Let it simmer while you **go about your day**, then enjoy!

With chunks of onion and green pepper, the main course is both satisfying and low in carbohydrates. The steak's tangy gravy is ideal over the home-style mashed potatoes, a tasty addition to any meal.

Slow-Cooked Sirloin

Vicki Tormaschy, Dickinson, North Dakota

PREP: 20 MIN.   **COOK:** 3-1/2 HOURS

- 1   boneless beef sirloin steak (1-1/2 pounds)
- 1   medium onion, cut into 1-inch chunks
- 1   medium green pepper, cut into 1-inch chunks
- 1   can (14-1/2 ounces) reduced-sodium beef broth
- 1/4   cup Worcestershire sauce
- 1/4   teaspoon dill weed
- 1/4   teaspoon dried thyme
- 1/4   teaspoon pepper

Dash crushed red pepper flakes
- 2   tablespoons cornstarch
- 2   tablespoons water

In a large nonstick skillet coated with nonstick cooking spray, brown beef on both sides. Place onion and green pepper in a 3-qt. slow cooker. Top with beef.

Combine the beef broth, Worcestershire sauce, dill, thyme, pepper and red pepper flakes; pour over the beef. Cover and cook on high for 3-4 hours or until the meat reaches desired doneness and the vegetables are crisp-tender. Remove the beef and keep warm.

Combine cornstarch and water until smooth; gradually stir into cooking juices. Cover and cook about 30 minutes longer or until slightly thickened. Return beef to the slow cooker; heat through. **YIELD:** 6 SERVINGS.

Nutrition Facts:
One serving (3 ounces cooked steak) equals:
- 199   calories
- 6 g   fat (2 g saturated fat)
- 68 mg   cholesterol
- 305 mg   sodium
- 8 g   carbohydrate
- 1 g   fiber
- 26 g   protein

Diabetic Exchanges: 3 lean meat, 1 vegetable.

Horseradish Mashed Potatoes

Melissa Merkle, Elizabeth, Illinois

PREP: 35 MIN.   **BAKE:** 20 MIN.

- 1-1/2   pounds Yukon gold potatoes, peeled and cubed
- 6   tablespoons reduced-fat sour cream, *divided*
- 3   tablespoons fat-free milk
- 2-1/4   teaspoons snipped chives, *divided*
- 1/2   teaspoon salt
- 4-1/2   teaspoons reduced-fat mayonnaise
- 2-1/4   teaspoons prepared horseradish
- 1/8   teaspoon pepper

Place potatoes in a large saucepan and cover with water. Bring to a boil. Reduce heat; cover and cook for 15-20 minutes or until tender. Drain.

Place potatoes in a large bowl; mash with 5 tablespoons sour cream, milk, 1-1/2 teaspoons chives and salt. Spoon into a 1-qt. baking dish coated with nonstick cooking spray.

In a small bowl, combine the mayonnaise, horseradish, pepper and remaining sour cream. Spread over potato mixture. Sprinkle with remaining chives. Bake, uncovered, at 400° for 20-25 minutes or until heated through. **YIELD:** 6 SERVINGS.

Nutrition Facts: One serving (1/2 cup) equals:
- 130   calories
- 3 g   fat (1 g saturated fat)
- 6 mg   cholesterol
- 204 mg   sodium
- 22 g   carbohydrate
- 1 g   fiber
- 4 g   protein

Diabetic Exchanges: 1-1/2 starch, 1/2 fat.

Appealing Partners

- Steamed brussels sprouts
- Coconut-Cherry Cream Squares, p. 329

Practical Tips

For a complete meal, add potatoes, carrots or mushrooms to the onions and peppers in the sirloin recipe.

Save time by mashing the potatoes a day early and storing them in the fridge. Before dinner, simply top them with the creamy spread and pop them in the oven to bake.

Harvest a bounty of compliments
with this **garden-fresh** meal that
cuts calories without sacrificing taste.

Beefy Tomatoes   `low carb`

Liz Gallagher, Gilbertsville, Pennsylvania

PREP: 20 MIN.   **BAKE:** 20 MIN.

The oven-warmed tomatoes make a pretty presentation when heaped with a ground beef and rice filling. Accompany this memorable main dish with warm slices of stuffed bread. It does double duty as a snack or appetizer, too.

- 6   medium tomatoes
- 1   pound lean ground beef
- 1   medium onion, chopped
- 2   teaspoons dried basil
- 1   teaspoon salt
- 1/4   teaspoon pepper
- 1/2   cup cooked rice
- 1/2   cup shredded reduced-fat cheddar cheese
- 1   egg, lightly beaten

Cut a thin slice off the top of each tomato and discard; remove core. Carefully scoop out pulp, leaving a 1/2-in. shell. Reserve 1 cup pulp (discard remaining pulp or save for another use). Invert tomatoes onto paper towels to drain.

In a nonstick skillet, cook beef and onion over medium heat until meat is no longer pink; drain. Stir in the basil, salt, pepper and reserved tomato pulp; bring to a boil. Reduce heat; simmer, uncovered, for 10-12 minutes or until the liquid has evaporated.

Stir in the rice, cheese and egg; heat through. Spoon into tomato shells. Place in a shallow 2-qt. baking dish coated with nonstick cooking spray. Bake, uncovered, at 350° for 20-25 minutes or until heated through. **YIELD:** 6 SERVINGS.

Nutrition Facts: One serving (1 tomato) equals:
- 215 calories
- 10 g fat (4 g saturated fat)
- 68 mg cholesterol
- 525 mg sodium
- 12 g carbohydrate
- 2 g fiber
- 21 g protein

Diabetic Exchanges: 2 lean meat, 1-1/2 fat, 1/2 starch.

Spinach-Stuffed Bread   `meat less`

Terry Byrne, Warwick, New York

PREP: 15 MIN. + RISING   **BAKE:** 25 MIN.

- 1   loaf (1 pound) frozen bread dough
- 1   medium onion, chopped
- 1   to 2 garlic cloves, minced
- 2   teaspoons olive oil
- 1   package (10 ounces) frozen chopped spinach, thawed and squeezed dry
- 2   cups (8 ounces) shredded reduced-fat cheddar *or* part-skim mozzarella

Thaw bread dough according to package directions; let rise until doubled. Meanwhile, in a skillet, saute onion and garlic in oil until tender. Stir in spinach.

On a lightly floured surface, roll dough into a 14-in. x 10-in. rectangle. Spread the spinach mixture to within 1/2 in. of edges; sprinkle with cheese. Roll up jelly-roll style, starting with a long side; pinch seam to seal. Place seam side down on a baking sheet coated with nonstick cooking spray; tuck ends under.

Bake at 350° for 25-30 minutes or until golden brown. Remove from pan to a wire rack; let stand for 10 minutes before slicing. Serve warm. **YIELD:** 6 SERVINGS.

Nutrition Facts: One serving (2 slices) equals:
- 240 calories
- 11 g fat (4 g saturated fat)
- 20 mg cholesterol
- 687 mg sodium
- 45 g carbohydrate
- 4 g fiber
- 21 g protein

Diabetic Exchanges: 2 starch, 2 lean meat, 1-1/2 fat.

Appealing Partners

- Carrot sticks
- Fresh fruit with yogurt dip

Practical Tips

Tomato pulp not used in the Beefy Tomatoes can be frozen up to 3 months. Use it to perk up tomato soup, spaghetti sauce or other tomato-based dishes.

The golden bread takes advantage of convenient frozen bread dough, so it's easy to assemble. But plan ahead—you'll need to thaw it first. Wrap it in plastic wrap and place in the fridge for 6-12 hours or on the counter for 2-3 hours until thawed but still cold.

Ease into your workweek with a nourishing classic you can have table-ready in record time.

This 30-minute mainstay starts with canned soup and ends with compliments! Serve it with these green beans, lightly seasoned with lemon, butter and parsley, for a comforting combination any day of the week.

Appealing Partners

- Mashed potatoes
- Peachy Fruit Salad, p. 263

Practical Tips

Use lean ground turkey instead of ground beef in the entree with equally tasty results. You can also use cream of celery soup rather than cream of mushroom soup.

To cut down on last-minute prep, mix and shape the patties early in the day, then cover and refrigerate until you're ready to cook them.

Replace the green beans with wax beans if you prefer, or use frozen beans instead of fresh.

Simple Salisbury Steak `low carb`

Elouise Bonar, Hanover, Illinois

PREP/TOTAL TIME: 30 MIN.

1	egg
1/3	cup dry bread crumbs
1	can (10-3/4 ounces) reduced-fat reduced-sodium condensed cream of mushroom soup, undiluted, *divided*
1/4	cup finely chopped onion
1	pound lean ground beef
1/2	cup fat-free milk
1/4	teaspoon browning sauce, optional
1/4	teaspoon salt
1-1/2	cups sliced fresh mushrooms

In a bowl, combine the egg, bread crumbs, 1/4 cup soup and onion. Crumble the beef over mixture and mix well. Shape into six patties. In a large nonstick skillet, brown the patties on both sides; drain.

In a bowl, combine milk, browning sauce if desired, salt and remaining soup; stir in mushrooms. Pour over patties. Reduce heat; cover and simmer for 15-20 minutes or until meat is no longer pink. **YIELD:** 6 SERVINGS.

Nutrition Facts:
One serving (1 patty with 1/4 cup sauce) equals:
- 212 calories
- 9 g fat (3 g saturated fat)
- 67 mg cholesterol
- 599 mg sodium
- 11 g carbohydrate
- trace fiber
- 20 g protein

Diabetic Exchanges: 3 lean meat, 1/2 starch, 1/2 fat.

Snappy Green Beans `low fat` `low carb` `meat less`

Tammy Neubauer, Ida Grove, Iowa

PREP/TOTAL TIME: 20 MIN.

2	pounds fresh green beans
2	teaspoons butter
2	tablespoons minced fresh parsley
2	teaspoons lemon juice
1/2	teaspoon salt
1/8	teaspoon pepper

Place beans in a large saucepan; cover with water. Bring to a boil. Reduce heat; simmer, uncovered, for 10-15 minutes or until crisp-tender. Drain.

In a large nonstick skillet, melt butter. Add beans; cook and stir until heated through. Remove from the heat. Add the parsley, lemon juice, salt and pepper; toss to coat. Serve immediately. **YIELD:** 6 SERVINGS.

Nutrition Facts: One serving (3/4 cup) equals:
- 58 calories
- 2 g fat (1 g saturated fat)
- 3 mg cholesterol
- 213 mg sodium
- 11 g carbohydrate
- 4 g fiber
- 3 g protein

Diabetic Exchange: 2 vegetable.

Simmer up a souper supper when you toss together a few **everyday ingredients** from your pantry.

Assemble the ingredients for this hearty soup the night before. In the morning, just combine them in the slow cooker, switch it on and let it simmer all day. Serve it with this moist loaf. No one will suspect that the secret ingredient in the bread is yogurt.

Appealing Partners

- Spinach salad
- Lime sherbet

Practical Tips

You can vary the slow-cooked soup by using lean ground turkey instead of the ground beef.

When seasoning Rustic Round Herb Bread, try different combinations of herbs, including basil, oregano and parsley.

For a change of pace, sprinkle the loaf with sesame or caraway seeds.

Beef Vegetable Soup

Jean Hutzell, Dubuque, Iowa

PREP: 15 MIN.   **COOK:** 9 HOURS

1 pound lean ground beef
1 medium onion, chopped
1/2 teaspoon salt
1/4 teaspoon pepper
3 cups water
3 medium potatoes, peeled and cut into 3/4-inch cubes
1 can (14-1/2 ounces) Italian diced tomatoes, undrained
1 can (11-1/2 ounces) V8 juice
1 cup chopped celery
1 cup sliced carrots
2 tablespoons sugar
1 tablespoon dried parsley flakes
2 teaspoons dried basil
1 bay leaf

In a nonstick skillet, cook beef and onion over medium heat until meat is no longer pink; drain. Stir in salt and pepper. Transfer to a 5-qt. slow cooker. Add the remaining ingredients. Cover and cook on low for 9-11 hours or until vegetables are tender. Discard bay leaf before serving. **YIELD:** 7 SERVINGS.

Nutrition Facts: One serving (1-1/3 cups) equals:
210 calories
5 g fat (2 g saturated fat)
32 mg cholesterol
537 mg sodium
26 g carbohydrate
3 g fiber
15 g protein

Diabetic Exchanges: 2 lean meat, 2 vegetable, 1 starch.

Rustic Round Herb Bread

meat less

Patricia Vatta, Norwood, Ontario

PREP/TOTAL TIME: 30 MIN.

2 cups all-purpose flour
1 cup (4 ounces) shredded reduced-fat cheddar cheese
1 tablespoon sugar
2 teaspoons baking powder
1/2 teaspoon baking soda
1/2 teaspoon salt
1/2 teaspoon rubbed sage
1/2 teaspoon dried thyme
1/2 teaspoon dill weed
3 tablespoons cold butter
1 egg
1/2 cup fat-free plain yogurt
1/2 cup fat-free milk
1/2 teaspoon poppy seeds

In a large bowl, combine the first nine ingredients; mix well. Cut in butter until mixture resembles fine crumbs. In another bowl, whisk the egg, yogurt and milk. Stir into dry ingredients until just moistened.

Spoon into a 9-in. round baking pan coated with nonstick cooking spray. Sprinkle with poppy seeds. Bake at 400° for 20-25 minutes or until golden brown. Cool in pan on a wire rack. Cut into wedges. **YIELD:** 10 SERVINGS.

Nutrition Facts: One serving (1 piece) equals:
185 calories
7 g fat (4 g saturated fat)
39 mg cholesterol
379 mg sodium
23 g carbohydrate
1 g fiber
7 g protein

Diabetic Exchanges: 1-1/2 starch, 1 fat.

Set your table in **style** when you serve
this **low-carb** continental cuisine
with an Asian **flair**.

*Create a robust blend
of seasonings to tenderize the
meat while it marinates.
Chinese cabbage gives the
coleslaw a fluffier texture.
Dress it with white
wine vinegar, sesame oil
and a touch of sugar.*

Teriyaki Flank Steak

`low carb`

Nancy Fairless, Clifton, New Jersey

PREP: 5 MIN. + MARINATING **GRILL:** 10 MIN.

- 1-1/2 pounds beef flank steak
- 3/4 cup reduced-sodium teriyaki sauce
- 2 tablespoons sesame oil
- 1-1/2 teaspoons ground ginger *or* 2 tablespoons minced fresh gingerroot
- 5 garlic cloves, minced
- 1/2 teaspoon Chinese five-spice powder
- 1/4 teaspoon pepper
- 2 green onions, thinly sliced

Score the surface of the steak with shallow diagonal cuts, making diamond shapes. In a bowl, combine the teriyaki sauce, oil, ginger, garlic, five-spice powder and pepper; mix well. Pour 2/3 cup marinade into a large resealable plastic bag; add the steak and green onions. Seal bag and turn to coat; refrigerate for at least 8 hours or overnight. Cover and refrigerate remaining marinade.

If grilling the steak, coat grill rack with nonstick cooking spray before starting the grill. Drain and discard marinade from meat. Grill steak, covered, over medium-hot heat or broil 4-6 in. from the heat for 5-6 minutes on each side or until meat reaches desired doneness (for medium-rare, a meat thermometer should read 145°; medium, 160°; well-done, 170°), brushing occasionally with reserved marinade. **YIELD:** 6 SERVINGS.

Nutrition Facts:
One serving (3 ounces cooked steak) equals:
- 207 calories
- 10 g fat (4 g saturated fat)
- 54 mg cholesterol
- 388 mg sodium
- 4 g carbohydrate
-      trace fiber
- 23 g protein

Diabetic Exchanges: 3 lean meat, 1/2 fat.

Asian Coleslaw

`low carb` `meat less`

Alta Goodman, Canton, South Dakota

PREP: 15 MIN. + CHILLING

- 5 cups Chinese *or* napa cabbage (1-1/4 pounds), thinly sliced and ribs removed
- 3 medium carrots, shredded
- 2 green onions, thinly sliced
- 1/4 cup minced fresh cilantro
- 1/3 cup white wine vinegar
- 1 tablespoon canola oil
- 1 tablespoon sesame oil
- 1 teaspoon sugar
- 1/2 teaspoon salt

In a large bowl, combine the cabbage, carrots, green onions and cilantro. In a small bowl, whisk together the remaining ingredients. Pour over cabbage mixture and toss to coat. Cover and refrigerate for 1 hour or until chilled. **YIELD:** 6 SERVINGS.

Nutrition Facts: One serving (1 cup) equals:
- 75 calories
- 5 g fat (1 g saturated fat)
- 0 cholesterol
- 223 mg sodium
- 8 g carbohydrate
- 3 g fiber
- 1 g protein

Diabetic Exchanges: 1 vegetable, 1 fat.

Appealing Partners

- Sesame Green Beans 'n' Water Chestnuts, p. 283
- Fresh orange wedges

Practical Tips

For the most tender results, our Test Kitchen recommends slicing the flank steak thinly across the grain.

When making the coleslaw, the type of sesame oil you choose will dictate its flavor. Light-colored sesame oil is milder while darker Oriental sesame oil has a bolder taste.

Add shredded turkey or chicken to the coleslaw and serve it as a light main dish.

Homemade sauce turns these meatballs into **moist, magnificent** fare, sure to please even the pickiest eaters at your table.

Served over steaming, hot cooked noodles, these tangy meatballs pack a lot of zip. Complete your meal with a tossed salad dolloped with this quick dressing.

Zesty Meatballs

Debbie Segate, Grande Prairie, Alberta

PREP/TOTAL TIME: 30 MIN.

- 1/3   cup finely chopped onion
-   2   egg whites, lightly beaten
- 1/4   cup fat-free milk
-   2   teaspoons prepared mustard
- 1/2   teaspoon salt
- 3/4   cup graham cracker crumbs (about 12 squares)
- 3/4   pound lean ground beef
- 3/4   pound lean ground turkey

BARBECUE SAUCE:

- 1/2   cup packed brown sugar
-   3   tablespoons cornstarch
- 1/2   cup cider vinegar
- 1/2   cup ketchup
- 1/2   cup molasses
- 1/4   cup orange juice concentrate
-   2   tablespoons Dijon mustard
-   2   tablespoons reduced-sodium soy sauce
- 1/4   teaspoon hot pepper sauce
-   6   cups hot cooked yolk-free noodles

Place onion in a small microwave-safe bowl; cover and microwave on high for 2 minutes or until tender. In a large bowl, combine the egg whites, milk, mustard, salt, cracker crumbs and onion. Crumble beef and turkey over mixture and mix well.

Shape into 1-1/4-in. balls. Place 1 in. apart on 15-in. x 10-in. x 1-in. baking pans coated with nonstick cooking spray. Bake at 375° for 15-18 minutes or until meat is no longer pink.

Meanwhile, in a large saucepan, combine brown sugar and cornstarch. Stir in vinegar until smooth. Add the ketchup, molasses, orange juice concentrate, mustard, soy sauce and hot pepper sauce. Bring to a boil; cook and stir for 2 minutes or until thickened. Add meatballs; heat through. Serve over noodles. **YIELD:** 6 SERVINGS.

Nutrition Facts: One serving (6 meatballs and 1/3 cup sauce with 1 cup noodles) equals:

672	calories
13 g	fat (4 g saturated fat)
66 mg	cholesterol
1,050 mg	sodium
105 g	carbohydrate
4 g	fiber
34 g	protein

Diabetic Exchanges: 7 starch, 2 lean meat.

Creamy French Dressing `low carb` `meat less`

Taste of Home Test Kitchen
Greendale, Wisconsin

PREP/TOTAL TIME: 10 MIN.

-   1   cup ketchup
- 1/2   cup reduced-fat mayonnaise
-   3   tablespoons cider vinegar
-   3   tablespoons honey
-   2   tablespoons water
-   1   tablespoon olive oil
-   1   teaspoon lemon juice
- 1/2   teaspoon ground mustard
- 1/4   teaspoon salt

In a blender or food processor, combine all the ingredients; cover and process until blended. Store in the refrigerator. **YIELD:** 1-3/4 CUPS.

Nutrition Facts:
One serving (2 tablespoons) equals:

70	calories
4 g	fat (1 g saturated fat)
3 mg	cholesterol
318 mg	sodium
10 g	carbohydrate
1 g	fiber
1 g	protein

Diabetic Exchanges: 1/2 starch, 1/2 fat.

Appealing Partners

- Chunky applesauce
- Ice water with a lemon wedge

Practical Tips

For your next party, serve Zesty Meatballs as an appetizer instead of a main dish. Or, for a change of pace, top the meatballs with the sauce of your choice. Try them covered in brown gravy or along with pineapple and green pepper chunks in a sweet-sour sauce.

When preparing the noodles to accompany the main dish, remember 2 ounces of dry medium egg noodles equals 1 cup of cooked noodles. So you'll need 12 ounces of uncooked noodles to get 6 cups of cooked noodles.

Combine two **memorable** flavors into one **mouth-watering** meal and watch your **hungry bunch** reach for seconds!

Tuck flavorful ground beef filling into jumbo pasta shells, then finish them off with sour cream, olives and other toppings. You'll need just four ingredients to round out the meal with this slushy drink. Serve the cool treat with a straw as a frosty beverage or with a spoon as a light, refreshing dessert.

Appealing Partners

- Parsley rice
- Mixed salad greens

Practical Tips

If you'd like the Mexican Stuffed Shells a little spicier, choose a hotter salsa or use hot turkey Italian sausage.

A 12-ounce box of jumbo pasta shells contains about 35 shells. Since some may break during cooking, cook the entire box. Use whole ones in your main dish, then top broken shells (and extras) with spaghetti sauce for lunch.

Mexican Stuffed Shells

Norma Jean Shaw, Stephens City, Virginia

PREP: 15 MIN. **BAKE:** 25 MIN.

- 24 uncooked jumbo pasta shells
- 1 pound lean ground beef
- 2 cups salsa
- 1 can (8 ounces) tomato sauce
- 1 cup frozen corn
- 1/2 cup canned black beans, rinsed and drained
- 1 cup (4 ounces) shredded reduced-fat Mexican cheese blend *or* cheddar cheese

TOPPINGS:

- 8 tablespoons reduced-fat sour cream
- 8 tablespoons salsa
- 1/4 cup sliced ripe olives
- 1/4 cup sliced green onions

Cook pasta shells according to package directions; drain. In a nonstick skillet, cook beef over medium heat until no longer pink; drain. Stir in the salsa, tomato sauce, corn and beans. Spoon into pasta shells.

Place in a 13-in. x 9-in. x 2-in. baking dish coated with nonstick cooking spray. Sprinkle with cheese. Cover and bake at 350° for 25-30 minutes or until heated through. Top with sour cream, salsa, olives and onions. **YIELD:** 8 SERVINGS.

Nutrition Facts: One serving (3 stuffed shells, calulated with 1 tablespoon each sour cream and salsa and 1-1/2 teaspoons each olives and onions) equals:

- 315 calories
- 9 g fat (5 g saturated fat)
- 43 mg cholesterol
- 696 mg sodium
- 33 g carbohydrate
- 2 g fiber
- 22 g protein

Diabetic Exchanges: 2 starch, 2 lean meat, 1 vegetable, 1 fat.

Watermelon Slush

Elizabeth Montgomery, Taylorville, Illinois

PREP: 5 MIN. + FREEZING

- 8 cups cubed seedless watermelon
- 1/4 cup lime juice
- 1/4 cup sugar
- 2 cups diet lemon-lime soda, chilled

In a blender or food processor, cover and process the watermelon, lime juice and sugar in batches until smooth. Pour into a freezer-proof container.

Cover and freeze for 30 minutes or until edges begin to freeze. Stir and return to freezer. Repeat every 20 minutes or until slushy, about 90 minutes. Spoon 3/4 cup into bowls or glasses; add 1/4 cup soda. **YIELD:** 8 SERVINGS.

Nutrition Facts: One serving (1 cup) equals:

- 75 calories
- 1 g fat (trace saturated fat)
- 0 cholesterol
- 12 mg sodium
- 18 g carbohydrate
- 1 g fiber
- 1 g protein

Diabetic Exchange: 1 fruit.

Take a break and **get grilling!**
You'll flip over these two-handed burgers
piled high with all your favorite fixings.

A short ingredient list makes these big burgers a winner on busy evenings. Boost the grilled flavor with beer, garlic, onion and Worcestershire sauce. The coleslaw is a change from regular recipes, too. Let it sit in the refrigerator for a couple of hours so the flavors blend.

Appealing Partners

• Mixed fresh fruit
• Fat-free fudge pops

Practical Tips

Topping your burgers with lettuce and tomato is an easy way to add vegetables to your meal. Among the tomatoes on the grocery list are two for tonight's meal. Simply cut each one in six slices and serve two slices with each burger.

Don't have a can of Mexicorn for the slaw? Feel free to substitute 1-1/4 cups canned or frozen corn instead. The salad will have much the same flavor.

Hearty Backyard Burgers

Paula LeFevre, Garden, Michigan

PREP/TOTAL TIME: 25 MIN.

1/2	cup finely chopped onion
1/4	cup beer *or* nonalcoholic beer
1	tablespoon Worcestershire sauce
2	garlic cloves, minced
1	teaspoon salt
1/4	teaspoon pepper
1-1/2	pounds lean ground beef
6	rye rolls *or* whole wheat hamburger buns, split
6	lettuce leaves
12	tomato slices

In a bowl, combine the first six ingredients. Crumble beef over mixture and mix well. Shape into six patties.

Coat grill rack with nonstick cooking spray before starting the grill. Cover and grill over medium-high heat for 4-5 minutes on each side or until no longer pink and a meat thermometer reads 160°. Serve on rolls with lettuce and tomato slices. **YIELD:** 6 SERVINGS.

Nutrition Facts: One serving (1 burger) equals:
307 calories
12 g fat (4 g saturated fat)
70 mg cholesterol
686 mg sodium
25 g carbohydrate
4 g fiber
25 g protein

Diabetic Exchanges: 3 lean meat, 1-1/2 starch.

Broccoli Slaw

Betty Kleberger, Florissant, Missouri

PREP/TOTAL TIME: 10 MIN. + CHILLING

4	cups broccoli coleslaw mix
1	can (11 ounces) Mexicorn, drained
1/2	cup salsa
2	tablespoons reduced-fat mayonnaise
2	teaspoons sugar
1/2	teaspoon salt
1/8	teaspoon coarsely ground pepper
3	tablespoons cider vinegar

In a bowl, combine the coleslaw mix, corn and salsa. In a small bowl, combine the mayonnaise, sugar, salt and pepper. Gradually whisk in vinegar. Pour over coleslaw mixture; toss to coat evenly. Cover and refrigerate for at least 2 hours. **YIELD:** 6 SERVINGS.

Editor's Note: Broccoli coleslaw mix may be found in the produce section of most grocery stores.

Nutrition Facts: One serving (3/4 cup) equals:
87 calories
2 g fat (trace saturated fat)
2 mg cholesterol
620 mg sodium
16 g carbohydrate
3 g fiber
3 protein

Diabetic Exchanges: 1/2 starch, 1 vegetable.

A **popular** restaurant entree garners great reviews
when **lightened up** for family-friendly dining.

*This version of a classic
restaurant dish gets its
rewarding flavor from broth
and wine, even though the
extra oil has been eliminated.
You'll need just moments to
toss together this pretty salad
and tangy classic dressing to
round out your meal.*

Chicken Marsala `low carb`

Nancy Granaman, Burlington, Iowa

PREP: 25 MIN. + MARINATING **BAKE:** 25 MIN.

- 6 boneless skinless chicken breast halves
  (4 ounces *each*)
- 1 cup fat-free Italian salad dressing
- 1 tablespoon all-purpose flour
- 1 teaspoon Italian seasoning
- 1/2 teaspoon garlic powder
- 1/4 teaspoon paprika
- 1/4 teaspoon pepper
- 2 tablespoons olive oil, *divided*
- 1 tablespoon butter
- 1/2 cup reduced-sodium chicken broth
- 1/2 cup Marsala wine *or* 3 tablespoons
  unsweetened apple juice plus
  5 tablespoons additional reduced-sodium
  chicken broth
- 1 pound sliced fresh mushrooms
- 1/2 cup minced fresh parsley

Flatten chicken to 1/2-in. thickness. Place in
a large resealable plastic bag; add salad
dressing. Seal bag and turn to coat; refrigerate for 8 hours or overnight.

Drain and discard marinade. Combine the
flour, Italian seasoning, garlic powder, paprika and pepper; sprinkle over both sides of
chicken. In a large nonstick skillet coated
with nonstick cooking spray, cook chicken
in 1 tablespoon oil and butter for 2 minutes
on each side or until browned. Transfer to a
13-in. x 9-in. x 2-in. baking dish coated with
nonstick cooking spray.

Gradually add broth and wine or apple
juice mixture to skillet, stirring to loosen
browned bits. Bring to a boil; cook and stir
for 2 minutes. Strain sauce; set aside. In the
same skillet, cook mushrooms in remaining
oil for 2 minutes; drain. Stir sauce into
mushrooms; heat through. Pour over chick-
en; sprinkle with parsley. Bake, uncovered,
at 350° for 25-30 minutes or until chicken
juices run clear. **YIELD:** 6 SERVINGS.

Nutrition Facts: One serving (1 chicken breast
half with 1/3 cup mushroom mixture) equals:
- 247 calories
- 9 g fat (3 g saturated fat)
- 68 mg cholesterol
- 348 mg sodium
- 9 g carbohydrate
- 1 g fiber
- 26 g protein

Diabetic Exchanges: 3 very lean meat, 1-1/2 fat,
1/2 starch.

Cranberry Spinach Salad `low sodium` `meat less`

Anne Smithson, Cary, North Carolina

PREP/TOTAL TIME: 20 MIN.

- 8 cups fresh baby spinach
- 1 cup dried cranberries
- 2 medium pears, cored and chopped
- 1/4 cup cider vinegar
- 5 tablespoons sugar
- 1 teaspoon dried minced onion
- 1/2 teaspoon Worcestershire sauce
- 1/2 teaspoon ground mustard
- 1/4 teaspoon paprika
- 1/4 cup olive oil
- 1 tablespoon sesame seeds
- 1 teaspoon poppy seeds
- 2 tablespoons chopped pecans, toasted

In a large bowl, combine the spinach, cranberries and pears. In a blender, combine the
vinegar, sugar, onion, Worcestershire sauce,
mustard and paprika; cover and process until blended. While processing, gradually add
oil in a steady stream. Add sesame seeds and
poppy seeds. Pour over salad and toss to
coat. Sprinkle with pecans. **YIELD:** 8 SERVINGS.

Nutrition Facts: One serving (1 cup) equals:
- 189 calories
- 9 g fat (1 g saturated fat)
- 0 cholesterol
- 28 mg sodium
- 29 g carbohydrate
- 3 g fiber
- 2 g protein

Diabetic Exchanges: 2 fat, 1 vegetable, 1 fruit,
1/2 starch.

Appealing Partners

- Crescent rolls
- Berry Nectarine Salad, p. 249

Practical Tips

To flatten boneless chicken
breasts, place between two pieces
of waxed paper or plastic wrap.
Starting in the center and
working out to the edges, pound
lightly with the flat side of a
meat mallet until the chicken is
even in thickness.

A bag of ready-to-use salad mix
can be substituted for the
spinach in the salad. If you don't
have dried cranberries on hand,
try other dried fruits, such as
pineapple tidbits or golden
raisins.

Make any meal a fiesta with a **south-of-the-border** specialty that adds **sizzle** without all of the extra calories!

Colorful sweet peppers and tenders strips of turkey fold nicely into warm flour tortillas for the perfect no-fuss meal! Flavored with cilantro, cumin and cayenne, this fun main dish is bursting with authentic Mexican flavor. Serve it with a moist and mildly seasoned rice for a filling spread.

Appealing Partners

- Fresh salsa
- Fruit juice popsicles

Practical Tips

For a change of pace, you can exchange chicken breast or sirloin steak with the turkey tenderloin in the fajitas.

You can use instant rice in place of the long grain rice in the Spanish Rice recipe. Instead of using 1 cup uncooked long grain rice, use 2 cups uncooked instant rice. Prepare it according to package directions using the same amount of broth called for in the recipe.

Turkey Fajitas

Bonnie Basinger, Lees Summit, Missouri

PREP/TOTAL TIME: 30 MIN.

- 1 pound boneless turkey tenderloins, cut into thin strips
- 1 tablespoon canola oil
- 1 *each* medium green, sweet red and yellow peppers, cut into 1/4-inch strips
- 1 medium onion, thinly sliced and separated into rings
- 1 garlic clove, minced
- 1/2 teaspoon salt
- 1/2 teaspoon ground cumin
- 1/2 teaspoon pepper
- 1/4 teaspoon cayenne pepper
- 1/2 cup minced fresh cilantro
- 1/4 cup lime juice
- 8 flour tortillas (6 inches), warmed

In a large nonstick skillet, saute turkey in oil for 2 minutes. Add the peppers, onion, garlic, salt, cumin, pepper and cayenne. Cook and stir for 5 minutes or until turkey is no longer pink and peppers are crisp-tender. Stir in cilantro and lime juice; cook 1 minute longer. Serve in tortillas. **YIELD:** 4 SERVINGS.

Nutrition Facts: One serving (2 fajitas) equals:
- 369 calories
- 7 g fat (trace saturated fat)
- 45 mg cholesterol
- 448 mg sodium
- 42 g carbohydrate
- 4 g fiber
- 37 g protein

Diabetic Exchanges: 3 lean meat, 2 vegetable, 2 starch.

Spanish Rice

Sharon Donat, Kalispell, Montana

PREP/TOTAL TIME: 30 MIN.

- 1 can (14-1/2 ounces) vegetable broth
- 1 can (14-1/2 ounces) stewed tomatoes
- 1 cup uncooked long grain rice
- 1 teaspoon olive oil
- 1 teaspoon chili powder
- 1/4 teaspoon dried oregano
- 1/4 teaspoon garlic salt

In a large saucepan, combine all ingredients. Bring to a boil. Reduce heat; cover and simmer for 20-25 minutes or until rice is tender and liquid is absorbed. **YIELD:** 6 SERVINGS.

Nutrition Facts: One serving (2/3 cup) equals:
- 156 calories
- 1 g fat (trace saturated fat)
- 0 cholesterol
- 350 mg sodium
- 32 g carbohydrate
- 1 g fiber
- 4 g protein

Diabetic Exchange: 2 starch.

One bite of this luscious, **low-fat** sandwich and you'll hand out **high marks** for its satisfying flavor.

Get a head start on dinner when you marinate the chicken breasts for this casual meal the previous night. For a colorful accompaniment, fix this 15-minute salad and place servings on lettuce leaves, then garnish with ripe tomato wedges.

Appealing Partners

- Sparkling water with lime
- Lemon sherbet

Practical Tips

If your family prefers pork over chicken, use 1/2-inch-thick boneless pork chops instead of chicken breasts in the sandwich recipe. There's no need to pound them. Just marinate and continue with the rest of the recipe directions. Be sure to cook the pork to 160°.

To cut down on last-minute preparation, you can assemble the Black-Eyed Pea Salad ahead of time. Cover it and keep it in the fridge until serving.

Ultimate Chicken Sandwiches

Gregg Voss, Emerson, Nebraska

PREP: 10 MIN. + MARINATING **BAKE:** 20 MIN.

  6 boneless skinless chicken breast halves (4 ounces *each*)
  1 cup buttermilk
1/2 cup reduced-fat biscuit/baking mix
1/2 cup cornmeal
1-1/2 teaspoons paprika
3/4 teaspoon salt
3/4 teaspoon poultry seasoning
1/2 teaspoon garlic powder
1/2 teaspoon pepper
1/4 teaspoon cayenne pepper
  6 onion *or* kaiser rolls, split
  6 lettuce leaves
12 tomato slices

Pound chicken to 1/2-in. thickness. Pour buttermilk into a large resealable plastic bag; add chicken. Seal bag and turn to coat; refrigerate for 8 hours or overnight.

In a shallow bowl, combine the biscuit mix, cornmeal, paprika, salt, poultry seasoning, garlic powder, pepper and cayenne. Remove chicken one piece at a time, allowing excess buttermilk to drain off. Discard buttermilk. Coat chicken with cornmeal mixture; place in a 13-in. x 9-in. x 2-in. baking dish coated with nonstick cooking spray.

Bake, uncovered, at 400° for 12 minutes. Turn chicken. Bake 8-12 minutes longer or until juices run clear and coating is lightly browned. Serve on rolls with lettuce and tomato. **YIELD:** 6 SERVINGS.

Nutrition Facts: One serving (1 sandwich) equals:
    372 calories
      7 g fat (3 g saturated fat)
   63 mg cholesterol
 759 mg sodium
    46 g carbohydrate
     3 g fiber
    31 g protein

Diabetic Exchanges: 3 starch, 3 lean meat.

Black-Eyed Pea Salad

Melinda Ewbank, Fairfield, Ohio

meatless

PREP: 15 MIN. + CHILLING

  6 ounces small shell pasta, cooked and drained
  1 can (15 ounces) black-eyed peas, rinsed and drained
  1 cup sliced green onions
3/4 cup diced seeded peeled cucumber
3/4 cup diced green pepper
3/4 cup diced seeded tomato
  1 small jalapeno pepper, seeded and finely chopped
DRESSING:
  3 tablespoons canola oil
1/4 cup red wine vinegar
  1 teaspoon sugar
  1 teaspoon dried basil
  1 teaspoon chili powder
  1 teaspoon hot pepper sauce
1/2 teaspoon seasoned salt

In a salad bowl, combine the first seven ingredients. In a jar with a tight-fitting lid, combine the oil, vinegar, sugar, basil, chili powder, hot pepper sauce and seasoned salt; shake well. Pour over salad and stir to coat. Cover and refrigerate for at least 2 hours before serving. **YIELD:** 6 SERVINGS.

Editor's Note: When cutting or seeding hot peppers, use rubber or plastic gloves to protect your hands. Avoid touching your face.

Nutrition Facts: One serving (1 cup) equals:
    186 calories
     6 g fat (1 g saturated fat)
     0 cholesterol
 269 mg sodium
    28 g carbohydrate
     4 g fiber
     6 g protein

Diabetic Exchanges: 1-1/2 starch, 1 vegetable, 1 fat.

Piping hot pizza is an easy option for fast family meals. Why settle for frozen when you can make it fresh?

For this pizza, traditional tomato sauce is replaced by a light-lemon spread on the golden crust, then topped with plenty of deli turkey, bacon, tomato and two kinds of cheese. For a heartier meal, also serve a bowl of this soup that stars cheese tortellini and beans.

Turkey Tomato Pizza

Michelle Beall, Westminster, Maryland

PREP/TOTAL TIME: 30 MIN.

- 1   tube (10 ounces) refrigerated pizza crust
- 2   teaspoons sesame seeds
- 1/4 cup reduced-fat mayonnaise
- 1/4 teaspoon grated lemon peel
- 1   cup (4 ounces) shredded reduced-fat Mexican cheese blend
- 1   teaspoon dried basil
- 1/4 pound thinly sliced deli turkey, julienned
- 3   bacon strips, cooked and crumbled
- 2   small tomatoes, thinly sliced
- 1   cup (4 ounces) shredded reduced-fat Swiss cheese
- 2   tablespoons thinly sliced green onions

Unroll the pizza crust onto a 15-in. x 10-in. x 1-in. baking pan coated with nonstick cooking spray. Flatten dough and build up edges slightly. Prick dough several times with a fork; sprinkle with sesame seeds. Bake at 425° for 10-12 minutes or until lightly browned.

Combine the mayonnaise and lemon peel; spread over crust. Sprinkle with Mexican cheese blend and basil. Top with turkey, bacon, tomatoes and Swiss cheese. Bake for 7-9 minutes or until the crust is golden brown and cheese is melted. Sprinkle with onion. **YIELD:** 6 SERVINGS.

Nutrition Facts: One serving (1 slice) equals:
- 284 calories
- 11 g fat (4 g saturated fat)
- 27 mg cholesterol
- 865 mg sodium
- 27 g carbohydrate
- 1 g fiber
- 19 g protein

Diabetic Exchanges: 2 meat, 1-1/2 starch, 1 vegetable, 1 fat.

Basil Tortellini Soup

Dwyer-Reff, Fort Wayne, Indiana

PREP/TOTAL TIME: 20 MIN.

- 4-1/2 cups chicken broth
- 1   package (9 ounces) refrigerated cheese tortellini
- 1   can (15 ounces) white kidney *or* cannellini beans, rinsed and drained
- 1   cup chopped fresh tomato
- 1/3 to 1/2 cup shredded fresh basil
- 1   to 2 tablespoons balsamic vinegar
- 1/4 teaspoon salt
- 1/8 to 1/4 teaspoon pepper
- 1/3 cup shredded Parmesan cheese

In a large saucepan, bring broth to a boil. Add tortellini; cook until tender, about 6 minutes. Stir in the beans, tomato and basil. Reduce heat; simmer, uncovered, for 5 minutes. Add the vinegar, salt and pepper. Serve with cheese. **YIELD:** 6 SERVINGS.

Nutrition Facts: One serving (1 cup) equals:
- 238 calories
- 6 g fat (3 g saturated fat)
- 20 mg cholesterol
- 1,170 mg sodium
- 33 g carbohydrate
- 4 g fiber
- 13 g protein

Diabetic Exchanges: 2 starch, 1 lean meat, 1/2 fat.

Appealing Partners

- Sparkling water
- Low-fat banana pudding

Practical Tips

Grate 1/4 teaspoon of peel from a lemon for the pizza. Then refrigerate the lemon so you can squeeze a bit of juice from it over cooked vegetables at a different meal.

The tortellini soup is nicely seasoned with fresh basil, but if you don't have any on hand, you can use 1 teaspoon dried basil instead.

Plan dinner at the table or **pack a picnic** to go.
Either way, this **classic** chicken dinner fits the bill.

With a sweet and tangy sauce, these tender chicken breasts make any meal special. To complement the entree, serve a medley of red pepper, red potatoes and green peas in a throw-together salad. When chilled, it's ready to go!

Appealing Partners

- Baked beans
- Tropical fruit salad

Practical Tips

Make an extra batch of the barbecue sauce and use it for burgers, ribs or chops.

If you don't have the salt-free garlic seasoning blend called for in the potato salad recipe, use an equal amount of regular salt-free seasoning blend and add between 1/8 and 1/4 teaspoon of garlic powder.

Oven Barbecued Chicken

Marge Wagner, Roselle, Illinois

PREP: 20 MIN. **BAKE:** 45 MIN.

6	bone-in chicken breast halves (8 ounces *each*)
1/3	cup chopped onion
3/4	cup ketchup
1/2	cup water
1/3	cup white vinegar
3	tablespoons brown sugar
1	tablespoon Worcestershire sauce
1	teaspoon ground mustard
1/4	teaspoon salt
1/8	teaspoon pepper

In a nonstick skillet coated with nonstick cooking spray, brown chicken over medium heat. Transfer to a 13-in. x 9-in. x 2-in. baking dish coated with nonstick cooking spray.

Recoat skillet with nonstick cooking spray; cook onion over medium heat until tender. Stir in the remaining ingredients. Bring to a boil. Reduce heat; simmer, uncovered, for 15 minutes. Pour over chicken. Bake, uncovered, at 350° for 45-55 minutes or until chicken juices run clear and a meat thermometer reads 170°. **YIELD:** 6 SERVINGS.

Nutrition Facts: One serving (1 chicken breast half) equals:

241	calories
4 g	fat (1 g saturated fat)
90 mg	cholesterol
563 mg	sodium
17 g	carbohydrate
1 g	fiber
34 g	protein

Diabetic Exchanges: 4 very lean meat, 1 starch.

Potato 'n' Pea Salad

`low fat` `meat less`

Taste of Home Test Kitchen
Greendale, Wisconsin

PREP: 10 MIN. **COOK:** 15 MIN. + CHILLING

9	unpeeled small red potatoes (1-1/4 pounds)
1/3	cup fat-free plain yogurt
1/3	cup reduced-fat sour cream
3	tablespoons chopped green onions
3	teaspoons minced fresh parsley, *divided*
3/4	teaspoon dried basil
1/2	teaspoon *each* salt and salt-free garlic seasoning blend
	Dash paprika
3/4	cup fresh *or* frozen peas, thawed
1/2	cup chopped sweet red pepper

Place potatoes in a large saucepan and cover with water. Bring to a boil. Reduce heat; cover and cook for 15-20 minutes or until tender. Drain and cool; slice potatoes.

In a large bowl, combine the yogurt, sour cream, onions, 1 teaspoon parsley, basil, salt, seasoning blend and paprika. Add the potatoes, peas and red pepper; toss to coat. Sprinkle with remaining parsley. Cover and refrigerate for at least 1 hour. **YIELD:** 6 SERVINGS.

Nutrition Facts:
One serving (1-1/2 cups) equals:

115	calories
1 g	fat (1 g saturated fat)
5 mg	cholesterol
246 mg	sodium
22 g	carbohydrate
3 g	fiber
5 g	protein

Diabetic Exchange: 1-1/2 starch.

No need to sacrifice flavor for **fewer calories.**
Try this **elegant option** when you want to
impress guests with a lighter dish.

Prepare these appealing roll-ups for family and company alike. Pop them in the oven along with the distinctive side dish. Both conveniently cook at the same oven temperature to save you time.

Appealing Partners

- Long grain and wild rice
- Apple slices with fat-free caramel dip

Practical Tips

To cut down on last-minute preparation, assemble the Breaded Turkey Rolls the night before. The next day, coat them with the bread crumb mixture right before baking.

Use another reduced-fat cheese, such as cheddar, instead of the Swiss cheese called for in the entree recipe.

If your family is fond of garlic, sprinkle the asparagus with a clove or two of minced garlic before roasting.

Breaded Turkey Rolls

low carb

Rita Pearl, Norwalk, Iowa

PREP/TOTAL TIME: 30 MIN.

- 8 uncooked turkey breast slices (1 pound)
- 8 thin slices deli turkey ham (1/4 ounce each)
- 8 slices reduced-fat Swiss cheese (1/2 ounce each)
- 1 tablespoon Dijon mustard
- 7 tablespoons dry bread crumbs
- 3/4 teaspoon salt
- 1/4 teaspoon pepper
- 1/8 teaspoon paprika
- 3 tablespoons reduced-fat mayonnaise

Flatten turkey slices to 1/8-in. thickness. Top each with a slice of ham and cheese; spread with mustard. Roll up tightly and secure with toothpicks.

In a shallow bowl, combine the bread crumbs, salt, pepper and paprika. Brush with turkey roll-ups with mayonnaise, then coat with crumb mixture. Place in an 11-in. x 7-in. x 2-in. baking dish coated with non-stick cooking spray. Bake, uncovered, at 425° for 20-25 minutes or until meat juices run clear. **YIELD:** 4 SERVINGS.

Nutrition Facts: One serving (2 rolls) equals:
- 315 calories
- 12 g fat (5 g saturated fat)
- 104 mg cholesterol
- 962 mg sodium
- 10 g carbohydrate
- trace fiber
- 40 g protein

Diabetic Exchanges: 4 lean meat, 1 fat, 1/2 starch.

Roasted Asparagus With Balsamic Vinegar

low fat | low carb | meat less

Natalie Peterson, Kirkland, Washington

PREP/TOTAL TIME: 15 MIN.

- 1-1/2 pounds fresh asparagus, trimmed
- 2 teaspoons olive oil
- 1/2 teaspoon salt
- 1/8 teaspoon white pepper
- 3 tablespoons balsamic vinegar

Place the asparagus in a 13-in. x 9-in. x 2-in. baking dish. Sprinkle with oil, salt and pepper; toss to coat. Bake, uncovered, at 425° for 10-15 minutes or until lightly browned. Drizzle with vinegar just before serving. **YIELD:** 4 SERVINGS.

Nutrition Facts: One serving (6 ounces) equals:
- 47 calories
- 3 g fat (trace saturated fat)
- 0 cholesterol
- 305 mg sodium
- 5 g carbohydrate
- 1 g fiber
- 2 g protein

Diabetic Exchanges: 1 vegetable, 1/2 fat.

For a **tried-and-true** palate pleaser, bake up a soothing casserole brimming with **down-home** goodness.

The creamy casserole topped with crunchy cornflake crumbs is just the beginning. Top off the meal with individual dishes of this fluffy dessert, sure to satisfy any sweet tooth.

Appealing Partners

- Spinach salad with low-fat dressing
- Hot apple cider

Practical Tips

You need 3 cups of cooked chicken for the Rotini Chicken Casserole. Purchase a pound of boneless chicken, then poach, microwave or grill it and cube it for the recipe. Or use leftover chicken if you have it on hand.

When preparing the casserole, feel free to use a 13-in. x 9-in. baking dish instead of a 3-quart dish.

For an extra treat, create a chocolate topping for the mousse. Melt 1/2 cup of milk chocolate chips and drizzle a bit on each serving.

Rotini Chicken Casserole

Ruth Lee, Troy, Ontario

PREP: 15 MIN.   **BAKE:** 25 MIN.

2-3/4 cups uncooked tricolor rotini *or* spiral pasta
  3/4 cup chopped onion
  1/2 cup chopped celery
    2 garlic cloves, minced
    1 tablespoon olive oil
    3 cups cubed cooked chicken breast
    1 can (10-3/4 ounces) reduced-fat reduced-sodium condensed cream of chicken soup, undiluted
1-1/2 cups fat-free milk
    1 package (16 ounces) frozen Italian-blend vegetables
    1 cup (4 ounces) shredded reduced-fat cheddar cheese
    2 tablespoons minced fresh parsley
1-1/4 teaspoons dried thyme
    1 teaspoon salt
  2/3 cup crushed cornflakes

Cook pasta according to package directions. Meanwhile, in a nonstick skillet, saute onion, celery and garlic in oil until tender. Drain pasta; place in a bowl. Add the onion mixture, chicken, soup, milk, frozen vegetables, cheese, parsley, thyme and salt.

Pour into a shallow 3-qt. baking dish coated with nonstick cooking spray. Cover and bake at 350° for 25 minutes. Sprinkle with cornflakes; spritz with nonstick cooking spray. Bake, uncovered, 10-15 minutes longer or until heated through. **YIELD:** 8 SERVINGS.

Nutrition Facts: One serving (1-1/3 cups) equals:
    341 calories
      7 g fat (3 g saturated fat)
    56 mg cholesterol
   698 mg sodium
     40 g carbohydrate
      3 g fiber
     28 g protein

Diabetic Exchanges: 3 lean meat, 2 starch, 1 vegetable.

Strawberry Mousse

Waydella Hart, Parsons, Kansas

PREP/TOTAL TIME: 20 MIN.

    4 cups quartered fresh strawberries *or* frozen unsweetened strawberries
  1/2 cup sugar
    1 package (1 ounce) sugar-free instant vanilla pudding mix
    1 carton (8 ounces) frozen reduced-fat whipped topping, thawed

In a food processor or blender, combine strawberries and sugar; cover and process until smooth. Strain and discard seeds. Return strawberry mixture to the food processor. Add pudding mix; cover and process until smooth. Transfer to a large bowl; fold in whipped topping. Spoon into dessert dishes. Refrigerate until serving. **YIELD:** 8 SERVINGS.

Nutrition Facts: One serving (1/2 cup) equals:
    145 calories
      3 g fat (3 g saturated fat)
      0 cholesterol
   148 mg sodium
     27 g carbohydrate
      2 g fiber
         trace protein

Diabetic Exchanges: 1 starch, 1 fruit, 1/2 fat.

Heat up **cool nights** with a **steaming** kettle of homemade stew. Everyone will leave the table satisfied and in **good spirits.**

Brimming with Italian sausage, pasta and beans, this hearty stew smells wonderful as it cooks. Bake a round loaf of this quick bread to serve tall, tasty wedges on the side.

Tomato Sausage Stew

Jeanette Jones, Muncie, Indiana

PREP: 10 MIN.   **COOK:** 45 MIN.

- 1/2 pound turkey Italian sausage links, casings removed
- 1 large onion, chopped
- 2 garlic cloves, minced
- 3/4 cup chopped carrots
- 1 fennel bulb, chopped
- 1/3 cup chopped celery
- 1 can (14-1/2 ounces) reduced-sodium chicken broth
- 3 medium tomatoes, peeled, seeded and chopped
- 1 teaspoon dried basil
- 1 teaspoon dried oregano
- 1/4 teaspoon salt
- 1 cup uncooked small pasta shells
- 1 can (15 ounces) navy beans, rinsed and drained
- 1/2 cup shredded Parmesan cheese

In a Dutch oven, cook the sausage, onion and garlic over medium heat until meat is no longer pink; drain. Add the carrots, fennel and celery; cook until vegetables are softened. Stir in the broth to loosen any browned bits from pan. Add tomatoes, basil, oregano and salt. Bring to a boil. Reduce heat; cover and simmer for 10 minutes or until vegetables are tender.

Stir in pasta and beans. Add enough water to cover. Bring to a boil. Reduce heat; cover and simmer for 10 minutes or until vegetables are tender. Sprinkle with Parmesan cheese. **YIELD:** 6 SERVINGS.

Nutrition Facts:
One serving (1-1/2 cups) equals:
- 247 calories
- 6 g fat (2 g saturated fat)
- 24 mg cholesterol
- 900 mg sodium
- 36 g carbohydrate
- 7 g fiber
- 17 g protein

Diabetic Exchanges: 2 lean meat, 2 vegetable, 1-1/2 starch.

Hearty Oat Loaf

meat less

Judi Havens, Denton, Texas

PREP: 15 MIN.   **BAKE:** 40 MIN.

- 2 cups all-purpose flour
- 1 cup whole wheat flour
- 1/2 cup plus 2 tablespoons quick-cooking oats, *divided*
- 1/4 cup sugar
- 3 teaspoons baking powder
- 3/4 teaspoon salt
- 1 egg
- 1-1/2 cups fat-free milk
- 3 tablespoons canola oil

In a large bowl, combine the flours, 1/2 cup oats, sugar, baking powder and salt.

In another bowl, combine the egg, milk and oil; stir into dry ingredients just until moistened. Spread batter into an 8- or 9-in. round baking pan coated with nonstick cooking spray. Sprinkle with remaining oats.

Bake at 350° for 40-50 minutes or until a toothpick inserted near the center comes out clean. Cool for 5 minutes before removing from pan to a wire rack. Serve warm. **YIELD:** 1 LOAF (10 WEDGES).

Nutrition Facts: One serving (1 slice) equals:
- 229 calories
- 6 g fat (1 g saturated fat)
- 22 mg cholesterol
- 272 mg sodium
- 38 g carbohydrate
- 3 g fiber
- 7 g protein

Diabetic Exchanges: 2-1/2 starch, 1 fat.

Appealing Partners

- Tossed salad with Hold-the-Oil French Dressing, p. 252
- Sugar-free vanilla pudding

Practical Tips

Feel free to substitute a 15-1/2-ounce can of great northern beans for the canned navy beans in the stew recipe.

Have any leftover stew? Jeanette says it's great reheated for lunch or another dinner. It will keep in the fridge for up to 2 days.

The Hearty Oat Loaf is best served warm. For a different look, sprinkle the loaf with sesame seeds, poppy seeds or toasted wheat germ before baking.

Calorie-conscious cooks appreciate the quick-fix burgers and low-fat fries. One taste and so will you!

Turkey and pineapple turn everyday burgers into something to talk about. The thick, skins-on potato wedges are covered in a nicely seasoned coating before they're baked to a golden crispness.

Hawaiian Turkey Burgers

Babette Watterson, Atglen, Pennsylvania

PREP/TOTAL TIME: 25 MIN.

- 1   can (8 ounces) sliced pineapple
- 1/2 cup dry bread crumbs
- 1/2 cup sliced green onions
- 1/2 cup chopped sweet red pepper
- 1   tablespoon reduced-sodium soy sauce
- 1/4 teaspoon salt
- 1   pound lean ground turkey
- 1/4 cup reduced-sodium teriyaki sauce
- 4   sesame hamburger buns

Coat grill rack with nonstick cooking spray before starting the grill. Drain pineapple, reserving 1/4 cup juice (discard remaining juice or save for another use); set pineapple aside. In a bowl, combine the bread crumbs, onions, red pepper, soy sauce, salt and reserved pineapple juice. Crumble turkey over mixture and mix well. Shape into four patties.

Grill, covered, over medium heat for 3 minutes on each side. Brush with teriyaki sauce. Grill 4-6 minutes longer on each side or until meat is no longer pink and a meat thermometer reads 165°. Grill pineapple slices for 2 minutes on each side, basting occasionally with teriyaki sauce. Warm buns on grill; top each with a burger and pineapple slice. **YIELD:** 4 SERVINGS.

Nutrition Facts: One serving (1 sandwich) equals:
- 391 calories
- 13 g fat (3 g saturated fat)
- 90 mg cholesterol
- 1,041 mg sodium
- 42 g carbohydrate
- 3 g fiber
- 27 g protein

Diabetic Exchanges: 3 lean meat, 2 starch, 1 fruit.

Oven-Baked Country Fries

LaDonna Reed, Ponca City, Oklahoma

PREP: 10 MIN.   **BAKE:** 40 MIN.

- 2   egg whites
- 1/4 cup all-purpose flour
- 1/3 cup dry bread crumbs
- 2   tablespoons grated Parmesan cheese
- 1-1/2 teaspoons onion salt
- 1-1/2 teaspoons Italian seasoning
- 1   teaspoon paprika
- 1/4 teaspoon pepper
- 3   medium unpeeled baking potatoes (1 pound)

In a shallow bowl, beat egg whites until foamy. In another shallow bowl, combine the flour, bread crumbs, Parmesan cheese and seasonings. Cut each potato lengthwise into eight wedges. Dip potatoes into egg whites, then coat with crumb mixture.

Place in a single layer on a baking sheet coated with nonstick cooking spray. Spray wedges evenly with nonstick cooking spray. Bake, uncovered, at 375° for 40-45 minutes or until golden brown. **YIELD:** 4 SERVINGS.

Nutrition Facts: One serving (6 wedges) equals:
- 185 calories
- 1 g fat (1 g saturated fat)
- 3 mg cholesterol
- 822 mg sodium
- 36 g carbohydrate
- 3 g fiber
- 7 g protein

Diabetic Exchange: 2-1/2 starch.

Appealing Partners

- Strawberries with Crisp Wontons, p. 334
- Mixed pepper strips with low-fat dressing

Practical Tips

When buying ground turkey, check the label. The lean ground turkey called for in the burger recipe is 93% lean. Some ground turkey has a higher percentage of fat.

For easy cleanup, line the baking sheet with aluminum foil before cooking the oven-fried potatoes.

Heat up the skillet for this simple stir-fry you'll have **table-ready** in just 20 minutes.

Extra cooked turkey gets a tasty treatment in this stir-fry which features a simple soy glaze. For a light dessert, serve slices of this super-moist cake. It's a boxed mix jazzed up with poppy seeds, orange juice, almond extract and cinnamon.

Turkey Stir-Fry

`low carb`

Kylene Konosky, Jermyn, Pennsylvania

PREP/TOTAL TIME: 20 MIN.

1-1/2 cups sliced fresh mushrooms
   1 cup sliced celery
  1/2 cup sliced onion
   2 tablespoons canola oil
   2 tablespoons cornstarch
   1 can (10-1/2 ounces) condensed chicken broth, undiluted
   1 tablespoon reduced-sodium soy sauce
   2 cups cubed cooked turkey breast
   2 cups fresh snow peas
  1/2 cup sliced water chestnuts
Hot cooked rice, optional

In a nonstick skillet, saute the mushrooms, celery and onion in oil until tender. Combine the cornstarch, broth and soy sauce until smooth; stir into vegetable mixture. Bring to a boil; cook and stir for 1-2 minutes or until thickened.

Reduce heat to medium-low. Add the turkey, peas and water chestnuts; cook until turkey is heated through and peas are tender. Serve over rice if desired. **YIELD:** 4 SERVINGS.

Nutrition Facts:
One serving (1 cup turkey mixture) equals:
   242 calories
    9 g fat (1 g saturated fat)
   61 mg cholesterol
  687 mg sodium
   13 g carbohydrate
    2 g fiber
   27 g protein

Diabetic Exchanges: 3 lean meat, 1 vegetable, 1/2 starch.

Orange Poppy Seed Cake

`low fat`

Brenda Craig, Spokane, Washington

PREP: 20 MIN.   **BAKE:** 45 MIN. + COOLING

   1 package (18-1/4 ounces) yellow cake mix
   2 tablespoons poppy seeds
   1 cup fat-free sour cream
  3/4 cup egg substitute
   1 can (6 ounces) frozen orange juice concentrate, thawed
  1/3 cup water
  1/4 teaspoon almond extract
   2 tablespoons sugar
  1/2 teaspoon ground cinnamon
GLAZE:
1-3/4 cups confectioners' sugar
   2 tablespoons fat-free milk
   1 tablespoon orange juice

In a large bowl, combine the cake mix and poppy seeds. In a small mixing bowl, combine the sour cream, egg substitute, orange juice concentrate, water and almond extract; beat until smooth. Stir into cake mix just until combined. Coat a 10-in. fluted tube pan with nonstick cooking spray. Combine the sugar and cinnamon; sprinkle evenly in pan. Pour batter into pan.

Bake at 350° for 40-45 minutes or until a toothpick inserted near the center comes out clean. Cool for 10 minutes before removing from pan to a wire rack. Combine glaze ingredients; drizzle over cooled cake. **YIELD:** 14 SERVINGS.

Nutrition Facts: One serving (1 piece) equals:
   247 calories
    1 g fat (1 g saturated fat)
      trace cholesterol
  283 mg sodium
   55 g carbohydrate
      trace fiber
    5 g protein

Appealing Partners

- Phyllo Turkey Egg Rolls, p. 201
- Iced tea

Practical Tips

The Turkey Stir-Fry is a breeze to make with leftover holiday turkey. In case you don't have any, buy a pound of turkey tenderloins. To cook them for this recipe, place them on a rack in a roasting pan and bake in a 350° oven for 20-30 minutes or until a meat thermometer reads 170°.

To round out the stir-fry, serve it with long grain rice.

Everyone will **say yes** to seconds when you
pass a platter of this classic chicken delight.

The crisp coating on this juicy chicken is created by baking it in the oven instead of frying it on the stove. The moist corn bread is a traditional Southern side to the chicken.

Appealing Partners

- Vegetable sticks
- Melon balls with sugar-free glaze

Practical Tips

For the chicken, you'll need about 3-1/2 cups of cornflakes to make 1 cup crushed cereal.

There are several ways to crush cornflakes quickly. Process them in a blender or food processor, place them in a plastic bag and crush them with a rolling pin, or place them in a bowl and crush them with the bottom of a glass.

To add some zip to the corn bread, stir a chopped jalapeno pepper or 1/8 teaspoon of hot pepper sauce into the batter before baking.

Crispy Baked Chicken `low carb`

Angela Capettini, Boynton Beach, Florida

PREP: 10 MIN.   **BAKE:** 30 MIN.

2	tablespoons butter, melted
1	cup crushed cornflakes
1	cup all-purpose flour
1-1/2	teaspoons seasoned salt
4	chicken drumsticks (4 ounces *each*), skin removed
4	chicken thighs (6 ounces *each*), skin removed
3/4	cup egg substitute

Drizzle butter in a 13-in. x 9-in. x 2-in. baking dish. In a shallow bowl, combine the cornflakes, flour and seasoned salt. Dip chicken in egg substitute, then roll in cornflake mixture. Dip again in egg substitute and roll in cornflake mixture.

Arrange chicken in prepared dish, meatier side down. Bake, uncovered, at 425° for 20 minutes. Turn chicken over; bake 10-15 minutes longer or until juices run clear and a meat thermometer reads 180°. **YIELD:** 4 SERVINGS.

Nutrition Facts:
One serving (1 drumstick and 1 thigh) equals:
- 237 calories
- 10 g fat (4 g saturated fat)
- 71 mg cholesterol
- 720 mg sodium
- 15 g carbohydrate
- trace fiber
- 21 g protein

Diabetic Exchanges: 3 lean meat, 1 starch.

Corn Bread Squares `meat less`

Amanda Andrews, Mansfield, Texas

PREP/TOTAL TIME: 30 MIN.

1	cup yellow cornmeal
1/4	cup all-purpose flour
2	teaspoons baking powder
1/2	teaspoon salt
1/4	teaspoon baking soda
1	egg, lightly beaten
1	carton (8 ounces) fat-free plain yogurt
1/2	cup fat-free milk
1/4	cup canola oil
1	tablespoon honey

In a large bowl, combine the first five ingredients. In another bowl, combine the egg, yogurt, milk, oil and honey. Stir into dry ingredients just until moistened. Pour into an 8-in. square baking dish coated with nonstick cooking spray. Bake at 425° for 16-20 minutes or until a toothpick comes out clean. **YIELD:** 9 SERVINGS.

Nutrition Facts: One serving (1 piece) equals:
- 157 calories
- 7 g fat (1 g saturated fat)
- 24 mg cholesterol
- 349 mg sodium
- 20 g carbohydrate
- 1 g fiber
- 4 g protein

Diabetic Exchanges: 1-1/2 starch, 1 fat.

Turn dinner into an **instant party** with a tasty travel theme. Tonight, head **south of the border** for dining inspiration.

A Tex-Mex supper is a favorite, fun addition to your weekday menu. Start with these cheesy enchiladas. Continue the theme with a colorful salad that includes corn, peas, tomatoes and black beans.

White Chicken Enchiladas

Sharon Welsh, Onsted, Michigan

PREP: 15 MIN.   **BAKE:** 35 MIN.

12	white *or* yellow corn tortillas (6 inches)
4	ounces reduced-fat cream cheese
1	tablespoon plus 1 cup fat-free milk, *divided*
1	teaspoon ground cumin
4	cups cubed cooked chicken breast
1/2	cup chopped green onions
1/2	cup chopped sweet red pepper
1	can (10-3/4 ounces) reduced-fat reduced-sodium condensed cream of chicken soup, undiluted
1	cup (8 ounces) fat-free sour cream
2	jalapeno peppers, seeded and chopped
1/4	teaspoon cayenne pepper
1/2	cup shredded reduced-fat cheddar cheese

Wrap tortillas in foil. Bake at 350° for 10 minutes or until softened. Meanwhile, in a large bowl, combine the cream cheese, 1 tablespoon milk and cumin until smooth. Stir in chicken. In a nonstick skillet coated with cooking spray, saute onions and red pepper until softened. Stir into chicken mixture.

In another bowl, combine the soup, sour cream, jalapenos, cayenne and remaining milk. Stir 2 tablespoons soup mixture into chicken mixture. Place 1/3 cup of chicken mixture down the center of each tortilla; roll up.

Place seam side down in a 13-in. x 9-in. x 2-in. baking dish coated with nonstick cooking spray. Top with remaining soup mixture. Cover and bake at 350° for 30 minutes or until heated through. Uncover; sprinkle with cheese. Bake 5 minutes longer or until cheese is melted. **YIELD:** 6 SERVINGS.

Nutrition Facts:
One serving (2 enchiladas) equals:
```
    405  calories
     10 g  fat (5 g saturated fat)
    108 mg  cholesterol
    435 mg  sodium
     35 g  carbohydrate
      3 g  fiber
     40 g  protein
```

Diabetic Exchanges: 4 lean meat, 1 starch, 1 fat-free milk, 1/2 fat.

Southwestern Barley Salad

meatless

Tommi Roylance, Charlo, Montana

PREP/TOTAL TIME: 20 MIN.

3	cups cooked medium pearl barley
1	can (15 ounces) black beans, rinsed and drained
1-1/2	cups frozen corn, thawed
1-1/2	cups diced seeded tomatoes
1	cup frozen peas, thawed
1/4	cup minced fresh cilantro
1	teaspoon salt
1/4	teaspoon pepper
1/2	cup water
3	tablespoons lemon juice
1	tablespoon finely chopped onion
1	tablespoon canola oil
2	garlic cloves, minced
8	lettuce leaves
1	ripe avocado, peeled and sliced
2	medium tomatoes, cut into wedges

In a bowl, combine the first eight ingredients. In a jar with a tight-fitting lid, combine the water, lemon juice, onion, oil and garlic; shake well. Pour over barley mixture and toss to coat. Serve on lettuce-lined plates. Garnish with avocado and tomatoes.
YIELD: 8 SERVINGS.

Nutrition Facts: One serving (1 cup) equals:
```
    233  calories
      7 g  fat (1 g saturated fat)
        0  cholesterol
    490 mg  sodium
     38 g  carbohydrate
      9 g  fiber
      7 g  protein
```

Diabetic Exchanges: 2 starch, 1 vegetable, 1 fat.

Appealing Partners

- Cut fruit
- Limeade

Practical Tips

The recipe for White Chicken Enchiladas calls for 4 cups of cooked chicken. Poach, microwave or grill 1-1/2 pounds of boneless chicken breasts, then cube it for the recipe.

To cut down on last-minute preparation for the salad, prepare a big batch of barley ahead of time. (A 16-ounce package will yield about 9 cups cooked barley.) Then divide it into 1-cup portions, place it in labeled freezer bags or containers, and store in the freezer until needed. It will keep for up to 3 months.

Here's a **healthy option** for hearty eating that's both **quick to fix** and packed with authentic Italian zest.

Fresh garlic, basil and caraway seeds subtly season this skillet supper. The light, airy dessert is a snap to whip together and pop in the fridge the night before.

Appealing Partners

- Spinach salad
- Italian bread

Practical Tips

In a hurry? Substitute 1-1/2 teaspoons of Italian seasoning for the basil, oregano and thyme called for in the main dish.

If your family likes dishes with some kick, add crushed red pepper flakes or cayenne pepper to the pasta toss.

Feel free to experiment with other flavors of yogurt when making the dessert. When using a citrus yogurt, add the corresponding citrus peel. When using other yogurt flavors, omit the peel altogether.

Italian Sausage 'n' Peppers Supper

Teresa Puszkar, Colorado Springs, Colorado

PREP/TOTAL TIME: 30 MIN.

- 2 cups uncooked penne pasta
- 1 pound turkey Italian sausage links
- 1/2 cup *each* julienned sweet red, yellow and green pepper
- 1 tablespoon minced fresh basil *or* 1 teaspoon dried basil
- 3 garlic cloves, minced
- 1/4 teaspoon dried oregano
- 1/4 teaspoon dried thyme
- 1/4 teaspoon caraway seeds
- 1 tablespoon olive oil
- 2 cans (14-1/2 ounces *each*) diced tomatoes, drained

Cook pasta according to package directions. In a large nonstick skillet, brown sausage over medium heat; drain. Cut sausage into 1/4-in. slices. In the same skillet, saute the peppers, basil, garlic, oregano, thyme, caraway seeds and sliced sausage in oil until peppers are crisp-tender. Stir in tomatoes. Cook and stir until heated through. Drain pasta; add to skillet and mix well. **YIELD:** 5 SERVINGS.

Nutrition Facts:
One serving (1-1/2 cups) equals:
- 327 calories
- 12 g fat (3 g saturated fat)
- 49 mg cholesterol
- 845 mg sodium
- 33 g carbohydrate
- 3 g fiber
- 21 g protein

Diabetic Exchanges: 2 vegetable, 2 lean meat, 1-1/2 starch, 1 fat.

Lemon Yogurt Cream Pie

low sodium

Susan Kostecke, St. Louis, Missouri

PREP: 15 MIN. + CHILLING

- 1 envelope unflavored gelatin
- 1/4 cup cold water
- Sugar substitute equivalent to 1/3 cup sugar
- 1/3 cup lemon juice
- 2 cartons (6 ounces *each*) fat-free lemon yogurt
- 1 teaspoon grated lemon peel
- 1 carton (8 ounces) frozen reduced-fat whipped topping, thawed
- 1 reduced-fat graham cracker crust (8 inches)
- Lemon slices and mint, optional

In a microwave-safe bowl, sprinkle gelatin over cold water; let stand for 1 minute. Microwave, uncovered, on high for 20 seconds. Stir in sugar substitute and lemon juice. Add yogurt and lemon peel; mix well. Fold in whipped topping; spoon into crust. Cover and refrigerate for 8 hours or overnight. Garnish with lemon slices and mint if desired. **YIELD:** 8 SERVINGS.

Editor's Note: This recipe was tested with Splenda No Calorie Sweetener.

Nutrition Facts: One serving (1 piece) equals:
- 226 calories
- 6 g fat (4 g saturated fat)
- 1 mg cholesterol
- 130 mg sodium
- 33 g carbohydrate
- trace fiber
- 7 g protein

Diabetic Exchanges: 2 starch, 1/2 fat-free milk, 1/2 fat.

Let your **slow cooker** do all the work
for this **supper saver** while you go about
your busy day **worry-free.**

*This tender turkey tastes just
like Italian beef, but without
the fat. The low-fat,
low-sodium salad medley
promises a rainbow of color
in every crunchy bite.*

Italian Turkey Sandwiches

Carol Riley, Galva, Illinois

PREP: 10 MIN.   **COOK:** 5 HOURS

- 1 bone-in turkey breast (5-1/2 pounds), skin removed
- 1/2 cup chopped green pepper
- 1 medium onion, chopped
- 1/4 cup chili sauce
- 3 tablespoons white vinegar
- 2 tablespoons dried oregano *or* Italian seasoning
- 4 teaspoons beef bouillon granules
- 11 kaiser *or* hard rolls, split

Cut turkey breast in half along the bone.
Place the turkey breast, green pepper and
onion in a 5-qt. slow cooker coated with
nonstick cooking spray. Combine the chili
sauce, vinegar, oregano and bouillon; pour
over turkey and vegetables. Cover and cook
on low for 5-6 hours or until meat juices run
clear and vegetables are tender.

Remove turkey, reserving cooking liquid.
Shred the turkey with two forks; return to
cooking juices. Spoon 1/2 cup onto each
roll. **YIELD:** 11 SERVINGS.

Nutrition Facts: One serving (1 sandwich) equals:
- 364 calories
- 4 g fat (1 g saturated fat)
- 102 mg cholesterol
- 576 mg sodium
- 33 g carbohydrate
- 1 g fiber
- 46 g protein

Diabetic Exchanges: 3-1/2 lean meat, 2 starch.

Seven-Vegetable Salad

Sara Lindler, Irmo, South Carolina

PREP/TOTAL TIME: 30 MIN.

- 1 cup cut fresh green beans
- 1 cup fresh sugar snap peas
- 1 cup sliced yellow summer squash
- 1 cup sliced zucchini
- 1/2 cup julienned onion
- 2 small tomatoes, seeded and chopped
- 1 cup coarsely grated carrots
- 2/3 cup reduced-fat Italian salad dressing
- 4 teaspoons minced chives
- 2 teaspoons dried basil

In a saucepan, bring 2 in. of water to a boil.
Add beans, peas, yellow squash, zucchini and
onion. Reduce heat; cover and simmer for
2-3 minutes or until vegetables are crisp-tender.
Drain; rinse with cold water and pat dry.

Place vegetables in a bowl; add the
remaining ingredients. Gently stir to coat.
Refrigerate until serving. **YIELD:** 12 SERVINGS.

Nutrition Facts: One serving (1/2 cup) equals:
- 47 calories
- 2 g fat (1 g saturated fat)
- 0 cholesterol
- 132 mg sodium
- 6 g carbohydrate
- 2 g fiber
- 1 g protein

Diabetic Exchange: 2 vegetable.

Appealing Partners

- Light strawberry yogurt
- Lemon iced tea

Practical Tips

If you'd like the Italian Turkey
Sandwiches to have more zip,
sprinkle crushed red pepper flakes
into the slow cooker when you
add the oregano.

When assembling the salad, swap
out seasonal veggies where
appropriate. Broccoli, cauliflower
and celery are easy options
available most any time of year.
Also, feel free to use a favorite
reduced-fat vinaigrette, such as
raspberry or red wine vinaigrette,
in place of the Italian salad
dressing.

Here's a **can-do idea** for easy summer entertaining or a **no-stress** weeknight family dinner.

Chili sauce packs a big punch on these moist chunks of turkey alternated with crisp-tender zucchini, peppers, mushrooms and cherry tomatoes. Have an extra 15 minutes? Whip together a fluffy finale and then chill while enjoying the kabobs. The mousse will be ready in time for dessert.

Appealing Partners

- Wild rice blend
- Three-bean salad

Practical Tips

You can also broil the kabobs in your oven instead. Broil the skewers 4-6 inches from the heat for 3-4 minutes on each side or until the juices run clear.

These savory skewers would also taste great with chicken, pork or beef.

For a change of pace, give the dessert a mocha taste. Instead of using frozen whipped topping, prepare an envelope of whipped topping mix with low-fat chocolate milk.

Grilled Turkey Kabobs

Marilyn Rodriguez, Fairbanks, Alaska

PREP: 10 MIN. + MARINATING **GRILL:** 10 MIN.

- 1/3 cup chili sauce
- 2 tablespoons lemon juice
- 1 tablespoon sugar
- 2 bay leaves
- 1 pound turkey breast tenderloins, cut into 1-1/2-inch cubes
- 2 medium zucchini, cut into 1/2-inch-slices
- 2 small green peppers, cut into 1-1/2-inch squares
- 2 small onions, quartered
- 8 medium fresh mushrooms
- 8 cherry tomatoes
- 1 tablespoon canola oil

In a bowl, combine the chili sauce, lemon juice, sugar and bay leaves; mix well. Pour 1/4 cup marinade into a large resealable plastic bag; add the turkey. Seal bag and turn to coat; refrigerate for at least 2 hours or overnight. Cover and refrigerate remaining marinade.

Coat grill rack with nonstick cooking spray before starting the grill. Drain and discard marinade. Discard bay leaves from reserved marinade. On eight metal or soaked wooden skewers, alternately thread turkey and vegetables. Brush lightly with oil. Grill, uncovered, over medium-hot heat for 3-4 minutes on each side or until juices run clear, basting frequently with reserved marinade and turning three times. **YIELD:** 4 SERVINGS.

Nutrition Facts: One serving (2 kabobs) equals:
- 254 calories
- 5 g fat (1 g saturated fat)
- 82 mg cholesterol
- 695 mg sodium
- 21 g carbohydrate
- 3 g fiber
- 33 g protein

Diabetic Exchanges: 3 lean meat, 2 vegetable, 1/2 starch.

Coffee Mousse

Vernette Dechaine, Pittsfield, Maine

PREP: 15 MIN. + CHILLING

- 1 envelope unflavored gelatin
- 1/4 cup cold water
- 2 teaspoons instant coffee granules
- 1/4 cup boiling water
- Sugar substitute equivalent to 2 teaspoons sugar
- 2 ice cubes
- 2 cups plus 4 tablespoons reduced-fat whipped topping, *divided*
- Additional coffee granules, crushed

In a small bowl, sprinkle gelatin over cold water; let stand for 2 minutes. In a small saucepan, dissolve coffee granules in boiling water. Add gelatin mixture; cook and stir just until gelatin is dissolved (do not boil).

Remove from the heat; stir in sugar substitute. Add ice cubes; stir until ice is melted and mixture begins to thicken. Transfer to a mixing bowl; add 2/3 cup whipped topping. Beat until blended. Fold in 1-1/3 cups whipped topping.

Spoon into four individual serving dishes; top each with 1 tablespoon whipped topping. Refrigerate for at least 2 hours. Just before serving, dust with crushed coffee granules. **YIELD:** 4 SERVINGS.

Editor's Note: This recipe was tested with Splenda No Calorie Sweetener.

Nutrition Facts: One serving (1/2 cup) equals:
- 101 calories
- 5 g fat (5 g saturated fat)
- 0 cholesterol
- 4 mg sodium
- 10 g carbohydrate
- 0 fiber
- 2 g protein

Diabetic Exchanges: 1 starch, 1/2 fat.

Beat the clock with time to spare when you add this **delicious duo** to your menu lineup.

The juicy chicken tenderloins and homemade tomato sauce come together in just half an hour on the stovetop. And what's an Italian meal without garlic? You'll find plenty of it in the creamy side.

Tasty Italian Chicken `low fat` `low carb`

Beth Ann Stein, Richmond, Indiana

PREP/TOTAL TIME: 30 MIN.

1/2	cup chopped onion
1-1/8	teaspoons paprika, *divided*
3	teaspoons olive oil, *divided*
1-1/4	cups water
1/4	cup tomato paste
1	bay leaf
1/2	teaspoon reduced-sodium chicken bouillon granules
1/2	teaspoon Italian seasoning
1/4	cup all-purpose flour
1-1/2	teaspoons grated Parmesan cheese
1/2	teaspoon salt
1/4	teaspoon garlic powder
1/4	teaspoon dried oregano
1-1/2	pounds chicken tenderloins

In a small saucepan, saute onion and 1/8 teaspoon paprika in 1 teaspoon oil until tender. Stir in the water, tomato paste, bay leaf, bouillon and Italian seasoning. Bring to a boil. Reduce heat; simmer, uncovered, for 10 minutes.

Meanwhile, in a large resealable plastic bag, combine the flour, Parmesan cheese, salt, garlic powder, oregano and remaining paprika. Add chicken; seal bag and shake to coat.

In a large nonstick skillet coated with non-stick cooking spray, cook half of the chicken in 1 teaspoon oil for 2-3 minutes on each side or until juices run clear. Remove and keep warm; repeat with remaining chicken and oil. Discard bay leaf from sauce. Serve over chicken. **YIELD:** 6 SERVINGS.

Nutrition Facts: One serving (4 ounces cooked chicken with 3 tablespoons sauce) equals:
- 163 calories
- 3 g fat (trace saturated fat)
- 67 mg cholesterol
- 287 mg sodium
- 8 g carbohydrate
- 1 g fiber
- 27 g protein

Diabetic Exchanges: 3 very lean meat, 1/2 starch, 1/2 fat.

Creamy Noodles `meat less`

Brenda Nolen, Folsom, Louisiana

PREP/TOTAL TIME: 25 MIN.

8	ounces uncooked thin spaghetti
3	garlic cloves, minced
3	tablespoons butter, *divided*
6	ounces fat-free cream cheese, cubed
3	tablespoons reduced-fat sour cream
3	tablespoons fat-free milk
3/4	teaspoon salt
1/2	teaspoon onion powder
1/4	teaspoon Cajun seasoning
1/4	teaspoon white pepper
4-1/2	teaspoons minced fresh parsley

Cook the spaghetti according to package directions. Meanwhile, in a saucepan, saute garlic in 1 tablespoon butter until tender. Add the cream cheese, sour cream, milk, salt, onion powder, Cajun seasoning, pepper and remaining butter. Cook and stir over low heat just until smooth (do not boil). Remove from the heat.

Drain spaghetti; toss with cream sauce. Sprinkle with parsley. Serve immediately. **YIELD:** 6 SERVINGS.

Nutrition Facts: One serving (1 cup) equals:
- 234 calories
- 7 g fat (4 g saturated fat)
- 20 mg cholesterol
- 547 mg sodium
- 32 g carbohydrate
- 1 g fiber
- 10 g protein

Diabetic Exchanges: 2 starch, 1 very lean meat, 1 fat.

Appealing Partners

- Steamed broccoli
- Fat-free chocolate pudding

Practical Tips

When shopping for chicken tenderloins, remember that some brands label the product as chicken tenders.

Got leftover rice? Finish it up by serving the saucy chicken over it.

For extra flavor and color, try stirring a little of your favorite salsa into the noodles.

Warm-weather cooking calls for smart planning, so pull out the grill to **cut down** calories and cleanup!

Start with an easy-to-make lime marinade to turn regular chicken breasts into an extraordinary grilled entree. The frosty, finishing touch keeps you cooled down and refreshed.

Appealing Partners

- Garlic Green and Wax Beans, p. 247
- Iced tea

Practical Tips

If the weather isn't conducive to grilling, simply broil the chicken 4-6 inches from the heat for the same amount of time directed in the recipe.

For a sensational slushy beverage, place a few scoops of Watermelon Ice in a tall glass and add club soda.

You can use cantaloupe or honeydew instead of watermelon in the dessert recipe for a tantalizing twist.

Herbed Lime Chicken   `low fat` `low carb`

Kay Alliman, Biggsville, Illinois

PREP: 5 MIN. + MARINATING   **GRILL:** 10 MIN.

- 1   bottle (16 ounces) fat-free Italian salad dressing
- 1/2   cup lime juice
- 1   lime, halved and sliced
- 3   garlic cloves, minced
- 1   teaspoon dried thyme
- 4   boneless skinless chicken breast halves (1 pound)

In a bowl, combine the first five ingredients. Remove 1/2 cup for basting; cover and refrigerate. Pour remaining marinade into a large resealable plastic bag; add chicken. Seal bag and turn to coat; refrigerate for 8-10 hours.

Drain and discard marinade. Grill chicken, uncovered, over medium heat for 5 minutes. Turn chicken; baste with reserved marinade. Grill 5-7 minutes longer or until juices run clear, basting occasionally. **YIELD:** 4 SERVINGS.

Nutrition Facts:
One serving (1 chicken breast) equals:
- 62 calories
- 2 g fat (1 g saturated fat)
- 67 mg cholesterol
- 718 mg sodium
- 8 g carbohydrate
- 1 g fiber
- 27 g protein

Diabetic Exchange: 4 very lean meat.

Watermelon Ice   `low fat` `low sodium`

Kaaren Jurack, Virginia Beach, Virginia

PREP: 10 MIN. + FREEZING

- 1   teaspoon unflavored gelatin
- 2   tablespoons water
- 4   cups seeded cubed watermelon, *divided*
- 2   tablespoons lime juice
- 2   tablespoons honey

In a microwave-safe bowl, sprinkle gelatin over water; let stand for 2 minutes. Microwave on high for 40 seconds; stir. Let stand for 2 minutes or until gelatin is dissolved.

Pour into a blender or food processor; add 1 cup watermelon, lime juice and honey. Cover and process until smooth. Add remaining melon, a cup at a time, and process until smooth.

Pour into a 9-in. square dish; freeze until almost firm. Transfer to a chilled bowl; beat with an electric mixer until mixture is bright pink. Pour into serving dishes; freeze until firm. Remove from the freezer 15-20 minutes before serving. **YIELD:** 4 SERVINGS.

Nutrition Facts: One serving (3/4 cup) equals:
- 85 calories
- 1 g fat (1 g saturated fat)
- 0 cholesterol
- 5 mg sodium
- 20 g carbohydrate
- 1 g fiber
- 2 g protein

Diabetic Exchange: 1-1/2 fruit.

Give leftovers a **mouth-watering** makeover.
Everyone will wonder how you create
such delectable **dinner magic.**

*Turn extra turkey or chicken
into a comforting main course
peppered with seasonal flavors.
Serve it with a simple salad
tossed with this five-ingredient
dressing. You won't go wrong!*

Appealing Partners

• Cranberry sauce
• Sunflower Wheat Rolls, p. 308

Practical Tips

If your family enjoys the taste of
whole grain bread, feel free to
increase the amount in the hot
bake, decreasing the amount of
white bread accordingly.

Spoon some sliced mushrooms
or cooked green beans into the
casserole before baking it.

Consider Celery Seed Salad
Dressing the next time you need a
thick, creamy dip for a vegetable
tray.

Leftover-Turkey Bake

Alice Slagter, Wyoming, Michigan

PREP: 20 MIN.   **BAKE:** 35 MIN.

1-1/2 cups finely chopped onion
 1/2   cup finely chopped celery
   1   can (14-1/2 ounces) reduced-sodium
       chicken broth, *divided*
   2   eggs, lightly beaten
   2   teaspoons poultry seasoning
 1/2   teaspoon salt
 1/4   teaspoon pepper
   3   cups cubed whole grain bread
   3   cups cubed white bread
   2   cups cubed cooked turkey breast
 1/2   cup chopped fresh *or* frozen cranberries

In a large saucepan, bring the onion, celery
and 1/2 cup broth to a boil. Reduce heat;
simmer, uncovered, for 5-8 minutes or until
vegetables are tender. Remove from the heat.
Stir in the remaining broth, then add the
eggs, poultry seasoning, salt and pepper; stir
until blended. Add the bread cubes, turkey
and cranberries; mix well. Spoon into a 2-qt.
baking dish coated with nonstick cooking
spray.
  Cover and bake at 350° for 15 minutes.
Uncover; bake 20-25 minutes longer or until
lightly browned and a knife inserted near
center comes out clean. **YIELD:** 4 SERVINGS.

Nutrition Facts: One serving (1-1/2 cups) equals:
      290 calories
        5 g fat (1 g saturated fat)
      154 mg cholesterol
      916 mg sodium
       34 g carbohydrate
        4 g fiber
       27 g protein

Diabetic Exchanges: 3 lean meat, 1-1/2 starch,
1 vegetable.

Celery Seed Salad Dressing

Tammie Lee Carter, Wheatfield, New York

PREP/TOTAL TIME: 10 MIN.

   1   cup reduced-fat mayonnaise
 1/2   cup sugar
 1/3   cup finely chopped onion
 1/3   cup red wine vinegar
   1   tablespoon celery seed

In a small bowl, whisk the mayonnaise, sugar,
onion, vinegar and celery seed. Cover and
refrigerate until serving. **YIELD:** 1-3/4 CUPS.

Nutrition Facts:
One serving (2 tablespoons) equals:
       90 calories
        6 g fat (1 g saturated fat)
        6 mg cholesterol
      138 mg sodium
        9 g carbohydrate
             trace fiber
             trace protein

Diabetic Exchanges: 1 fat, 1/2 starch.

With just **minutes to spare,** you can whip together a meal that **tastes great** and is **good for you,** too!

The tasty tortilla wedges are chock-full of seasoned ground turkey, zucchini, corn, red pepper and just enough melted cheese. For the side, use cooked rice to hurry along the preparation.

Turkey Quesadillas

Wendy Greinke, Round Rock, Texas

PREP/TOTAL TIME: 20 MIN.

- 1 pound lean ground turkey
- 1 cup chopped red onion
- 1 to 2 garlic cloves, minced
- 2 cups julienned zucchini
- 1 cup salsa
- 1 cup frozen corn
- 1 cup julienned sweet red pepper
- 1 can (4 ounces) chopped green chilies
- 2 tablespoons minced fresh cilantro
- 1/2 teaspoon dried oregano
- 1/2 teaspoon ground cumin
- 1/4 teaspoon salt
- 1/8 teaspoon cayenne pepper
- 8 flour tortillas (8 inches)
- 2 cups (8 ounces) shredded reduced-fat Mexican cheese blend

In a nonstick skillet, cook turkey, onion and garlic over medium heat until meat is no longer pink; drain. Add zucchini, salsa, corn, red pepper and chilies. Reduce heat; cover and simmer until vegetables are tender. Stir in seasonings.

For each quesadilla, place one tortilla in an ungreased nonstick skillet. Top with 1/2 cup filling, then sprinkle with another 1/4 cup cheese. Cover with another tortilla. Cook over medium heat, carefully turning once, until lightly browned on both sides and cheese begins to melt. Cut into eight wedges. **YIELD:** 4 QUESADILLAS (8 WEDGES EACH).

Nutrition Facts: One serving (2 wedges) equals:
- 179 calories
- 7 g fat (2 g saturated fat)
- 32 mg cholesterol
- 388 mg sodium
- 18 g carbohydrate
- 1 g fiber
- 12 g protein

Diabetic Exchanges: 2 starch, 2 lean meat, 1-1/2 fat.

Lemon Fried Rice

meat less

Janice Mitchell, Aurora, Colorado

PREP/TOTAL TIME: 20 MIN.

- 1/2 cup sliced green onions
- 1/4 cup minced fresh parsley
- 1/4 cup butter
- 4 cups cold cooked rice
- 1 package (10 ounces) frozen peas, thawed
- 2 tablespoons reduced-sodium soy sauce
- 2 teaspoons grated lemon peel
- 1/2 teaspoon salt
- 1/8 teaspoon hot pepper sauce

In a large nonstick skillet or wok, stir-fry onions and parsley in butter for 1 minute. Add the remaining ingredients; stir-fry for 4-6 minutes or until peas are tender and rice is heated through. **YIELD:** 8 SERVINGS.

Nutrition Facts: One serving (2/3 cup) equals:
- 186 calories
- 6 g fat (4 g saturated fat)
- 16 mg cholesterol
- 391 mg sodium
- 28 g carbohydrate
- 2 g fiber
- 4 g protein

Diabetic Exchanges: 2 starch, 1/2 fat.

Appealing Partners

- Chopped tomatoes and cucumbers in a fat-free vinaigrette
- Low-fat chocolate muffins

Practical Tips

Feel free to use fresh corn for the frozen corn called for in the quesadillas recipe. Cut the kernels from 2 medium ears of corn to equal 1 cup.

Be sure to start with cold rice when making the fried rice. Chilling the rice helps keep the grains separate and prevents it from sticking to the skillet. Simply break up the clumps of rice before adding to the skillet.

Put together this **time-honored** comfort food when someone you love needs a **pick-me-up.**

Turkey lends a lighter, yet tempting twist to a classic meat loaf. Ideal for a cozy dinner, the specialty potatoes have so much buttery goodness that no one will suspect they're light.

Appealing Partners

- Frozen mixed vegetables
- Banana Chocolate Cake, p. 336

Practical Tips

Freeze any leftover turkey loaf for fast dinners on future nights or use extra slices for lunch sandwiches the next day.

Pick up a package of chopped onions from the grocery store's freezer case or produce department. They'll speed up tonight's main course, and you can use the extras to hurry along future meals, too.

Terrific Turkey Meat Loaf `low carb`

Wanda Bannister, New Bern, North Carolina

PREP: 15 MIN. **BAKE:** 55 MIN.

 1 egg white
 3 tablespoons ketchup
 1 tablespoon Worcestershire sauce
1/2 teaspoon Dijon mustard
1/2 cup oat bran
1/2 cup chopped green pepper
1/4 cup finely chopped onion
 2 tablespoons chopped ripe olives
 1 garlic clove, minced
1/4 teaspoon celery salt
1/4 teaspoon dried marjoram
1/4 teaspoon rubbed sage
1/4 teaspoon pepper
 1 pound ground turkey

In a large bowl, combine the egg white, ketchup, Worcestershire sauce and mustard. Stir in the oat bran, green pepper, onion, olives, garlic, celery salt, marjoram, sage and pepper. Crumble turkey over mixture and mix well.

Pat into a loaf in an 11-in. x 7-in. x 2-in. baking dish coated with nonstick cooking spray. Bake, uncovered, at 350° for 55-65 minutes or until a meat thermometer reads 165°. **YIELD:** 4 SERVINGS.

Nutrition Facts: One serving (1 slice) equals:
   253 calories
   12 g fat (3 g saturated fat)
   82 mg cholesterol
  421 mg sodium
   14 g carbohydrate
    3 g fiber
   26 g protein

Diabetic Exchanges: 3 lean meat, 1 starch.

Herbed Twice-Baked Potatoes `meat less`

Ruth Andrewson, Peck, Idaho

PREP: 15 MIN. **BAKE:** 1-1/4 HOURS + COOLING

 2 medium baking potatoes
1-1/2 ounces reduced-fat cream cheese, cubed
 1 tablespoon snipped chives
1/4 teaspoon salt
1/4 teaspoon dried basil
Dash cayenne pepper
 3 tablespoons fat-free milk
 3 teaspoons butter, melted, *divided*
Dash garlic powder
Dash paprika

Scrub and pierce potatoes. Bake at 375° for 1 hour or until tender. Cool for 10 minutes. Cut potatoes in half. Scoop out pulp, leaving a thin shell.

In a bowl, mash the pulp with cream cheese, chives, salt, basil and cayenne. Add milk and 1-1/2 teaspoons butter; mash. Spoon into potato shells. Drizzle with remaining butter; sprinkle with garlic powder and paprika. Place on an ungreased baking sheet. Bake for 15-20 minutes or until heated through. **YIELD:** 4 SERVINGS.

Nutrition Facts:
One serving (1 potato half) equals:
   150 calories
    5 g fat (3 g saturated fat)
   15 mg cholesterol
  234 mg sodium
   23 g carbohydrate
    2 g fiber
    4 g protein

Diabetic Exchanges: 1-1/2 starch, 1 fat.

A **classy** casserole comes together in
mere minutes, but leaves a
lasting impression when served.

*Tender chicken breast
and fluffy rice get added color
from vegetables and extra
crunch from almonds
sprinkled over the top.
Finish off the meal with a
tossed green salad
drizzled with a low-fat,
low-carb vinaigrette.*

Chicken Rice Casserole

Mary Louise Chubb, Perkasie, Pennsylvania

PREP: 20 MIN. **BAKE:** 25 MIN.

- 6 boneless skinless chicken breast halves (1-1/2 pounds)
- 1 tablespoon canola oil
- 3/4 cup chopped sweet red pepper
- 3/4 cup chopped green pepper
- 1/2 cup chopped onion
- 1/2 cup chopped fresh mushrooms
- 1 garlic clove, minced
- 2 cups uncooked instant brown rice
- 2 cups chicken broth
- 1-1/2 cups frozen corn, thawed
- 1/4 teaspoon salt
- 1/8 teaspoon pepper
- 1/4 cup slivered almonds, toasted
- 2 tablespoons minced parsley

In a large skillet, brown chicken in oil for 4 minutes on each side. Remove and keep warm. In the same skillet, saute peppers, onion, mushrooms and garlic until tender. Stir in the rice, broth, corn, salt and pepper; bring to a boil.

Transfer to an 11-in. x 7-in. x 2-in. baking dish coated with nonstick cooking spray. Top with chicken. Cover and bake at 350° for 20 minutes. Uncover; bake 5 minutes longer or until chicken juices run clear. Sprinkle with almonds and parsley. **YIELD:** 6 SERVINGS.

Nutrition Facts: One serving (1 chicken breast half and mixture) equals:
- 351 calories
- 8 g fat (1 g saturated fat)
- 66 mg cholesterol
- 493 mg sodium
- 37 g carbohydrate
- 4 g fiber
- 33 g protein

Diabetic Exchanges: 3 lean meat, 2 starch, 1 vegetable.

Dill Vinaigrette

Joyce Clifford, Mansfield, Ohio

PREP/TOTAL TIME: 5 MIN.

- 1/4 cup cider vinegar
- 2 tablespoons water
- 2 tablespoons olive oil
- 2 tablespoons honey
- 1/2 teaspoon garlic powder
- 1/2 teaspoon dill weed
- 1/2 teaspoon dried parsley flakes
- 1/4 teaspoon salt
- 1/8 teaspoon pepper
- 1/8 teaspoon celery seed

Salad greens and vegetables of your choice

In a jar with a tight-fitting lid, combine the first 10 ingredients; shake well. Serve with salad. Refrigerate leftovers; shake well before serving. **YIELD:** 1 CUP.

Nutrition Facts:
One serving (2 tablespoons) equals:
- 48 calories
- 3 g fat (trace saturated fat)
- 0 cholesterol
- 74 mg sodium
- 5 g carbohydrate
- trace fiber
- trace protein

Diabetic Exchanges: 1/2 fruit, 1/2 fat.

Appealing Partners

- Banana bread
- Herbed peas

Practical Tips

When assembling the dish for company, you may also substitute portobello mushrooms for the regular mushrooms and pine nuts for the almonds to give it special flavor.

You can use ready-to-serve salad greens with Dill Vinaigrette, but you may also want to add other fixings (cucumbers, tomatoes, carrots, etc.).

For a meal that **sticks to your ribs** and not your waistline, ladle up **steaming bowls** of chili with a **sassy kick**.

With a little prep work in advance, you can put the chili mixture into the slow cooker to simmer in the morning and have dinner ready when you come home. Accompany it with squares of seasoned warm corn bread.

Appealing Partners

- Spinach salad with low-fat French dressing
- Sugar-free hot cocoa

Practical Tips

Save time in the kitchen by purchasing packages of ready-to-serve grilled chicken breast strips. You can cube the precooked poultry and use just what you need. Omit the 1 teaspoon of salt and just season to taste.

For zestier chili, increase the cayenne pepper, cumin and garlic.

If you like your corn bread a little spicier, use chopped jalapeno peppers instead of the canned chilies.

Flavorful White Chili

Wilda Bensenhaver, Deland, Florida

PREP: 10 MIN. + STANDING **COOK:** 8 HOURS

1	pound dry great northern beans, rinsed and sorted
4	cups chicken broth
2	cups chopped onions
3	garlic cloves, minced
2	teaspoons ground cumin
1-1/2	teaspoons dried oregano
1	teaspoon ground coriander
1/8	teaspoon ground cloves
1/8	teaspoon cayenne pepper
1	can (4 ounces) chopped green chilies
1/2	pound boneless skinless chicken breast, grilled and cubed
1	teaspoon salt
3/4	cup shredded reduced-fat Mexican cheese blend

Place beans in a soup kettle or Dutch oven; add water to cover by 2 in. Bring to a boil; boil for 2 minutes. Remove from the heat; cover and let stand for 1 hour. Drain and rinse beans, discarding liquid.

Place beans in a slow cooker. Add the broth, onions, garlic and seasonings. Cover and cook on low for 7-8 hours or until beans are almost tender. Add the chilies, chicken and salt; cover and cook for 1 hour or until the beans are tender. Serve with cheese. **YIELD:** 6 SERVINGS.

Nutrition Facts: One serving (1-1/3 cups chili with 2 tablespoons cheese) equals:
384 calories
5 g fat (2 g saturated fat)
37 mg cholesterol
1,224 mg sodium
53 g carbohydrate
16 g fiber
34 g protein

Diabetic Exchanges: 4 very lean meat, 3 starch.

Southwestern Corn Bread

meat less

Tena Edyvean, Rapid City, South Dakota

PREP: 15 MIN. **BAKE:** 40 MIN.

1	can (15-1/4 ounces) whole kernel corn, drained
1	cup all-purpose flour
1	cup cornmeal
1/2	teaspoon baking soda
1/2	teaspoon salt
1	egg
2	egg whites
3/4	cup fat-free milk
1/4	cup canola oil
1	cup (4 ounces) shredded reduced-fat cheddar cheese
1	can (4 ounces) chopped green chilies

Place corn in a food processor or blender; cover and process until coarsely chopped. Set aside. In a bowl, combine the flour, cornmeal, baking soda and salt.

In a small bowl, combine the egg, egg whites, milk and oil. Stir into dry ingredients just until moistened. Add the cheese, chilies and corn.

Pour into a 9-in. square baking dish coated with nonstick cooking spray. Bake at 350° for 40-45 minutes or until a toothpick inserted near the center comes out clean. Serve warm. **YIELD:** 9 SERVINGS.

Nutrition Facts: One serving (1 slice) equals:
243 calories
10 g fat (3 g saturated fat)
33 mg cholesterol
598 mg sodium
30 g carbohydrate
3 g fiber
10 g protein

Diabetic Exchanges: 2 starch, 2 fat.

Head to the bayou with a **spicy sandwich** selection that's sure to **liven up** lunch for family or friends.

You'll have lunch or dinner well in hand when you serve this robust grilled chicken sandwich. Dessert is easy, too! Try this quick-batter peanut butter cookie dotted with mini baking bits.

Appealing Partners

• Vegetable sticks with dip
• Potato salad

Practical Tips

When preparing the Cajun Chicken Sandwiches, make a very large batch of seasoning and use it on a variety of items besides chicken. Try it on pork, fish or even beef.

If the weather isn't nice enough for grilling, broil the chicken breasts in your oven instead. Broil 4-6 inches from the heat for 3-4 minutes on each side or until the juices run clear.

When making the bar cookies, use chips instead of baking bits.

Cajun Chicken Sandwiches

Amber Peterson, Oakes, North Dakota

PREP: 10 MIN. + MARINATING   **GRILL:** 10 MIN.

  6 boneless skinless chicken breast halves (4 ounces *each*)
  1 tablespoon olive oil
1/2 teaspoon celery salt
1/2 teaspoon garlic salt
1/2 teaspoon lemon-pepper seasoning
1/4 teaspoon cayenne pepper
1/4 teaspoon paprika
1/4 teaspoon pepper
  6 kaiser rolls, split and toasted
 12 slices tomato
  6 lettuce leaves

Flatten chicken to 1/2-in. thickness. Brush both sides with oil. Combine the seasonings; rub over both sides of chicken. Arrange in a 13-in. x 9-in. x 2-in. baking dish. Cover and refrigerate for at least 2 hours or overnight.

   Coat grill rack with nonstick cooking spray before starting the grill. Grill, covered, over medium heat for 3-5 minutes on each side or until chicken juices run clear. Serve on rolls with tomato and lettuce. **YIELD:** 6 SERVINGS.

Nutrition Facts: One serving (1 sandwich) equals:
      323 calories
        6 g fat (1 g saturated fat)
       66 mg cholesterol
      701 mg sodium
       33 g carbohydrate
        2 g fiber
       32 g protein

Diabetic Exchanges: 3 lean meat, 2 starch.

Candy Chip Bar Cookies   `low sodium`

Wendy Budlong, Acton, Massachusetts

PREP: 15 MIN.   **BAKE:** 15 MIN. + COOLING

1/2 cup canola oil
1/2 cup packed brown sugar
Sugar substitute equal to 1/2 cup sugar
1/4 cup reduced-fat peanut butter
  1 egg
  1 teaspoon vanilla extract
  2 cups all-purpose flour
1/2 teaspoon baking soda
1/4 teaspoon salt
3/4 cup miniature semisweet M&M baking bits

In a bowl, combine the oil, brown sugar, sugar substitute, peanut butter, egg and vanilla. Combine the flour, baking soda and salt; stir into the peanut butter mixture. Stir in baking bits.

   Spread in a 13-in. x 9-in. x 2-in. baking pan coated with nonstick cooking spray. Bake at 350° for 12-15 minutes or until lightly browned. Cool on a wire rack. **YIELD:** 1-1/2 DOZEN.

   Editor's Note: This recipe was tested with Splenda No Calorie Sweetener.

Nutrition Facts: One serving (1 piece) equals:
      204 calories
       10 g fat (2 g saturated fat)
       13 mg cholesterol
      108 mg sodium
       25 g carbohydrate
        1 g fiber
        3 g protein

Diabetic Exchanges: 2 fat, 1-1/2 starch.

Every cook should have a **signature dish**,
and this **elegant entree** fits the bill perfectly.

This tender meat loaf has pretty spirals of spinach throughout and spaghetti sauce on top for a fast final touch. To complement the entree, consider this potato side dish coated with a creamy ranch sauce.

Appealing Partners

- Tossed garden salad with low-fat dressing
- Green beans

Practical Tips

You'll need two slices of wheat bread to make a cup of soft bread crumbs for the Spinach Turkey Roll. Simple tear the bread into pieces and pulse in a blender or food processor to create soft crumbs.

We recommend using the red potatoes called for in the Creamy Skillet Potatoes recipe, because they retain their shape best when boiled.

Spinach Turkey Roll

`low carb`

Delia Kennedy, Deer Park, Washington

PREP: 25 MIN. **BAKE:** 50 MIN.

- 1 cup meatless spaghetti sauce, *divided*
- 2 eggs, lightly beaten
- 1 cup soft whole wheat bread crumbs
- 1/4 cup finely chopped onion
- 2 garlic cloves, minced
- 1 teaspoon dried basil
- 1 teaspoon dried oregano
- 1 teaspoon ground mustard
- 1 pound lean ground turkey
- 1 package (10 ounces) frozen chopped spinach, thawed and squeezed dry
- 1/2 cup shredded part-skim mozzarella cheese

In a bowl, combine 1/4 cup spaghetti sauce, eggs, bread crumbs, onion, garlic, basil, oregano and mustard. Crumble turkey over mixture and mix well.

On a sheet of waxed paper, pat turkey mixture into a 12-in. x 8-in. rectangle. Sprinkle with spinach and cheese. Roll up jelly-roll style, starting with a short side and peeling waxed paper away while rolling. Seal seam and ends. Place seam side down in a 15-in. x 10-in. x 1-in. baking pan coated with nonstick cooking spray.

Bake, uncovered, at 350° for 50-60 minutes or until a meat thermometer reads 165°. Let stand for 5 minutes before slicing. Heat remaining spaghetti sauce; serve over turkey. **YIELD:** 6 SERVINGS.

Nutrition Facts: One serving (1 slice) equals:
230 calories
11 g fat (4 g saturated fat)
137 mg cholesterol
395 mg sodium
12 g carbohydrate
3 g fiber
20 g protein

Diabetic Exchanges: 3 lean meat, 2 vegetable.

Creamy Skillet Potatoes

Denise Pritchard, Seminole, Oklahoma

PREP/TOTAL TIME: 30 MIN.

- 7 cups cubed uncooked red potatoes
- 1/3 cup chopped onion
- 2 tablespoons all-purpose flour
- 1 envelope (1 ounce) ranch salad dressing mix
- 1/2 teaspoon dried parsley flakes
- 1/4 teaspoon salt
- 1/4 cup reduced-fat sour cream
- 2 cups fat-free milk

Place 1 in. of water and potatoes in a large nonstick skillet; bring to a boil. Reduce heat; cover and simmer for 10 minutes or until tender; drain. Coat skillet with nonstick cooking spray; add potatoes and onion. Cook over medium-high heat for 5-7 minutes or until golden brown.

In a saucepan, combine the flour, salad dressing mix, parsley and salt. Stir in the sour cream. Gradually add the milk, stirring until blended. Bring to a boil; cook and stir for 2 minutes or until thickened. Pour over potatoes; toss to coat. **YIELD:** 8 SERVINGS.

Nutrition Facts: One serving (3/4 cup) equals:
160 calories
1 g fat (1 g saturated fat)
5 mg cholesterol
365 mg sodium
32 g carbohydrate
2 g fiber
5 g protein

Diabetic Exchange: 2 starch.

Revisit the **soothing flavors** of Grandma's **cherished recipes** every time you serve this classic **one-dish wonder** to your family.

After a busy day, it's tough to resist bubbling comfort foods...and with this star dish you can dig in without guilt. Enjoy the 30-minute entree alongside crisp greens, featuring this delicious six-ingredient dressing guaranteed to perk up any salad.

Appealing Partners

- Reduced-fat crackers
- Meringue cookies

Practical Tips

Streamline the main course with three boxes (6 ounces each) of cooked chicken cubes.

You'll need three medium carrots for the chicken dinner's 1 cup of sliced carrots.

Use the salad dressing to top greens tossed with shredded cabbage, sliced zucchini, water chestnuts and fat-free croutons.

Easy Chicken and Dumplings

Nancy Tuck, Elk Falls, Kansas

PREP/TOTAL TIME: 30 MIN.

- 3 celery ribs, chopped
- 1 cup sliced fresh carrots
- 3 cans (14-1/2 ounces *each*) reduced-sodium chicken broth
- 1/2 teaspoon poultry seasoning
- 1/8 teaspoon pepper
- 3 cups cubed cooked chicken breast
- 1-2/3 cups reduced-fat biscuit/baking mix
- 2/3 cup fat-free milk

In a Dutch oven coated with nonstick cooking spray, saute celery and carrots for 5 minutes. Stir in the broth, poultry seasoning and pepper. Bring to a boil. Reduce heat; simmer, uncovered. Add the chicken.

For dumplings, combine biscuit mix and milk. Drop by tablespoonfuls onto simmering broth. Cover and simmer for 10-15 minutes or until a toothpick inserted into a dumpling comes out clean (do not lift cover while simmering). **YIELD:** 6 SERVINGS.

Nutrition Facts: One serving (1 cup chicken mixture with 3 dumplings) equals:
- 282 calories
- 5 g fat (1 g saturated fat)
- 60 mg cholesterol
- 1,022 mg sodium
- 29 g carbohydrate
- 1 g fiber
- 28 g protein

Diabetic Exchanges: 3 very lean meat, 1-1/2 starch, 1 vegetable, 1/2 fat.

Salad Dressing With a Kick

Joyce Courser, Greenacres, Washington

PREP: 10 MIN. + CHILLING

- 1/2 cup fat-free plain yogurt
- 1/4 cup chili sauce
- 1 teaspoon prepared horseradish
- 1 teaspoon steak sauce
- 1/2 teaspoon Worcestershire sauce
- 1/8 teaspoon garlic powder

In a small bowl, whisk all of the ingredients. Chill for at least 30 minutes before serving. **YIELD:** 3/4 CUP.

Editor's Note: This recipe was tested with Heinz 57 steak sauce.

Nutrition Facts:
One serving (2 tablespoons) equals:
- 20 calories
- trace fat (0 saturated fat)
- trace cholesterol
- 187 mg sodium
- 5 g carbohydrate
- trace fiber
- 1 g protein

Diabetic Exchange: Free food.

The **secret ingredient** in this
sandwich selection will keep your hungry
bunch guessing and **coming back** for more!

*Give leftover turkey
a makeover with a few
ingredients, including picante
sauce. Toss together a
crunchy combination of
veggies, chopped nuts
and a mild dressing for
gobble-it-up results.*

Turkey Barbecue

Arlene Anderson, San Antonio, Texas

PREP: 15 MIN. **COOK:** 25 MIN.

- 1 celery rib, chopped
- 1 medium onion, chopped
- 1/4 cup chopped green pepper
- 1 tablespoon canola oil
- 1/4 cup packed brown sugar
- 1/4 cup ketchup
- 1/4 cup picante sauce
- 2 tablespoons Worcestershire sauce
- 1-1/2 teaspoons chili powder
- 1 teaspoon salt
- 1/8 teaspoon pepper
- Dash hot pepper sauce
- 4 cups cubed cooked turkey
- 8 whole wheat hamburger buns, split

In a large nonstick skillet, saute the celery, onion and green pepper in oil for 3-4 minutes or until tender. Stir in the brown sugar, ketchup, picante sauce, Worcestershire sauce, chili powder, salt, pepper and pepper sauce; bring to a boil. Reduce heat; simmer, uncovered, for 3-4 minutes. Add turkey; simmer 10 minutes longer or until heated through. Serve on buns. **YIELD:** 8 SERVINGS.

Nutrition Facts: One serving (1 sandwich) equals:
- 295 calories
- 7 g fat (2 g saturated fat)
- 53 mg cholesterol
- 758 mg sodium
- 33 g carbohydrate
- 4 g fiber
- 25 g protein

Diabetic Exchanges: 3 lean meat, 2 starch.

Crunchy Peanut Coleslaw

`low carb` `meat less`

Judy Madsen, Ellis, Idaho

PREP/TOTAL TIME: 20 MIN.

- 1 cup (8 ounces) reduced-fat sour cream
- 1/2 cup fat-free mayonnaise
- 1 tablespoon sugar
- 1 tablespoon tarragon vinegar
- 1/2 teaspoon salt
- 1/4 teaspoon white pepper
- 4 cups finely chopped cabbage
- 1 cup coarsely chopped cauliflower
- 1 cup chopped celery
- 1/4 cup finely chopped onion
- 1/4 cup chopped green pepper
- 1/4 cup finely chopped cucumber
- 1/2 cup chopped peanuts

Combine the sour cream, mayonnaise, sugar, vinegar, salt and pepper; stir until blended. In a large bowl, combine the cabbage, cauliflower, celery, onion, green pepper and cucumber. Pour dressing over vegetables; toss to coat. Sprinkle with peanuts. **YIELD:** 8 SERVINGS.

Nutrition Facts: One serving (3/4 cup) equals:
- 121 calories
- 7 g fat (2 g saturated fat)
- 12 mg cholesterol
- 323 mg sodium
- 14 g carbohydrate
- 3 g fiber
- 4 g protein

Diabetic Exchanges: 1 vegetable, 1 fat, 1/2 starch.

Appealing Partners

- Carrot sticks
- Canned pears

Practical Tips

Make the Turkey Barbecue filling ahead of time and keep it in the freezer for up to 3 months.

If you don't have tarragon vinegar on hand to use for the coleslaw dressing, simply substitute the same amount of white wine vinegar and a dash of tarragon.

Feast on a **traditional** turkey dinner
any time of the year with this **sumptuous**
entree as your dining centerpiece.

*Don't heat up the oven
for this turkey breast.
Simply switch on the slow
cooker and let it roast.
The mashed spuds taste
so good, your family won't
even need to add butter.*

Lemony Turkey Breast

Lynn Laux, Ballwin, Missouri

PREP: 10 MIN. **COOK:** 5 HOURS

 1 bone-in turkey breast (5 pounds), halved
 1 medium lemon, halved
 1 teaspoon salt-free lemon-pepper seasoning
 1 teaspoon garlic salt
 4 teaspoons cornstarch
 1/2 cup reduced-sodium chicken broth

Remove skin from turkey. Pat turkey dry with paper towels; spray turkey with non-stick cooking spray. Place breast side up in a slow cooker. Squeeze half of the lemon over turkey; sprinkle with lemon-pepper and garlic salt. Place lemon halves under turkey. Cover and cook on low for 5-7 hours or until meat is no longer pink and a meat thermometer reads 170°. Remove turkey and keep warm. Discard lemon.

For gravy, pour cooking liquid into a measuring cup; skim fat. In a saucepan, combine cornstarch and broth until smooth. Gradually stir in cooking liquid. Bring to a boil; cook and stir for 2 minutes or until thickened. Serve with turkey. **YIELD:** 14 SERVINGS.

Nutrition Facts: One serving (4 ounces cooked turkey with 2 tablespoons gravy) equals:
       154 calories
         1 g fat (trace saturated fat)
      92 mg cholesterol
     149 mg sodium
         1 g carbohydrate
              trace fiber
        34 g protein

Diabetic Exchange: 4 very lean meat.

Garlic-Rosemary Mashed Potatoes

Kathy Rairigh, Milford, Indiana

PREP: 15 MIN. **BAKE:** 45 MIN.

 6 medium baking potatoes (about 3 pounds)
 1 large whole garlic bulb
 4-1/2 teaspoons olive oil, *divided*
 1 teaspoon minced fresh rosemary
 3/4 cup fat-free milk
 3/4 teaspoon salt

Scrub and pierce potatoes. Bake at 400° for 45-55 minutes or until tender. Meanwhile, remove papery outer skin from garlic bulb (do not peel or separate cloves); cut top off bulb. Place on a piece of heavy-duty foil; drizzle with 1/2 teaspoon oil. Wrap foil around bulb. Bake at 400° for 30-35 minutes or until softened. Cool for 10 minutes.

Squeeze softened garlic into a large mixing bowl. Cut potatoes in half; scoop out pulp and add to garlic. Discard potato skins. mash potatoes. In a small saucepan, saute rosemary in remaining oil for 2 minutes; add to potato mixture. Add milk and salt; beat until fluffy. **YIELD:** 8 SERVINGS.

Nutrition Facts: One serving (3/4 cup) equals:
       153 calories
         3 g fat (trace saturated fat)
              trace cholesterol
     239 mg sodium
        30 g carbohydrate
         2 g fiber
         4 g protein

Diabetic Exchanges: 2 starch, 1/2 fat.

Appealing Partners

• Sauteed yellow summer squash
• Fresh fruit salad

Practical Tips

The entree makes a lot, so make the most of the leftovers. Extra cooked turkey can be stored in the refrigerator for 1-2 days or in the freezer for up to 3 months. Use it to make sandwiches, salads, casseroles or quick stir-fries.

Save rosemary from your summer garden with the mashed potato recipe in mind. To freeze rosemary, rinse whole sprigs, then pat dry with paper towels. Place a few sprigs in each of several small plastic freezer bags.

Enjoy a **saucy slice** of this main course tonight, then look forward to **tummy-tempting** leftovers for tomorrow's **light lunch**.

A tasty noodle layer covered with creamy cottage cheese and a hearty ground turkey mixture makes for a mouth-watering pie. For dessert, bite into these sweet squares that are so simple to make ahead and freeze. No need to thaw—just pull out a few to enjoy!

Appealing Partners

- Crusty French bread
- Steamed carrots

Practical Tips

For more authentic Italian flavor, use 3/4 pound of turkey Italian sausage (with the casings removed) in place of the ground turkey. Or, for a zippier taste, try hot turkey Italian sausage.

Instead of using chocolate graham crackers in the dessert, sandwich the creamy filling between regular or cinnamon graham crackers.

Turkey Spaghetti Pie

Anita Cunningham, Blaine, Washington

PREP: 30 MIN.   **BAKE:** 25 MIN. + STANDING

6	ounces uncooked spaghetti
5	tablespoons grated Parmesan cheese
1/2	cup egg substitute
3/4	pound lean ground turkey breast
1	medium onion, chopped
1/2	medium green pepper, chopped
1-1/2	cups meatless spaghetti sauce
1	cup fat-free cottage cheese
1/2	cup shredded part-skim mozzarella cheese

Cook spaghetti according to package directions. Drain well and cool to room temperature. In a bowl, combine the spaghetti, Parmesan cheese and egg substitute. Transfer to a 9-in. pie plate coated with nonstick cooking spray and form into a crust; set aside.

In a nonstick skillet over medium heat, cook turkey, onion and green pepper until turkey is no longer pink; drain. Add spaghetti sauce; heat through. Spread cottage cheese over crust; top with turkey mixture.

Bake, uncovered, at 350° for 20 minutes. Sprinkle with mozzarella cheese. Bake 5 minutes longer or until cheese is melted. Let stand for 5 minutes before cutting. **YIELD:** 6 SERVINGS.

Nutrition Facts: One serving (1 wedge) equals:
274 calories
11 g fat (4 g saturated fat)
57 mg cholesterol
710 mg sodium
19 g carbohydrate
2 g fiber
25 g protein

Diabetic Exchanges: 3 lean meat, 1 starch, 1 vegetable.

Mock Ice Cream Sandwiches

Tony Kern, Milwaukee, Wisconsin

PREP: 15 MIN. + FREEZING

2	cups fat-free whipped topping
1/2	cup miniature semisweet chocolate chips
8	whole chocolate graham crackers

In a bowl, combine whipped topping and chocolate chips. Break or cut graham crackers in half. Spread whipped topping mixture over half of the crackers; top with remaining crackers. Wrap in plastic wrap and freeze for at least 1 hour. **YIELD:** 8 SANDWICHES.

Nutrition Facts: One serving (1 sandwich) equals:
180 calories
7 g fat (3 g saturated fat)
0 cholesterol
88 mg sodium
28 g carbohydrate
1 g fiber
2 g protein

Diabetic Exchanges: 2 starch, 1/2 fat.

A picture-perfect meal requires only minutes to assemble, but promises long-lasting flavor.

One pan is all it takes to pull together a complete pork and veggie meal. You'll need only three ingredients for the thick, creamy dressing that's an inviting topping for any green salad.

Appealing Partners

- Hot spiced apple cider
- Fat-free vanilla ice cream

Practical Tips

When preparing the pork and veggies, vary the flavor by combining your own blend of herbs in place of the rosemary and sage. Experiment with mint and marjoram or basil and rosemary.

To save time at dinner, make the Buttermilk Salad Dressing early in the day.

Roasted Pork Tenderloin And Vegetables

Diane Martin, Brown Deer, Wisconsin

PREP: 10 MIN.   **BAKE:** 30 MIN.

- 2   pork tenderloins (3/4 pound *each*)
- 2   pounds red potatoes, quartered
- 1   pound carrots, halved and cut into 2-inch pieces
- 1   medium onion, cut into wedges
- 1   tablespoon olive oil
- 2   teaspoons dried rosemary, crushed
- 1   teaspoon rubbed sage
- 1/2 teaspoon salt
- 1/4 teaspoon pepper

Place the pork in a shallow roasting pan coated with nonstick cooking spray; arrange the potatoes, carrots and onion around pork. Drizzle with oil. Combine the seasonings; sprinkle over meat and vegetables.

Bake, uncovered, at 450° for 30-40 minutes or until a meat thermometer reads 160°, stirring vegetables occasionally. **YIELD:** 6 SERVINGS.

Nutrition Facts: One serving (3 ounces cooked meat with 1 cup vegetables) equals:
- 331 calories
- 7 g fat (2 g saturated fat)
- 67 mg cholesterol
- 299 mg sodium
- 40 g carbohydrate
- 5 g fiber
- 28 g protein

Diabetic Exchanges: 3 lean meat, 2 starch, 1 vegetable.

Buttermilk Salad Dressing

Vicki Floden, Story City, Iowa

PREP: 10 MIN. + CHILLING

- 3/4 cup buttermilk
- 2   cups (16 ounces) 2% cottage cheese
- 1   envelope ranch salad dressing mix

Salad greens and vegetables of your choice

In a blender or food processor, combine the buttermilk, cottage cheese and salad dressing mix; cover and process for 20 seconds or until smooth. Pour into a small pitcher or bowl. Cover and refrigerate for 1 hour. Stir before serving with salad. **YIELD:** 2-3/4 CUPS.

Nutrition Facts:
One serving (2 tablespoons) equals:
- 23 calories
- 1 g fat (1 g saturated fat)
- 3 mg cholesterol
- 177 mg sodium
- 2 g carbohydrate
- 0 fiber
- 3 g protein

Diabetic Exchange: 1/2 fat-free milk.

Spending a **few minutes** in the kitchen the night before is worth it when this **dazzling duo** is on your menu.

Start by marinating chops overnight in a pleasant lime mixture. A comforting counterpart to the hearty pork is this whip-together, super spud side.

Honey-Lime Pork Chops   `low carb`

Janice Mitchell, Aurora, Colorado

PREP: 20 MIN. + MARINATING   **GRILL:** 15 MIN.

- 1/2   cup lime juice
- 1/2   cup reduced-sodium soy sauce
- 2   tablespoons honey
- 2   garlic cloves, minced
- 6   boneless pork loin chops (4 ounces *each*)

SAUCE:
- 3/4   cup reduced-sodium chicken broth
- 1   garlic clove, minced
- 1-1/2   teaspoons honey
- 1/2   teaspoon lime juice
- 1/8   teaspoon browning sauce

Dash pepper
- 2   teaspoons cornstarch
- 2   tablespoons water

In a large resealable plastic bag, combine the first four ingredients. Add pork chops. Seal bag and turn to coat; refrigerate for 8 hours or overnight. Drain and discard marinade. Grill chops, covered, over medium heat or broil 4 in. from the heat for 6-7 minutes on each side or until juices run clear.

For sauce, combine the broth, garlic, honey, lime juice, browning sauce and pepper in a small saucepan. Bring to a boil. Combine cornstarch and water until smooth; stir into broth mixture. Return to a boil; cook and stir for 1-2 minutes or until thickened. Serve with pork chops. **YIELD:** 6 SERVINGS.

Nutrition Facts: One serving (1 pork chop with 2 tablespoons sauce) equals:
- 200   calories
- 5 g   fat (2 g saturated fat)
- 71 mg   cholesterol
- 884 mg   sodium
- 11 g   carbohydrate
-       trace fiber
- 26 g   protein

Diabetic Exchanges: 3 lean meat, 1/2 fruit.

Garlic Mashed Red Potatoes   `meat less`

Val Mitchell, Hudson, Ohio

PREP/TOTAL TIME: 30 MIN.

- 8   medium red potatoes, quartered
- 3   garlic cloves, peeled
- 2   tablespoons butter
- 1/2   cup fat-free milk, warmed
- 1/2   teaspoon salt
- 1/4   cup grated Parmesan cheese

Place potatoes and garlic in a large saucepan; cover with water. Bring to a boil. Reduce heat; cover and simmer for 20-25 minutes or until the potatoes are very tender. Drain well. Add the butter, milk and salt; mash. Stir in Parmesan cheese. **YIELD:** 6 SERVINGS.

Nutrition Facts: One serving (1 cup) equals:
- 190   calories
- 5 g   fat (3 g saturated fat)
- 14 mg   cholesterol
- 275 mg   sodium
- 36 g   carbohydrate
- 4 g   fiber
- 8 g   protein

Diabetic Exchanges: 2 starch, 1/2 fat.

Appealing Partners

- Steamed baby carrots
- Emerald Fruit Salad, p. 260

Practical Tips

Dovetail some of the recipe steps. For example, fix the sauce for the entree while the chops are cooking on the grill or under the broiler.

Cut down on prep time when making the marinade. Instead of mincing fresh garlic cloves, take advantage of convenient minced garlic available in jars. A half teaspoon is equal to one clove of minced garlic.

Healthy fare with home-style taste is both scrumptious and calorie-smart.

Skillet-warmed ham steaks with sweet pineapple sauce pack big taste without added calories. Carrot, celery and red pepper lend crispness to the potato salad. You'll want to remember the salad recipe for picnics, too!

Appealing Partners

• Steamed brussels sprouts

• Raspberry Pie with Oat Crust, p. 328

Practical Tips

For the entree, you need 1 cup of pineapple juice so buy a six-pack of 6-ounce cans. Then store the extra cans in your pantry to use later.

For a pretty presentation, line the bowl that holds the Crunchy Potato Salad with lettuce leaves.

Spiced Pineapple Ham

Betty Claycomb, Alverton, Pennsylvania

PREP/TOTAL TIME: 20 MIN.

  1 cup unsweetened pineapple juice
1/2 teaspoon whole cloves
  1 cinnamon stick (3 inches)
  3 tablespoons brown sugar
  1 tablespoon cornstarch
  2 tablespoons cider vinegar
  1 cup unsweetened pineapple tidbits, drained
  6 boneless fully cooked ham steaks (4 ounces *each*)

In a saucepan, bring pineapple juice, cloves and cinnamon stick to a boil. Reduce heat; cook, uncovered, for 5 minutes. Strain juice, discarding cloves and cinnamon. Return juice to the pan.

In a bowl, combine brown sugar and cornstarch; stir in vinegar until smooth. Stir into pineapple juice. Bring to a boil; cook and stir for 2 minutes or until thickened. Stir in pineapple; heat through.

In a large nonstick skillet, cook ham steaks until browned and heated through. Serve with the pineapple sauce. **YIELD:** 6 SERVINGS.

Nutrition Facts:
One serving (1 ham steak) equals:
185 calories
4 g fat (1 g saturated fat)
58 mg cholesterol
1,180 mg sodium
17 g carbohydrate
trace fiber
21 g protein

Diabetic Exchanges: 3 lean meat, 1 fruit.

Crunchy Potato Salad

meat less

Janis Plagerman, Lynden, Washington

PREP: 25 MIN. + CHILLING

1-1/2 pounds red potatoes, cubed
  1 celery rib, chopped
1/4 cup chopped sweet red pepper
  1 medium carrot, shredded
  1 green onion, chopped
1/4 cup reduced-fat mayonnaise
1/4 cup reduced-fat plain yogurt
  1 tablespoon sweet pickle relish
3/4 teaspoon prepared mustard
1/2 teaspoon salt
1/2 teaspoon lemon-pepper seasoning
1/2 teaspoon dill weed
Lettuce leaves, optional

Place potatoes in a saucepan and cover with water; bring to a boil. Reduce heat; cover and simmer for 15-20 minutes or until tender. Drain and cool; place in a bowl. Add the celery, red pepper, carrot and onion.

In a small bowl, combine the mayonnaise, yogurt, pickle relish, mustard, salt, lemon-pepper and dill; pour over vegetables and toss to coat. Cover and refrigerate for at least 1 hour. Serve in a lettuce-lined bowl if desired. **YIELD:** 6 SERVINGS.

Nutrition Facts: One serving (3/4 cup) equals:
143 calories
4 g fat (1 g saturated fat)
4 mg cholesterol
371 mg sodium
25 g carbohydrate
3 g fiber
3 g protein

Diabetic Exchanges: 1-1/2 starch, 1/2 fat.

Southern-style sandwiches make it tastier than ever to ease into the weekend.

For an informal soup and sandwich supper, start with this combo. You'll get plenty of veggies with the coleslaw sandwich topping and the garden-fresh gazpacho ingredients.

Appealing Partners

- Limeade (from frozen concentrate)
- Watermelon slices

Practical Tips

You can easily substitute turkey tenderloin for the pork tenderloin when making the Pork 'n' Slaw Sandwiches. Just be sure you broil the turkey to 170°.

To cut down on prep time, use about 2 cups coleslaw mix from your supermarket's produce department rather than shredding the green and red cabbage and carrot.

If your family prefers a less zippy gazpacho, use regular V8 juice instead of the spicy hot variety.

Pork 'n' Slaw Sandwiches

Taste of Home Test Kitchen
Greendale, Wisconsin

PREP/TOTAL TIME: 30 MIN.

3	tablespoons cider vinegar
4	teaspoons sugar
2	teaspoons canola oil
1	teaspoon Dijon mustard
1/4	teaspoon celery seed
1/4	teaspoon mustard seed
1/4	teaspoon salt
1/8	teaspoon pepper
1	cup shredded green cabbage
1	cup shredded cabbage
1	large carrot, shredded
1-1/2	pounds pork tenderloin
1	cup barbecue sauce
6	kaiser rolls, split

For coleslaw, in a bowl, whisk together the first eight ingredients. Add cabbage and carrot; toss to coat. Set aside.

Broil pork 4-6-in. from the heat for 6-7 minutes on each side or until a meat thermometer reads 160°. Let stand for 5 minutes. Cut into strips or shred with two forks; place in a bowl. Add barbecue sauce and toss to coat. Serve 1/2 cup pork mixture and 1/3 cup coleslaw on each roll. **YIELD:** 6 SERVINGS.

Nutrition Facts: One serving (1 sandwich) equals:
- 377 calories
- 9 g fat (2 g saturated fat)
- 67 mg cholesterol
- 828 mg sodium
- 41 g carbohydrate
- 1 g fiber
- 31 g protein

Diabetic Exchanges: 3 lean meat, 2-1/2 starch, 1 vegetable.

Black Bean Zucchini Gazpacho

meat less

Julie Wilson, Grand Rapids, Ohio

PREP: 10 MIN. + CHILLING

3	cans (5-1/2 ounces *each*) spicy hot V8 juice
1	can (15 ounces) black beans, rinsed and drained
1	medium onion, chopped
2	large tomatoes, seeded and chopped
2	medium zucchini, chopped
2	tablespoons olive oil
2	tablespoons white wine vinegar
1	garlic clove, minced
1/4	teaspoon salt
1/4	teaspoon pepper
1/4	teaspoon cayenne pepper

In a large bowl, combine all ingredients. Cover and refrigerate for 8 hours or overnight. **YIELD:** 6 SERVINGS.

Nutrition Facts: One serving (1 cup) equals:
- 149 calories
- 5 g fat (1 g saturated fat)
- 0 cholesterol
- 574 mg sodium
- 20 g carbohydrate
- 6 g fiber
- 6 g protein

Diabetic Exchanges: 2 vegetable, 1 fat, 1/2 starch.

A **traditional** meal does delicious double duty as a weeknight **staple** or as a company's-coming **celebration**.

Marinate the entree for just on hour, then take it to the grill. Even the eye-catching, chilled rice salad is a breeze to make— and a pleasure to eat.

Honey-Herb Pork

Arlene Anderson, San Antonio, Texas

PREP: 10 MIN. + MARINATING
GRILL: 25 MIN. + STANDING

1	cup beer *or* ginger ale
1/2	cup prepared mustard
1/2	cup honey
2	tablespoons canola oil
2	tablespoons onion powder
1-1/2	teaspoons dried rosemary, crushed
1	teaspoon salt
1	teaspoon garlic powder
1/4	teaspoon pepper
2	pork tenderloins (1 pound *each*)

In a small bowl, combine the first nine ingredients. Pour 1 cup marinade into a large resealable plastic bag; add the pork. Seal bag and turn to coat; refrigerate for at least 1 hour. Cover and refrigerate the remaining marinade for basting.

Coat grill rack with nonstick cooking spray before preparing the grill for indirect heat. Drain and discard marinade from pork. Grill, covered, over indirect medium heat for 25-30 minutes or until a meat thermometer reads 160°, basting occasionally with reserved marinade. Let stand for 10 minutes before slicing. Serve with any remaining marinade if desired. **YIELD:** 6 SERVINGS.

Nutrition Facts: One serving (4 ounces cooked pork) equals:

274	calories
8 g	fat (2 g saturated fat)
84 mg	cholesterol
432 mg	sodium
17 g	carbohydrate
1 g	fiber
31 g	protein

Diabetic Exchanges: 4 lean meat, 1 starch.

Wild Rice Pepper Salad

`meat less`

Judy Madsen, Ellis, Idaho

PREP: 10 MIN. **COOK:** 1 HOUR + CHILLING

2/3	cup uncooked wild rice
3	cups water
1	cup chopped green pepper
1	cup chopped sweet red pepper
1	cup chopped sweet yellow pepper
1/2	cup sunflower kernels
1/3	cup chopped onion
1/3	cup raisins
1/2	cup fat-free Italian salad dressing

In a small saucepan, bring the rice and water to a boil. Reduce heat; cover and simmer for 1 hour or until rice is tender. Drain and place in a bowl. Refrigerate until chilled. Add the remaining ingredients; toss to coat. **YIELD:** 6 SERVINGS.

Nutrition Facts: One serving (3/4 cup) equals:

206	calories
7 g	fat (1 g saturated fat)
1 mg	cholesterol
357 mg	sodium
32 g	carbohydrate
3 g	fiber
6 g	protein

Diabetic Exchanges: 1 starch, 1 vegetable, 1 fat, 1/2 fruit.

Appealing Partners:

- Grilled mushrooms and sliced onions
- Fresh fruit with whipped topping

Practical Tips

To help streamline the tenderloins' preparation, substitute 1 cup of prepared honey-mustard from the grocery store for the honey and mustard in the ingredients.

When red and yellow peppers aren't in season, you can make the side dish with chopped carrots and celery instead.

One **creamy** bite and you'll be convinced that **light** dining doesn't mean you have to sacrifice **luscious flavor.**

Creamy filling with diced ham and Swiss cheese is tucked into tender pasta shells, then served with a side of fresh green beans, simply seasoned with onion, allspice and garlic.

Ham-Stuffed Jumbo Shells

Leona Reuer, Medina, North Dakota

PREP: 20 MIN. BAKE: 30 MIN.

- 24 jumbo pasta shells
- 3 tablespoons all-purpose flour
- 2 cups 1% milk
- 1/2 pound fresh mushrooms, halved and sliced
- 1/2 cup chopped onion
- 1/2 cup chopped green pepper
- 1 tablespoon canola oil
- 3 cups cubed fully cooked lean ham
- 1 cup (4 ounces) shredded reduced-fat Swiss cheese, *divided*
- 3 tablespoons grated Parmesan cheese
- 2 tablespoons minced fresh parsley
- 1/4 teaspoon paprika

Cook pasta according to package directions. Meanwhile, in a small saucepan, combine flour and milk until smooth. Bring to a boil; cook and stir for 2 minutes or until thickened. Remove from the heat; set aside.

In a large nonstick skillet, saute the mushrooms, onion and green pepper in oil until tender. Reduce heat; add the ham, 1/2 cup Swiss cheese and Parmesan cheese. Cook and stir until cheese is melted. Remove from the heat. Stir in 1/2 cup of the reserved sauce.

Drain pasta; stuff each shell with about 3 tablespoons of filling. Place in a 13-in. x 9-in. x 2-in. baking dish coated with nonstick cooking spray. Top with remaining sauce. Cover and bake at 350° for 30 minutes or until heated through. Sprinkle with parsley, paprika and remaining Swiss cheese. **YIELD:** 8 SERVINGS.

Nutrition Facts:
One serving (3 stuffed shells) equals:
- 274 calories
- 7 g fat (2 g saturated fat)
- 26 mg cholesterol
- 703 mg sodium
- 30 g carbohydrate
- 2 g fiber
- 23 g protein

Diabetic Exchanges: 2 starch, 2 lean meat.

Green Beans With Tomatoes

Clara Coulston, Washington Court House, Ohio

PREP/TOTAL TIME: 25 MIN.

- 1/2 cup reduced-sodium chicken broth *or* vegetable broth
- 1 cup chopped onion
- 2 garlic cloves, minced
- 2 pounds fresh green beans, cut into 2-inch pieces
- 4 medium ripe tomatoes, seeded and chopped
- 3/4 teaspoon seasoned salt
- 1/8 teaspoon ground allspice
- 1/8 teaspoon pepper

In a large nonstick skillet, bring the broth, onion and garlic to a boil. Add beans; return to a boil. Reduce heat; cover and simmer for 15 minutes. Add the tomatoes, seasoned salt, allspice and pepper; cook 2-3 minutes longer or until beans are tender. Serve with a slotted spoon. **YIELD:** 8 SERVINGS.

Nutrition Facts: One serving (3/4 cup) equals:
- 61 calories
- trace fat (trace saturated fat)
- 0 cholesterol
- 184 mg sodium
- 12 g carbohydrate
- 5 g fiber
- 2 g protein

Diabetic Exchange: 2 vegetable.

Appealing Partners

- Romaine lettuce salad
- Fruit juice bars

Practical Tips

When preparing Ham-Stuffed Jumbo Shells, you may also use manicotti instead of jumbo pasta shells.

The main dish calls for 3 cups cubed fully cooked lean ham. You can cut up a ham steak or cut a portion from a small boneless ham and save the rest for other meals. In a hurry? Pick up two 1-pound packages of ham that's already been cubed.

Get ready for plenty of **"seconds, please"**
comments when you bring this **low-carb** star to the table.

A sprinkling of oregano and basil provides the pleasant Italian flavor you'll find in this main dish. When a guiltless dessert is in order, grab these frosty snacks that are easy to assemble and so much fun to munch on.

Appealing Partners

- Green peas
- Cucumber salad

Practical Tips

The pork chop recipe calls for 2 cups hot cooked noodles, so you'll need to boil 4 ounces uncooked noodles (about 3 cups).

When making the dessert, you can press the edges of the sandwiches in grated chocolate or M&M miniature baking bits instead of mini chocolate chips.

For variety, substitute chocolate or cinnamon-topped graham crackers.

Pork Chops With Pizza Sauce

low carb

Joanna Iovino, Commack, New York

PREP/TOTAL TIME: 30 MIN.

- 2 to 4 teaspoons dried oregano, *divided*
- 2 to 4 teaspoons dried basil, *divided*
- 1/2 teaspoon salt, *divided*
- 1/2 teaspoon pepper, *divided*
- 4 bone-in center loin pork chops (7 ounces *each*)
- 1 tablespoon olive oil
- 3 medium onions, thinly sliced
- 4 garlic cloves, minced
- 2 cans (8 ounces *each*) tomato sauce
- 1/2 cup water
- 2 cups hot cooked noodles

In a small bowl, combine 1-1/2 to 3 teaspoons oregano, 1-1/2 to 3 teaspoons basil, 1/4 teaspoon salt and 1/4 teaspoon pepper. Sprinkle over both sides of chops. In a large nonstick skillet, brown pork on both sides in oil over medium heat; remove from skillet.

In the same skillet, saute onions and garlic until tender. Add the tomato sauce, water and the remaining oregano, basil, salt and pepper. Bring to a boil. Return pork to the skillet. Reduce heat; cover and simmer for 15-20 minutes or until a meat thermometer reads 160°. Serve with hot noodles. **YIELD:** 4 SERVINGS.

Nutrition Facts: One serving (1 pork chop and 3/4 cup sauce with 1/2 cup noodles) equals:
302 calories
12 g fat (4 g saturated fat)
86 mg cholesterol
882 mg sodium
14 g carbohydrate
3 g fiber
33 g protein

Diabetic Exchanges: 4 lean meat, 3 vegetable.

Pudding Grahamwiches

low fat

Anissa DeGrasse
Mountain Home Air Force Base, Idaho

PREP: 20 MIN. + FREEZING

- 1-1/2 cups cold fat-free milk
- 1 package (1 ounce) sugar-free instant vanilla pudding mix
- 1 carton (8 ounces) frozen reduced-fat whipped topping, thawed
- 1 cup miniature marshmallows
- 24 graham crackers (about 5 inches x 2-1/2 inches *each*), broken in half
- 5 tablespoons miniature semisweet chocolate chips

In a large bowl, whisk milk and pudding mix for 2 minutes. Let stand for 2 minutes or until soft-set. Fold in whipped topping and marshmallows. Spread pudding mixture over half of graham crackers. Top with remaining crackers.

Place chocolate chips in a shallow dish. Press edges of sandwich into chips to coat. Wrap each sandwich in plastic wrap; place in an airtight container and freeze. Remove from the freezer about 5 minutes before serving. **YIELD:** 2 DOZEN.

Nutrition Facts: One serving (1 sandwich) equals:
108 calories
3 g fat (2 g saturated fat)
trace cholesterol
143 mg sodium
18 g carbohydrate
1 g fiber
2 g protein

Diabetic Exchanges: 1 starch, 1/2 fat.

A **stick-to-your-ribs** supper the whole family will love starts with everyday **fiber-rich** ingredients.

A golden bread crumb topping completes this full-flavored meal-in-one. A warm dressing made with sauteed mushrooms, onions and garlic is a light change from heavier bacon dressings and sparks big flavor on fresh spinach.

Appealing Partners

- Vegetable soup
- Angel food cake with berry sauce

Practical Tips

Instead of great northern beans, you can use other white beans, such as white kidney or cannellini beans.

To make soft bread crumbs for the casserole's topping, tear three slices of white bread into pieces. Use a blender or food processor to process them into crumbs to yield 1-1/2 cups.

If you don't have balsamic vinegar on hand for the salad dressing, try red wine vinegar instead.

Oven Cassoulet

Diane Molberg, Emerald Park, Saskatchewan

PREP: 20 MIN. **BAKE:** 30 MIN.

- 1/2 pound reduced-fat fully cooked kielbasa *or* Polish sausage, cut into 1/2-inch cubes
- 1 cup chopped onion
- 2 medium carrots, thinly sliced
- 2 celery ribs, chopped
- 1 garlic clove, minced
- 1 can (14-1/2 ounces) diced tomatoes, drained
- 3/4 cup reduced-sodium chicken broth
- 1 bay leaf
- 1/2 teaspoon dried thyme
- 1/4 teaspoon pepper
- 1/8 teaspoon ground cloves
- 2 cans (15-1/2 ounces *each*) great northern beans, rinsed and drained
- 1-1/2 cups soft bread crumbs
- 2 tablespoons butter, melted
- 2 tablespoons minced fresh parsley

In a nonstick saucepan coated with nonstick cooking spray, cook and stir the sausage, onion, carrots, celery and garlic for 4-5 minutes or until onion is tender. Stir in the tomatoes, broth, bay leaf, thyme, pepper and cloves. Bring to a boil. Reduce heat; simmer, uncovered, for about 15 minutes or until carrots are tender and liquid is slightly thickened. Discard bay leaf. Stir in beans.

Transfer to a 2-qt. baking dish coated with nonstick cooking spray. Combine the bread crumbs, butter and parsley. Sprinkle over sausage mixture. Bake, uncovered, at 350° for 30-35 minutes or until edges are bubbly and top is golden brown. **YIELD:** 6 SERVINGS.

Nutrition Facts:
One serving (1-1/4 cups) equals:

270	calories
6 g	fat (3 g saturated fat)
23 mg	cholesterol
809 mg	sodium
40 g	carbohydrate
10 g	fiber
14 g	protein

Diabetic Exchanges: 2 lean meat, 2 vegetable, 1-1/2 starch.

Chive-Mushroom Spinach Salad

Amber Kimmich, Powhatan, Virginia

PREP/TOTAL TIME: 15 MIN.

- 8 cups fresh baby spinach
- 2 cups sliced fresh mushrooms
- 1 tablespoon chopped onion
- 1 garlic clove, minced
- 2 tablespoons olive oil
- 3 tablespoons minced chives
- 2 tablespoons lemon juice
- 2 tablespoons balsamic vinegar
- 1 teaspoon sugar
- 1-1/2 cups seasoned salad croutons
- 1/4 cup shredded Parmesan cheese

Place spinach in a large salad bowl; set aside. In a large skillet, saute the mushrooms, onion and garlic in oil for 2-4 minutes. In a small bowl, combine the chives, lemon juice, vinegar and sugar. Pour into the skillet. Cook and stir 1 minute longer or until mushrooms are tender. Add to spinach with croutons and Parmesan cheese; toss to coat. Serve immediately. **YIELD:** 6 SERVINGS.

Nutrition Facts:
One serving (1-1/3 cups) equals:

117	calories
6 g	fat (1 g saturated fat)
2 mg	cholesterol
235 mg	sodium
11 g	carbohydrate
1 g	fiber
5 g	protein

Diabetic Exchanges: 1 vegetable, 1 fat, 1/2 starch.

You'll win a **standing ovation** for this sumptuous sit-down dinner. Any extras will make for a tasty **encore** meal.

This slow-cooked meat is moist and tender with a pleasant, fruity taste. For an attractive yet simple side dish, dress up noodles with lemon peel, orange peel and basil. You'll love the burst of refreshing flavor...and color!

Appealing Partners

- Steamed broccoli
- Fresh fruit cups

Practical Tips

When preparing the pork roast, dried rosemary can be substituted for fresh. Put the rosemary in a tied cheesecloth bag and place the bag in the slow cooker with the roast.

Apple cider and apple juice can be used interchangeably in the Cider Pork Roast recipe.

Cider Pork Roast

Terry Danner, Rochelle, Illinois

PREP: 20 MIN. **COOK:** 5 HOURS 10 MIN.

- 1 boneless pork loin roast (2 pounds)
- 3/4 teaspoon salt
- 1/4 teaspoon pepper
- 2 cups apple cider *or* unsweetened apple juice, *divided*
- 3 sprigs fresh rosemary
- 1/2 cup dried cherries
- 5 teaspoons cornstarch

Sprinkle pork with salt and pepper. In a nonstick skillet coated with nonstick cooking spray, brown pork for about 4 minutes on each side. Pour 1 cup apple cider in a 3-qt. slow cooker. Place two sprigs rosemary in slow cooker; top with meat and remaining rosemary. Place cherries around roast. Cover and cook on low for 5-6 hours or until a meat thermometer reads 160°.

Remove meat; keep warm. Strain cooking liquid; reserve liquid and transfer to a small saucepan. Stir in 3/4 cup cider; bring to a boil. Combine cornstarch and remaining cider until smooth. Gradually whisk into cider mixture. Bring to a boil; cook and stir for 1-2 minutes or until thickened. Serve with meat. **YIELD:** 6 SERVINGS.

Nutrition Facts: One serving (4 ounces cooked pork with 1/4 cup gravy) equals:

    298 calories
      9 g fat (3 g saturated fat)
    89 mg cholesterol
  368 mg sodium
    20 g carbohydrate
     1 g fiber
    32 g protein

Diabetic Exchanges: 4 lean meat, 1-1/2 fruit.

Sesame Seed Citrus Noodles

Trisha Kruse, Boise, Idaho

PREP/TOTAL TIME: 25 MIN.

- 4 cups wide no-yolk noodles
- 2 tablespoons chopped fresh basil *or* 2 teaspoons dried basil
- 4-1/2 teaspoons butter, melted
- 1 tablespoon lemon juice
- 1/2 teaspoon salt
- 1/2 teaspoon grated lemon peel
- 1/2 teaspoon grated orange peel
- 1-1/2 teaspoons sesame seeds, toasted

Cook noodles according to package directions. Drain, reserving 1/2 cup cooking water. Return noodles to pan. Add the basil, butter, lemon juice, salt and lemon and orange peels. Toss to coat, adding reserved cooking liquid if needed to moisten noodles. Sprinkle with sesame seeds. **YIELD:** 6 SERVINGS.

Nutrition Facts: One serving (2/3 cup) equals:

  136 calories
    3 g fat (2 g saturated fat)
    8 mg cholesterol
  241 mg sodium
    21 g carbohydrate
    2 g fiber
    4 g protein

Diabetic Exchanges: 1-1/2 starch, 1/2 fat.

Plan ahead and you can come home to the **savory aroma** of a slow-cooked meal, **ready to eat** when you are.

Slow-Cooked Sweet 'n' Sour Pork

Martha Nickerson, Hancock, Maine

PREP: 20 MIN. **COOK:** 6-1/2 HOURS

There's nothing complicated about this tender pork dish, especially when served with fluffy white rice. For dessert, treat yourself to a moist slice of these pan bars. The recipe makes a batch that should be enough to last a few days.

- 2 tablespoons plus 1-1/2 teaspoons paprika
- 1-1/2 pounds boneless pork loin roast, cut into 1-inch strips
- 1 tablespoon canola oil
- 1 can (20 ounces) unsweetened pineapple chunks
- 1 medium onion, chopped
- 1 medium green pepper, chopped
- 1/4 cup cider vinegar
- 3 tablespoons brown sugar
- 3 tablespoons reduced-sodium soy sauce
- 1 tablespoon Worcestershire sauce
- 1/2 teaspoon salt
- 2 tablespoons cornstarch
- 1/4 cup cold water

Hot cooked rice, optional

Place paprika in a large resealable plastic bag. Add pork, a few pieces at a time, and shake to coat. In a nonstick skillet, brown pork in oil in batches over medium-high heat. Transfer to a 3-qt. slow cooker.

Drain pineapple, reserving juice; refrigerate the pineapple. Add the pineapple juice, onion, green pepper, vinegar, brown sugar, soy sauce, Worcestershire sauce and salt to slow cooker; mix well. Cover and cook on low for 6-8 hours or until meat is tender.

Combine cornstarch and water until smooth; stir into pork mixture. Add pineapple. Cover and cook 30 minutes longer or until sauce is thickened. Serve over rice if desired. **YIELD:** 6 SERVINGS.

Nutrition Facts:
One serving (1 cup pork mixture) equals:
- 312 calories
- 10 g fat (3 g saturated fat)
- 73 mg cholesterol
- 592 mg sodium
- 28 g carbohydrate
- 2 g fiber
- 27 g protein

Diabetic Exchanges: 3 lean meat, 1 fruit, 1/2 starch, 1/2 fat.

Oatmeal Date Bars

low sodium

Helen Cluts, Sioux Falls, South Dakota

PREP: 25 MIN. **BAKE:** 20 MIN. + COOLING

- 1 cup chopped dates
- 1/2 cup water
- 1/4 cup sugar
- 1-1/2 cups quick-cooking oats
- 1 cup all-purpose flour
- 1 cup packed brown sugar
- 1/2 teaspoon baking soda
- 1/4 teaspoon salt
- 1/3 cup butter, melted
- 1 egg white

In a small saucepan, combine the dates, water and sugar. Cook and stir until mixture comes to a boil. Reduce heat; simmer, uncovered, for 5 minutes or until mixture is smooth and thickened, stirring constantly.

In a large bowl, combine the oats, flour, brown sugar, baking soda and salt. Stir in the butter and egg white until blended. Pat half of the mixture into an 8-in. square baking dish coated with nonstick cooking spray. Carefully spread with date mixture. Gently pat remaining oat mixture over date mixture. Bake at 350° for 20-25 minutes or until lightly browned. Cool on a wire rack. Cut into bars. **YIELD:** 16 SERVINGS.

Nutrition Facts: One serving (1 bar) equals:
- 186 calories
- 4 g fat (2 g saturated fat)
- 10 mg cholesterol
- 124 mg sodium
- 36 g carbohydrate
- 2 g fiber
- 2 g protein

Diabetic Exchanges: 1-1/2 starch, 1 fat, 1/2 fruit.

Appealing Partners

- Spinach salad
- Pineapple wedges

Practical Tips

To trim time in the morning, slice the pork and chop the onion and green pepper the night before.

While you're chopping the vegetables for the entree, cut up extra veggies to use for a salad or other dish later in the week.

For a change of pace, replace half of the dates in the oat bars with an equal amount of dried apricots.

If your day is **spinning** out of control,
take a **deep breath** and slow it down
with a stovetop **solution.**

Here's a dish so versatile that it can be adapted to most everyone's taste buds. The vegetable side salad is a healthy alternative to pasta and potato sides—and it's a snap to toss together.

Appealing Partners

- Corn muffins
- Oven-baked steak fries

Practical Tips

For a streamlined version of the entree, substitute cubed cooked chicken for the pork. Also, the spiciness can be toned down by adding more brown sugar and less chili powder.

When assembling Asparagus Pepper Salad, feel free to experiment with another flavor of store-bought or homemade vinaigrette. And if asparagus isn't your family's favorite vegetable, try cut green beans.

Easy Barbecued Pork Chops

Jorie Welch, Acworth, Georgia

PREP: 5 MIN.　**COOK:** 40 MIN.

- 4　bone-in pork loin chops (6 ounces *each*)
- 2　teaspoons canola oil
- 1　medium green pepper, chopped
- 2/3　cup chopped celery
- 1/3　cup chopped onion
- 1　cup ketchup
- 1/4　cup packed brown sugar
- 1/4　cup reduced-sodium chicken broth
- 2　tablespoons chili powder

In a large nonstick skillet, brown pork chops in oil over medium-high heat. Remove chops and keep warm. Add green pepper, celery and onion to the skillet; cook and stir until vegetables begin to soften.

Return pork chops to the pan. In a bowl, combine the ketchup, brown sugar, broth and chili powder. Pour over chops and vegetables. Bring to a boil. Reduce heat; cover and simmer for 30 minutes or until meat is tender. **YIELD:** 4 SERVINGS.

Nutrition Facts: One serving (1 pork chop with 1/3 cup sauce) equals:

　　　312　calories
　　　　9 g　fat (2 g saturated fat)
　　　66 mg　cholesterol
　　867 mg　sodium
　　　　35 g　carbohydrate
　　　　3 g　fiber
　　　　24 g　protein

Diabetic Exchanges: 3 lean meat, 2 starch.

Asparagus Pepper Salad

Beverly Scalise, Bend, Oregon

PREP: 15 MIN. + CHILLING

- 10　cups water
- 1　pound fresh asparagus, trimmed and cut into 1-inch pieces
- 1/2　cup *each* chopped green, sweet red and yellow pepper
- 2　green onions (white portion only), thinly sliced
- 1/3　cup reduced-fat raspberry salad dressing

In a large saucepan, bring water to a boil. Add asparagus; cover and boil for 3 minutes. Drain and immediately place asparagus in ice water. Drain and pat dry.

In a bowl, combine the peppers, onions and asparagus. Drizzle with salad dressing; toss to coat. Cover and refrigerate for 3-4 hours before serving. **YIELD:** 4 SERVINGS.

Nutrition Facts: One serving (1 cup) equals:

　　　73　calories
　　　3 g　fat (trace saturated fat)
　　　　　trace cholesterol
　　154 mg　sodium
　　　9 g　carbohydrate
　　　2 g　fiber
　　　4 g　protein

Diabetic Exchanges: 2 vegetable, 1/2 fat.

Scoop up a **heaping platter** of pasta
and indulge! This **slimmed-down**
version is yours to enjoy **guilt-free!**

Eating right doesn't mean sacrificing flavor. With this dreamy pasta tossed with red peppers and bacon, your family will never guess they're eating light. Partnered with fresh greens jazzed up with pears and dried cherries, it's a meal that's sure to satisfy everyone around the table.

Appealing Partners

- Breadsticks
- Rainbow sherbet

Practical Tips

You'll need two strips of bacon for the pasta dish. So fry two strips, then wrap and freeze the rest of the package for up to 1 month.

When preparing the entree, try 1/2 cup frozen mixed vegetables in place of the peas.

Dried cherries for the salad can be found near the raisins in larger grocery stores. Or, use dried cranberries or golden raisins instead.

Light Linguine Carbonara

Mary Jo Nikolaus, Mansfield, Ohio

PREP/TOTAL TIME: 20 MIN.

8 ounces uncooked linguine
1 egg, lightly beaten
1 cup fat-free evaporated milk
1/4 cup finely chopped sweet red pepper
1/8 teaspoon crushed red pepper flakes
1/8 teaspoon pepper
1/2 cup grated Parmesan cheese, *divided*
1/2 cup frozen peas, thawed
2 bacon strips, cooked and crumbled

Cook linguine according to package directions. Meanwhile, in a small saucepan, combine the next five ingredients. Cook and stir over medium-low heat until mixture reaches 160° and coats the back of a metal spoon. Stir in 1/4 cup Parmesan cheese, peas and bacon; heat through. Drain linguine; toss with sauce. Sprinkle with the remaining Parmesan cheese. **YIELD:** 4 SERVINGS.

Nutrition Facts: One serving (1 cup) equals:
352 calories
7 g fat (3 g saturated fat)
66 mg cholesterol
349 mg sodium
52 g carbohydrate
3 g fiber
20 g protein

Diabetic Exchanges: 3 starch, 1 lean meat, 1 fat, 1/2 fat-free milk.

Fruity Green Salad

Hope Ralph, Woburn, Massachusetts

PREP/TOTAL TIME: 10 MIN.

6 cups torn mixed salad greens *or* 1 package (10 ounces) fresh spinach, torn
2 medium ripe pears, thinly sliced
1/3 cup dried cherries *or* cranberries
1/4 cup balsamic vinegar
2 tablespoons honey, warmed
1/4 teaspoon salt
1/8 teaspoon pepper

In a salad bowl, toss the greens, pears and cherries. In a small bowl, combine the vinegar, honey, salt and pepper. Drizzle over salad and toss to coat. Serve immediately. **YIELD:** 4 SERVINGS.

Nutrition Facts:
One serving (1-1/2 cups) equals:
134 calories
1 g fat (trace saturated fat)
0 cholesterol
170 mg sodium
32 g carbohydrate
5 g fiber
2 g protein

Diabetic Exchanges: 2 fruit, 1 vegetable.

A **sensible** dinner starts with **healthy** choices...
and here are two **time-saving** dishes
to help you head in the right direction.

The mildly seasoned chops on this menu will bake up in half an hour or less. While they're in the oven, grab a can of green chilies and fresh herbs to spice up this rice side dish.

Appealing Partners

• Steamed baby carrots
• Chilled grapefruit segments

Practical Tips

If you like your food with a bit more heat, add cayenne pepper to the coating for the pork chops.

To trim minutes from the side dish, replace the long grain rice with 3 cups instant rice (use the same amount of broth called for in the recipe). Simply add rice to the boiling broth and green chilies, cover and let it stand for 5 minutes before fluffing. There's no need to simmer.

Don't have time to grate the peel of a fresh lemon? Buy a jar of grated lemon peel available in the spice aisle.

Texas-Flavored Pork Chops

Andrea Keith, Kentwood, Michigan

PREP/TOTAL TIME: 30 MIN.

  3/4   cup seasoned bread crumbs
    3   tablespoons chili powder
  1/2   teaspoon seasoned salt
    1   egg
  1/4   cup fat-free milk
    6   bone-in pork rib chops (about 7 ounces *each*, 3/4 inch thick)

In a shallow bowl, combine the bread crumbs, chili powder and seasoned salt. In another shallow bowl, combine the egg and milk. Dip chops in egg mixture, then coat with crumbs.

Transfer to a 15-in. x 10-in. x 1-in. baking pan coated with nonstick cooking spray. Bake at 350° for 20-25 minutes or until a meat thermometer reads 160°. **YIELD:** 6 SERVINGS.

Nutrition Facts: One serving (1 pork chop) equals:
      299 calories
       12 g fat (4 g saturated fat)
      120 mg cholesterol
      448 mg sodium
       12 g carbohydrate
        1 g fiber
       34 g protein

Diabetic Exchanges: 4 lean meat, 1 starch.

Lemony Herbed Rice

Connie Rank-Smith, Sherwood, Wisconsin

PREP/TOTAL TIME: 25 MIN.

    3   cups reduced-sodium chicken broth *or* vegetable broth
 1-1/3 cups uncooked long grain rice
    1   can (4-1/2 ounces) chopped green chilies, drained
  3/4   teaspoon salt
    1   tablespoon *each* minced fresh parsley, cilantro and chives
  1/2   teaspoon grated lemon peel
  1/4   teaspoon pepper

In a large saucepan, combine the broth, rice, chilies and salt; bring to a boil. Reduce heat; cover and simmer for 15-20 minutes or until rice is tender. Remove from the heat; let stand for 5 minutes. Fluff with a fork and stir in the remaining ingredients. **YIELD:** 7 SERVINGS.

Nutrition Facts: One serving (2/3 cup) equals:
      151 calories
           trace fat (trace saturated fat)
        0 cholesterol
      578 mg sodium
       32 g carbohydrate
        1 g fiber
        4 g protein

Diabetic Exchange: 2 starch.

Stay in for dinner to indulge in a **Chinese-style** meal that's **loaded** with flavor, but **lighter** in calories.

Why bother with the fuss of dining out when you can make this tasty Oriental dinner at home? Marinate the pork overnight for best results. Then partner it with a broccoli stir-fry that includes crunchy almonds and plenty of garlic.

Appealing Partners

• Herbed breadsticks
• Hot tea

Practical Tips

The grilled pork is equally delicious when served cold for a light summer supper. You can also serve the slices on a bun as an easy sandwich for lunch.

Before making the side dish, grate the peel from a lemon and freeze it for future use. Then squeeze 2 teaspoons of juice from the lemon to use in the broccoli recipe.

Grilled Pork With Hot Mustard

`low carb`

Kyle Spencer, Havre, Montana

PREP: 5 MIN. + MARINATING   **GRILL:** 15 MIN.

- 1/4 cup reduced-sodium soy sauce
- 2 tablespoons dry red wine *or* chicken broth
- 1 tablespoon brown sugar
- 1 tablespoon honey
- 1/2 teaspoon ground cinnamon
- 2 pork tenderloins (3/4 pound *each*)

HOT MUSTARD:

- 1/4 cup Dijon mustard
- 1 tablespoon honey
- 1 teaspoon prepared horseradish
- 2 teaspoons sesame seeds, toasted

In a large resealable plastic bag, combine the soy sauce, wine or broth, sugar, honey and cinnamon; add pork. Seal bag and turn to coat; refrigerate for 8 hours or overnight. Drain and discard marinade.

Grill pork, covered, over indirect medium-hot heat for 25-40 minutes or until a meat thermometer reads 160°. Let stand for 5 minutes before slicing. In a small bowl, combine the mustard, honey and horseradish. Slice pork; sprinkle with sesame seeds. Serve with hot mustard. **YIELD:** 6 SERVINGS.

Nutrition Facts:
One serving (4 ounces cooked pork) equals:
- 197 calories
- 7 g fat (2 g saturated fat)
- 62 mg cholesterol
- 408 mg sodium
- 6 g carbohydrate
- 1 g fiber
- 26 g protein

Diabetic Exchanges: 3 lean meat, 1/2 fat.

Almond Broccoli Stir-Fry

`low carb` `meat less`

Margery Bryan, Moses Lake, Washington

PREP/TOTAL TIME: 15 MIN.

- 10 cups broccoli florets
- 2 tablespoons canola oil
- 2 to 3 garlic cloves, minced
- 1/4 cup reduced-sodium soy sauce
- 2 tablespoons sugar
- 1/2 teaspoon ground ginger
- 2 teaspoons lemon juice
- 1/2 cup chopped almonds, toasted

In a nonstick skillet or wok, stir-fry broccoli in oil for 2 minutes or until crisp-tender. Add garlic; stir-fry for 1 minute. Stir in the soy sauce, sugar and ginger; cook for 1-2 minutes or until sugar is dissolved. Sprinkle with lemon juice and almonds. **YIELD:** 8 SERVINGS.

Nutrition Facts: One serving (3/4 cup) equals:
- 132 calories
- 8 g fat (1 g saturated fat)
- 0 cholesterol
- 333 mg sodium
- 12 g carbohydrate
- 2 g fiber
- 6 g protein

Diabetic Exchanges: 2 vegetable, 2 fat.

Only have a **half hour** to spare? No need to worry!
This menu will be **table-ready** in no time at all.

Sage, rosemary and garlic brighten these moist and tender chops. For a refreshing complement to the entree, serve this crisp, citrusy salad. Company will love it!

Braised Pork Chops `low carb`

Marilyn Larsen, Port Orange, Florida

PREP/TOTAL TIME: 30 MIN.

1	teaspoon rubbed sage
1	teaspoon dried rosemary, crushed
1	garlic clove, minced
1/2	teaspoon salt
1/8	teaspoon pepper
4	boneless pork loin chops (1/2-inch thick and 4 ounces *each*)
1	tablespoon butter
1	tablespoon olive oil
3/4	cup dry white wine *or* apple juice, *divided*
1	tablespoon minced fresh parsley

Combine the sage, rosemary, garlic, salt and pepper; rub over both sides of pork chops. In a large nonstick skillet, brown chops on both sides in butter and oil. Remove.

Add 1/2 cup wine or juice to the skillet; bring to a boil. Return chops to pan. Reduce heat; cover and simmer for 8-10 minutes or until meat juices run clear, basting occasionally. Remove chops to a serving platter and keep warm.

Add the remaining wine or juice to the skillet. Bring to a boil, loosening any browned bits from the pan. Cook, uncovered, until liquid is reduced to 1/2 cup. Pour over pork chops; sprinkle with parsley. **YIELD:** 4 SERVINGS.

Nutrition Facts:
One serving (1 pork chop) equals:
- 232 calories
- 11 g fat (4 g saturated fat)
- 79 mg cholesterol
- 383 mg sodium
- 1 g carbohydrate
- trace fiber
- 24 g protein

Diabetic Exchanges: 3 lean meat, 1-1/2 fat.

Fennel Orange Salad `meat less`

Nina Hall, Citrus Heights, California

PREP/TOTAL TIME: 30 MIN.

1	fennel bulb with fronds (about 3/4 pound)
4	medium navel oranges, peeled and sectioned
1/3	cup orange juice
4	teaspoons olive oil
1	tablespoon grated orange peel
1/4	teaspoon salt
1/8	teaspoon pepper

Finely chop enough fennel fronds to measure 1/4 cup; set aside. Cut fennel bulb in half lengthwise; remove and discard the tough outer layer, fennel core and any green stalks. Cut widthwise into thin slices and measure 3 cups; place in a large bowl. Add orange sections.

In a jar with a tight-fitting lid, combine the orange juice, oil, orange peel, salt and pepper; shake well. Pour over fennel and oranges; toss gently. Sprinkle with reserved fronds. **YIELD:** 4 SERVINGS.

Nutrition Facts: One serving (1 cup) equals:
- 143 calories
- 5 g fat (1 g saturated fat)
- 0 cholesterol
- 193 mg sodium
- 25 g carbohydrate
- 6 g fiber
- 3 g protein

Diabetic Exchanges: 1 vegetable, 1 fruit, 1 fat.

Appealing Partners

- Hot cooked bow tie pasta
- Green beans

Practical Tips

Be sure to grate 1 tablespoon orange peel for the Fennel Orange Salad before sectioning the oranges.

Not familiar with fresh fennel? The white or pale green bulb has overlapping ribs, similar to celery, with feathery dill-like green leaves growing from the middle. Eaten raw, it has a licorice-like flavor and celery-like crunch. It's sold in the produce section of many supermarkets.

Imagine yourself on a tropical vacation as you savor this island-inspired pair.

Break up the weekday doldrums with a dinnertime getaway. Supper sizzles with onions, tomatoes, green peppers and pork in this sauteed attraction. Served with an eye-appealing frosty beverage, it's sure to hit the spot.

Lime Pork with Peppers

Shonda Ford, DeRidder, Louisiana

PREP: 15 MIN. + MARINATING **COOK:** 20 MIN.

      2 medium limes
    1/4 cup reduced-sodium soy sauce
      4 garlic cloves, minced
      1 teaspoon dried oregano
    1/2 teaspoon dried thyme
    1/8 teaspoon cayenne pepper
      2 to 3 sprigs fresh parsley, stems removed
      1 pork tenderloin (1 pound), cut into 1-inch cubes
      1 bay leaf
      1 tablespoon olive oil
      1 teaspoon brown sugar
      2 medium onions, *each* cut into 8 wedges
      2 small green peppers, cut into 1-inch pieces
      2 medium tomatoes, *each* cut into 8 wedges

Finely grate lime peel, reserving 2 tablespoons peel. Juice the limes. In a bowl, combine the soy sauce, garlic, oregano, thyme, cayenne, parsley, lime juice and reserved lime peel. Pour 1/2 cup marinade into a large resealable plastic bag; add the pork and bay leaf. Seal bag and turn to coat; refrigerate for at least 2 hours. Cover and refrigerate remaining marinade.

   Drain pork and discard marinade. Discard bay leaf. In a large nonstick skillet, heat oil over medium-high heat. Add sugar; stir until bubbly. Add the meat; cook and stir for 3-4 minutes or until browned. Reduce heat; add the onions, peppers and the reserved lime mixture. Cook, uncovered, for 10-15 minutes or until vegetables are tender. Add the tomatoes; cook 1 minute longer. **YIELD:** 4 SERVINGS.

Nutrition Facts: One serving (1-1/2 cups) equals:
         240 calories
           8 g fat (2 g saturated fat)
          63 mg cholesterol
         540 mg sodium
          18 g carbohydrate
           3 g fiber
          26 g protein

Diabetic Exchanges: 3 lean meat, 2 vegetable, 1/2 fat.

Pineapple Smoothies

Darlene Brenden, Salem, Oregon

PREP/TOTAL TIME: 10 MIN.

  1-1/2 cups unsweetened pineapple juice
      1 cup buttermilk
      2 cups ice cubes
      2 cans (8 ounces *each*) unsweetened crushed pineapple
    1/4 cup sugar

Combine all ingredients in a blender or food processor; cover and process until smooth. Pour into glasses; serve immediately. **YIELD:** 6 SERVINGS.

Nutrition Facts: One serving (1 cup) equals:
         133 calories
              trace fat (trace saturated fat)
           1 mg cholesterol
          50 mg sodium
          31 g carbohydrate
           1 g fiber
           2 g protein

Diabetic Exchanges: 1-1/2 fruit, 1/2 starch.

Appealing Partners

• Hawaiian bread
• Seasoned rice

Practical Tips

If you don't have a grater for the lime peel, use a vegetable peeler instead. Finely dice the strips of peel and continue with the recipe.

There's no need to purchase buttermilk just for the smoothies. As an alternative, combine 2/3 cup of plain nonfat or low-fat yogurt with 1/2 cup 1% milk. Add this mixture to the blender instead of the buttermilk.

Dining in on a Saturday night or planning a small meal for friends? Consider a carb-conscious choice like these chops.

A simmered sauce takes pork loin chops to a new level of satisfaction, while old-fashioned snack cake bars with a vanilla glaze satisfy the sweet tooth.

Sweet 'n' Tangy Pork Chops `low carb`

Michelle Bishop, Peru, Indiana

PREP/TOTAL TIME: 25 MIN.

- 1/4 cup sherry *or* chicken broth
- 2 tablespoons brown sugar
- 2 tablespoons reduced-sodium soy sauce
- 1/4 teaspoon crushed red pepper flakes
- 4 boneless pork loin chops (4 ounces *each*)
- 1 teaspoon olive oil
- 2 teaspoons cornstarch
- 2 tablespoons water
- 1/4 cup diced green pepper
- 1/4 cup diced sweet red pepper

In a bowl, combine the sherry or broth, brown sugar, soy sauce and red pepper flakes; set aside. In a large nonstick skillet, brown pork chops in oil. Top with sauce. Reduce heat; cover and simmer for 10-12 minutes or until meat juices run clear.

Combine the cornstarch and water until smooth; add to the skillet. Bring to a boil; cook and stir for 1-2 minutes or until thickened. Garnish with diced peppers. **YIELD:** 4 SERVINGS.

Nutrition Facts: One serving (1 pork chop with 2 tablespoons sauce) equals:
- 229 calories
- 9 g fat (3 g saturated fat)
- 63 mg cholesterol
- 342 mg sodium
- 10 g carbohydrate
- 1 g fiber
- 26 g protein

Diabetic Exchanges: 3 lean meat, 1/2 starch.

Raisin Cinnamon Bars `low sodium`

Jean Morgan, Roscoe, Illinois

PREP: 20 MIN.   **BAKE:** 20 MIN.

- 1/4 cup butter
- 1 cup packed brown sugar
- 1 egg
- 1/2 cup hot brewed coffee
- 1-1/2 cups all-purpose flour
- 1 teaspoon baking powder
- 1/2 teaspoon ground cinnamon
- 1/4 teaspoon baking soda
- 1/4 teaspoon salt
- 1/2 cup raisins
- 1/4 cup chopped pecans

ICING:
- 1 cup confectioners' sugar
- 1/2 teaspoon vanilla extract
- 4 to 5 teaspoons water

In a mixing bowl, combine butter and brown sugar until crumbly, about 2 minutes. Add egg; mix well. Gradually beat in coffee. Combine the flour, baking powder, cinnamon, baking soda and salt. Add to the coffee mixture; mix well. Stir in raisins and pecans. Transfer to a 13-in. x 9-in. x 2-in. baking pan coated with nonstick cooking spray. Bake at 350° for 18-20 minutes or until edges begin to pull away from the sides of the pan and a toothpick inserted near the center comes out clean. Cool on a wire rack for 5 minutes.

Meanwhile for icing, in a bowl, combine the confectioners' sugar, vanilla and enough water to achieve spreading consistency. Spread over warm bars. **YIELD:** 18 SERVINGS (1-1/2 DOZEN).

Nutrition Facts: One serving (1 bar) equals:
- 158 calories
- 4 g fat (2 g saturated fat)
- 19 mg cholesterol
- 112 mg sodium
- 30 g carbohydrate
- 1 g fiber
- 2 g protein

Diabetic Exchanges: 1-1/2 starch, 1 fat, 1/2 fruit.

Appealing Partners

- Stir-fry vegetable blend
- Baked sweet potato

Practical Tips

Extra pineapple tidbits on hand? Drain the pineapple and add 1/4 cup to the sauce. The calories will be slightly higher, but the taste is worth it!

You can use bone-in pork chops instead of boneless, but it may take a bit longer. Cook them until a meat thermometer reads 160°.

Time and taste are on your side with an orchard-fresh entree and garden-grown side.

Why spend hours slaving over a meal just to make it light? Start with the right recipes and the task is easy! The sweetened pork medallions and seasoned veggies prove that dinner can be done in under half an hour.

Appealing Partners

- Sauerkraut
- Mulled cider

Practical Tips

The pork calls for a little unsweetened apple juice. If you don't want to purchase a large bottle of juice, consider buying small juice boxes instead. The unopened boxes are easy to store.

When preparing the green onions for the entree, chop more than you need. Use 1/4 cup for the medallions and store the rest in the fridge or freezer for future use.

Pork Medallions With Sauteed Apples

Clara Coulston, Washington Court House, Ohio

PREP/TOTAL TIME: 30 MIN.

- 1 pork tenderloin (1 pound), cut into 1-inch slices
- 3/4 teaspoon dried thyme
- 1/2 teaspoon paprika
- 1/4 teaspoon salt
- 1/4 teaspoon pepper
- 1/4 cup sliced green onions
- 1 garlic clove, minced
- 1 tablespoon butter
- 2 medium apples, cut into wedges
- 2 teaspoons cornstarch
- 2/3 cup reduced-sodium chicken broth
- 1/4 cup unsweetened apple juice

Flatten pork to 1/2-in. thickness. Combine the thyme, paprika, salt and pepper; sprinkle over both sides of pork. Broil 3-4 in. from the heat for 3-4 minutes on each side or until meat juices run clear; keep warm.

In a nonstick skillet, saute onions and garlic in butter until tender. Add apples; cook and stir for 2 minutes or until apples are crisp-tender. Combine the cornstarch, broth and apple juice until smooth; stir into apple mixture. Bring to a boil; cook and stir for 1-2 minutes or until thickened. Serve with pork. **YIELD:** 4 SERVINGS.

Nutrition Facts: One serving (3 ounces cooked pork with 1/2 cup apples) equals:
- 251 calories
- 10 g fat (4 g saturated fat)
- 85 mg cholesterol
- 335 mg sodium
- 15 g carbohydrate
- 3 g fiber
- 25 g protein

Diabetic Exchanges: 3 lean meat, 1 fruit.

Herbed Green Beans

Lucinda Walker, Somerset, Pennsylvania

PREP/TOTAL TIME: 15 MIN.

- 1 pound fresh green beans, trimmed
- 4-1/2 teaspoons butter, melted
- 1/4 teaspoon salt
- 1/4 teaspoon dried savory
- 1/8 teaspoon dried oregano
- 1/8 teaspoon pepper

Place green beans in a microwave-safe dish. Combine the remaining ingredients; pour over beans and toss to coat evenly.

Cover and microwave on high for 6-8 minutes or until beans are tender. **YIELD:** 4 SERVINGS.

Editor's Note: This recipe was tested in a 1,100-watt microwave.

Nutrition Facts: One serving (3/4 cup) equals:
- 69 calories
- 4 g fat (3 g saturated fat)
- 11 mg cholesterol
- 197 mg sodium
- 7 g carbohydrate
- 3 g fiber
- 2 g protein

Diabetic Exchanges: 1 vegetable, 1 fat.

Need a lighter **potluck** dish to pass?
Pack up this **comforting combo** for the road.

Friends and family will beg you for the secret to this soul-satisfying duo. The creamy casserole and delicious soup will keep everyone guessing how you manage to whip up healthy yet hearty dishes.

Appealing Partners

- Herbed baked pita chips
- Strawberry shortcake

Practical Tips

Instead of buying two bags of frozen vegetables for the casserole, consider purchasing a 24-ounce bag of frozen California blend, and you'll benefit from the addition of sliced carrots. Use 6-1/4 cups of the blend for the casserole.

You can pick up cubed fully cooked ham for the hot dish at the supermarket. Look for it near the bacon or sliced lunchmeat area of your grocery store.

Cheesy Broccoli Cauliflower Casserole
Nancy Whitford, Edwards, New York
PREP: 35 MIN. **BAKE:** 25 MIN.

- 1 tablespoon butter
- 4-1/2 teaspoons all-purpose flour
- 1-1/4 cups 1% milk
- 3/4 cup shredded reduced-fat cheddar cheese
- 1/3 cup grated Parmesan cheese
- 1 package (10 ounces) frozen broccoli florets, thawed
- 1 package (10 ounces) frozen cauliflowerets, thawed
- 1 cup cubed fully cooked lean ham
- 1 cup soft bread crumbs
- Butter-flavored nonstick cooking spray

In a saucepan, melt butter. Stir in flour until smooth; gradually add the milk. Bring to a boil; cook and stir for 1-2 minutes or until thickened. Remove from the heat. Add cheeses; stir until melted.

Place vegetables in a 2-qt. baking dish coated with nonstick cooking spray; sprinkle with ham. Pour sauce over ham. Place bread crumbs in a bowl; spray with butter-flavored spray. Sprinkle around the edge of casserole. Bake, uncovered, at 350° for 25-30 minutes or until heated through and bubbly. **YIELD:** 5 SERVINGS.

Nutrition Facts: One serving (1 cup) equals:
- 227 calories
- 10 g fat (6 g saturated fat)
- 34 mg cholesterol
- 707 mg sodium
- 16 g carbohydrate
- 3 g fiber
- 18 g protein

Diabetic Exchanges: 2 lean meat, 1 vegetable, 1 fat, 1/2 starch.

Vegetable Bean Barley Soup
Tina Dierking, Canaan, Maine
PREP: 20 MIN. **COOK:** 1 HOUR

- 1 medium onion, chopped
- 1 garlic clove, minced
- 1/2 teaspoon dried basil
- 1/2 teaspoon dill weed
- 2 tablespoons canola oil
- 2 cans (14-1/2 ounces *each*) reduced-sodium chicken broth
- 1-3/4 cups water
- 1 cup chopped carrots
- 1/2 cup medium pearl barley
- 1 can (16 ounces) pork and beans
- 2 small zucchini, sliced
- 1/2 teaspoon salt
- 1/4 teaspoon pepper
- 1 can (14-1/2 ounces) diced tomatoes, undrained
- 1 teaspoon cider vinegar

In a large saucepan or Dutch oven, saute the onion, garlic, basil and dill in oil until onion is tender. Add the broth, water, carrots and barley. Bring to a boil. Reduce heat; cover and simmer for 30 minutes.

Add the pork and beans, zucchini, salt and pepper. Cover and simmer 10-15 minutes longer or until vegetables and barley are tender. Just before serving, stir in tomatoes and vinegar; heat through. **YIELD:** 6 SERVINGS.

Nutrition Facts: One serving (1-1/2 cups) equals:
- 218 calories
- 6 g fat (1 g saturated fat)
- 5 mg cholesterol
- 1,003 mg sodium
- 36 g carbohydrate
- 9 g fiber
- 9 g protein

Diabetic Exchanges: 2 starch, 1 vegetable, 1 fat.

Here's a **six-ingredient** supper that will appeal to
picky **kids** and impress **dinner guests** alike.

Liven up a weekday dinner with a swift sauce over succulent pork tenderloin. You'll capture the sunny flavors of fresh citrus in a fruit medley topped with crunchy almonds. Together, they tantalize the taste buds.

Glazed Pork Tenderloin

Bernice Dean, Garland, Texas

PREP/TOTAL TIME: 30 MIN.

1/4	teaspoon salt
1/4	teaspoon pepper
1	pork tenderloin (1 pound)
2	sprigs fresh rosemary
1/2	cup pineapple preserves
1	tablespoon prepared horseradish

Combine salt and pepper; rub over pork. Place in a 13-in. x 9-in. x 2-in. baking pan coated with nonstick cooking spray. Place one sprig of rosemary under the pork and one on top. Bake, uncovered, at 425° for 10 minutes.

Meanwhile, in a saucepan, heat preserves and horseradish until preserves are melted; stir until blended. Remove top rosemary sprig. Brush pork with 1/4 cup pineapple sauce. Bake 10-20 minutes longer or until meat thermometer reads 160°. Let stand for 5 minutes before slicing. Serve with the remaining sauce. **YIELD:** 4 SERVINGS.

Nutrition Facts: One serving (3 ounces cooked pork with 2 tablespoons gravy) equals:
242 calories
4 g fat (1 g saturated fat)
67 mg cholesterol
226 mg sodium
29 g carbohydrate
trace fiber
24 g protein

Diabetic Exchanges: 3 lean meat, 2 fruit.

Almond Sunshine Citrus

Geri Barr, Calgary, Alberta

PREP: 20 MIN. + CHILLING

3	large navel oranges
1	medium red grapefruit
1	medium white grapefruit
1	small lemon
1	small lime
1/3	cup sugar
1/8	teaspoon almond extract
2	tablespoons sliced almonds, toasted

Grate enough peel from the oranges, grapefruit, lemon and lime to measure 1 tablespoon of mixed citrus peel; set peel aside. To section citrus fruit, cut a thin slice off the bottom and top of the oranges, grapefruit, lemon and lime. Place each fruit cut side down on a cutting board. With a sharp knife, remove peel and white pith. Holding fruit over a bowl, slice between the membrane of each section and the fruit until the knife reaches the center; remove sections and place in a glass bowl. Set 1/2 cup juice aside.

In a small saucepan, combine the sugar and reserved peel and juice. Bring to a boil. Reduce heat; simmer, uncovered for 10 minutes. Cool; stir in extract. Pour over fruit. Refrigerate overnight. Just before serving, sprinkle with almonds. **YIELD:** 4 SERVINGS.

Nutrition Facts: One serving (3/4 cup) equals:
197 calories
2 g fat (trace saturated fat)
0 cholesterol
1 mg sodium
47 g carbohydrate
6 g fiber
3 g protein

Diabetic Exchanges: 3 fruit, 1/2 fat.

Appealing Partners

- Sauteed zucchini
- Baked sweet potatoes

Practical Tips

If your grocery store does not stock the pineapple preserves needed for the Glazed Pork Tenderloin, peach or apricot preserves are a nice substitute.

Before grating the citrus peel for the salad, wash all fruit thoroughly. Grate only the top layer of peel; the white pith will give the dish a bitter taste.

To save the time you would spend sectioning grapefruit for the salad, buy a jar of grapefruit sections from the produce department instead.

Low-sodium cooks crave rich, **rewarding** flavor without the extra salt. So look no further than this supper **solution.**

A little planning helps you start marinating the pork chops a day in advance. Since the veggie side dish takes only 20 minutes from start to finish, you won't be rushed as dinnertime nears.

Appealing Partners

- Sauteed apples
- Mashed Winter Vegetables, p. 284

Practical Tips

If you'd rather season the pork with fresh rosemary instead of dried, use 1-1/2 teaspoons of the finely chopped herb.

Not crazy about pineapple? Substitute orange juice for the pineapple juice in the main course's marinade.

Dress up the beans for company by topping them with a sprinkling of sesame seeds.

Moist Herbed Pork Chops

Linda Austin, Allen, Texas

PREP: 5 MIN. + MARINATING   **GRILL:** 10 MIN.

- 1 cup unsweetened pineapple juice
- 2/3 cup dry white wine *or* chicken broth
- 2 tablespoons brown sugar
- 1 garlic clove, minced
- 1/2 teaspoon dried rosemary, crushed
- 4 bone-in center-cut pork loin chops (3/4-inch thick and 7 ounces *each*)

In a bowl, combine the first five ingredients; stir until sugar is dissolved. Pour 1-1/2 cups into a large resealable plastic bag; add the pork chops. Seal bag and turn to coat; refrigerate for 8 hours or overnight. Cover and refrigerate remaining marinade for basting.

If grilling, coat grill rack with nonstick cooking spray before starting the grill. Drain and discard marinade. Grill pork, covered, over medium heat or broil 4-6 in. from the heat for 4-5 minutes on each side or until a meat thermometer reads 160°, basting frequently with reserved marinade. **YIELD:** 4 SERVINGS.

Nutrition Facts: One serving (1 pork chop) equals:
```
       237  calories
         9 g  fat (3 g saturated fat)
        87 mg  cholesterol
        65 mg  sodium
         5 g  carbohydrate
              trace fiber
        31 g  protein
```

Diabetic Exchange: 4 lean meat.

Lemon-Garlic Green Beans

Gail Orsillo, Lynnwood, Washington

PREP/TOTAL TIME: 20 MIN.

- 2 garlic cloves, minced
- 2 teaspoons olive oil
- 1 pound fresh green beans, trimmed and cut into 2-inch pieces
- 1 tablespoon lemon juice
- 1/4 teaspoon coarsely ground pepper
- 1/8 teaspoon salt

In a large nonstick skillet coated with nonstick cooking spray, cook the garlic in olive oil over medium heat for 30 seconds. Add the green beans; cook and stir for 10-13 minutes or until crisp-tender. Stir in the lemon juice, pepper and salt. **YIELD:** 4 SERVINGS.

Nutrition Facts: One serving (3/4 cup) equals:
```
       54  calories
        2 g  fat (trace saturated fat)
         0  cholesterol
       80 mg  sodium
        8 g  carbohydrate
        3 g  fiber
        2 g  protein
```

Diabetic Exchanges: 1 vegetable, 1/2 fat.

The **best** part about this tantalizing **meal-in-one** might just be the **dreamy dessert** you can look forward to!

You'll have most of your meal taken care of when you put this skillet wonder on your menu. It's easy to make and tastes good, too. End the evening on a sweet note with decadent brownies. This recipe makes a big pan, so you'll have plenty for later or to share with friends.

Asparagus Ham Dinner

Rhonda Zavodny, David City, Nebraska

PREP/TOTAL TIME: 25 MIN.

2	cups uncooked spiral pasta
3/4	pound fresh asparagus, cut into 1-inch pieces
1	medium sweet yellow pepper, julienned
1	tablespoon olive oil
3	cups diced fresh tomatoes (about 6 medium)
6	ounces reduced-sodium fully cooked ham, cubed
1/4	cup minced fresh parsley
1/2	teaspoon salt
1/2	teaspoon dried oregano
1/2	teaspoon dried basil
1/8	to 1/4 teaspoon cayenne pepper
1/4	cup shredded Parmesan cheese

Cook pasta according to package directions. Meanwhile, in a nonstick skillet, saute asparagus and yellow pepper in oil until tender. Add tomatoes and ham; heat through. Drain pasta; add to the vegetable mixture. Stir in seasonings. Sprinkle with Parmesan cheese. **YIELD:** 6 SERVINGS.

Nutrition Facts: One serving (1-1/3 cups) equals:
238 calories
6 g fat (1 g saturated fat)
18 mg cholesterol
522 mg sodium
33 g carbohydrate
3 g fiber
14 g protein

Diabetic Exchanges: 2 vegetable, 1-1/2 starch, 1 lean meat, 1/2 fat.

Appealing Partners

- Spinach salad with low-fat ranch dressing
- Crusty Italian bread

Practical Tips

If fresh asparagus isn't available or you don't have any on hand, you can substitute a 10-ounce package of frozen cut asparagus. Just thaw it before sauteing with the yellow pepper.

Make the brownies the night before; cool and cut into squares. Set aside enough for the next day's dessert, then freeze the rest in a freezer container for up to 3 months. Thaw them to pack into bag lunches or to serve when you need a sweet treat for company.

Fudgy Peanut Butter Brownies

Martha Domeny, Overland Park, Kansas

PREP: 20 MIN. **BAKE:** 25 MIN. + COOLING

2	cups sugar
1-1/2	cups all-purpose flour
3/4	cup baking cocoa
1/2	teaspoon salt
2/3	cup unsweetened applesauce
3/4	cup egg substitute
2	teaspoons vanilla extract

FILLING:

3	ounces reduced-fat cream cheese, softened
1/3	cup reduced-fat peanut butter
1/4	cup sugar
1/4	cup egg substitute
1	teaspoon vanilla extract

FROSTING:

1	cup confectioners' sugar
3	tablespoons baking cocoa
2	tablespoons 2% milk
1	teaspoon vanilla extract
1	teaspoon water

In a large bowl, combine the sugar, flour, cocoa and salt. Stir in applesauce, egg substitute and vanilla; mix well. Pour about half of the batter into a 13-in. x 9-in. x 2-in. baking pan coated with nonstick cooking spray.

In a mixing bowl, combine the filling ingredients; beat until smooth. Drop by tablespoonfuls onto batter. Spoon remaining batter over the top; cut through batter with a knife to swirl peanut butter mixture.

Bake at 325° for 25-30 minutes or until edges are firm and center is almost set. Cool on a wire rack.

In a small bowl, combine the frosting ingredients until smooth. Spread over brownies. **YIELD:** 20 BROWNIES.

Nutrition Facts: One serving (1 brownie) equals:
201 calories
3 g fat (1 g saturated fat)
3 mg cholesterol
119 mg sodium
40 g carbohydrate
2 g fiber
5 g protein

Diabetic Exchanges: 2-1/2 starch, 1/2 fat.

For a **fill-you-up** meal, try this easy entree…
a meaty main dish and sweet side in
one **fast-to-fix** recipe.

Apple slices and caramelized onions are simmered with choice cut loin chops. For a seasoned side to balance the sweetness, toss together fresh green beans and a bit of olive oil with garlic.

Apples 'n' Onion Topped Chops

Beverly McLain, Endicott, New York

PREP/TOTAL TIME: 30 MIN.

- 4 boneless lean pork loin chops (5 ounces each)
- 3 cups sweet onion slices
- 1 teaspoon canola oil
- 2 medium Granny Smith apples, peeled and sliced
- 1/2 cup water
- 2 tablespoons brown sugar
- 1 tablespoon cider vinegar
- 1 teaspoon garlic powder
- 1/2 teaspoon salt
- 1/4 to 1/2 teaspoon pepper
- 1/4 teaspoon dried rosemary, crushed

In a large nonstick skillet coated with nonstick cooking spray, cook chops for about 3 minutes on each side or until browned. Remove meat; set aside and keep warm.

In same skillet, cook and stir onion in oil for 7 minutes or until golden brown. Add apple slices; cook and stir 3 minutes longer. Combine the water, brown sugar, vinegar, garlic powder, salt, pepper and rosemary. Stir into skillet. Bring to a boil. Return meat to pan. Reduce heat; cover and simmer for 8-10 minutes or until apples are crisp-tender and a meat thermometer reads 160°. **YIELD:** 4 SERVINGS.

Nutrition Facts: One serving (1 pork chop with 1/2 cup apple-onion mixture) equals:
- 326 calories
- 11 g fat (4 g saturated fat)
- 79 mg cholesterol
- 344 mg sodium
- 25 g carbohydrate
- 2 g fiber
- 33 g protein

Diabetic Exchanges: 4 lean meat, 2 vegetable, 1 fruit.

Garlic Green Beans

Howard Levine, Arleta, California

PREP/TOTAL TIME: 20 MIN.

- 1 pound fresh green beans, trimmed
- 1 to 2 garlic cloves, minced
- 1/2 teaspoon salt
- 1/8 teaspoon white pepper
- 2 teaspoons olive oil

Place beans and enough water to cover in a saucepan; bring to a boil. Cook, uncovered, for 8-10 minutes or until crisp-tender; drain. Toss beans with garlic, salt and pepper. Drizzle with oil. Serve immediately. **YIELD:** 4 SERVINGS.

Nutrition Facts: One serving (3/4 cup) equals:
- 61 calories
- 3 g fat (trace saturated fat)
- 0 cholesterol
- 298 mg sodium
- 9 g carbohydrate
- 4 g fiber
- 2 g protein

Diabetic Exchanges: 1 vegetable, 1/2 fat.

Appealing Partners

- Bakery rolls
- Lemon Cream Pie, p. 324

Practical Tips

The recipe for Apples 'n' Onion Topped Chops calls for sweet onion slices. When buying sweet onions, look for them in the produce section under the names Vidalia, Maui, Walla Walla, Rio Sweet or OSO Sweet.

To boost the flavor of the main dish, add 1/4 teaspoon of caraway seeds…or use two minced cloves of garlic instead of the garlic powder.

Remember the **stick-to-your-ribs** casseroles
Mom made? Now you can enjoy
platefuls of flavor again—minus the extra fat!

The traditional pasta bake gets its creamy texture from cottage cheese. When you're finished, why not snuggle up to warm mugs of citrus-spiced cider?

Appealing Partners

- Tomato soup
- Fat-free pound cake

Practical Tips

When making the casserole, you can substitute cubed cooked chicken for the ham and dried oregano for the dill.

Use a few Jolly Rancher "fire" candies instead of red hots in the cider. The individually wrapped hard candies have an intense cinnamon taste.

The cider recipe can easily be doubled for large gatherings, but be sure to use a 5-quart slow cooker.

Ham and Noodle Casserole

Ruth Hastings, Louisville, Illinois

PREP: 15 MIN.   **BAKE:** 35 MIN. + STANDING

  6 ounces uncooked yolk-free fine noodles
1-1/2 cups (12 ounces) 1% small-curd cottage cheese
  1 package (10 ounces) frozen mixed vegetables, thawed and drained
  1 cup cubed fully cooked lean ham
3/4 cup reduced-fat sour cream
1/4 cup fat-free milk
  3 tablespoons grated Parmesan cheese
  2 teaspoons all-purpose flour
  1 teaspoon dill weed *or* 1 tablespoon snipped fresh dill
1/4 teaspoon salt

Cook noodles according to package directions; drain. In a large bowl, combine the remaining ingredients. Add noodles and toss to coat. Transfer to a 2-qt. baking dish coated with nonstick cooking spray.

  Cover and bake at 350° for 30 minutes. Uncover; bake 5-10 minutes longer or until heated through. Let stand for 5 minutes before serving. **YIELD:** 4 SERVINGS.

Nutrition Facts:
One serving (1-1/2 cups) equals:
  266 calories
    5 g fat (3 g saturated fat)
  21 mg cholesterol
702 mg sodium
  32 g carbohydrate
    3 g fiber
  21 g protein

Diabetic Exchanges: 2 lean meat, 1-1/2 starch, 1 vegetable.

Orange Spiced Cider

Erika Reinhard, Colorado Springs, Colorado

PREP: 5 MIN.   **COOK:** 2 HOURS

  4 cups unsweetened apple juice
  1 can (12 ounces) orange juice concentrate, thawed
1/2 cup water
  1 tablespoon red-hot candies
1/2 teaspoon ground nutmeg
  1 teaspoon whole cloves
Fresh orange slices and cinnamon sticks, optional

In a slow cooker, combine the first five ingredients. Place cloves in a double thickness of cheesecloth; bring up corners of cloth and tie with kitchen spring to form a bag. Add bag to slow cooker. Cover and cook on low for 2-3 hours or until heated through. Before serving, discard spice bag and stir cider. Garnish with orange slices and cinnamon sticks if desired. **YIELD:** 8 SERVINGS.

Nutrition Facts: One serving (3/4 cup) equals:
  128 calories
       trace fat (trace saturated fat)
    0 cholesterol
  6 mg sodium
  31 g carbohydrate
    1 g fiber
    1 g protein

Diabetic Exchange: 2 fruit.

A slice of **lemony, sweet** cake tastes even better when it follows a plate of **spicy, succulent** scallops stir-fried to perfection.

Ready in just 25 minutes, this speedy entree is specially seasoned with lime juice, sesame oil and hot pepper sauce. Dessert is equally easy since it starts with a packaged cake mix.

Stir-Fried Scallops And Asparagus

Barbara Schindler, Napolean, Ohio

PREP/TOTAL TIME: 25 MIN.

- 1 package (3 ounces) chicken ramen noodles
- 1 pound fresh asparagus, trimmed and cut into 1-inch pieces
- 1 garlic clove, minced
- 1 tablespoon olive oil
- 1 medium sweet red pepper, julienned
- 3 green onions, thinly sliced
- 1 pound sea scallops, halved horizontally
- 1 tablespoon lime juice
- 2 tablespoons reduced-sodium soy sauce
- 1 teaspoon sesame oil
- 1 teaspoon hot pepper sauce

Discard seasoning package from ramen noodles or save for another use. Cook ramen noodles according to package directions; keep warm.

Meanwhile, in a nonstick skillet or wok, cook and stir asparagus and garlic in oil for 2 minutes. Add red pepper; cook and stir 1 minute longer. Add green onions; cook and stir 2 minutes longer. Stir in scallops. Cook for 3 minutes or until scallops are firm and opaque.

Combine the lime juice, soy sauce, sesame oil and hot pepper sauce; stir into skillet. Serve over ramen noodles. **YIELD:** 4 SERVINGS.

Nutrition Facts: One serving (1 cup scallop mixture and 1/4 cup noodles) equals:
- 269 calories
- 9 g fat (3 g saturated fat)
- 37 mg cholesterol
- 578 mg sodium
- 22 g carbohydrate
- 2 g fiber
- 24 g protein

Diabetic Exchanges: 3 very lean meat, 1 starch, 1 vegetable, 1 fat.

Lemon Cake

Bonita Giesbrecht, Glenn, California

PREP: 20 MIN.   **BAKE:** 25 MIN. + COOLING

- 1 package (18-1/4 ounces) white cake mix
- 1 package (3 ounces) lemon gelatin
- 1 cup plus 2 tablespoons water
- 4 egg whites
- 1/3 cup unsweetened applesauce
- 1 tablespoon canola oil
- 1 teaspoon lemon extract
- 4 drops yellow food coloring, optional

LEMON GLAZE:

- 1-1/2 cups confectioners' sugar
- 1/3 cup lemon juice

In a large mixing bowl, combine the dry cake mix, gelatin, water, egg whites, applesauce, oil, lemon extract and food coloring if desired. Beat on medium speed for 2 minutes. Pour into a 13-in. x 9-in. x 2-in. baking pan coated with nonstick cooking spray. Bake at 350° for 25-30 minutes or until edges are lightly browned and a toothpick inserted near the center comes out clean. Cool on a wire rack for 10 minutes.

Meanwhile, for glaze, in a bowl, combine the confectioners' sugar and lemon juice until smooth. Drizzle about a third of glaze over cake; carefully spread evenly. Repeat with remaining glaze. Cool completely. **YIELD:** 15 SERVINGS.

Nutrition Facts: One serving (1 piece) equals:
- 225 calories
- 5 g fat (1 g saturated fat)
- 0 cholesterol
- 266 mg sodium
- 43 g carbohydrate
- trace fiber
- 3 g protein

Appealing Partners

- Baked egg rolls
- Egg drop soup

Practical Tips

If you do not have the ramen noodles called for in the stir-fry, use spaghetti or angel hair pasta.

You'll need to slice three green onions for the main course. While you're at it, finely chop the rest of the bunch, and store the onions in a resealable bag in your refrigerator. This will give you a head start when preparing a quick tossed salad later in the week.

Stay in for a **simple seafood feast** that will be **ready to impress** family or guests in record time.

Dress up tender fish with sour cream, sauteed peppers and onions to make this quick entree. For a swift stovetop side dish, this combination of orzo and peas will do the trick.

Appealing Partners

- Honey Lime Fruit Toss, p. 242
- Cut asparagus

Practical Tips

When grating the lemon peel for the side dish, grate all the peel. Place any extra in a heavy-duty resealable plastic bag and freeze for future use.

Feel free to use long grain rice instead of orzo in the side dish if your family prefers it. The taste will still be delicious!

Onion Peppered Roughy

`low carb`

Elizabeth Harrer, Lockport, New York

PREP/TOTAL TIME: 20 MIN.

- 6 orange roughy *or* whitefish fillets (6 ounces *each*)
- 2 tablespoons butter, melted, *divided*
- 1/4 teaspoon salt
- 1/4 teaspoon pepper
- 1/2 cup each julienned sweet red, yellow and green pepper
- 1/2 cup thinly sliced onion
- 3/4 cup reduced-fat sour cream

Paprika, optional

Pat fish fillets dry with paper towels; place in a 15-in. x 10-in. x 1-in. baking pan coated with nonstick cooking spray. Drizzle fish with 1 tablespoon butter; sprinkle with salt and pepper. Bake, uncovered, at 350° for 10 minutes or until fish flakes easily with a fork.

Meanwhile, in a skillet, saute sweet peppers and onion in remaining butter until almost tender. Dollop fish with sour cream; top with vegetable mixture. Bake 2-3 minutes longer or until heated through. Sprinkle with paprika if desired. **YIELD:** 6 SERVINGS.

Nutrition Facts: One serving (1 fillet) equals:
- 206 calories
- 8 g fat (4 g saturated fat)
- 54 mg cholesterol
- 363 mg sodium
- 6 g carbohydrate
- 1 g fiber
- 28 g protein

Diabetic Exchanges: 4 very lean meat, 1 vegetable, 1 fat.

Minty Orzo and Peas

`meat less`

Kristen Dunphy, Haverhill, Massachusetts

PREP/TOTAL TIME: 20 MIN.

- 1 cup uncooked orzo pasta
- 1 small onion, finely chopped
- 1 garlic clove, minced
- 2 tablespoons butter
- 2 cups frozen peas
- 1 teaspoon grated lemon peel
- 1/4 teaspoon salt
- 1/8 teaspoon pepper
- 2 tablespoons finely chopped fresh mint

Prepare orzo according to package directions. Drain and set aside. In a large skillet, saute onion and garlic in butter until tender. Add peas; cook for 2 minutes or until tender. Add the lemon peel, salt, pepper and orzo; heat through. Stir in mint. Serve immediately. **YIELD:** 6 SERVINGS.

Nutrition Facts: One serving (2/3 cup) equals:
- 200 calories
- 5 g fat (3 g saturated fat)
- 10 mg cholesterol
- 194 mg sodium
- 33 g carbohydrate
- 3 g fiber
- 7 g protein

Diabetic Exchanges: 2 starch, 1 fat.

Make a **healthy choice** for a family dinner
with this **delectable** fish and vegetable duo.

It doesn't take long for these fillets to bake in the oven. A light coating, which has a mild cornmeal flavor, helps the delicate fish stay moist. Dried apricots are a colorful and tasty addition to the green bean side dish.

Appealing Partners

- Cucumber Fennel Salad, p. 260
- Sliced strawberries and bananas

Practical Tips

The breading also would be good on other types of fish, such as orange roughy, grouper or sole.

Don't have fresh gingerroot for the side dish? In a pinch, you can use 1/2 teaspoon ground ginger in place of the 2 teaspoons minced fresh gingerroot called for in the recipe.

It's easy to toast sesame seeds on the stovetop. Place them in a dry skillet over medium heat. Cook them, stirring occasionally, just until golden brown.

Breaded Flounder Fillets   low fat | low carb

Michelle Smith, Sykesville, Maryland

PREP/TOTAL TIME: 20 MIN.

- 1/4 cup all-purpose flour
- 1/4 cup cornmeal
- 1   teaspoon salt
- 1/2 teaspoon paprika
- 1/2 teaspoon pepper
- 2   egg whites
- 1/4 cup fat-free milk
- 4   flounder fillets (6 ounces *each*)
- 1   tablespoon grated Parmesan cheese

In a shallow bowl, combine the flour, cornmeal, salt, paprika and pepper. In another shallow bowl, beat egg whites and milk. Coat fish with cornmeal mixture, then dip into egg white mixture. Coat fish again in cornmeal mixture.

In a 15-in. x 10-in. x 1-in. baking pan coated with nonstick cooking spray, arrange fish in a single layer. Sprinkle with Parmesan cheese. Bake, uncovered, at 425° for 8-10 minutes or until fish flakes easily with a fork. **YIELD:** 4 SERVINGS.

Nutrition Facts: One serving (1 fillet) equals:
236 calories
3 g fat (1 g saturated fat)
83 mg cholesterol
789 mg sodium
14 g carbohydrate
1 g fiber
37 g protein

Diabetic Exchanges: 5 very lean meat, 1 starch.

Stir-Fry Sesame Green Beans   meat less

Taste of Home Test Kitchen
Greendale, Wisconsin

PREP/TOTAL TIME: 20 MIN.

- 1   pound fresh green beans, cut into 1-inch pieces
- 1   tablespoon canola oil
- 1   cup julienned sweet red pepper
- 1   cup sliced fresh mushrooms
- 1/4 cup thinly sliced green onions
- 2   garlic cloves, minced
- 3   tablespoons reduced-sodium soy sauce
- 2   teaspoons minced fresh gingerroot
- 1/4 cup sliced dried apricots
- 1   teaspoon sesame oil
- 2   teaspoons sesame seeds, toasted

In a large nonstick skillet or wok, stir-fry beans over medium-high heat in oil for 2 minutes. Add sweet pepper and mushrooms; stir-fry 2 minutes longer. Add green onions and garlic; stir-fry for 1-2 minutes.

Combine the soy sauce and ginger; stir into skillet. Bring to a boil. Reduce heat; simmer, uncovered, for 2 minutes. Stir in apricots; cook and stir for 1 minute longer. Remove from the heat; stir in sesame oil and sesame seeds. Serve immediately. **YIELD:** 4 SERVINGS.

Nutrition Facts: One serving (1 cup) equals:
135 calories
6 g fat (trace saturated fat)
0 cholesterol
463 mg sodium
18 g carbohydrate
5 g fiber
4 g protein

Diabetic Exchanges: 2 vegetable, 1 fat, 1/2 fruit.

For **satisfying light fare** when time is tight, turn to these **savory stovetop** creations.

Pretzel and whole-wheat bread crumbs create the unusual coating on these pan-fried patties, while jalapeno pepper gives them just the right amount of kick. It's sweet red peppers that make this spinach side a great choice.

Spicy Salmon Patties

Barbara Coston, Little Rock, Arkansas

PREP/TOTAL TIME: 30 MIN.

- 2   slices whole wheat bread
- 12 fat-free pretzel twists
- 2   teaspoons Italian seasoning
- 2   teaspoons salt-free spicy seasoning blend
- 1/2 teaspoon pepper
- 1/2 cup egg substitute
- 1   can (14-3/4 ounces) salmon, drained, bones and skin removed
- 1/2 cup finely chopped onion
- 1/3 cup finely chopped green pepper
- 1   tablespoon finely chopped jalapeno pepper
- 2   garlic cloves, minced
- 2   tablespoons olive oil

Place the first five ingredients in a blender or food processor; cover and process until mixture resembles fine crumbs.

In a bowl, combine the egg substitute, salmon, onion, green pepper, jalapeno, garlic and 1/2 cup of the crumb mixture. Shape into eight 1/2-in.-thick patties. Coat with remaining crumb mixture.

In a large nonstick skillet over medium heat, cook patties in oil for 4-5 minutes on each side or until lightly browned. **YIELD:** 4 SERVINGS.

Editor's Note: When cutting or seeding hot peppers, use rubber or plastic gloves to protect your hands. Avoid touching your face.

Nutrition Facts:
One serving (2 patties) equals:
- 304 calories
- 14 g fat (2 g saturated fat)
- 58 mg cholesterol
- 870 mg sodium
- 18 g carbohydrate
- 2 g fiber
- 26 g protein

Diabetic Exchanges: 3 lean meat, 1-1/2 fat, 1 starch.

Sauteed Spinach And Peppers

Mary Lou Moon, Beaverton, Oregon

PREP/TOTAL TIME: 15 MIN.

- 1   large sweet red pepper, coarsely chopped
- 1   tablespoon olive oil
- 1   small red onion, finely chopped
- 3   garlic cloves, minced
- 8   cups packed fresh spinach
- 1/2 teaspoon salt
- 1/4 teaspoon pepper
- 1/8 teaspoon sugar

In a large nonstick skillet, saute red pepper in oil for 1 minute. Add onion and garlic; saute until tender, about 1-1/2 minutes longer. Stir in the spinach, salt, pepper and sugar; saute for 1-2 minutes or until spinach is wilted and tender. Serve with a slotted spoon. **YIELD:** 4 SERVINGS.

Nutrition Facts: One serving (1/2 cup) equals:
- 65 calories
- 4 g fat (1 g saturated fat)
- 0 cholesterol
- 342 mg sodium
- 7 g carbohydrate
- 3 g fiber
- 2 g protein

Diabetic Exchanges: 1 vegetable, 1/2 fat.

Appealing Partners

- Chunky Applesauce
- Lemon Pecan Pilaf, p. 275

Practical Tips

To save time later in the week, chop the whole green pepper, use 1/3 cup for the salmon patties and place the rest in a plastic bag in the freezer. Later, take out just the amount of chopped pepper you need for other recipes.

Not familiar with the salt-free spicy seasoning blend in the recipe for the salmon patties? It's available under the brand name Mrs. Dash Extra Spicy in the spice aisle of most grocery stores.

Unwind after a busy day with an **impressive** yet simple seafood mainstay.

This catfish dish comes together quickly and gets its flavor from an abundance of seasonings. Enjoy it with a glass of the refreshing cooler with hints of vanilla.

Catfish with Spiced Fruit Salsa

Karen Martis, Merrillville, Indiana

PREP/TOTAL TIME: 30 MIN.

4	catfish fillets (6 ounces *each*)
2	teaspoons canola oil
2	teaspoons ground coriander
1	teaspoon ground cumin
1/4	teaspoon ground cinnamon
1/4	teaspoon cayenne pepper
3/4	teaspoon salt
1/2	cup dried tropical fruit
1/3	cup unsweetened apple juice
1	tablespoon cider vinegar
1	tablespoon 100% apricot spreadable fruit
2	tablespoons minced fresh parsley

Rub both sides of fillets with oil. Combine the coriander, cumin, cinnamon and cayenne; set aside 1/2 teaspoon. Add salt to remaining spice mixture; rub over both sides of fillets.

In a saucepan, combine the tropical fruit, apple juice, vinegar and reserved spice mixture. Bring to a boil; stir in spreadable fruit. Remove from the heat; let stand for 5 minutes.

In a large nonstick skillet coated with nonstick cooking spray, cook fillets over medium-high heat for 3-4 minutes on each side or until fish flakes easily with a fork. Serve with fruit salsa; sprinkle with parsley. **YIELD:** 4 SERVINGS.

Nutrition Facts:
One serving (1 fillet with 2 tablespoons salsa) equals:

349	calories
16 g	fat (4 g saturated fat)
80 mg	cholesterol
561 mg	sodium
22 g	carbohydrate
2 g	fiber
27 g	protein

Diabetic Exchanges: 4 lean meat, 1 fruit, 1 fat, 1/2 starch.

Pineapple Cooler

low fat low sodium

Ashley Braswell, Huntsville, Alabama

PREP: 5 MIN. + CHILLING

4	cups unsweetened pineapple juice
2	teaspoons lemon juice
1	teaspoon vanilla extract
1/2	teaspoon coconut extract
2	cups carbonated water

In a pitcher, combine the pineapple juice, lemon juice and extracts; chill. Just before serving, stir in carbonated water. Serve over ice. **YIELD:** 3 SERVINGS.

Nutrition Facts: One serving (1 cup) equals:

120	calories
	trace fat (trace saturated fat)
0	cholesterol
5 mg	sodium
30 g	carbohydrate
	trace fiber
1 g	protein

Diabetic Exchanges: 1-1/2 fruit, 1/2 starch.

Appealing Partners

- Green beans
- Corn bread

Practical Tips

If catfish isn't a family favorite, fix the main course using orange roughy instead.

To cut dinnertime prep, use the microwave to prepare the salsa for the fish.

Keep the salsa in mind for future recipes. You'll find that it's a light yet lip-smacking way to jazz up grilled chicken, pork or even steak.

Serve bowlfuls of a **steamy, hearty** soup alongside slices of this **wholesome** bread.

Break up the dinnertime routine with a filling gumbo with a hint of cayenne pepper. The hearty bread calls for a handful of ingredients and bakes up easily in a bread machine.

Southern Seafood Gumbo

Susan Wright, Champaign, Illinois

PREP: 25 MIN.   **COOK:** 25 MIN.

- 1 medium onion, chopped
- 2 celery ribs with leaves, chopped
- 1 medium green pepper, chopped
- 3 garlic cloves, minced
- 1 tablespoon olive oil
- 1 bottle (46 ounces) spicy hot V8 juice
- 1 can (14-1/2 ounces) diced tomatoes, undrained
- 1/4 teaspoon cayenne pepper
- 1 package (16 ounces) frozen sliced okra, thawed
- 1 pound catfish fillets, cut into 3/4-inch cubes
- 3/4 pound uncooked medium shrimp, peeled and deveined
- 3 cups cooked long grain rice

In a large saucepan, saute the onion, celery, green pepper and garlic in oil until tender. Stir in the V8 juice, tomatoes and cayenne; bring to a boil. Reduce heat; cover and simmer for 10 minutes.

Stir in okra and catfish; cook 8 minutes longer. Add the shrimp; cook about 7 minutes longer or until fish flakes easily with a fork and shrimp turn pink. Place rice in individual serving bowls; top with gumbo.
YIELD: 12 SERVINGS.

Nutrition Facts:
One serving (1 cup gumbo with 1/4 cup rice) equals:

180	calories
5 g	fat (1 g saturated fat)
60 mg	cholesterol
512 mg	sodium
22 g	carbohydrate
3 g	fiber
14 g	protein

Diabetic Exchanges: 2 very lean meat, 2 vegetable, 1 starch.

Four-Grain Bread

^{low fat} ^{meat less}

John Reed, Lees Summit, Missouri

PREP: 10 MIN.   **BAKE:** 3 TO 4 HOURS

- 1-1/2 cups water (70° to 80°)
- 1/2 cup honey
- 1-1/2 teaspoons salt
- 2 cups bread flour
- 1 cup whole wheat flour
- 3/4 cup rye flour
- 3/4 cup cornmeal
- 2-1/4 teaspoons active dry yeast

In bread machine pan, place all ingredients in order suggested by manufacturer. Select basic bread setting. Choose crust color and loaf size if available.

Bake according to bread machine directions (check dough after 5 minutes of mixing; add 1 to 2 tablespoons of water or flour if needed).
YIELD: 1 LOAF (2 POUNDS, 24 SLICES).

Nutrition Facts: One serving (1 slice) equals:

108	calories
	trace fat (trace saturated fat)
0	cholesterol
148 mg	sodium
24 g	carbohydrate
2 g	fiber
3 g	protein

Diabetic Exchange: 1-1/2 starch.

Appealing Partners

- Steamed brussels sprouts
- Fat-free pound cake with sliced strawberries

Practical Tips

You can prepare the gumbo with your family's favorite seafood, such as crab or cod.

Clear out the fridge by stirring extra veggies into the gumbo. If you have carrots or tomatoes left over from a meal earlier in the week, finish them up here.

To give the bread extra flair, add a couple of tablespoons of sunflower kernels just before the final kneading.

For **less mess** in the kitchen, go ahead and **get grilling!** This favorite fillet is ideal for **fuss-free** cooking.

Baste a salmon fillet with a light glaze while grilling. Then serve it with a colorful rice side seasoned with oregano and fresh parsley. Dinner guests will be impressed!

Appealing Partners

- Honeydew melon balls
- Steamed carrots

Practical Tips

For a marvelous main-dish salad, serve the grilled salmon over mixed baby greens tossed with a store-bought Asian-style dressing.

Salmon can be part of a healthy menu plan. While it's higher in total fat, it's low in saturated fat. Plus, salmon is high in omega-3 fatty acids, which help reduce the risk of heart disease.

Glazed Salmon Fillet

`low carb`

Sherry West, New River, Arizona

PREP: 10 MIN.   **GRILL:** 10 MIN.

- 1/4 cup reduced-sodium soy sauce
- 2 tablespoons brown sugar
- 1/4 teaspoon crushed red pepper flakes
- 1/4 teaspoon ground ginger
- 1/8 teaspoon sesame oil
- 1 salmon fillet (1-1/2 pounds)

In a bowl, combine the first five ingredients. If grilling the salmon, coat grill rack with nonstick cooking spray before starting the grill. Grill salmon, covered, over medium heat or broil 4-6 in. from the heat for 5-6 minutes on each side or until salmon flakes easily with a fork, basting frequently with glaze. **YIELD:** 6 SERVINGS.

Nutrition Facts:
One serving (4 ounces cooked salmon) equals:
- 233 calories
- 12 g fat (3 g saturated fat)
- 67 mg cholesterol
- 472 mg sodium
- 5 g carbohydrate
- trace fiber
- 23 g protein

Diabetic Exchanges: 3 lean meat, 1/2 fat, 1/2 starch.

Confetti Rice

`low fat`

Dorothy Bayes, Sardis, Ohio

PREP: 15 MIN.   **COOK:** 15 MIN. + STANDING

- 1 can (14-1/2 ounces) reduced-sodium chicken broth
- 1 cup uncooked long grain rice
- 1/4 cup water
- 1/4 teaspoon salt
- 1/4 teaspoon dried oregano
- 1/8 teaspoon pepper
- 1/2 cup diced sweet red pepper
- 1/2 cup diced green pepper
- 1/2 cup frozen green peas, thawed
- 2 tablespoons minced fresh parsley

In a large saucepan, combine the first six ingredients. Bring to a boil. Stir in sweet peppers. Reduce heat; cover and simmer for 15-20 minutes or until rice is tender. Remove from the heat. Stir in peas. Cover and let stand for about 5 minutes or until heated through and liquid is absorbed. Stir in parsley. **YIELD:** 6 SERVINGS.

Nutrition Facts:
One serving (3/4 cup) equals:
- 144 calories
- trace fat (trace saturated fat)
- 0 cholesterol
- 294 mg sodium
- 30 g carbohydrate
- 1 g fiber
- 4 g protein

Diabetic Exchanges: 1-1/2 starch, 1 vegetable.

Show off your stir-fry skill with this lightened-up dish that's ready in a dash.

Sassy Shrimp Stir-Fry

Taste of Home Test Kitchen
Greendale, Wisconsin

PREP/TOTAL TIME: 30 MIN.

- 2 tablespoons cornstarch
- 1-1/2 cups reduced-sodium chicken broth
- 3 tablespoons reduced-sodium soy sauce
- 2 tablespoons rice wine vinegar
- 1 tablespoon honey
- 2 teaspoons sesame oil
- 1 teaspoon grated orange peel
- 1 teaspoon canola oil
- 1 pound uncooked medium shrimp, peeled and deveined
- 1-1/2 teaspoons minced fresh gingerroot
- 2 garlic cloves, minced
- 1/2 teaspoon crushed red pepper flakes
- 1/2 cup julienned carrot
- 2-1/2 cups chopped Chinese *or* napa cabbage
- 2 cups fresh pea pods
- 1/4 cup thinly sliced green onions
- Hot cooked rice, optional

In a bowl, combine cornstarch and broth until smooth. Stir in the soy sauce, vinegar, honey, sesame oil and orange peel; set aside.

In a large nonstick skillet or wok, heat canola oil; stir-fry shrimp for 30 seconds. Add ginger, garlic and red pepper flakes; stir-fry 1-2 minutes longer or until shrimp turn pink. Remove and keep warm.

In the same pan, stir-fry the carrot for 1 minute. Stir broth mixture and stir into pan. Bring to a boil; cook and stir for 1-2 minutes or until thickened. Add the cabbage, peas, onions and shrimp mixture; heat through. Serve over rice if desired. **YIELD:** 10 SERVINGS.

Nutrition Facts:
One serving (1-1/4 cups stir-fry mixture) equals:
- 219 calories
- 5 g fat (1 g saturated fat)
- 168 mg cholesterol
- 896 mg sodium
- 20 g carbohydrate
- 4 g fiber
- 24 g protein

Diabetic Exchanges: 3 very lean meat, 1 starch, 1 vegetable, 1/2 fat.

Velvety Orange Gelatin Pie

Jean Shourds, Sault Sainte Marie, Michigan

PREP: 20 MIN. + CHILLING

- 1 package (.3 ounce) sugar-free orange gelatin
- 1/2 cup boiling water
- 1 can (14 ounces) fat-free sweetened condensed milk
- 1 cup (8 ounces) reduced-fat sour cream
- 3 tablespoons grated orange peel
- 1 carton (8 ounces) frozen reduced-fat whipped topping, thawed
- 1 extra-servings-size graham cracker crust (9 ounces)

In a large bowl, dissolve gelatin in boiling water. Stir in the milk, sour cream and orange peel. Fold in the whipped topping. Spoon into crust. Cover and refrigerate for at least 4 hours. **YIELD:** 10 SERVINGS.

Nutrition Facts: One serving (1 piece) equals:
- 321 calories
- 11 g fat (5 g saturated fat)
- 10 mg cholesterol
- 224 mg sodium
- 48 g carbohydrate
- 1 g fiber
- 6 g protein

Appealing Partners

- Green tea
- Vegetable egg rolls

Practical Tips

When stir-frying carrots for the entree, feel free to toss in water chestnuts or diced green pepper.

Substitute Asian rice noodles for hot cooked rice with the stir-fry to make a fun change of pace.

For extra flair, garnish the top of the pie with curls of orange peel.

Turn up the heat on the grill and your table with a flavor-packed combo sure to please!

No need to turn on the stove with this meal that cooks entirely on the grill! To save time, zap potatoes in the microwave instead, then top them with grilled veggies.

Firecracker Salmon Steaks

Phyllis Schmalz, Kansas City, Kansas

PREP/TOTAL TIME: 20 MIN.

- 1/4 cup balsamic vinegar
- 1/4 cup chili sauce
- 1/4 cup packed brown sugar
- 3 garlic cloves, minced
- 2 teaspoons minced fresh parsley
- 1 teaspoon minced fresh gingerroot
- 1/4 to 1/2 teaspoon cayenne pepper
- 1/4 to 1/2 teaspoon crushed red pepper flakes, optional
- 4 salmon steaks (6 ounces *each*)

Coat grill rack with nonstick cooking spray before starting the grill. In a small bowl, combine the vinegar, chili sauce, sugar, garlic, parsley and seasonings. Grill salmon, covered, over medium heat for 4-5 minutes on each side or until fish flakes easily with a fork, brushing occasionally with sauce.
YIELD: 4 SERVINGS.

Nutrition Facts: One serving (1 steak) equals:

373	calories
17 g	fat (4 g saturated fat)
106 mg	cholesterol
565 mg	sodium
22 g	carbohydrate
	trace fiber
32 g	protein

Diabetic Exchanges: 5 lean meat, 1-1/2 starch.

Appealing Partners

- Corn muffins
- Orange sherbet

Practical Tips

Do you favor foods on the spicy side? Be sure to include the crushed red pepper flakes when fixing the sauce for the Firecracker Salmon Steaks.

You can use salmon fillets in place of steaks. Simply cook skin side down for 8-10 minutes or until fish flakes easily with a fork.

If the weather isn't conducive to grilling, both the entree and side dish can be cooked in the oven by broiling 4-6 inches from the heat.

Grilled Vegetable Potato Skins

Karen Hemminger, Mansfield, Massachusetts

PREP: 30 MIN. + COOLING   **GRILL:** 20 MIN.

- 2 large baking potatoes
- 1 cup sliced yellow summer squash
- 1 cup sliced zucchini
- 1/2 large sweet red pepper, julienned
- 1/2 large green pepper, julienned
- 1 small red onion, cut into 1/4-inch wedges
- 1/4 cup reduced-fat olive oil and vinegar salad dressing *or* Italian salad dressing
- 1-1/2 teaspoons olive oil
- 1/2 teaspoon salt, *divided*
- 1/4 cup shredded reduced-fat cheddar cheese

Pierce potatoes several times with a fork and place on a microwave-safe plate. Microwave on high for 18-20 minutes or until tender, rotating the potatoes once. Let stand until cool enough to handle.

In a large resealable plastic bag, combine squash, zucchini, peppers and onion. Pour salad dressing over vegetables. Seal bag and turn to coat; marinate for 20 minutes.

Cut each potato in half lengthwise. Scoop out pulp, leaving a thin shell (discard pulp or save for another use). Brush inside of shells with oil and sprinkle with 1/4 teaspoon salt.

Coat grill rack with nonstick cooking spray. Place potato shells skin side up on grill rack. Grill, covered, over indirect medium heat for 10 minutes or until golden brown.

Drain vegetables, reserving marinade. Grill vegetables in a grill basket, uncovered, over medium heat for 10 minutes or until tender, basting with reserved marinade.

Sprinkle potato skins with cheese. Fill with grilled vegetables; sprinkle with remaining salt. Grill 5 minutes longer or until cheese is melted. **YIELD:** 4 SERVINGS.

Editor's Note: This recipe was tested with an 850-watt microwave.

Nutrition Facts:
One serving (1 potato half) equals:

107	calories
6 g	fat (2 g saturated fat)
4 mg	cholesterol
497 mg	sodium
11 g	carbohydrate
3 g	fiber
4 g	protein

Diabetic Exchanges: 1 vegetable, 1 fat, 1/2 starch.

This **effortless** entree delights guests
and **satisfies** everyone in the family.

*You'll make your week a little
more special when you serve
this light fettuccine coated with
a basil-seasoned sauce. The
snappy side is sure to please
even the pickiest eaters.*

Basil Shrimp Fettuccine

Cathy Carroll, Bossier City, Louisiana

PREP/TOTAL TIME: 30 MIN.

    8   ounces uncooked fettuccine
    1/2 cup chopped onion
    1/4 cup *each* chopped sweet yellow and red
        pepper
    1   to 2 garlic cloves, minced
    2   tablespoons olive oil
    1/4 cup all-purpose flour
    1   can (12 ounces) fat-free evaporated milk
    1/2 teaspoon salt
    1/4 teaspoon white pepper
    1/8 teaspoon cayenne pepper
    1   pound uncooked shrimp, peeled and
        deveined
    2   tablespoons minced fresh basil *or* 2
        teaspoons dried basil

Cook pasta according to package directions.
Meanwhile, in a nonstick skillet, saute the
onion, peppers and garlic in oil until tender.
In a small bowl, combine flour and milk
until smooth. Add to vegetable mixture. Stir
in the seasonings. Bring to a boil; cook and
stir for 2 minutes or until thickened.
   Reduce heat; add shrimp and basil.
Simmer, uncovered, for 3 minutes or until
shrimp turn pink. Drain pasta; place in a
large bowl. Add shrimp mixture and toss to
coat. **YIELD:** 6 SERVINGS.

Nutrition Facts:
One serving (1-1/4 cups) equals:
        306 calories
          7 g fat (1 g saturated fat)
        115 mg cholesterol
        465 mg sodium
         37 g carbohydrate
          2 g fiber
         24 g protein

Diabetic Exchanges: 2 starch, 2 very lean meat,
1 fat, 1/2 fat-free milk.

Broccoli with Orange Sauce

Estelle Hardin, Santa Ana, California

PREP/TOTAL TIME: 20 MIN.

    1   pound fresh *or* frozen broccoli spears
    4-1/2 teaspoons sugar
    2   teaspoons cornstarch
    1/2 teaspoon chicken bouillon granules
    1/4 cup water
    1/4 cup orange juice
    1   teaspoon grated orange peel
    1   medium navel orange, thinly sliced

Place broccoli and a small amount of water
in a saucepan; bring to a boil. Reduce heat;
cover and cook for 5-8 minutes or until
crisp-tender. Meanwhile, in a small
saucepan, combine the sugar, cornstarch and
bouillon. Stir in water, orange juice and peel
until blended. Bring to a boil; cook and stir
for 2 minutes or until thickened.
   Drain broccoli and place in a serving
bowl. Garnish with orange slices and drizzle
with sauce. **YIELD:** 6 SERVINGS.

Nutrition Facts: One serving (1 cup) equals:
         54 calories
            trace fat (trace saturated fat)
            trace cholesterol
        108 mg sodium
         13 g carbohydrate
          3 g fiber
          3 g protein

Diabetic Exchanges: 1 vegetable, 1/2 fruit.

Appealing Partners

• Iced tea
• Light chocolate cake

Practical Tips

Most any kind of pasta you have
on hand can be used in place of
fettuccine. Just be sure to use 8
ounces and cook it according to
package directions.

Grate the peel of one orange and
use some in the side dish. Freeze
the rest for future use.

Try this new **taste twist** on a classic
Mexican dish partnered with a traditional side,
both sure to **spice up** any meal.

Cumin and red pepper flakes give these enchiladas satisfying zip. The salsa's colorful blend of cucumber and mango is a refreshing change of pace, too.

Black Bean And Rice Enchiladas

Christie Ladd, Mechanicsburg, Pennsylvania

PREP: 40 MIN.   **BAKE:** 30 MIN.

- 1 green pepper, chopped
- 1 medium onion, chopped
- 3 garlic cloves, minced
- 1 tablespoon olive oil
- 1 can (15 ounces) black beans, rinsed and drained
- 1 can (14-1/4 ounces) diced tomatoes with green chilies
- 1/4 cup picante sauce
- 1 tablespoon chili powder
- 1 teaspoon ground cumin
- 1/4 teaspoon crushed red pepper flakes
- 2 cups cooked brown rice
- 8 flour tortillas (6 inches), warmed
- 1 cup salsa
- 1 cup (4 ounces) reduced-fat shredded cheddar cheese
- 3 tablespoons chopped fresh cilantro

In a large nonstick skillet, saute the green pepper, onion and garlic in oil until tender. Add the beans, tomatoes, picante sauce, chili powder, cumin and red pepper flakes; bring to a boil. Reduce heat; simmer, uncovered, until heated through and mixture thickens. Add rice; cook 5 minutes longer or until heated through.

Spoon a rounded 1/2 cup down the center of each tortilla. Fold sides over filling and roll up. Place in a 13-in. x 9-in. x 2-in. baking dish coated with nonstick cooking spray. Spoon salsa over each tortilla. Cover and bake at 350° for 25 minutes. Uncover; sprinkle with cheese and cilantro. Bake 2-3 minutes longer or until cheese is melted. **YIELD:** 8 SERVINGS.

Nutrition Facts: One serving (1 enchilada) equals:
- 279 calories
- 8 g fat (2 g saturated fat)
- 10 mg cholesterol
- 807 mg sodium
- 39 g carbohydrate
- 5 g fiber
- 11 g protein

Diabetic Exchanges: 2-1/2 starch, 1 lean meat, 1 vegetable.

Chunky Cucumber Salsa

Sarah Lubner, Milwaukee, Wisconsin

PREP: 20 MIN. + CHILLING

- 3 medium cucumbers, peeled and coarsely chopped
- 1 medium mango, coarsely chopped
- 1 cup frozen corn, thawed
- 1 medium sweet red pepper, coarsely chopped
- 1 small red onion, coarsely chopped
- 1 jalapeno pepper, finely chopped
- 3 garlic cloves, minced
- 2 tablespoons white wine vinegar
- 1 tablespoon minced fresh cilantro
- 1 teaspoon salt
- 1/2 teaspoon sugar
- 1/4 to 1/2 teaspoon cayenne pepper

In a large bowl, combine all the ingredients. Cover and refrigerate for 2-3 hours before serving. **YIELD:** 4 CUPS.

Editor's Note: When cutting or seeding hot peppers, use rubber or plastic gloves to protect your hands. Avoid touching your face.

Nutrition Facts: One serving (1/2 cup) equals:
- 57 calories
- trace fat (trace saturated fat)
- 0 cholesterol
- 297 mg sodium
- 13 g carbohydrate
- 2 g fiber
- 2 g protein

Diabetic Exchanges: 1 vegetable, 1/2 fruit.

Appealing Partners

- Baked tortilla chips
- Chicken soup

Practical Tips

The main dish recipe calls for 2 cups cooked brown rice. If you don't have leftover brown rice, consider preparing a big batch, then divide the extras into 1-cup portions and freeze for up to 3 months to use later in soups and casseroles. If you're in a hurry, cook instant brown rice instead.

The salsa recipe makes 4 cups, so it's perfect when you need a crowd-pleaser for parties and buffets. Serve it with lime-flavored tortilla chips for extra zing.

A wedge of **savory**, fresh-baked bread
and this cheesy favorite make for a
satisfying celebration any weeknight.

*The secret to the manicotti
is in the sauce! Chunky salsa
replaces an ordinary tomato
sauce. And you'll trim time
on the focaccia by starting with
a convenient hot roll mix,
then simply adding
your own seasonings.*

Spinach Manicotti

Mary Steiner, West Bend, Wisconsin

PREP: 15 MIN. **BAKE:** 1 HOUR 10 MIN.

- 1 carton (15 ounces) fat-free ricotta cheese
- 2 cups (8 ounces) shredded part-skim mozzarella cheese, *divided*
- 1 package (10 ounces) frozen chopped spinach, thawed and squeezed dry
- 1/2 cup reduced-fat sour cream
- 1/4 cup dry bread crumbs
- 1 tablespoon Italian seasoning
- 1 teaspoon garlic powder
- 1 teaspoon onion powder
- 2 cups tomato juice
- 1 cup chunky salsa
- 1 can (15 ounces) crushed tomatoes
- 14 uncooked manicotti shells

In a large bowl, combine the ricotta, 1-1/2 cups mozzarella cheese, spinach, sour cream, bread crumbs, Italian seasoning, garlic powder and onion powder.

Combine the tomato juice, salsa and crushed tomatoes; spread 1 cup sauce in an ungreased 13-in. x 9-in. x 2-in. baking dish. Stuff uncooked manicotti with spinach mixture; arrange over sauce. Pour remaining sauce over manicotti.

Cover and bake at 350° for 55 minutes. Uncover; sprinkle with remaining mozzarella cheese. Bake 15 minutes longer or until noodles are tender. **YIELD:** 7 SERVINGS.

Nutrition Facts:
One serving (2 stuffed manicotti) equals:

345	calories
8 g	fat (5 g saturated fat)
34 mg	cholesterol
782 mg	sodium
45 g	carbohydrate
4 g	fiber
22 g	protein

Diabetic Exchanges: 2 starch, 2 lean meat, 2 vegetable.

Appealing Partners

- Minestrone Soup, p. 220
- Italian green beans

Practical Tips

Assemble the Spinach Manicotti the day before and refrigerate it overnight. If you do make the manicotti ahead, wait until just before baking to pour on the final layer of sauce.

To give Herb Focaccia Bread a different flavor, try other combinations of herbs such as basil and oregano instead of rosemary and thyme.

Herb Focaccia Bread

Taste of Home Test Kitchen
Greendale, Wisconsin

PREP: 30 MIN. + RISING **BAKE:** 15 MIN.

- 1 package (16 ounces) hot roll mix
- 1 cup warm water (120° to 130°)
- 1 egg, lightly beaten
- 2 tablespoons plus 2 teaspoons olive oil, *divided*
- 1 cup finely chopped onion
- 1 teaspoon dried rosemary, crushed
- 1 teaspoon dried thyme

In a large mixing bowl, combine the hot roll mix and contents of yeast packet; mix well. Stir in the warm water, egg and 2 tablespoons oil; beat for 2 minutes or until dough pulls away from sides of bowl. Turn onto a floured surface; knead until smooth and elastic, about 5 minutes. Place in a bowl coated with nonstick cooking spray, turning once to grease top. Let rest for 5 minutes.

Divide dough in half. Roll each half into a 12-in. circle. Transfer to two 12-in. pizza pans coated with nonstick cooking spray. Using fingertips, make indentations 1 in. apart on dough; cover. In a small skillet, saute the onion, rosemary and thyme in the remaining oil for 3-4 minutes or until tender. Spread evenly on dough. Cover and let rise in a warm place until doubled, about 30 minutes.

Bake at 375° for 14-18 minutes or until golden brown. Remove from pans to wire racks. **YIELD:** 2 BREADS (10 WEDGES EACH).

Nutrition Facts: One serving (1 wedge) equals:

104	calories
3 g	fat (trace saturated fat)
11 mg	cholesterol
154 mg	sodium
16 g	carbohydrate
1 g	fiber
3 g	protein

Diabetic Exchanges: 1 starch, 1/2 fat.

For **dinner in a dash**, toss together this
pasta pleaser, then serve it with a **simple salad**
for guaranteed family raves.

*Feta cheese adds the finishing
touch to this speedy stovetop
entree. It's so delicious,
you won't miss the meat!
The quick-fix salad dressing
gets its unique flavor from
tasty tarragon vinegar.*

Appealing Partners

• Italian Wedding Soup,
  p. 239
• Crunchy breadsticks

Practical Tips

If you have a family of confirmed
meat lovers, feel free to add slices
of leftover grilled steak or strips
of cooked chicken to the pasta.

Spiral or medium shell pasta can
be used in place of the penne
pasta.

For the herb dressing, use fresh
tarragon from the garden to
make the flavored vinegar. You
should also be able to find
prepared tarragon vinegar in the
vinegar section at your supermarket.

Bell Peppers and Pasta

Sharon Csuhta, Wadsworth, Ohio

PREP/TOTAL TIME: 25 MIN.

2-1/4 cups uncooked penne
3/4 cup chopped onion
1 tablespoon olive oil
3 garlic cloves, minced
1 cup chopped sweet red pepper
1 cup chopped green pepper
1/4 cup sliced ripe olives
1 teaspoon dried oregano
1/4 teaspoon salt
1/8 teaspoon cayenne pepper
1/4 cup water
1/2 cup crumbled feta cheese

Cook pasta according to package directions.
In a nonstick skillet, saute onion in oil for
1-1/2 minutes. Add garlic; cook 30 seconds
longer. Add the sweet peppers; cook and stir
for 2-3 minutes or until vegetables are
tender. Stir in the olives, oregano, salt and
cayenne. Add water; cook and stir until
mixture comes to a boil. Drain pasta and stir
into skillet. Remove from the heat. Stir in
cheese. Serve immediately. **YIELD:** 4 SERVINGS.

Nutrition Facts: One serving (1-1/4 cups) equals:
274 calories
9 g fat (4 g saturated fat)
17 mg cholesterol
434 mg sodium
40 g carbohydrate
4 g fiber
9 g protein

Diabetic Exchanges: 2 starch, 2 vegetable,
1-1/2 fat.

Mixed Greens Salad with Tarragon Dressing

Janice Mitchell, Aurora, Colorado

PREP/TOTAL TIME: 10 MIN.

2 tablespoons tarragon vinegar
2 tablespoons canola oil
2 teaspoons sugar
1 garlic clove, minced
1/2 teaspoon salt
1/4 teaspoon ground mustard
1/4 teaspoon pepper
1/4 teaspoon lemon juice
1/4 teaspoon Worcestershire sauce
6 cups torn mixed salad greens
2 radishes, thinly sliced
1 cup salad croutons
2 tablespoons sesame seeds, toasted

In a small bowl, whisk together the first nine
ingredients. In a large salad bowl, toss salad
greens, radishes, croutons and sesame seeds.
Drizzle with dressing; toss to coat. **YIELD:** 4
SERVINGS.

Nutrition Facts: One serving (1-1/2 cups) equals:
147 calories
10 g fat (1 g saturated fat)
0 cholesterol
370 mg sodium
11 g carbohydrate
2 g fiber
3 g protein

Diabetic Exchanges: 2 fat, 1 vegetable,
1/2 starch.

East meets West with the **fresh flavors** in this updated main dish and the **zesty tang** of its crunchy side salad.

If you like traditional egg foo young, you'll enjoy this recipe with its mushroom and noodle topping. It goes well with this low-carb side that turns basic broccoli into a sensational salad.

Oriental Oven Omelet

Edna Hoffman, Hebron, Indiana

PREP: 35 MIN. **BAKE:** 10 MIN.

- 2 packages (3 ounces *each*) ramen noodles
- 1/2 cup thinly sliced celery
- 2 teaspoons canola oil
- 1 package (8 ounces) sliced fresh mushrooms
- 4 tablespoons green onions, thinly sliced, *divided*
- 2 tablespoons minced fresh gingerroot
- 3 eggs
- 6 egg whites
- 1 teaspoon sesame oil
- 1/2 teaspoon sugar
- 1/2 teaspoon salt
- 2 tablespoons reduced-sodium soy sauce

Discard seasoning packet from ramen noodles or save for another use. Cook noodles according to package directions. Drain and rinse in cold water; transfer to a bowl and set aside.

Meanwhile, in a large nonstick ovenproof skillet over medium heat, cook celery in canola oil for 1 minute. Stir in the mushrooms, 2 tablespoons green onions and the ginger; cook and stir for 7 minutes or until mushrooms are lightly browned. Stir into the noodles.

Whisk the eggs, egg whites, sesame oil, sugar and salt. Stir into noodle mixture; spread into an even layer in the skillet. Cook on medium for 2 minutes.

Bake, uncovered at 350° for 10-12 minutes or until set. Cut into wedges. Sprinkle with remaining green onions. Drizzle with soy sauce. **YIELD:** 6 SERVINGS.

Nutrition Facts: One serving (1 wedge) equals:
- 221 calories
- 10 g fat (4 g saturated fat)
- 160 mg cholesterol
- 597 mg sodium
- 21 g carbohydrate
- 1 g fiber
- 11 g protein

Diabetic Exchanges: 1-1/2 starch, 1 lean meat, 1 fat.

Sunflower Broccoli Salad

Rick and Sheila Ellison, Prattville, Alabama

PREP/TOTAL TIME: 25 MIN.

- 6 cups fresh broccoli florets
- 3 tablespoons rice wine vinegar
- 3 tablespoons reduced-sodium soy sauce
- 3 tablespoons sesame oil
- Sugar substitute equivalent to 1 tablespoon sugar
- 1/4 cup unsalted sunflower kernels

In a large saucepan, bring 8 cups water to a boil. Add broccoli; cover and cook for 3 minutes. Drain and immediately place broccoli in ice water. Drain and pat dry.

In a small bowl, whisk the vinegar, soy sauce, oil and sugar substitute. Pour over broccoli; toss to coat evenly. Cover and refrigerate for at least 1 hour, stirring several times. Just before serving, stir in sunflower kernels. **YIELD:** 6 SERVINGS.

Editor's Note: This recipe was tested with Splenda Sugar Blend for Baking.

Nutrition Facts: One serving (3/4 cup) equals:
- 121 calories
- 10 g fat (1 g saturated fat)
- 0 cholesterol
- 322 mg sodium
- 6 g carbohydrate
- 3 g fiber
- 4 g protein

Diabetic Exchanges: 2 fat, 1 vegetable.

Appealing Partners

- Vegetable Fried Rice, p. 272
- Green tea

Practical Tips

Use extra seasoning packets from ramen noodles when you're short on bouillon cubes.

Experiment with taste and try this salad with cauliflower instead of broccoli. Add extra color by tossing in some shredded carrot or red cabbage.

Discover plenty of **garden goodness**
in this ultimate **summer sampler**
loaded with just-picked flavor.

*Served chilled, this quick
soup is suitable for either a
summer lunch or lighter
family dinner. Add a little
heat to both with these
jalapeno-flavored muffins.*

Appealing Partners

• Citrus Tossed Salad,
  p. 242
• Cheddar cheese wedges

Practical Tips

Serve other gazpacho toppers,
like sour cream, diced fresh
veggies or grated Parmesan
cheese in small dishes so
everyone can create their own
combination.

Chill gazpacho overnight in the
fridge for a better blend of
flavors.

Try substituting red or yellow
peppers instead of green for a
bolder soup flavor.

Easy Gazpacho

[meat less]

Marlene Muckenhirn, Delano, Minnesota

PREP: 5 MIN. + CHILLING

2-1/2	cups reduced-sodium tomato juice
3	tablespoons white vinegar
3	tablespoons olive oil
2	garlic cloves, minced
1/4	teaspoon salt
2	to 3 drops hot pepper sauce
4	large tomatoes, chopped and *divided*
1	medium onion, chopped
1	medium cucumber, peeled, seeded and chopped
1	medium green pepper, chopped
1/4	cup fat-free croutons

In a blender or food processor, combine the
tomato juice, vinegar, oil, garlic, salt, hot
pepper sauce and half of the tomatoes; cover
and process until smooth. Transfer to a
bowl. Add the onion, cucumber, green
pepper and remaining tomatoes. Cover and
refrigerate for 4 hours or until chilled.
Garnish with croutons. **YIELD:** 4 SERVINGS.

Nutrition Facts:
One serving (1-1/2 cups) equals:
203 calories
11 g fat (2 g saturated fat)
trace cholesterol
285 mg sodium
24 g carbohydrate
4 g fiber
4 g protein

Diabetic Exchanges: 5 vegetable, 2 fat.

Spinach Corn Muffins

[low sodium] [meat less]

Jane Shapton, Tustin, California

PREP: 15 MIN.   **BAKE:** 20 MIN. + COOLING

1	cup cornmeal
1	cup all-purpose flour
1/4	cup packed brown sugar
2	teaspoons baking powder
1/4	teaspoon salt
1	egg
1	cup fat-free milk
2	tablespoons canola oil
1	cup chopped fresh spinach
3/4	cup shredded reduced-fat cheddar cheese
2	jalapeno peppers, seeded and chopped

In a large bowl, combine the cornmeal,
flour, brown sugar, baking powder and salt.
In another bowl, beat the egg, milk and oil;
stir into dry ingredients just until moistened.
Fold in the spinach, cheese and jalapenos.

Coat muffin cups with nonstick cooking
spray; fill two-third full with batter. Bake at
400° for 18-22 minutes or until a toothpick
comes out clean. Cool for 2 minutes before
removing from pan to a wire rack. **YIELD:**
1 DOZEN.

Editor's Note: When cutting or seeding hot
peppers, use rubber or plastic gloves to
protect your hands. Avoid touching your
face.

Nutrition Facts: One serving (1 muffin) equals:
153 calories
5 g fat (1 g saturated fat)
23 mg cholesterol
108 mg sodium
23 g carbohydrate
1 g fiber
5 g protein

Diabetic Exchanges: 1-1/2 starch, 1 fat.

The next time you're in the mood for a satisfying snack or a thirst-quenching beverage, try one of these tempting treats. You'll find plenty of lighter options for appealing appetizers, pack-and-go snacks and refreshing drinks.

Hot Mexican Dip

Heather O'Neill, Dudley, Massachusetts

PREP: 15 MIN. **BAKE:** 25 MIN. + COOLING

1	pound lean ground turkey
1-1/2	teaspoons chili powder
1	teaspoon onion powder
1/4	teaspoon salt
1	can (16 ounces) fat-free refried beans
1	can (4 ounces) chopped green chilies
3/4	cup taco sauce
2	cups (8 ounces) shredded reduced-fat Mexican cheese blend, *divided*
1	cup (8 ounces) fat-free sour cream
1/3	cup chopped green onions

Baked tortilla chips

Crumble turkey into a large nonstick skillet. Cook over medium heat until no longer pink; drain. Add the chili powder, onion powder and salt; set aside. In a 13-in. x 9-in. x 2-in. baking dish coated with nonstick cooking spray, layer the beans, turkey mixture, green chilies, taco sauce and 1-1/2 cups cheese.

Cover and bake at 400° for 25-30 minutes or until cheese is melted and bubbles around edges. Cool for 5 minutes. Spread sour cream on top; sprinkle with green onions and remaining cheese. Serve with tortilla chips. **YIELD:** 15 SERVINGS.

Nutrition Facts: One serving (1/2 cup dip) equals:
 133 calories
 5 g fat (2 g saturated fat)
 32 mg cholesterol
 389 mg sodium
 9 g carbohydrate
 2 g fiber
 12 g protein

Diabetic Exchanges: 2 lean meat, 1/2 starch.

Striped Fruit Pops

Taste of Home Test Kitchen
Greendale, Wisconsin

PREP: 15 MIN. + FREEZING

2	cups sliced fresh strawberries
3/4	cup honey, *divided*
12	plastic cups *or* Popsicle molds (3 ounces each)
6	kiwifruit, peeled and sliced
12	Popsicle sticks
1-1/3	cups sliced fresh ripe peaches

In a blender or food processor, place the strawberries and 1/4 cup honey; cover and process until smooth. Pour into cups or molds. Freeze for 30 minutes or until firm. In a blender or food processor, place kiwi and 1/4 cup honey; cover and process until smooth. Pour over frozen strawberry layer; insert Popsicle sticks. Freeze until firm. Repeat with peaches and remaining honey; pour over kiwi layer. Freeze until firm. **YIELD:** 1 DOZEN.

Nutrition Facts: One serving (1 pop) equals:
 106 calories
 trace fat (trace saturated fat)
 0 cholesterol
 1 mg sodium
 27 g carbohydrate
 2 g fiber
 1 g protein

Diabetic Exchange: 2 fruit.

Peanut Shrimp Kabobs

Helen Gilden, Middletown, Delaware

PREP/TOTAL TIME: 15 MIN.

1/4	cup sugar
1/4	cup reduced-sodium soy sauce
1/4	cup reduced-fat creamy peanut butter
1	tablespoon water
1	tablespoon canola oil
3	garlic cloves, minced
1-1/2	pounds uncooked medium shrimp, peeled and deveined

In a small saucepan, combine the first six ingredients until smooth. Cook and stir over medium-low heat until blended and sugar is dissolved. Set aside 6 tablespoons sauce.

If grilling the kabobs, coat the grill rack with nonstick cooking spray before starting the grill. On eight metal or soaked wooden skewers, thread the shrimp. Brush with remaining peanut sauce.

Grill kabobs, uncovered, over medium heat or broil 4 in. from the heat for 2-3 minutes on each side or until shrimp turn pink, turning once. Brush with reserved sauce before serving. **YIELD:** 8 SERVINGS.

Nutrition Facts: One serving (1 kabob) equals:
 151 calories
 5 g fat (1 g saturated fat)
 126 mg cholesterol
 492 mg sodium
 10 g carbohydrate
 1 g fiber
 16 g protein

Diabetic Exchanges: 2 lean meat, 1/2 starch.

Striped Fruit Pops

Seafood Nachos

Linda McKee, Big Prairie, Ohio

PREP/TOTAL TIME: 20 MIN.

- 30 baked tortilla chips
- 1 package (8 ounces) imitation crabmeat, chopped
- 1/4 cup reduced-fat sour cream
- 1/4 cup reduced-fat mayonnaise
- 2 tablespoons finely chopped onion
- 1/4 teaspoon dill weed
- 1 cup (4 ounces) shredded reduced-fat cheddar cheese
- 1/4 cup sliced ripe olives
- 1/4 teaspoon paprika

Arrange tortilla chips in a single layer on an ungreased baking sheet. In a bowl, combine the crab, sour cream, mayonnaise, onion and dill; spoon about 1 tablespoon onto each chip. Sprinkle with cheese, olives and paprika. Bake at 350° for 6-8 minutes or until cheese is melted. **YIELD:** 6 SERVINGS.

Nutrition Facts: One serving (5 pieces) equals:
- 190 calories
- 9 g fat (3 g saturated fat)
- 25 mg cholesterol
- 531 mg sodium
- 16 g carbohydrate
- 1 g fiber
- 13 g protein

Diabetic Exchanges: 1 starch, 1 lean meat, 1 fat.

Seafood Nachos

Asparagus Guacamole [low fat] [low carb] [meat less]

Judi Hummer, Lititz, Pennsylvania

PREP/TOTAL TIME: 20 MIN.

- 1 pound fresh asparagus, trimmed and cut into 1-inch pieces
- 1/3 cup chopped onion

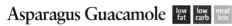

Asparagus Guacamole

- 1 garlic clove
- 1/3 cup chopped seeded tomato
- 2 tablespoons reduced-fat mayonnaise
- 1 tablespoon lemon juice
- 1/2 teaspoon salt
- 3/4 teaspoon minced fresh cilantro
- 1/4 teaspoon chili powder
- 6 drops hot pepper sauce

Assorted raw vegetables and baked tortilla chips

Place 1/2 in. of water and asparagus in a saucepan; bring to a boil. Reduce heat; cover and simmer for 5 minutes or until tender. Drain; place asparagus in a blender or food processor. Add onion and garlic; cover and process until smooth.

In a bowl, combine tomato, mayonnaise, lemon juice, salt, cilantro, chili powder and hot pepper sauce. Stir in the asparagus mixture until blended. Serve with vegetables and chips. Refrigerate leftovers; stir before serving. **YIELD:** 2 CUPS.

Nutrition Facts:
One serving (1/3 cup dip) equals:
- 42 calories
- 2 g fat (1 g saturated fat)
- 2 mg cholesterol
- 240 mg sodium
- 5 g carbohydrate
- 1 g fiber
- 3 g protein

Diabetic Exchange: 1-1/2 vegetable.

Spinach Cheese Mushrooms

Debbie Hert, Columbus, Indiana

PREP/TOTAL TIME: 25 MIN.

- 1/2 pound fresh torn spinach
- 2 tablespoons water
- 3/4 cup reduced-fat ricotta cheese
- 3 tablespoons butter, softened
- 1 egg
- 2/3 cup grated Parmesan cheese
- 1/2 cup water chestnuts, chopped
- 1/3 cup finely chopped pecans, *divided*
- 56 large fresh mushrooms (about 3-1/2 pounds)

Refrigerated butter-flavored spray

In a saucepan, bring spinach and water to a boil. Reduce heat; cover and cook for 3 minutes. Drain; squeeze dry and finely chop.

In a mixing bowl, beat ricotta and butter until smooth. Beat in egg. Stir in Parmesan cheese, water chestnuts, 3 tablespoons pecans and chopped spinach. Remove stems from mushrooms (discard or save for another use). Spray inside of mushroom caps with butter-flavored spray. Place caps on a baking sheet coated with nonstick cooking spray. Stuff with spinach mixture; sprinkle with remaining pecans.

Bake, uncovered, at 400° for 15-20 minutes or until lightly browned. **YIELD:** 28 SERVINGS.

Spinach Cheese Mushrooms

Editor's Note: This recipe was tested with I Can't Believe It's Not Butter Spray.

Nutrition Facts:
One serving (2 stuffed mushrooms) equals:
- 59 calories
- 4 g fat (2 g saturated fat)
- 15 mg cholesterol
- 82 mg sodium
- 3 g carbohydrate
- 1 g fiber
- 4 g protein

Diabetic Exchange: 2 vegetable.

Apple Cheese Wraps

Grace Malone, Lafayette, Colorado

PREP: 25 MIN. **BAKE:** 10 MIN.

- 1 tablespoon butter
- 1/4 cup packed brown sugar
- 3 cups thinly sliced peeled Golden Delicious apples (about 2 medium)
- 1/4 cup golden raisins
- 1/2 teaspoon ground cinnamon
- 1/8 teaspoon ground nutmeg
- 1/2 teaspoon vanilla extract
- 5 flour tortillas (8 inches), warmed
- 1/3 cup shredded reduced-fat cheddar cheese

TOPPING:
- 1/2 teaspoon sugar

Dash ground cinnamon

- 10 tablespoons reduced-fat whipped topping

In a small saucepan, melt butter over medium-low heat; stir in brown sugar until dissolved. Add the apples, raisins, cinnamon and nutmeg. Cook and stir over medium heat until apples are tender. Remove from the heat; stir in vanilla. Cool slightly.

Place each tortilla on a 12-in. square piece of foil. Top with about 1/4 cup apple mixture; sprinkle with cheese. Fold in sides of tortilla and roll up. Wrap in foil.

Bake at 350° for 10-12 minutes or until heated through. Combine sugar and cinnamon; sprinkle over wraps. Serve warm with whipped topping. **YIELD:** 5 SERVINGS.

Nutrition Facts: One serving (1 tortilla) equals:
- 302 calories
- 8 g fat (3 g saturated fat)
- 9 mg cholesterol
- 313 mg sodium
- 54 g carbohydrate
- 2 g fiber
- 6 g protein

Italian Ranch Chicken Strips

LaDonna Reed, Ponca City, Oklahoma

PREP: 15 MIN. **BAKE:** 15 MIN.

- 2/3 cup cornflake crumbs
- 1 teaspoon Italian seasoning

Phyllo Turkey Egg Rolls

1/2 teaspoon garlic powder

1/3 cup reduced-fat ranch salad dressing

1 teaspoon water

1/2 pound boneless skinless chicken breasts, cut into strips

In a shallow bowl, combine the cornflake crumbs, Italian seasoning and garlic powder. In another shallow bowl, combine dressing and water. Dip chicken into dressing mixture, then coat with crumb mixture.

Arrange chicken on a baking sheet coated with nonstick cooking spray. Lightly spray top of chicken with nonstick cooking spray. Bake, uncovered, at 400° for 12-15 minutes or until juices run clear. **YIELD:** 4 SERVINGS.

Nutrition Facts:
One serving (about 2 strips) equals:
- 147 calories
- 2 g fat (trace saturated fat)
- 33 mg cholesterol
- 413 mg sodium
- 17 g carbohydrate
- trace fiber
- 15 g protein

Diabetic Exchanges: 2 very lean meat, 1 starch.

Phyllo Turkey Egg Rolls

low carb

Kara de la Vega, Somerset, California

PREP: 30 MIN. **BAKE:** 25 MIN.

1 pound ground turkey breast

4 cups coleslaw mix (about 8 ounces)

1/4 cup chopped green onions

3 tablespoons reduced-sodium soy sauce

2 garlic cloves, minced

1/2 teaspoon Chinese five-spice powder

1 teaspoon grated fresh gingerroot

12 phyllo dough sheets (18 inches x 14 inches)

Refrigerated butter-flavored spray

Sweet-and-sour sauce *and/or* hot mustard, optional

Crumble turkey into a large nonstick skillet. Cook over medium heat until no longer pink; drain. Add the coleslaw mix, onions, soy sauce, garlic, five-spice powder and ginger. Cook for 2-3 minutes or until coleslaw is wilted. Remove from the heat.

Place one sheet of phyllo dough on a work surface with a long side facing you; spritz with butter spray and brush to evenly distribute. Repeat with two more sheets of phyllo, spritzing and brushing each layer. (Keep remaining phyllo dough covered with waxed paper to avoid drying out.) Cut the stack widthwise into four 14-in. x 4-1/2-in. strips. Place 1/4 cup of turkey mixture along one short side of each rectangle. Fold in long sides; starting at the filling edge, roll up tightly. Place seam side down on ungreased baking sheets. Spritz top with butter spray. Repeat with remaining phyllo and filling.

Bake at 350° for 25-30 minutes, then broil 6 in. from the heat for 5 minutes or until golden brown. Serve warm with sweet-and-sour sauce and/or mustard if desired. **YIELD:** 16 EGG ROLLS.

Editor's Note: This recipe was tested with I Can't Believe It's Not Butter Spray.

Nutrition Facts: One serving (1 egg roll) equals:
- 108 calories
- 4 g fat (1 g saturated fat)
- 22 mg cholesterol
- 236 mg sodium
- 12 g carbohydrate
- 1 g fiber
- 7 g protein

Diabetic Exchanges: 1 starch, 1 lean meat.

Yogurt Breakfast Drink

low fat low sodium

Renee Gastineau, Seattle, Washington

PREP/TOTAL TIME: 5 MIN.

2 cups (16 ounces) reduced-fat vanilla yogurt

2 cups (16 ounces) reduced-fat peach yogurt

1/2 cup frozen orange juice concentrate

1/2 cup fat-free milk

2 cups ice cubes

In a blender or food processor, combine the first four ingredients; cover and process until smooth. Add ice cubes; cover and process until smooth. Pour into glasses; serve immediately. **YIELD:** 6 SERVINGS.

Nutrition Facts: One serving (1 cup) equals:
- 166 calories
- 2 g fat (1 g saturated fat)
- 10 mg cholesterol
- 100 mg sodium
- 30 g carbohydrate
- 0 fiber
- 8 g protein

Diabetic Exchanges: 1 fruit, 1 fat-free milk.

Yogurt Breakfast Drink

Herbed Cheese Dip

Sun-Dried Tomato-Flavored Hummus

Kathleen Tribble, Buellton, California

PREP/TOTAL TIME: 10 MIN.

   1 can (15 ounces) garbanzo beans *or* chickpeas, rinsed and drained

1/3 cup reduced-fat mayonnaise

   1 tablespoon sun-dried tomato pesto sauce mix

   1 teaspoon lemon juice

Assorted crackers

In a food processor or blender, combine the beans, mayonnaise, sauce mix and lemon juice; cover and process until blended. Transfer to a small bowl. Serve with crackers. Store in the refrigerator. **YIELD:** 1-1/4 CUPS.

Nutrition Facts:
One serving (1/4 cup hummus) equals:
       139 calories
         7 g fat (1 g saturated fat)
        6 mg cholesterol
   363 mg sodium
      16 g carbohydrate
       3 g fiber
       4 g protein

Diabetic Exchanges: 1 starch, 1 fat.

Herbed Cheese Dip

`low fat` `low carb` `meat less`

Trace Morgan, Louisville, Tennessee

PREP: 10 MIN. + CHILLING

2/3 cup 1% cottage cheese

   1 package (8 ounces) reduced-fat cream cheese, cubed

   1 teaspoon red wine vinegar

1/2 teaspoon Worcestershire sauce

   1 garlic clove, minced

1/4 teaspoon garlic salt

1/8 teaspoon *each* dried basil, marjoram, savory and thyme

   1 tablespoon minced fresh parsley

Green and sweet red pepper strips *or* raw vegetables of your choice

Place cottage cheese in a blender or food processor; cover and process until smooth. Add the cream cheese, vinegar, Worcestershire sauce, garlic and seasonings; cover and process until smooth.

   Transfer to a bowl. Cover and refrigerate for at least 1 hour. Sprinkle with parsley. Serve with vegetables. **YIELD:** 1-1/2 CUPS.

Nutrition Facts:
One serving (2 tablespoons dip) equals:
        53 calories
        3 g fat (2 g saturated fat)
     11 mg cholesterol
   147 mg sodium
       2 g carbohydrate
            trace fiber
       4 g protein

Diabetic Exchanges: 1/2 lean meat, 1/2 fat.

Hot Crab Dip

`low fat` `low carb`

Cammy Brittingham, Cambridge, Maryland

PREP: 15 MIN. BAKE: 25 MIN.

   1 package (8 ounces) fat-free cream cheese

1/2 cup fat-free sour cream

   2 tablespoons fat-free mayonnaise

   1 teaspoon Worcestershire sauce

1/2 teaspoon seafood seasoning

1/2 teaspoon spicy brown mustard

1/2 teaspoon reduced-sodium soy sauce

1/8 teaspoon garlic salt

   2 cans (6 ounces *each*) crabmeat, drained, flaked and cartilage removed *or* 1/2 pound imitation crabmeat, flaked

1/3 cup plus 2 tablespoons shredded reduced-fat cheddar cheese, *divided*

1/3 cup plus 2 tablespoons shredded part-skim mozzarella cheese, divided

Melba rounds

In a large mixing bowl, beat cream cheese until smooth. Add the sour cream, mayonnaise, Worcestershire sauce, seafood seasoning, mustard, soy sauce and garlic salt; mix well. Stir in crab, 1/3 cup cheddar cheese and 1/3 cup mozzarella cheese.

   Place in a shallow 1-qt. baking dish coated with nonstick cooking spray. Sprinkle the remaining cheese on top. Bake at 350° for 25-30 minutes or until mixture bubbles around the edges. Serve warm with melba rounds. **YIELD:** 2-1/2 CUPS.

Nutrition Facts: One serving (1/2 cup dip) equals:
- 91 calories
- 3 g fat (2 g saturated fat)
- 31 mg cholesterol
- 320 mg sodium
- 5 g carbohydrate
- trace fiber
- 12 g protein

Diabetic Exchange: 2 lean meat.

Cheesy Pita Crisps

`low carb` `meat less`

Christine Mattiko, Dallastown, Pennsylvania

PREP/TOTAL TIME: 25 MIN.

- 2 whole wheat pita breads (6 inches)
- 1/4 cup reduced-fat margarine, melted
- 1/2 teaspoon garlic powder
- 1/2 teaspoon onion powder
- 1/4 teaspoon salt
- 1/4 teaspoon pepper
- 3 tablespoons grated Parmesan cheese
- 1/2 cup shredded part-skim mozzarella cheese

Split each pita bread into two rounds. Cut each round into four triangles; place inside side up on a baking sheet coated with nonstick cooking spray.

In a bowl, combine the margarine, garlic powder, onion powder, salt and pepper; stir in the Parmesan cheese. Spread over triangles. Sprinkle with mozzarella cheese. Bake at 400° for 12-15 minutes or until golden brown. **YIELD:** 8 SERVINGS.

Nutrition Facts: One serving (2 triangles) equals:
- 95 calories
- 5 g fat (2 g saturated fat)
- 6 mg cholesterol
- 264 mg sodium
- 9 g carbohydrate
- 1 g fiber
- 4 g protein

Diabetic Exchanges: 1 fat, 1/2 starch.

Cheesy Pita Crisps

Broccoli Chicken Cups

Broccoli Chicken Cups

`low carb`

Marty Kingery, Point Pleasant, West Virginia

PREP: 15 MIN. **BAKE:** 25 MIN.

- 2-1/2 cups diced cooked chicken breast
- 1 can (10-3/4 ounces) reduced-fat reduced-sodium condensed cream of chicken soup, undiluted
- 1 cup frozen chopped broccoli, thawed and drained
- 2 small plum tomatoes, seeded and chopped
- 1 small carrot, grated
- 1 tablespoon Dijon mustard
- 1 garlic clove, minced
- 1/4 teaspoon pepper
- 1 sheet frozen puff pastry, thawed
- 1/4 cup grated Parmesan cheese

In a large bowl, combine the first eight ingredients; set aside. On a lightly floured surface, roll pastry into a 12-in. x 9-in. rectangle. Cut lengthwise into four strips and widthwise into three strips. Gently press puff pastry squares into muffin cups coated with nonstick cooking spray.

Spoon chicken mixture into pastry cups. Sprinkle with Parmesan cheese. Bake at 375° for 25-30 minutes or until golden brown. Serve warm. **YIELD:** 1 DOZEN.

Nutrition Facts: One serving (1 piece) equals:
- 182 calories
- 10 g fat (3 g saturated fat)
- 23 mg cholesterol
- 310 mg sodium
- 13 g carbohydrate
- 1 g fiber
- 10 g protein

Diabetic Exchanges: 2 lean meat, 1-1/2 starch, 1/2 fat.

Olive Pepper Pinwheels

Kristin Manley, Montesano, Washington

PREP: 15 MIN. + CHILLING

    1   package (8 ounces) reduced-fat cream
        cheese
    1   teaspoon fat-free milk
  1/3   cup *each* finely chopped sweet red, green
        and yellow pepper
    1   can (2-1/4 ounces) chopped ripe olives,
        drained
    2   tablespoons ranch salad dressing mix
    6   flour tortillas (6 inches)

In a mixing bowl, beat cream cheese and
milk until smooth; stir in the peppers, olives
and dressing mix. Spread over tortillas. Roll
up jelly-roll style; wrap tightly in plastic
wrap.

Refrigerate for 2 hours or until firm. Just
before serving, cut into 1-in. pieces. **YIELD:**
3 DOZEN.

Nutrition Facts: One serving (2 pieces) equals:
         68   calories
          4 g fat (1 g saturated fat)
          7 mg cholesterol
        226 mg sodium
          6 g carbohydrate
          1 g fiber
          2 g protein

Diabetic Exchanges: 1 vegetable, 1/2 starch.

Olive Pepper Pinwheels

Baked Sausage Wontons

Karen Rolfe, Dayton, Ohio

PREP/TOTAL TIME: 30 MIN.

  1/2   pound bulk pork sausage
  1/2   cup finely shredded carrot
  1/4   cup finely chopped water chestnuts
    2   teaspoons cornstarch
  1/2   teaspoon ground ginger
  1/3   cup chicken broth
    1   tablespoon sherry *or* additional chicken
        broth
    1   tablespoon reduced-sodium soy sauce
   40   wonton wrappers

In a large skillet, cook sausage over medium
heat until no longer pink; drain. Stir in
carrot and water chestnuts.

Meanwhile, in a bowl, combine cornstarch and ginger. Stir in the broth, sherry or
additional broth and soy sauce until smooth.
Stir into sausage mixture. Bring to a boil;
cook and stir for 1-2 minutes or until thickened.

Gently press wonton wrappers into miniature muffin cups coated with nonstick
cooking spray. Lightly coat wontons with
nonstick cooking spray. Bake at 350° for
5 minutes.

Remove wontons from cups and arrange
upside down on greased baking sheets. Bake
5 minutes longer or until light golden. Turn
wontons; fill each with about 1 teaspoon
sausage mixture. Bake for 2-3 minutes or
until filling is heated through. **YIELD:**
40 WONTONS.

Nutritional Facts: One serving (2 pieces) equals:
         77   calories
          2 g fat (1 g saturated fat)
         10 mg cholesterol
        196 mg sodium
         10 g carbohydrate
               trace fiber
          3 g protein

Diabetic Exchange: 1 starch.

Asparagus in Puff Pastry

Dianne Werdegar, Naperville, Illinois

PREP: 30 MIN. + CHILLING   **BAKE:** 10 MIN.

    2   cups water
   24   fresh asparagus spears (about 1 pound),
        trimmed
    1   package (8 ounces) reduced-fat cream
        cheese
  1/2   teaspoon salt
    1   package (17-1/4 ounces) frozen puff
        pastry dough, thawed
  1/4   cup egg substitute

Asparagus in Puff Pastry

In a large nonstick skillet, bring water to a boil. Add asparagus; cover and cook for 3 minutes. Drain asparagus and immediately place in ice water; drain and pat dry. In a mixing bowl, beat cream cheese and salt until smooth; set aside.

Unfold the dough on a lightly floured surface. Cut each sheet in half widthwise. For each rectangle, spread cream cheese mixture lengthwise over half of the dough to within 1/2 in. of edges. Arrange two rows of three asparagus spears lengthwise in a single layer over cream cheese.

Brush edges of dough with some of the egg substitute; fold dough over filling and press edges together to seal. Cover and refrigerate for 1 hour.

Cut widthwise into 1-1/4-in. pieces. Place 1 in. apart on a baking sheet coated with nonstick cooking spray. Brush with remaining egg substitute. Bake at 425° for 8-12 minutes or until golden. Serve warm. **YIELD:** 28 SERVINGS.

Nutrition Facts: One serving (2 pieces) equals:
  87 calories
  6 g fat (3 g saturated fat)
  9 mg cholesterol
 156 mg sodium
  6 g carbohydrate
  1 g fiber
  3 g protein

Diabetic Exchanges: 1 vegetable, 1/2 starch, 1/2 fat.

Cinnamon Toasties

Diane Marshall
Winston Salem, North Carolina

PREP/TOTAL TIME: 20 MIN.

 8 slices bread
1/4 cup reduced-fat cream cheese
Refrigerated butter-flavored spray
 3 tablespoons sugar
1-1/2 teaspoons ground cinnamon

Flatten bread with a rolling pin. Spread cream cheese on one side of half of the slices; top with remaining bread. Cut each into four squares. Spritz both sides with butter-flavored spray.

In a small bowl, combine sugar and cinnamon; add bread squares and turn to coat both sides. Place on an ungreased baking sheet. Bake at 350° for 8-10 minutes or until puffed and golden. Serve immediately. **YIELD:** 4 SERVINGS.

Editor's Note: This recipe was tested with I Can't Believe It's Not Butter Spray.

Nutrition Facts: One serving (4 squares) equals:
 233 calories
  5 g fat (2 g saturated fat)
  9 mg cholesterol
 368 mg sodium
  41 g carbohydrate
  2 g fiber
  7 g protein

Apricot Peach Smoothies

DeAnn Alleva, Hudson, Wisconsin

PREP/TOTAL TIME: 10 MIN.

 1 can (5-1/2 ounces) apricot nectar
 1 medium ripe banana, frozen and cut into chunks
 1 cup (8 ounces) fat-free vanilla yogurt
 2 cups sliced fresh *or* frozen unsweetened peaches
 1 tablespoon lemon juice
 1 tablespoon honey
 1 teaspoon grated lemon peel
 6 ice cubes

In a blender or food processor, combine all ingredients. Cover and process until smooth. Pour into glasses; serve immediately. **YIELD:** 4 SERVINGS.

Nutrition Facts: One serving (1 cup) equals:
 160 calories
   trace fat (0 saturated fat)
  2 mg cholesterol
 35 mg sodium
  37 g carbohydrate
  3 g fiber
  4 g protein

Diabetic Exchanges: 2 fruit, 1/2 starch.

Apricot Peach Smoothies

Apple Pie Tartlets

Mary Kelley, Minneapolis, Minnesota

PREP: 35 MIN. + COOLING

- 1 sheet refrigerated pie pastry
- 1 tablespoon sugar

Dash ground cinnamon

FILLING:

- 2 teaspoons butter
- 2 cups diced peeled tart apples
- 3 tablespoons sugar
- 3 tablespoons fat-free caramel ice cream topping
- 2 tablespoons all-purpose flour
- 1/2 teaspoon ground cinnamon
- 1/2 teaspoon lemon juice
- 1/8 teaspoon salt

Roll out pastry on a lightly floured surface; cut into twenty 2-1/2-in. circles. Press onto the bottom and up the sides of miniature muffin cups coated with nonstick cooking spray. Prick pastry with a fork. Spray lightly with nonstick cooking spray. Combine sugar and cinnamon; sprinkle over pastry. Bake at 350° for 6-8 minutes or until golden brown. Cool for 5 minutes before removing from pans to wire racks.

In a saucepan, melt butter. Add apples; cook and stir over medium heat for 4-5 minutes or until crisp-tender. Stir in the sugar, caramel topping, flour, cinnamon, lemon juice and salt. Bring to a boil; cook and stir for 2 minutes or until sauce is thickened and apples are tender. Cool for 5 minutes. Spoon into tart shells. **YIELD:** 10 SERVINGS.

Nutrition Facts: One serving (2 tartlets) equals:

- 150 calories
- 6 g fat (3 g saturated fat)
- 6 mg cholesterol
- 126 mg sodium
- 22 g carbohydrate
- 1 g fiber
- 1 g protein

Diabetic Exchanges: 1-1/2 starch, 1 fat.

Apple Pie Tartlets

Fruity Granola

Nancy Chapman
Center Harbor, New Hampshire

PREP: 20 MIN. BAKE: 15 MIN. + COOLING

- 3 cups old-fashioned oats
- 1/2 cup sliced almonds
- 1-1/4 cups honey
- 1/2 cup Grape-Nuts
- 1 tablespoon butter
- 1 teaspoon ground cinnamon
- 2-1/2 cups Wheaties
- 1/2 cup dried cranberries
- 1/2 cup raisins
- 1/2 cup dried banana chips

Combine oats and almonds; spread evenly in a 15-in. x 10-in. x 1-in. baking pan coated with nonstick cooking spray. Bake at 325° for 15 minutes. In a large bowl, combine the honey, Grape-Nuts, butter and cinnamon. Add oat mixture; stir to combine. Return mixture to the pan. Bake 15-20 minutes longer or until golden. Cool on wire rack.

When cool enough to handle, break granola into pieces. Place in a large bowl; stir in the Wheaties, cranberries, raisins and banana chips. Store in an airtight container in a cool dry place for up to 2 months. **YIELD:** 10 CUPS.

Nutrition Facts: One serving (1/2 cup) equals:

- 183 calories
- 4 g fat (1 g saturated fat)
- 2 mg cholesterol
- 51 mg sodium
- 38 g carbohydrate
- 3 g fiber
- 3 g protein

Diabetic Exchanges: 1-1/2 fruit, 1 starch, 1/2 fat.

Festive Stuffed Dates

Diana Debruyn, Cincinnati, Ohio

PREP: 15 MIN. + CHILLING

- 3 ounces reduced-fat cream cheese
- 1/4 cup confectioners' sugar
- 2 teaspoons grated orange peel
- 30 pitted dates

In a small mixing bowl, beat the cream cheese, confectioners' sugar and orange peel until blended. Carefully make a slit in the center of each date; fill with cream cheese mixture. Cover and refrigerate for at least 1 hour before serving. **YIELD:** 10 SERVINGS.

Nutrition Facts: One serving (3 pieces) equals:

- 102 calories
- 2 g fat (1 g saturated fat)
- 6 mg cholesterol
- 37 mg sodium
- 22 g carbohydrate
- 2 g fiber
- 1 g protein

Diabetic Exchanges: 1 fruit, 1/2 fat.

Mediterranean Salsa

Margaret Potempa, Oshkosh, Wisconsin

PREP: 15 MIN. COOK: 15 MIN. + CHILLING

- 2 cups cubed peeled eggplant (1/2-inch cubes)
- 1 cup cubed sweet red pepper (1/2-inch cubes)

1 cup cubed green pepper (1/2-inch cubes)
1 cup cubed zucchini (1/2-inch cubes)
3 garlic cloves, minced
2 tablespoons olive oil
1 large tomato, cut into 1/2-inch cubes
2 tablespoons cider vinegar
1 tablespoon dried basil
1 teaspoon dried thyme
1/2 teaspoon sugar
1/2 teaspoon salt
1/4 to 1/2 teaspoon coarsely ground pepper
Toasted bread rounds

In a large nonstick skillet, saute the eggplant, peppers, zucchini and garlic in oil for 8 minutes. Add the tomato, vinegar, basil, thyme, sugar, salt and pepper. Cook 4-5 minutes longer or until vegetables are tender. Cover and refrigerate for at least 4 hours. Serve with toasted bread. **YIELD:** ABOUT 2-1/2 CUPS.

Nutrition Facts:
One serving (1/4 cup salsa) equals:
45 calories
3 g fat (trace saturated fat)
0 cholesterol
121 mg sodium
5 g carbohydrate
1 g fiber
1 g protein

Diabetic Exchanges: 1 vegetable, 1/2 fat.

Italian Red Pepper Bruschetta

meat less

Josephine Piro, Easton, Pennsylvania
PREP/TOTAL TIME: 30 MIN.

1 loaf (1 pound) unsliced Italian bread
3 garlic cloves, minced, *divided*
3 tablespoons olive oil, *divided*

Mediterranean Salsa

Italian Red Pepper Bruschetta

2 large sweet red peppers, chopped
1 medium onion, chopped
1-1/2 teaspoons Italian seasoning
2 tablespoons plus 1/4 cup coarsely chopped fresh basil, *divided*
2 tablespoons minced fresh parsley
1 tablespoon minced fresh oregano
6 plum tomatoes, sliced
3/4 cup shredded part-skim mozzarella cheese
2 ounces reduced-fat provolone cheese, shredded
1/4 cup shredded Parmesan cheese

Cut bread in half lengthwise; place on a baking sheet. In a nonstick skillet, saute 2 garlic cloves in 2 tablespoons oil until tender. Brush over cut side of bread.

In the same skillet, saute the red peppers, onion, Italian seasoning and remaining garlic in remaining oil until vegetables are tender; remove from the heat. Add 2 tablespoons basil, parsley and oregano; cool slightly. Place in a blender or food processor; cover and process until pureed. Spread over bread.

Top with tomato slices and cheese. Sprinkle with remaining basil. Bake at 400° for 10-13 minutes or until cheese is melted and edges are golden brown. **YIELD:** 12 SERVINGS.

Nutrition Facts: One serving (1 slice) equals:
190 calories
7 g fat (2 g saturated fat)
8 mg cholesterol
309 mg sodium
24 g carbohydrate
2 g fiber
8 g protein

Diabetic Exchanges: 1-1/2 starch, 1-1/2 fat.

Light Guacamole

Marlene Tokarski, Mesa, Arizona
PREP/TOTAL TIME: 10 MIN.

- 2 large ripe avocados, peeled, *divided*
- 1 cup (8 ounces) fat-free sour cream
- 1/4 cup chopped onion
- 3 jalapeno peppers, seeded and chopped
- 6 tablespoons minced fresh cilantro
- 4 teaspoons lemon juice
- 1/2 teaspoon salt
- 1/2 teaspoon ground cumin
- 1/8 teaspoon pepper
- 1 large tomato, seeded and chopped

Baked tortilla chips *or* fresh vegetables

In a food processor, combine one avocado, sour cream, onion, jalapenos, cilantro, lemon juice, salt, cumin and pepper; cover and process until smooth.

In a bowl, mash the remaining avocado with a fork. Stir in the pureed avocado mixture. Gently fold in tomato. Serve with tortilla chips or vegetables. **YIELD:** 3 CUPS.

Editor's Note: When cutting or seeding hot peppers, use rubber or plastic gloves to protect your hands. Avoid touching your face.

Nutrition Facts: One serving (1/4 cup dip) equals:
- 79 calories
- 5 g fat (1 g saturated fat)
- 2 mg cholesterol
- 119 mg sodium
- 7 g carbohydrate
- 2 g fiber
- 2 g protein

Diabetic Exchanges: 1 vegetable, 1 fat.

Light Guacamole

Easy Smoked Salmon

Norma Fell, Boyne City, Michigan
PREP: 10 MIN. + MARINATING
BAKE: 35 MIN. + CHILLING

- 1 salmon fillet (about 2 pounds)
- 2 tablespoons brown sugar
- 2 teaspoons salt
- 1/2 teaspoon pepper
- 1 to 2 tablespoons Liquid Smoke

Place salmon, skin side down, in an 11-in. x 7-in. x 2-in. baking pan coated with nonstick cooking spray. Sprinkle with brown sugar, salt and pepper. Drizzle with Liquid Smoke. Cover and refrigerate for 4-8 hours.

Drain and discard liquid. Bake, uncovered, at 350° for 35-45 minutes or until fish flakes easily with a fork. Cool to room temperature. Cover and refrigerate for 8 hours or overnight. **YIELD:** 16 SERVINGS.

Nutrition Facts: One serving (2 ounces) equals:
- 110 calories
- 6 g fat (1 g saturated fat)
- 33 mg cholesterol
- 327 mg sodium
- 2 g carbohydrate
- 1 g fiber
- 11 g protein

Diabetic Exchange: 2 lean meat.

Cantaloupe Ice Pops

Taste of Home Test Kitchen
Greendale, Wisconsin
PREP: 10 MIN. + FREEZING

- 4 cups cubed cantaloupe
- 1/4 cup sugar
- 2 tablespoons lemon juice
- 1 tablespoon chopped fresh mint *or*
  1 teaspoon dried mint
- 1/2 teaspoon grated lemon peel

Cantaloupe Ice Pops

12 plastic cups *or* Popsicle molds (3 ounces each)
12 Popsicle sticks

In a blender or food processor, combine the first five ingredients; cover and process until smooth. Pour 1/4 cup into each cup or mold; insert Popsicle sticks. Freeze until firm. **YIELD:** 1 DOZEN.

Nutrition Facts: One serving (1 pop) equals:
    36 calories
        trace fat (trace saturated fat)
     0 cholesterol
    5 mg sodium
    9 g carbohydrate
        trace fiber
        trace protein

Diabetic Exchange: 1/2 fruit.

Almond Tea

Susan Wilson, Lamesa, Texas

PREP/TOTAL TIME: 5 MIN.

2 cups diet ginger ale, chilled
2 cups cold water
1/4 cup sugar-free instant lemon iced tea mix
1/2 teaspoon almond extract
1/2 teaspoon vanilla extract

In a pitcher, combine all ingredients. Serve immediately over ice. **YIELD:** 4 SERVINGS.

Nutrition Facts: One serving (1 cup) equals:
    11 calories
     0 fat (0 saturated fat)
     0 cholesterol
   18 mg sodium
    2 g carbohydrate
     0 fiber
     0 protein

Creamy Mocha Drink `low sodium`

Taste of Home Test Kitchen
Greendale, Wisconsin

PREP: 15 MIN. + CHILLING

Sugar substitute equivalent to 6 tablespoons sugar
2 tablespoons baking cocoa
2 tablespoons instant coffee granules
1 cup boiling water
1 cup 2% milk
1/4 teaspoon vanilla extract
1-1/2 cups no-sugar-added reduced-fat vanilla ice cream
4 tablespoons whipped topping
1/4 teaspoon ground cinnamon

In a small bowl, combine the sugar substitute, cocoa and coffee. Add boiling water; stir until coffee and cocoa are dissolved. Stir in milk and vanilla. Cover and refrigerate for at least 1 hour.

Place the coffee mixture in a blender; add ice cream. Cover and process until smooth. Pour into mugs or glasses; garnish with whipped topping and cinnamon. **YIELD:** 4 SERVINGS.

Editor's Note: This recipe was tested with Splenda No Calorie Sweetener.

Nutrition Facts: One serving (2/3 cup with 1 tablespoon whipped topping) equals:
   138 calories
    5 g fat (3 g saturated fat)
  13 mg cholesterol
  74 mg sodium
  18 g carbohydrate
   1 g fiber
   5 g protein

Diabetic Exchanges: 1-1/2 starch, 1/2 fat.

Creamy Mocha Drink

Roasted Red Pepper Dip

Roasted Red Pepper Dip

Priscilla Gilbert
Indian Harbour Beach, Florida

PREP/TOTAL TIME: 15 MIN.

- 1 cup (8 ounces) fat-free sour cream
- 1/2 cup reduced-fat mayonnaise
- 1/2 teaspoon prepared horseradish
- 1/8 teaspoon cayenne pepper
- 4 drops hot pepper sauce
- 1 jar (7 ounces) roasted sweet red peppers, drained and chopped
- 1 medium sweet red pepper

Assorted fresh vegetables

In a small bowl, combine the first five ingredients. Stir in the roasted red peppers. Cut a thin slice off one long side of sweet red pepper; remove seeds. Spoon dip into pepper cup. Serve with vegetables. **YIELD:** 2 CUPS.

Nutrition Facts: One serving (1/4 cup dip) equals:
- 90 calories
- 5 g fat (1 g saturated fat)
- 10 mg cholesterol
- 192 mg sodium
- 9 g carbohydrate
- trace fiber
- 2 g protein

Diabetic Exchanges: 1 fat, 1/2 starch.

Rosemary Zucchini Sticks

Betty Jackson, White Pine, Tennessee

PREP/TOTAL TIME: 30 MIN.

- 2 medium zucchini, peeled
- 1 cup seasoned bread crumbs
- 1 tablespoon minced fresh rosemary *or* 1 teaspoon dried rosemary, crushed
- 1 egg
- 1 tablespoon water

Cut each zucchini in half widthwise, then cut each half lengthwise into quarters. In a shallow bowl, combine bread crumbs and rosemary. In another bowl, beat egg and water.

Dip zucchini in egg mixture, then coat with crumb mixture. Coat again in egg and crumbs. Arrange on a baking sheet coated with nonstick cooking spray. Bake at 375° for 20-25 minutes or until tender and golden, turning once. **YIELD:** 4 SERVINGS.

Nutrition Facts: One serving (4 pieces) equals:
- 144 calories
- 2 g fat (1 g saturated fat)
- 53 mg cholesterol
- 814 mg sodium
- 24 g carbohydrate
- 2 g fiber
- 7 g protein

Diabetic Exchanges: 1-1/2 starch, 1/2 fat.

Ruby Fruit Slush

Sarah Gingerich, Unionville, Missouri

PREP: 5 MIN. + FREEZING

- 3 quarts tropical fruit punch
- 1 can (46 ounces) unsweetened pineapple juice
- 1 bottle (48 ounces) cranberry-apple juice
- 4-1/2 cups water
- 1 can (12 ounces) frozen orange juice concentrate, thawed
- 2 liters diet ginger ale *or* lemon-lime soda, chilled

In a very large bowl or bowls, combine the first five ingredients. Transfer to four 2-qt. freezer containers. Freeze, stirring several times to make slushy. Remove containers from freezer 1-2 hours before serving; stir until slushy. Stir a fourth of ginger ale into each container. **YIELD:** 2 GALLONS.

Nutrition Facts: One serving (1 cup) equals:
- 108 calories
- trace fat (0 saturated fat)
- 0 cholesterol
- 30 mg sodium
- 27 g carbohydrate
- trace fiber
- trace protein

Diabetic Exchanges: 1 fruit, 1/2 starch.

Garlic Bean Dip

Nancy Testin, Harrington, Delaware

PREP/TOTAL TIME: 10 MIN.

- 1 can (15 ounces) white kidney *or* cannellini beans, rinsed and drained
- 1 tablespoon cider vinegar
- 2 garlic cloves, minced
- 1/2 teaspoon salt
- 1/2 teaspoon ground cumin
- 1/3 cup reduced-fat mayonnaise
- 2 tablespoons minced fresh parsley

Baked pita chips *or* assorted raw vegetables

In a food processor, combine the beans, vinegar, garlic, salt and cumin; cover and process until almost smooth. Add mayonnaise and parsley; cover and process just until blended. Serve with pita chips or vegetables. **YIELD:** 1-1/2 CUPS.

Nutritional Facts:
One serving (1/4 cup dip) equals:
- 102 calories
- 5 g fat (1 g saturated fat)
- 4 mg cholesterol
- 450 mg sodium
- 11 g carbohydrate
- 3 g fiber
- 3 g protein

Diabetic Exchanges: 1 starch, 1 fat.

Mushroom-Stuffed Shrimp

low fat | low carb

Karolee Plock, Burwell, Nebraska

PREP/TOTAL TIME: 25 MIN.

- 12 uncooked shell-on jumbo shrimp (about 1 pound)
- 1/2 teaspoon chicken bouillon granules
- 1 tablespoon hot water
- 3/4 cup soft bread crumbs
- 2 tablespoons finely chopped fresh mushrooms
- 2 tablespoons finely chopped celery
- 1 teaspoon reduced-fat butter
- 1/4 teaspoon garlic powder
- 4 drops hot pepper sauce

Peel and devein shrimp, leaving the tails on. Butterfly each shrimp along the outside curve. Open shrimp flat and place with tails up in an 8-in. square baking dish coated with nonstick cooking spray.

In a small bowl, dissolve bouillon in hot water. Stir in the remaining ingredients. Spoon about 1 teaspoon onto each shrimp. Bake at 375° for 5-8 minutes or until shrimp turn pink. Serve warm. **YIELD:** 1 DOZEN.

Editor's Note: This recipe was tested with Land O' Lakes light stick butter.

Nutritional Facts: One serving (3 shrimp) equals:
- 115 calories
- 2 g fat (1 g saturated fat)
- 170 mg cholesterol
- 353 mg sodium
- 5 g carbohydrate
- trace fiber
- 19 g protein

Diabetic Exchange: 3 very lean meat.

Mushroom-Stuffed Shrimp

Bottoms-Up Cherry Limeade

Bottoms-Up Cherry Limeade

low fat | low sodium | low carb

Awynne Thurstenson
Siloam Springs, Arkansas

PREP/TOTAL TIME: 10 MIN.

- 3/4 cup lime juice
- Sugar substitute equivalent to 1 cup sugar
- 2 liters lime carbonated water, chilled
- 1/2 cup maraschino cherry juice
- 8 maraschino cherries with stems
- 8 lime slices

In a bowl, combine lime juice and sugar substitute. Cover and refrigerate. Just before serving, stir carbonated water into lime juice mixture.

For each serving, place 1 tablespoon cherry juice in a glass. Add crushed ice and about 1 cup of lime juice mixture. Garnish with a maraschino cherry and a lime slice. **YIELD:** 8 SERVINGS.

Editor's Note: This recipe was tested with Splenda No Calorie Sweetener.

Nutrition Facts: One serving (1 cup) equals:
- 52 calories
- 1 g fat (1 g saturated fat)
- 0 cholesterol
- 1 mg sodium
- 14 g carbohydrate
- 1 g fiber
- 1 g protein

Diabetic Exchange: 1 fruit.

Maple Fruit Dip

Cathy Liebert, Hartland, Wisconsin

PREP/TOTAL TIME: 10 MIN.

- 1/2 cup fat-free vanilla yogurt
- 1/2 cup reduced-fat whipped topping
- 4 teaspoons reduced-calorie pancake syrup

Dash ground cinnamon

Assorted berries and fruit chunks

In a bowl, combine the first four ingredients. Cover and refrigerate until serving. Serve with fruit. **YIELD:** 1 CUP.

Nutrition Facts:
One serving (2 tablespoons dip) equals:
- 22 calories
- 1 g fat (1 g saturated fat)
- trace cholesterol
- 16 mg sodium
- trace carbohydrate
- 0 fiber
- trace protein

Crab-Filled Veggie Bites

Debbie Bloomer, Omaha, Nebraska

PREP: 20 MIN. + STANDING

- 12 cherry tomatoes
- 12 fresh snow peas

Crab-filled Veggie Bites

- 1 can (6 ounces) crabmeat, drained, flaked and cartilage removed *or* 1 cup finely chopped imitation crabmeat
- 2 tablespoons reduced-fat cream cheese
- 1 tablespoon finely chopped green onion
- 2 teaspoons reduced-fat sour cream
- 2 teaspoons chili sauce
- 1 teaspoon lemon juice
- 1/2 teaspoon prepared horseradish

Cut the top of each tomato; scoop out pulp with a small spoon and discard. Invert tomatoes on paper towels to drain; let stand for 1-3 hours.

Place 1 in. of water in a saucepan; add snow peas. Bring to a boil. reduce heat; cover and simmer for 1-2 minutes or until crisp-tender. Drain and immediately place peas in ice water. Drain and pat dry; refrigerate.

In a bowl, combine the remaining ingredients; mix well. Using a sharp knife, make a slit down the side of each pea pod. Fill peas and tomatoes with crab mixture. Arrange on a serving platter; cover and refrigerate for at least 30 minutes. **YIELD:** 4 SERVINGS.

Nutrition Facts: One serving (3 pieces) equals:
- 82 calories
- 2 g fat (1 g saturated fat)
- 43 mg cholesterol
- 254 mg sodium
- 5 g carbohydrate
- 1 g fiber
- 10 g protein

Diabetic Exchanges: 1 very lean meat, 1 vegetable, 1/2 fat.

Savory Swiss Cheesecake

Marjorie Turner, Poquoson, Virginia

PREP: 15 MIN. **BAKE:** 40 MIN. + CHILLING

- 1 cup finely crushed thin wheat crackers
- 3 tablespoons butter, melted
- 12 ounces reduced-fat cream cheese
- 2 cartons (8 ounces *each*) reduced-fat plain yogurt
- 1 egg
- 1 egg yolk
- 1/4 teaspoon dried basil
- 1/8 teaspoon dried rosemary, crushed
- 2 cups (8 ounces) shredded reduced-fat Swiss cheese

Assorted crackers

In a small bowl, combine cracker crumbs and butter. Press onto the bottom of a 9-in. springform pan; set aside. In a large mixing bowl, beat cream cheese until smooth. Add the yogurt, egg, egg yolk, basil and rosemary; beat on low speed just until blended. Stir in Swiss cheese.

Savory Swiss Cheesecake

Pour into prepared crust. Place pan on a baking sheet. Bake at 350° for 40-50 minutes or until center is almost set. Cool on a wire rack for 10 minutes. Carefully run a knife around edge of pan to loosen; cool 1 hour longer.

Refrigerate overnight. Remove sides of pan. Cut into wedges; serve with crackers. Refrigerate leftovers. **YIELD:** 16 SERVINGS.

Nutrition Facts: One serving (1 wedge) equals:
- 169 calories
- 11 g fat (7 g saturated fat)
- 57 mg cholesterol
- 170 mg sodium
- 7 g carbohydrate
- trace fiber
- 9 g protein

Diabetic Exchanges: 1-1/2 fat, 1 lean meat, 1/2 starch.

Cheesy Bagel Bites

Becky Ruff, Monona, Iowa

PREP/TOTAL TIME: 20 MIN.

- 1/3 cup reduced-fat mayonnaise
- 1/4 cup grated Parmesan cheese
- 1 tablespoon prepared mustard
- 2 green onions, finely chopped
- 1/4 teaspoon garlic powder
- 3 whole wheat bagels, split and toasted

In a small bowl, combine mayonnaise, Parmesan cheese, mustard, onions and garlic powder. Spread over bagels.

Place on a baking sheet. Broil 4-6 in. from the heat for 1-2 minutes or until golden brown and bubbly. Cut each bagel half into six pieces. **YIELD:** 12 SERVINGS.

Nutrition Facts: One serving (3 pieces) equals:
- 105 calories
- 3 g fat (1 g saturated fat)
- 4 mg cholesterol
- 248 mg sodium
- 16 g carbohydrates
- 3 g fiber
- 4 g protein

Diabetic Exchanges: 1 starch, 1/2 fat.

Lemon Fruit Dip

Regina King, Watertown, Wisconsin

PREP/TOTAL TIME: 5 MIN.

- 2 cups (16 ounces) reduced-fat sour cream
- 1 package (1 ounce) sugar-free instant vanilla pudding mix
- 1/4 cup fat-free milk
- 4 teaspoons lemon juice
- 1 teaspoon grated lemon peel

Assorted fresh fruit

In a bowl, whisk the sour cream, pudding mix, milk, lemon juice and peel until blended. Serve with fruit. **YIELD:** 2 CUPS.

Nutrition Facts: One serving (1/3 cup dip) equals:
- 127 calories
- 7 g fat (5 g saturated fat)
- 27 mg cholesterol
- 255 mg sodium
- 10 g carbohydrate
- 1 g fiber
- 6 g protein

Diabetic Exchanges: 1 starch, 1 fat.

Lemon Fruit Dip

Blue Cheese Appetizer Pizza

Blue Cheese Appetizer Pizza

Kathy Stanaway, DeWitt, Michigan

PREP: 15 MIN. + RISING **BAKE:** 20 MIN.

  1 loaf (1 pound) frozen bread dough, thawed
  3 tablespoons olive oil
  2 teaspoons dried basil
  2 teaspoons dried oregano
  1 teaspoon garlic powder
  1 small red onion, thinly sliced and separated into rings
  2 plum tomatoes, chopped
  1 cup (4 ounces) shredded part-skim mozzarella cheese, *divided*
  3 ounces crumbled blue cheese
  2 tablespoons grated Parmesan cheese

Divide bread dough in half. Press each portion onto the bottom of a 12-in. pizza pan coated with nonstick cooking spray; build up edges slightly. Prick dough several times with a fork. Cover and let rise in a warm place for 30 minutes.

  Brush dough with oil. Combine the basil, oregano and garlic powder; sprinkle over dough. Bake at 425° for 10 minutes. Arrange onion and tomatoes over crust; sprinkle with cheeses. Bake 8-10 minutes longer or until golden brown. **YIELD:** 2 PIZZAS (10 SLICES EACH).

Nutrition Facts: One serving (1 slice) equals:
    118 calories
      5 g fat (2 g saturated fat)
      7 mg cholesterol
    228 mg sodium
     13 g carbohydrate
      1 g fiber
      5 g protein

Diabetic Exchanges: 1 starch, 1 fat.

Chicken Salad Wonton Stars

Starr Tharp, Parchment, Michigan

PREP/TOTAL TIME: 30 MIN.

  1 package (8 ounces) reduced-fat cream cheese
  3 tablespoons fat-free milk
1/2 teaspoon garlic salt
1/4 teaspoon pepper
  2 cups cubed cooked chicken breast
  2 tablespoons chopped green onion
 36 wonton wrappers
Refrigerated butter-flavor spray
Paprika

In a mixing bowl, beat the cream cheese, milk, garlic salt and pepper until smooth. Stir in chicken and green onion; set aside. Spritz one side of each wonton wrapper with butter spray; press into mini muffin cups, buttered side down.

  Bake at 350° for 4-5 minutes or until golden brown. Fill each cup with about 1 tablespoon chicken salad. Bake 5 minutes longer. Sprinkle with paprika. **YIELD:** 3 DOZEN.

Nutrition Facts: One serving (1 piece) equals:
     46 calories
      1 g fat (1 g saturated fat)
     10 mg cholesterol
    101 mg sodium
      5 g carbohydrate
      1 g fiber
      4 g protein

Diabetic Exchange: 1 meat.

Banana Mocha Cooler

Cassandra Corridon, Frederick, Maryland

PREP/TOTAL TIME: 5 MIN.

  1 cup reduced-fat frozen vanilla yogurt
3/4 cup fat-free milk
  1 medium ripe banana, sliced
  1 teaspoon instant coffee granules
  1 cup ice cubes (7 to 8)

In a blender, combine all ingredients. Cover and process for 45-60 seconds or until frothy. Pour into glasses; serve immediately. **YIELD:** 3 SERVINGS.

Nutrition Facts: One serving (1 cup) equals:
    122 calories
      1 g fat (1 g saturated fat)
      5 mg cholesterol
     72 mg sodium
     24 g carbohydrate
      1 g fiber
      6 g protein

Diabetic Exchanges: 1 reduced-fat milk, 1/2 fruit.

Mini Rice Cake Snacks

Taste of Home Test Kitchen
Greendale, Wisconsin

PREP/TOTAL TIME: 10 MIN.

- 3 ounces reduced-fat cream cheese
- 1/4 cup orange marmalade
- 24 miniature honey-nut *or* cinnamon-apple rice cakes
- 2 medium fresh strawberries, sliced
- 3 tablespoons fresh blueberries
- 3 tablespoons mandarin orange segments
- 3 tablespoons pineapple tidbits

In a small mixing bowl, combine the cream cheese and marmalade until blended. Spread over rice cakes; top with fruit. **YIELD:** 2 DOZEN.

Nutrition Facts: One serving (3 pieces) equals:
- 81 calories
- 2 g fat (1 g saturated fat)
- 6 mg cholesterol
- 57 mg sodium
- 15 g carbohydrate
- 1 g fiber
- 2 g protein

Diabetic Exchanges: 1-1/2 starch, 1/2 fruit.

Hot Spinach Artichoke Dip

Michelle Wentz, Fort Polk, Louisiana

PREP/TOTAL TIME: 15 MIN.

- 1 small onion, finely chopped
- 2 packages (10 ounces *each*) frozen chopped spinach, thawed and squeezed dry
- 1 package (8 ounces) fat-free cream cheese, cubed
- 1 cup (8 ounces) reduced-fat sour cream

Mini Rice Cake Snacks

Hot Spinach Artichoke Dip

- 1 can (14 ounces) water-packed artichoke hearts, rinsed, drained and chopped
- 3/4 cup grated Parmesan cheese
- 1/4 teaspoon salt
- 1/8 teaspoon pepper
- 1/8 to 1/4 teaspoon crushed red pepper flakes
- 1/4 cup shredded reduced-fat cheddar cheese

Assorted reduced-fat melba toast *or* pita chips

In a large nonstick skillet coated with nonstick cooking spray, cook and stir onion until tender. Add spinach; cook and stir over medium heat until heated through. Reduce heat to low; stir in cream cheese and sour cream. Add artichoke hearts, Parmesan cheese, salt, pepper and red pepper flakes; cook for 1-2 minutes or until heated through.

Transfer to an ungreased 1-1/2-qt. microwave-safe dish; sprinkle with cheddar cheese. Cover and microwave on high for 2-3 minutes or until cheese is melted. Serve warm with melba toast or pita chips. **YIELD:** 4-1/2 CUPS.

Nutrition Facts: One serving (1/4 cup dip) equals:
- 71 calories
- 3 g fat (2 g saturated fat)
- 9 mg cholesterol
- 342 mg sodium
- 6 g carbohydrate
- 2 g fiber
- 6 g protein

Diabetic Exchanges: 1 lean meat, 1 vegetable.

Cheesy Zucchini Bites

Fudge Slush

Taste of Home Test Kitchen
Greendale, Wisconsin

PREP: 10 MIN. + FREEZING

   3/4 cup sugar
   1/2 cup baking cocoa
2-2/3 cups plus 2 tablespoons 1% milk, *divided*

In a saucepan, combine sugar and cocoa. Gradually stir in 2-2/3 cups milk; cook and stir over low heat until sugar is dissolved. Pour into a shallow pan or ice cube trays. Cover and freeze for 6 hours or overnight.

   Break frozen mixture into chunks; place in a blender or food processor. Add remaining milk; cover and process until smooth and slushy. **YIELD:** 6 SERVINGS.

Nutrition Facts: One serving (1/2 cup) equals:
            164 calories
              2 g fat (1 g saturated fat)
              7 mg cholesterol
            61 mg sodium
            35 g carbohydrate
              2 g fiber
              6 g protein

Diabetic Exchanges: 2 starch, 1/2 reduced-fat milk.

Cheesy Zucchini Bites

Amy Frombach, Bradford, Pennsylvania

PREP/TOTAL TIME: 30 MIN.

   5 medium zucchini (about 6 inches long)
   4 ounces blue cheese, crumbled
   3 tablespoons grated Parmesan cheese
   1 teaspoon dried basil
1/8 teaspoon pepper
   1 pint cherry tomatoes, thinly sliced

Cut zucchini into 3/4-in. slices. Using a melon baller or small spoon, scoop out the insides and discard, leaving the bottom intact. Place zucchini on an ungreased baking sheet; spoon 1/2 teaspoon crumbled blue cheese into each.

   Combine Parmesan cheese, basil and pepper; sprinkle half over blue cheese. Top each with a tomato slice; sprinkle with remaining Parmesan mixture.

   Bake at 400° for 5-7 minutes or until cheese is melted. Serve warm. **YIELD:** 35 APPETIZERS.

Nutrition Facts: One serving (1 piece) equals:
            19 calories
              1 g fat (1 g saturated fat)
              3 mg cholesterol
            58 mg sodium
              1 g carbohydrate
              1 g fiber
              1 g protein

Couscous-Stuffed Mushrooms

Lee Bremson, Kansas City, Missouri

PREP: 30 MIN.   **BAKE:** 15 MIN.

   18 medium fresh mushrooms
     3 green onions, chopped
     2 garlic cloves, minced
     1 tablespoon olive oil
     1 cup dry white wine *or* chicken broth
     2 tablespoons reduced-sodium soy sauce
FILLING:
   1/2 cup reduced-sodium chicken broth
   1/4 cup uncooked couscous
   1/3 cup minced fresh parsley
     2 tablespoons chopped fresh basil *or*
         2 teaspoons dried basil
   1/4 cup grated Romano cheese
     1 egg white, lightly beaten
     2 tablespoons chopped walnuts, toasted
   1/4 teaspoon salt
   1/8 teaspoon pepper

Remove mushroom stems; discard or save for another use. Set caps aside. In a large nonstick skillet, saute onions and garlic in oil for 1 minute. Stir in wine or broth and soy sauce; add mushroom caps. Bring to a boil. Reduce heat; cover and simmer for 5-6 minutes or until mushrooms are tender. Remove mushrooms with a slotted spoon, reserving liquid in skillet. Place mushrooms stem side down on paper towels.

In a saucepan, bring broth to a boil. Stir in couscous. Remove from the heat; cover and let stand for 5 minutes. Fluff with fork; add to reserved mushroom liquid. Cover and cook on low until liquid is absorbed, about 5 minutes. Add the next five ingredients and toss gently.

Sprinkle inside of mushroom caps with salt and pepper. Stuff with couscous mixture. Place in an 11-in. x 7-in. x 2-in. baking pan coated with nonstick cooking spray. Bake at 350° for 15-20 minutes or until stuffing is lightly browned. **YIELD:** 6 SERVINGS.

Nutrition Facts:
One serving (3 mushrooms) equals:

113	calories
5 g	fat (1 g saturated fat)
4 mg	cholesterol
416 mg	sodium
10 g	carbohydrate
2 g	fiber
5 g	protein

Diabetic Exchanges: 1 vegetable, 1 fat, 1/2 starch

Couscous-Stuffed Mushrooms

Feta-Spinach Melts

Alina Abbott, Mesa, Arizona

PREP/TOTAL TIME: 25 MIN.

- 3 packages (6 ounces *each*) fresh baby spinach, chopped
- 1 teaspoon water

Feta-Spinach Melts

- 1/2 cup crumbled feta cheese
- 1 plum tomatoes, seeded and chopped
- 1/4 cup finely chopped red onion
- 3 tablespoons fat-free mayonnaise
- 3 tablespoons fat-free sour cream
- 1 garlic cloves, minced
- 1/2 teaspoon salt
- 1/2 teaspoon dill weed
- 20 slices French baguette (1/2 inch thick)

In a large microwave-safe bowl, combine spinach and water. Cover and microwave on high for 1-1/2 to 2 minutes or until spinach is wilted, stirring twice; drain and squeeze dry. Add the feta cheese, tomato, onion, mayonnaise, sour cream, garlic, salt and dill weed; set aside.

Arrange bread on a baking sheet. Broil 4 in. from the heat for 1-2 minutes or until lightly toasted. Spread each with about 1 tablespoonful spinach mixture. Broil 3-4 minutes longer or until heated through. **YIELD:** 10 SERVINGS.

Editor's Note: This recipe was tested in a 1,100-watt microwave.

Nutrition Facts: One serving (2 slices) equals:

100	calories
3 g	fat (1 g saturated fat)
8 mg	cholesterol
400 mg	sodium
15 g	carbohydrate
2 g	fiber
4 g	protein

Diabetic Exchanges: 1 starch, 1/2 fat.

Savory Soups.

Whether it's a cool soup in summer or a steaming pot of hearty chili on a winter's day, soup is good for the body—and the spirit! Enjoy these naturally nutritious soups, stews and chilies in any season.

Apple Squash Soup

Apple Squash Soup

Crystal Ralph-Haughn, Bartlesville, Oklahoma

PREP/TOTAL TIME: 30 MIN.

1	large onion, chopped
1/2	teaspoon rubbed sage
2	tablespoons butter
1	can (14-1/2 ounces) chicken broth
3/4	cup water
2	medium Granny Smith *or* other tart apples, peeled and finely chopped
1	package (12 ounces) frozen mashed squash, thawed
1	teaspoon ground ginger
1/2	teaspoon salt
1/2	cup fat-free milk

In a saucepan, saute onion and sage in butter for 3 minutes or until tender. Add the broth, water and apples; bring to a boil. Reduce heat; cover and simmer for 12 minutes. Add the squash, ginger and salt; return to a boil. Reduce heat; simmer, uncovered, for 10 minutes. Cool until lukewarm.

In a food processor or blender, cover and process soup in batches until smooth; return to pan. Add milk; heat through (do not boil). **YIELD:** 5 SERVINGS.

Nutrition Facts: One serving (1 cup) equals:
142 calories
6 g fat (3 g saturated fat)
13 mg cholesterol
647 mg sodium
22 g carbohydrate
2 g fiber
3 g protein

Diabetic Exchanges: 1 fat, 1 starch, 1/2 fruit.

Broccoli Cheddar Soup

Jean Komlos, Plymouth, Michigan

PREP/TOTAL TIME: 20 MIN.

1	medium bunch broccoli, coarsely chopped (4 cups)
5	teaspoons cornstarch
1-1/2	cups fat-free milk
1	cup chicken broth
1	tablespoon butter
1	tablespoon sherry, optional
1/4	teaspoon salt
1/8	teaspoon pepper
1/8	teaspoon ground nutmeg
1	cup (4 ounces) shredded reduced-fat cheddar cheese
	Dash paprika

In a saucepan, bring 1 in. of water to a boil. Place broccoli in a steamer basket over water. Cover and steam for 5-8 minutes or until crisp-tender. Meanwhile, in another saucepan, combine the cornstarch, milk and broth until smooth. Bring to a boil; cook and stir for 2 minutes or until thickened.

Stir in the butter, sherry if desired, salt, pepper and nutmeg. Reduce heat. Add cheese and broccoli; heat just until cheese is melted. Sprinkle with paprika. **YIELD:** 3 SERVINGS.

Nutrition Facts: One serving (1 cup) equals:
203 calories
7 g fat (4 g saturated fat)
21 mg cholesterol
873 mg sodium
18 g carbohydrate
1 g fiber
18 g protein

Diabetic Exchanges: 2 vegetable, 1 lean meat, 1 fat, 1/2 fat-free milk.

Chicken Dumpling Soup

Brenda White, Morrison, Illinois

PREP: 15 MIN. COOK: 50 MIN.

1	pound boneless skinless chicken breasts, cut into 1-1/2-inch cubes
3	cans (14-1/2 ounces *each*) reduced-sodium chicken broth
3	cups water
4	medium carrots, chopped
1	medium onion, chopped
1	celery rib, chopped
1	teaspoon minced fresh parsley
1/2	teaspoon salt
1/4	teaspoon garlic powder
1/4	teaspoon poultry seasoning
1/4	teaspoon pepper
	DUMPLINGS:
3	egg whites
1/2	cup 1% cottage cheese
2	tablespoons water
1/4	teaspoon salt
1	cup all-purpose flour

In a large nonstick skillet coated with nonstick cooking spray, cook chicken until no longer pink. Add the broth, water, vegetables and seasonings. Bring to a boil. Reduce heat simmer, uncovered, for 30 minutes.

Meanwhile, for dumplings, beat the egg whites and cottage cheese in a mixing bowl. Add water and salt. Stir in the flour; mix well.

Bring soup to a boil. Drop dumplings by tablespoonfuls onto the boiling soup. Reduce heat; cover and simmer for 15 minutes or until a toothpick inserted in dumplings comes out clean (do not lift cover while simmering). Serve immediately. **YIELD:** 4 SERVINGS.

Nutrition Facts:
One serving (1-1/2 cups) equals:

363	calories
4 g	fat (2 g saturated fat)
73 mg	cholesterol
900 mg	sodium
39 g	carbohydrate
4 g	fiber
42 g	protein

Diabetic Exchanges: 4 lean meat, 2-1/2 starch.

Chicken Dumpling Soup

White Bean Fennel Soup `low fat` `meat less`

Donna Quinn, Salem, Wisconsin

PREP: 5 MIN.   **COOK:** 40 MIN.

- 1 large onion, chopped
- 1 small fennel bulb, thinly sliced
- 1 tablespoon olive oil
- 5 cups reduced-sodium chicken broth *or* vegetable broth
- 1 can (15 ounces) white kidney *or* cannellini beans, rinsed and drained
- 1 can (14-1/2 ounces) diced tomatoes, undrained
- 1 teaspoon dried thyme
- 1/4 teaspoon pepper
- 1 bay leaf
- 3 cups shredded fresh spinach

White Bean Fennel Soup

In a large saucepan, saute onion and fennel in oil until tender. Add the broth, beans, tomatoes, thyme, pepper and bay leaf; bring to a boil.

Reduce heat; cover and simmer for 30 minutes or until fennel is tender. Discard bay leaf. Add spinach; cook 3-4 minutes longer or until spinach is wilted. **YIELD:** 5 SERVINGS.

Nutrition Facts: One serving (1-1/2 cups) equals:

152	calories
3 g	fat (trace saturated fat)
0	cholesterol
976 mg	sodium
23 g	carbohydrate
7 g	fiber
8 g	protein

Diabetic Exchanges: 1 starch, 1 very lean meat, 1 vegetable.

Curry Carrot-Leek Soup

low fat

Valerie Engel, San Jose, California

PREP: 15 MIN. **COOK:** 30 MIN.

- 1 pound leeks (white portion only), thinly sliced
- 1 pound carrots, coarsely chopped
- 2 teaspoons butter
- 1 medium potato, peeled and diced
- 1/2 teaspoon curry powder
- 4 cups reduced-sodium chicken broth
- 1/4 teaspoon salt
- 1/4 teaspoon pepper

In a large saucepan, saute leeks and carrots in butter until leeks are tender. Add potato and curry powder; cook and stir for 2 minutes. Add broth, salt and pepper; bring to a boil.

Reduce heat; cover and simmer for 15-20 minutes or until the vegetables are very tender. Cool slightly.

In a food processor or blender, cover and process soup in batches until smooth. Return to the pan; heat through. **YIELD:** 6 SERVINGS.

Nutrition Facts: One serving (1 cup) equals:
- 108 calories
- 2 g fat (1 g saturated fat)
- 3 mg cholesterol
- 579 mg sodium
- 21 g carbohydrate
- 4 g fiber
- 4 g protein

Diabetic Exchanges: 1 starch, 1 vegetable.

Minestrone Soup

Minestrone Soup

low fat | meat less

Heather Ryan, Brown Deer, Wisconsin

PREP/TOTAL TIME: 30 MIN.

- 4 medium carrots, chopped
- 1 medium zucchini, sliced
- 1/4 cup chopped onion
- 1 garlic clove, minced
- 1 tablespoon olive oil
- 2 cans (14-1/2 ounces *each*) vegetable broth
- 3 cups V8 juice
- 1 can (15 ounces) garbanzo beans *or* chickpeas, rinsed and drained
- 1 can (14-1/2 ounces) diced tomatoes, undrained
- 1 cup frozen cut green beans
- 1/2 cup uncooked elbow macaroni
- 1 teaspoon dried basil
- 1 tablespoon minced fresh parsley

In a Dutch oven, cook the carrots, zucchini, onion and garlic in oil for 7 minutes or until onion is tender. Add the broth, V8 juice, garbanzo beans, tomatoes, green beans, macaroni and basil. Bring to a boil.

Reduce heat; simmer, uncovered, for 15 minutes. Stir in parsley. Cook 5 minutes longer or until macaroni is tender. **YIELD:** 8 SERVINGS.

Nutrition Facts:
One serving (1-1/2 cups) equals:
- 166 calories
- 3 g fat (trace saturated fat)
- 0 cholesterol
- 900 mg sodium
- 30 g carbohydrate
- 5 g fiber
- 6 g protein

Diabetic Exchanges: 3 vegetable, 1 starch, 1/2 fat.

Sunset Tomato Soup

meat less

Emily Beebe, Stoughton, Wisconsin

PREP: 5 MIN. **COOK:** 1 HOUR AND 5 MIN.

- 4 medium carrots, sliced
- 1 medium onion, chopped
- 1 tablespoon olive oil
- 3 to 4 large yellow tomatoes, peeled and coarsely chopped
- 4 plum tomatoes, peeled and coarsely chopped
- 1 can (14-1/2 ounces) reduced-sodium chicken broth *or* vegetable broth
- 1/2 teaspoon salt
- 1/4 teaspoon pepper
- 1-1/2 teaspoons snipped fresh dill *or* 3/4 teaspoon dill weed

In a Dutch oven or large kettle, saute carrots and onion in oil until onion is tender. Add

Cream of Wild Rice Soup

1 cup fat-free evaporated milk
1/4 cup minced chives

In a large saucepan, saute the onion, carrot and celery in butter until tender. Stir in flour until blended. Gradually add broth. Stir in the rice, chicken, salt and pepper. Bring to a boil over medium heat; cook and stir for 2 minutes or until thickened. Stir in milk; cook 3-5 minutes longer. Garnish with chives. **YIELD:** 10 SERVINGS (2-1/2 QUARTS).

Nutrition Facts: One serving (1 cup) equals:
　　　180 calories
　　　6 g fat (3 g saturated fat)
　　25 mg cholesterol
　899 mg sodium
　　　22 g carbohydrate
　　　2 g fiber
　　　11 g protein

Diabetic Exchanges: 1 starch, 1 very lean meat, 1 vegetable, 1 fat.

Chilled Bean Soup

Betty Nickels, Tampa, Florida

PREP: 15 MIN. + CHILLING

　4 cups chopped seeded tomatoes
　2 cups picante V8 juice
　1 can (15 ounces) black beans, rinsed and drained
　1 cup chopped cucumber
　1 cup chopped sweet red or yellow pepper
　1/2 cup chopped red onion
　2 tablespoons balsamic vinegar
　1 teaspoon sugar
　1/4 to 12 teaspoon hot pepper sauce
　1/4 teaspoon ground cumin
　1/4 teaspoon salt
　1/4 teaspoon pepper
　7 tablespoons reduced-fat sour cream
Sliced cucumber, optional

In a blender or food processor, combine tomatoes and V8 juice; cover and process just until blended. Transfer to a large bowl. Stir in the beans, chopped cucumber, sweet pepper, onion, vinegar, sugar and seasonings.

Cover and refrigerate for at least 4 hours or overnight. Serve with sour cream. Garnish with sliced cucumber if desired. **YIELD:** 7 SERVINGS.

Nutrition Facts: One serving (1 cup with 1 tablespoon sour cream) equals:
　　　122 calories
　　　2 g fat (1 g saturated fat)
　　4 mg cholesterol
　485 mg sodium
　　　21 g carbohydrate
　　　5 g fiber
　　　6 g protein

Diabetic Exchanges: 1 starch, 1 vegetable.

the tomatoes, broth, salt and pepper. Bring to a boil. Reduce heat; simmer, uncovered, for 45-60 minutes or until liquid is slightly reduced. Stir in dill; simmer 15 minutes longer. **YIELD:** 4 SERVINGS.

Nutrition Facts:
One serving (1-1/2 cups) equals:
　　　125 calories
　　　4 g fat (1 g saturated fat)
　　　0 cholesterol
　650 mg sodium
　　　20 g carbohydrate
　　　5 g fiber
　　　5 g protein

Diabetic Exchanges: 4 vegetable, 1/2 fat.

Cream of Wild Rice Soup

J. Beatrice Hintz, Neenah, Wisconsin

PREP/TOTAL TIME: 30 MIN.

　1 large onion, chopped
　1 large carrot, shredded
　1 celery rib, chopped
　1/4 cup butter
　1/2 cup all-purpose flour
　8 cups chicken broth
　3 cups cooked wild rice
　1 cup cubed cooked chicken breast
　1/4 teaspoon salt
　1/4 teaspoon pepper

Chilled Bean Soup

Cream of Cauliflower Soup

Cream of Cauliflower Soup
low carb

Karen Brown, West Lafayette, Ohio
PREP/TOTAL TIME: 20 MIN.

- 1/3 cup green onions (tops only)
- 2 tablespoons butter
- 2 tablespoons all-purpose flour
- 1/2 teaspoon salt
- 2 cups chicken broth
- 1 package (10 ounces) frozen cauliflower, thawed and chopped
- 2 cups 1% milk
- 1-1/2 cups (6 ounces) shredded reduced-fat cheddar cheese
- 2 tablespoons dry sherry, optional
- 1 tablespoon minced chives

In a saucepan, saute onions in butter until tender. Stir in flour and salt until blended. Gradually add broth. Bring to a boil; cook and stir for 2 minutes or until thickened. Reduce heat.

Add cauliflower; simmer for 2 minutes. Add the milk and cheese; cook and stir until cheese is melted. Stir in sherry if desired. Garnish with chives. **YIELD:** 6 SERVINGS.

Nutrition Facts: One serving (1 cup) equals:
- 190 calories
- 10 g fat (6 g saturated fat)
- 32 mg cholesterol
- 706 mg sodium
- 10 g carbohydrate
- 1 g fiber
- 15 g protein

Diabetic Exchanges: 2 lean meat, 1 vegetable, 1 fat.

Crab Bisque

Corney Welsh, Baton Rouge, Louisiana
PREP: 25 MIN.　**COOK:** 40 MIN.

- 2 cups chopped onions
- 1 cup chopped celery
- 1 cup chopped green pepper
- 4 garlic cloves, minced
- 1/4 cup reduced-fat margarine
- 4 cups diced peeled potatoes
- 2 cups fat-free milk
- 4 cups fat-free half-and-half
- 10 ounces reduced-fat process cheese (Velveeta), cut into 1-inch cubes
- 1 can (1 pound) crabmeat, drained, flaked and cartilage removed
- 3/4 teaspoon salt
- 1/4 teaspoon white pepper

In a soup kettle or Dutch oven, saute the onions, celery, green pepper and garlic in margarine until tender. Reduce heat to medium; add the potatoes and milk. Cook, uncovered, for 20 minutes or until potatoes are just tender, stirring occasionally.

Remove 1-1/2 cups of the potato mixture; mash and return to the pan. Reduce heat to low. Stir in half-and-half and process cheese. Cook and stir until cheese is melted. Add the crab, salt and pepper. Cook 10 minutes longer or until heated through. **YIELD:** 12 SERVINGS (3 QUARTS).

Nutrition Facts: One serving (1 cup) equals:
- 237 calories
- 5 g fat (2 g saturated fat)
- 44 mg cholesterol
- 802 mg sodium
- 27 g carbohydrate
- 2 g fiber
- 18 g protein

Diabetic Exchanges: 1 lean meat, 1 vegetable, 1 fat-free milk, 1/2 starch, 1/2 fat.

Meatball Alphabet Soup

Taste of Home Test Kitchen
Greendale, Wisconsin
PREP: 20 MIN.　**COOK:** 25 MIN.

- 1 egg, lightly beaten
- 2 tablespoons quick-cooking oats
- 2 tablespoons grated Parmesan cheese
- 1/4 teaspoon garlic powder
- 1/4 teaspoon Italian seasoning
- 1/2 pound lean ground turkey
- 1 cup chopped onion
- 1 cup chopped celery
- 1 cup chopped carrots
- 1 cup diced peeled potatoes
- 1 tablespoon olive oil
- 2 garlic cloves, minced

4 cans (14-1/2 ounces *each*) reduced-sodium chicken broth

1 can (28 ounces) diced tomatoes, undrained

1 can (6 ounces) tomato paste

1/4 cup minced fresh parsley

1 teaspoon dried basil

1 teaspoon dried thyme

3/4 cup uncooked alphabet pasta

In a bowl, combine the first five ingredients. Crumble turkey over mixture and mix well. Shape into 1/2-in. balls. In a nonstick skillet, cook meatballs in small batches over medium heat until no longer pink. Remove from the heat; set aside.

In a large saucepan or Dutch oven, saute the onion, celery, carrots and potatoes in oil for 5 minutes or until crisp-tender. Add garlic; saute 1 minute longer. Add the broth, tomatoes, tomato paste, parsley, basil and thyme; bring to a boil. Add pasta; cook for 5-6 minutes. Reduce heat; add meatballs. Simmer, uncovered, for 15-20 minutes or until vegetables are tender. **YIELD:** 9 SERVINGS.

Nutrition Facts:
One serving (1-1/2 cups) equals:
- 191 calories
- 5 g fat (1 g saturated fat)
- 44 mg cholesterol
- 679 mg sodium
- 26 g carbohydrate
- 4 g fiber
- 12 g protein

Diabetic Exchanges: 2 vegetable, 1 starch, 1 lean meat.

Harvest Corn Chicken Chowder

Janet Boote, Hull, Iowa

PREP: 20 MIN. **COOK:** 35 MIN.

1/2 cup chopped onion

1/2 cup chopped sweet red pepper

2 garlic cloves, minced

Meatball Alphabet Soup

Harvest Corn Chicken Chowder

1 tablespoon olive oil

1 cup cubed fully cooked ham

2 cups water

2 cups cubed red potatoes

1-1/2 cups fresh *or* frozen corn

1 teaspoon reduced-sodium chicken bouillon granules

3/4 teaspoon dried thyme

1/2 teaspoon poultry seasoning

1/2 teaspoon salt

1/4 teaspoon pepper

1 cup cubed cooked chicken breast

1 can (12 ounces) fat-free evaporated milk

3/4 cup 1% milk, divided

1/4 cup all-purpose flour

In a large saucepan, saute the onion, red pepper and garlic in oil until onion is tender. Add ham; cook and stir for 2 minutes. Stir in the water, potatoes, corn, bouillon, thyme, poultry seasoning, salt and pepper. Bring to a boil. Reduce heat; cover and simmer for 15 minutes or until potatoes are tender.

Add chicken; heat through. Stir in the evaporated milk and 1/2 cup milk; bring to a boil. Combine flour and remaining milk until smooth; gradually stir into soup. Cook and stir for 2 minutes or until thickened. **YIELD:** 5 SERVINGS.

Nutrition Facts: One serving (1-1/3 cups) equals:
- 306 calories
- 6 g fat (2 g saturated fat)
- 37 mg cholesterol
- 763 mg sodium
- 39 g carbohydrate
- 3 g fiber
- 25 g protein

Diabetic Exchanges: 2 lean meat, 1-1/2 starch, 1 fat-free milk.

Old-Fashioned Turkey Noodle Soup

Taste of Home Test Kitchen
Greendale, Wisconsin

PREP: 3-1/2 HOURS + CHILLING **COOK:** 45 MIN.

BROTH:

- 1 leftover turkey carcass (from a 12- to 14-pound turkey)
- 2 cooked turkey wings, meat removed
- 2 cooked turkey drumsticks, meat removed
- 1 turkey neck bone
- 1 medium unpeeled onion, cut into wedges
- 2 small unpeeled carrots, cut into chunks
- 6 to 8 garlic cloves, peeled
- 4 quarts plus 1 cup cold water, *divided*

SOUP:

- 3 quarts water
- 5 cups uncooked egg noodles
- 2 cups diced carrots
- 2 cups diced celery
- 3 cups cubed cooked turkey
- 1/4 cup minced fresh parsley
- 2-1/2 teaspoons salt
- 2 teaspoons dried thyme
- 1 teaspoon pepper

Place the turkey carcass, bones from wings and drumsticks, neck bone, onion, carrots and garlic in a 15-in. x 10-in. x 1-in. baking pan coated with nonstick cooking spray.

Bake, uncovered, at 400° for 1 hour, turning once.

Transfer the carcass, bones and vegetables to an 8-qt. soup kettle. Add 4 qts. cold water; set aside. Pour remaining cold water into baking pan, stirring to loosen browned bits. Add to kettle. Bring to a boil. Reduce heat; cover and simmer for 3-4 hours.

Cool slightly. Strain broth; discard bones and vegetables. Set soup kettle in an ice-water bath until cooled, stirring occasionally. Cover and refrigerate overnight.

Skim fat from broth. Cover and bring to a boil. Reduce heat to a simmer. Meanwhile, in a Dutch oven, bring 3 qts. water to a boil. Add noodles and carrots; cook for 4 minutes. Add celery; cook 5-7 minutes longer or until noodles and vegetables are tender. Drain; add to simmering broth. Add cubed turkey; heat through. Stir in the parsley, salt, thyme and pepper. **YIELD:** 10 SERVINGS (ABOUT 4 QUARTS).

Nutrition Facts:
One serving (1-1/2 cups) equals:
188 calories
4 g fat (1 g saturated fat)
69 mg cholesterol
663 mg sodium
17 g carbohydrate
2 g fiber
20 g protein

Diabetic Exchanges: 2 lean meat, 1 starch.

Old-Fashioned Turkey Noodle Soup

Zippy Three-Bean Chili

Agnes Hamilton, Scott Depot, West Virginia

PREP: 10 MIN. **COOK:** 1 HOUR 20 MIN.

- 1 pound lean ground beef
- 1/2 cup chopped onion
- 1 cup chopped fresh mushrooms
- 1/2 cup chopped green pepper
- 1/2 cup chopped sweet red pepper
- 1 garlic clove, minced
- 2 cups water
- 1 can (14-1/2 ounces) diced tomatoes and green chilies, undrained
- 1 envelope reduced-sodium taco seasoning
- 1 can (15-1/2 ounces) great northern beans, rinsed and drained
- 1 can (15 ounces) black beans, rinsed and drained
- 1 can (15 ounces) pinto beans, rinsed and drained
- 8 tablespoons shredded reduced-fat cheddar cheese, *divided*

In a large saucepan, cook beef and onion over medium heat until meat is no longer pink; drain. Add the mushrooms, peppers and garlic; cook and stir 3 minutes longer or until vegetables are almost tender. Stir in the water, tomatoes and taco seasoning.

3 cups fat-free milk

2 cups shredded zucchini

2 tablespoons cornstarch

1/4 cup cold water

In a large saucepan, saute onions and garlic in butter until tender. Add celery and carrots; cook and stir for 4 minutes. Stir in the water, bouillon, salt and thyme. Add potatoes. Bring to a boil.

Reduce heat; cover and simmer about 15 minutes or until potatoes are tender. Stir in milk and zucchini. Bring to a boil. In a small bowl, combine cornstarch and cold water until smooth. Gradually whisk into soup. Return to a boil; cook and stir for 2 minutes or until slightly thickened. **YIELD:** 6 SERVINGS.

Nutrition Facts: One serving (1-1/2 cups) equals:
- 175 calories
- 4 g fat (2 g saturated fat)
- 13 mg cholesterol
- 651 mg sodium
- 28 g carbohydrate
- 3 g fiber
- 7 g protein

Diabetic Exchanges: 1 starch, 1 vegetable, 1 fat, 1/2 fat-free milk.

Zippy Three-Bean Chili

Bring to boil. Reduce heat; simmer, uncovered, for 30 minutes. Add beans; simmer 30 minutes longer. Sprinkle each serving with 1 tablespoon cheese. **YIELD:** 8 SERVINGS (2 QUARTS).

Nutrition Facts: One serving (1 cup chili with 1 tablespoon cheese) equals:
- 269 calories
- 6 g fat (3 g saturated fat)
- 33 mg cholesterol
- 738 mg sodium
- 32 g carbohydrate
- 8 g fiber
- 21 g protein

Diabetic Exchanges: 2 lean meat, 1-1/2 starch, 1 vegetable.

Celery Zucchini Soup

meat less

Alyson Sprague, Sewickley, Pennsylvania

PREP/TOTAL TIME: 30 MIN.

3 green onions, thinly sliced

2 garlic cloves, minced

2 tablespoons butter

4 celery ribs, chopped

2 medium carrots, chopped

2 cups water

1 tablespoon reduced-sodium chicken bouillon granules *or* 3 vegetable bouillon cubes

3/4 teaspoon salt

3/4 teaspoon dried thyme

5 medium red potatoes, cut into small chunks (about 1 pound)

Summer Soup

low fat · meat less

Liz Fick, Litchville, North Dakota

PREP: 15 MIN. + CHILLING

1 bottle (46 ounces) reduced-sodium V8 juice

2 cans (14-1/2 ounces *each*) Italian diced tomatoes, undrained

2 cans (5-1/2 ounces *each*) spicy hot V8 juice

1 medium green pepper, chopped

1 cup shredded carrots

1/2 cup chopped green onions

1/2 cup reduced-fat zesty Italian salad dressing

2 tablespoons lemon juice

1 tablespoon sugar

2 teaspoons Worcestershire sauce

1 garlic clove, minced

3/4 teaspoon celery salt

1/2 teaspoon salt

In a large bowl, combine all of the ingredients. Cover and refrigerate for at least 2 hours before serving. **YIELD:** 12 SERVINGS.

Nutrition Facts: One serving (1 cup) equals:
- 95 calories
- 2 g fat (trace saturated fat)
- 0 cholesterol
- 695 mg sodium
- 16 g carbohydrate
- 2 g fiber
- 2 g protein

Diabetic Exchanges: 3 vegetable, 1/2 fat.

Summer Soup

Peppery Sweet Potato Soup `low fat`

Suzan Wiener, Spring Hill, Florida

PREP: 35 MIN. + COOLING   **COOK:** 40 MIN.

- 1   jalapeno pepper
- 2   medium sweet red peppers
- 5   garlic cloves
- 1   teaspoon olive oil
- 5   cups reduced-sodium chicken broth
- 4   cups cold mashed sweet potatoes (prepared without milk *or* butter)
- 1/2 teaspoon salt
- 1   cup fat-free milk

Broil whole jalapeno and red peppers 4 in. from the heat until the skins blister, about 7 minutes. With tongs, rotate peppers a quarter turn. Broil and rotate until all sides are blistered and blackened. Immediately place peppers in a bowl; cover with plastic wrap. Let stand for 15-20 minutes. Peel off and discard charred skin; remove stems and seeds. Finely chop peppers.

Place garlic on a double thickness of heavy-duty foil; drizzle with oil. Wrap foil around garlic. Bake at 425° for 15-20 minutes. Cool for 10-15 minutes. Squeeze softened garlic from skins into a small bowl and mash.

In a large saucepan or soup kettle, combine the peppers, garlic, broth, sweet potatoes and salt. Bring to a boil. Reduce heat; simmer, uncovered, for 25 minutes, stirring occasionally. Stir in milk; heat through. Cool slightly.

In a food processor or blender, cover and process soup in batches until smooth; return all to the pan and heat through. **YIELD:** 10 SERVINGS (2-1/2 QUARTS).

Editor's Note: When cutting or seeding hot peppers, use rubber or plastic gloves to protect your hands. Avoid touching your face.

Nutrition Facts: One serving (1 cup) equals:
- 166   calories
- 1 g   fat (trace saturated fat)
- 1 mg cholesterol
- 613 mg sodium
- 36 g carbohydrate
- 3 g   fiber
- 4 g   protein

Diabetic Exchange: 2 starch.

Tomato Green Bean Soup

Tomato Green Bean Soup `low fat` `low carb`

Bernice Nolan, Granite City, Illinois

PREP: 10 MIN.   **COOK:** 25 MIN.

- 1   cup chopped onion
- 1   cup chopped carrots
- 2   teaspoons butter
- 6   cups chicken broth
- 1   pound fresh green beans, cut into 1-inch pieces
- 1   garlic clove, minced
- 3   cups diced fresh tomatoes
- 1/4 cup minced fresh basil *or* 1 tablespoon dried basil
- 1/2 teaspoon salt
- 1/4 teaspoon pepper

In a large saucepan, saute onion and carrots in butter for 5 minutes. Stir in the broth, beans and garlic; bring to a boil.

Reduce heat; cover and simmer for 20 minutes or until vegetables are tender. Stir in the tomatoes, basil, salt and pepper. Cover and simmer 5 minutes longer. **YIELD:** 9 SERVINGS.

Nutrition Facts: One serving (1 cup) equals:
- 71   calories
- 1 g   fat (1 g saturated fat)
- 2 mg cholesterol
- 779 mg sodium
- 12 g carbohydrate
- 4 g   fiber
- 3 g   protein

Diabetic Exchanges: 2 vegetable, 1/2 fat.

Creamy Asparagus Soup low carb meat less

Adele Long, Sterling Heights, Michigan

PREP/TOTAL TIME: 30 MIN.

- 2 green onions, chopped
- 1 garlic clove, minced
- 1 tablespoon butter
- 2 cans (14-1/2 ounces *each*) reduced-sodium chicken broth *or* vegetable broth
- 1 pound fresh asparagus, trimmed and cut into 1-inch pieces
- 1/2 teaspoon salt
- 1/2 to 3/4 teaspoon dried thyme
- 1/8 teaspoon pepper
- 1 bay leaf
- 2 tablespoons all-purpose flour
- 3 tablespoons water
- 1/4 cup reduced-fat sour cream
- 1 teaspoon grated lemon peel

In a large saucepan, saute onions and garlic in butter until tender. Add the broth, asparagus, salt, thyme, pepper and bay leaf. Bring to a boil. Reduce heat; cover and simmer for 8-10 minutes or until asparagus is tender. Drain asparagus, reserving cooking liquid. Discard bay leaf. Cool slightly.

In a food processor or blender, combine asparagus and 1/2 cup cooking liquid; cover and process until smooth. Return pureed asparagus and remaining cooking liquid to pan.

Combine the flour and water until smooth; stir into soup. Bring to a boil; cook and stir for 1-2 minutes or until thickened. Garnish each serving with sour cream and lemon peel. **YIELD:** 4 SERVINGS.

Nutrition Facts: One serving (1 cup soup with 1 tablespoon sour cream) equals:

- 107 calories
- 4 g fat (3 g saturated fat)
- 13 mg cholesterol
- 876 mg sodium
- 11 g carbohydrate
- 3 g fiber
- 7 g protein

Diabetic Exchanges: 1 vegetable, 1 fat, 1/2 starch.

Skinny Tortilla Soup

Sharon Adams, Columbus, Ohio

PREP/TOTAL TIME: 30 MIN.

- 1 can (16 ounces) fat-free refried beans
- 1 can (15 ounces) black beans, rinsed and drained
- 1 can (14-1/2 ounces) reduced-sodium chicken broth
- 1-1/2 cups frozen corn
- 3/4 cup chunky salsa

Skinny Tortilla Soup

- 3/4 cup cubed cooked chicken breast
- 1/2 cup water
- 2 cups (8 ounces) shredded reduced-fat cheddar cheese, *divided*
- 28 baked tortilla chips, *divided*

In a large saucepan, combine the first seven ingredients. Bring to a boil. Reduce heat; cover and simmer for 10 minutes. Add 1 cup cheese; cook and stir over low heat until melted.

Crumble half of the tortilla chips into soup bowls. Ladle soup over chips. Top each serving with two crumbled chips; sprinkle with remaining cheese. **YIELD:** 7 SERVINGS.

Nutrition Facts: One serving (1 cup) equals:

- 295 calories
- 7 g fat (5 g saturated fat)
- 34 mg cholesterol
- 900 mg sodium
- 35 g carbohydrate
- 1 g fiber
- 25 g protein

Diabetic Exchanges: 2-1/2 starch, 2 lean meat.

Tomato Basil Soup

Tomato Basil Soup

Chris Baker, South Lake Tahoe, California

PREP: 10 MIN. **COOK:** 1 HOUR 20 MIN.

4	medium carrots, peeled and finely chopped
1	large onion, finely chopped
1/4	cup butter
1	can (49 ounces) reduced-sodium chicken broth *or* 6 cups vegetable broth, *divided*
1	can (29 ounces) tomato puree
5	teaspoons dried basil
1-1/2	teaspoons sugar
1/2	teaspoon salt
1/2	teaspoon white pepper
1	can (12 ounces) fat-free evaporated milk

In a Dutch oven, cook carrots and onion in butter over medium-low heat for 30 minutes or until vegetables are tender, stirring occasionally. Remove from the heat and cool slightly.

In a blender or food processor, place 1/2 broth and the cooled vegetables; cover and process until blended. Return to the Dutch oven. Stir in the tomato puree, basil, sugar, salt, pepper and remaining broth. Bring to a boil.

Reduce heat; simmer, uncovered, for 30 minutes. Reduce heat to low. Gradually stir in evaporated milk; heat through (do not boil). **YIELD:** 6 SERVINGS (2-1/4 QUARTS).

Nutrition Facts:
One serving (1-1/2 cups) equals:
- 201 calories
- 8 g fat (5 g saturated fat)
- 23 mg cholesterol
- 1,004 mg sodium
- 24 g carbohydrate
- 3 g fiber
- 10 g protein

Diabetic Exchanges: 3 vegetable, 1-1/2 fat, 1/2 fat-free milk.

Fresh Corn Chowder

Margaret Olien, New Richmond, Wisconsin

PREP/TOTAL TIME: 30 MIN.

4	large ears sweet corn, husks removed
1	large onion, chopped
1	celery rib, chopped
1	tablespoon butter
1-1/2	cups diced peeled potatoes
1	cup water
2	teaspoons chicken bouillon granules
1/4	teaspoon dried thyme
1/4	teaspoon pepper
6	tablespoons all-purpose flour
3	cups 2% milk

Cut corn off the cob; set aside. In a large saucepan, saute onion and celery in butter until tender. Add the potatoes, water, bouillon, thyme, pepper and corn. Bring to a boil.

Reduce heat; cover and simmer for 15 minutes or until potatoes are tender. Combine the flour and milk until smooth; gradually stir into soup. Bring to a boil; cook and stir for 2 minutes or until thickened. **YIELD:** 7 SERVINGS.

Nutrition Facts: One serving (1 cup) equals:
- 204 calories
- 5 g fat (3 g saturated fat)
- 13 mg cholesterol
- 410 mg sodium
- 35 g carbohydrate
- 4 g fiber
- 8 g protein

Diabetic Exchanges: 2 starch, 1/2 reduced-fat milk.

Thrive-on-Five Soup

Robert Hermann, Stockton, California

PREP: 25 MIN. **COOK:** 70 MIN.

1	cup chopped onion
1/2	cup chopped celery
1/2	cup chopped green pepper
1/2	cup chopped peeled turnip
1/3	cup sliced fresh carrot
1	tablespoon olive oil
3	cups reduced-sodium chicken broth
1	can (14-1/2 ounces) stewed tomatoes, cut up
1-1/2	teaspoons dried thyme
1	bay leaf
1	cup coarsely chopped green cabbage
1	cup cut fresh green beans (2-inch pieces)
1-1/2	cups cubed cooked turkey breast
1	tablespoon cider vinegar
1/2	teaspoon salt
1/8	teaspoon pepper

In a large saucepan, saute the onion, celery, green pepper, turnip and carrot in oil for 7 minutes. Stir in the broth, tomatoes, thyme and bay leaf. Bring to a boil. Reduce heat; cover and simmer for 30 minutes.

Stir in cabbage and beans; return to a boil. Reduce heat; cover and simmer for 10 minutes. Stir in turkey; simmer 5 minutes longer. Stir in the vinegar, salt and pepper; heat through. Discard bay leaf. **YIELD:** 7 SERVINGS.

Nutrition Facts: One serving (1 cup) equals:
- 112 calories
- 3 g fat (1 g saturated fat)
- 26 mg cholesterol
- 550 mg sodium
- 9 g carbohydrate
- 3 g fiber
- 12 g protein

Diabetic Exchanges: 2 vegetable, 1 very lean meat, 1/2 fat.

Sausage Kale Soup

Susan Pursell, Fountain Valley, California

PREP: 10 MIN. **COOK:** 25 MIN.

- 3/4 cup chopped onion
- 2 garlic cloves, minced
- 1 tablespoon olive oil
- 4 cups reduced-sodium chicken broth
- 2 medium potatoes, peeled and cubed
- 1/4 teaspoon salt
- 1/4 teaspoon pepper
- 1 pound fresh kale, trimmed and chopped
- 1 can (15 ounces) white kidney *or* cannellini beans, rinsed and drained
- 1/2 pound reduced-fat fully cooked Polish sausage *or* turkey kielbasa, sliced

In a large saucepan or Dutch oven, saute onion and garlic in oil until tender. Add the broth, potatoes, salt and pepper. Bring to a boil. Reduce heat; cover and simmer for 10-15 minutes or until potatoes are tender.

Using a potato masher, mash potatoes slightly. Add the kale, beans and sausage; cook over medium-low heat until kale is tender. **YIELD:** 7 SERVINGS.

Nutrition Facts: One serving (1 cup) equals:
- 194 calories
- 4 g fat (1 g saturated fat)
- 14 mg cholesterol
- 823 mg sodium
- 28 g carbohydrate
- 50 g fiber
- 11 g protein

Diabetic Exchanges: 1-1/2 starch, 1 lean meat, 1 vegetable.

Seafood Soup

low carb

Valerie Bradley, Beaverton, Oregon

PREP: 20 MIN. **COOK:** 50 MIN.

- 1/2 cup chopped onion
- 1/2 cup chopped green pepper

Sausage Kale Soup

Seafood Soup

- 3 tablespoons minced fresh parsley
- 1 tablespoon olive oil
- 1 cup chopped carrots
- 1 garlic clove, minced
- 1 can (15 ounces) tomato sauce
- 1 can (14-1/2 ounces) diced tomatoes
- 3/4 cup white wine *or* chicken broth
- 1 bay leaf
- 1/2 teaspoon dried oregano
- 1/4 teaspoon dried basil
- 1/4 teaspoon pepper
- 3/4 pound salmon fillets, skinned and cut into 3/4-inch cubes
- 1/2 pound uncooked medium shrimp, peeled and deveined

In a large saucepan, saute the onion, green pepper and parsley in oil until tender. Add carrots and garlic; cook and stir for 3 minutes. Stir in the tomato sauce, tomatoes, wine or broth and seasonings. Bring to a boil.

Reduce heat; cover and simmer for 30 minutes. Stir in salmon and shrimp. Cover and cook 7-10 minutes longer or until fish flakes easily with a fork and shrimp turn pink. Discard bay leaf. **YIELD:** 6 SERVINGS.

Nutrition Facts: One serving (1 cup) equals:
- 212 calories
- 9 g fat (2 g saturated fat)
- 87 mg cholesterol
- 620 mg sodium
- 13 g carbohydrate
- 3 g fiber
- 19 g protein

Diabetic Exchanges: 3 lean meat, 2 vegetable.

Spinach Lentil Stew

Alice McEachern, Surrey, British Columbia

PREP: 10 MIN. **COOK:** 40 MIN.

- 1/2 cup chopped onion
- 2 garlic cloves, minced
- 1 tablespoon canola oil
- 5 cups water
- 1 cup lentils, rinsed
- 4 teaspoons vegetable *or* chicken bouillon granules
- 3 teaspoons Worcestershire sauce
- 1/2 teaspoon salt
- 1/2 teaspoon dried thyme
- 1/4 teaspoon pepper
- 1 bay leaf
- 1 cup chopped carrots
- 1 can (14-1/2 ounces) diced tomatoes, undrained
- 1 package (10 ounces) frozen chopped spinach, thawed and squeezed dry
- 1 tablespoon red wine vinegar

In a large saucepan, saute onion and garlic in oil until tender. Add the water, lentils, bouillon, Worcestershire sauce, salt, thyme, pepper and bay leaf; bring to a boil. Reduce heat; cover and simmer for 20 minutes.

Add carrots, tomatoes and spinach; return to a boil. Reduce heat; cover and simmer 15-20 minutes longer or until lentils are tender. Stir in vinegar. Discard bay leaf before serving. **YIELD:** 6 SERVINGS.

Nutrition Facts:
One serving (1-1/4 cups) equals:
- 168 calories
- 3 g fat (trace saturated fat)
- trace cholesterol
- 1,123 mg sodium
- 27 g carbohydrate
- 10 g fiber
- 10 g protein

Diabetic Exchanges: 2 vegetable, 1 starch, 1 lean meat.

Green Chili Stew

Doris Johns, Hurst, Texas

PREP: 10 MIN. **COOK:** 35 MIN.

- 1-1/2 pounds boneless pork loin roast, cut into 3/4-inch cubes
- 2 tablespoons olive oil
- 1 large onion, diced
- 1 to 2 jalapeno peppers, seeded and chopped
- 3 garlic cloves, minced
- 1-1/2 teaspoons ground cumin
- 1 teaspoon salt
- 1/4 teaspoon white pepper
- 1 bay leaf
- 5 medium potatoes, peeled and cubed
- 3 cups water
- 1 can (14-1/2 ounces) diced tomatoes, undrained
- 3 cans (4 ounces *each*) chopped green chilies

In a Dutch oven or large saucepan, cook pork in oil until no longer pink. Add the onion, jalapenos, garlic, cumin, salt, pepper and bay leaf; saute until onion is tender. Add potatoes and water; bring to boil.

Reduce heat; cover and simmer for 15-20 minutes or until potatoes are tender. Add tomatoes and chilies; simmer 10 minutes longer. Discard bay leaf before serving. **YIELD:** 8 SERVINGS.

Editor's Note: When cutting or seeding hot peppers, use rubber or plastic gloves to protect your hands. Avoid touching your face.

Nutrition Facts: One serving (1-1/3 cups) equals:
- 253 calories
- 8 g fat (2 g saturated fat)
- 47 mg cholesterol
- 707 mg sodium
- 24 g carbohydrate
- 4 g fiber
- 22 g protein

Diabetic Exchanges: 2-1/2 meat, 1-1/2 vegetable, 1 starch.

Spinach Lentil Stew

Chilled Cucumber Soup

Savory Mushroom-Barley Soup

Christine Wright, Franklinton, North Carolina

PREP: 5 MIN.   COOK: 45 MIN.

- 4 cups water
- 3/4 cup uncooked medium pearl barley
- 4 medium onions, chopped
- 2 celery ribs, chopped
- 1 tablespoon olive oil
- 1-1/2 pounds sliced fresh mushrooms
- 6 cups reduced-sodium beef broth *or* vegetable broth
- 2 cups sliced carrots
- 1 can (6 ounces) tomato paste
- 1/2 teaspoon salt
- 1/4 teaspoon pepper
- 1/2 cup minced fresh parsley

In a large saucepan, bring water and barley to a boil. Reduce heat; cover and simmer for 30 minutes or until barley is partially cooked (do not drain).

Meanwhile, in a soup kettle or Dutch oven, saute onions and celery in oil until tender. Add mushrooms; cook and stir for 5 minutes. Stir in the broth, carrots, tomato paste and barley mixture. Bring to a boil over medium heat.

Reduce heat; cover and simmer for 30 minutes, stirring occasionally. Stir in salt and pepper. Sprinkle with parsley. YIELD: 10 SERVINGS (ABOUT 3-1/2 QUARTS).

Nutrition Facts:
One serving (1-1/2 cups) equals:
- 136 calories
- 2 g fat (1 g saturated fat)
- 3 mg cholesterol
- 416 mg sodium
- 26 g carbohydrate
- 6 g fiber
- 6 g protein

Diabetic Exchanges: 2 vegetable, 1 starch.

Chilled Cucumber Soup

Shirley Kidd, New London, Minnesota

PREP: 10 MIN. + CHILLING

- 2 medium cucumbers
- 2 cups buttermilk
- 1/2 cup reduced-fat sour cream
- 1-1/2 teaspoons sugar
- 1 teaspoon dill weed
- 1/2 teaspoon salt
- 1/8 teaspoon white pepper
- 2 green onions, chopped
- Fresh dill, optional

Cut four thin slices of cucumber; set aside for garnish. Peel and finely chop remaining cucumbers. In a bowl, combine the buttermilk, sour cream, sugar, dill, salt, pepper, green onions and chopped cucumbers; mix well. Refrigerate for 4 hours or overnight. Garnish with cucumber slices and fresh dill if desired. YIELD: 4 SERVINGS.

Nutrition Facts: One serving (1 cup) equals:
- 110 calories
- 4 g fat (3 g saturated fat)
- 15 mg cholesterol
- 445 mg sodium
- 13 g carbohydrate
- 1 g fiber
- 7 g protein

Diabetic Exchanges: 1 vegetable, 1/2 reduced-fat milk.

Savory Mushroom-Barley Soup

Taco Twist Soup

Colleen Zertler, Menomonie, Wisconsin

PREP/TOTAL TIME: 20 MIN.

    1   medium onion, chopped
    2   garlic cloves, minced
    2   teaspoons olive oil
    3   cups reduced-sodium beef broth *or*
         vegetable broth
    1   can (15 ounces) black beans, rinsed and
         drained
    1   can (14-1/2 ounces) diced tomatoes
1-1/2   cups picante sauce
    1   cup uncooked spiral pasta
    1   small green pepper, chopped
    2   teaspoons chili powder
    1   teaspoon ground cumin
  1/2   cup shredded reduced-fat cheddar cheese
    3   tablespoons reduced-fat sour cream

In a large saucepan, saute onion and garlic in oil until tender. Add the broth, beans, tomatoes, picante sauce, pasta, green pepper and seasonings. Bring to a boil, stirring frequently. Reduce heat; cover and simmer for 10-12 minutes or until pasta is tender, stirring occasionally. Serve with cheese and sour cream. **YIELD:** 6 SERVINGS.

Nutrition Facts: One serving (1 cup) equals:
       216   calories
         5 g fat (2 g saturated fat)
        12 mg cholesterol
     1,052 mg sodium
        33 g carbohydrate
         6 g fiber
        10 g protein

Diabetic Exchanges: 2 vegetable, 1-1/2 starch, 1 lean meat, 1/2 fat.

Tuscan Turkey Sausage Soup

Thomas Licking, Green Lake, Wisconsin

PREP/TOTAL TIME: 30 MIN.

   12   ounces turkey Italian sausage links
    4   cups reduced-sodium chicken broth
    1   can (10-3/4 ounces) reduced-fat reduced-
         sodium condensed cream of chicken soup,
         undiluted
    1   can (8 ounces) mushroom stems and
         pieces, drained
    1   small onion, chopped
    1   tablespoon Italian seasoning
  1/4   teaspoon salt-free garlic and herb
         seasoning
  1/8   teaspoon caraway seeds
  1/8   teaspoon fennel seed, crushed
    1   can (15-1/2 ounces) great northern beans,
         rinsed and drained
    1   small leek (white potion only), cut into
         1-inch strips

In a nonstick skillet coated with nonstick cooking spray, cook sausage over medium heat until no longer pink; drain. Let cool and slice.

In a large saucepan, whisk together the broth, soup, mushrooms, onion, Italian seasoning, garlic and herb seasoning, caraway seeds and fennel seed. Add sausage. Bring to a boil.

Reduce heat; simmer, uncovered, for 5 minutes. Add beans and leek. Simmer 10 minutes longer or until vegetables are tender. **YIELD:** 8 SERVINGS.

Nutrition Facts: One serving (1 cup) equals:
       181   calories
         5 g fat (2 g saturated fat)
        26 mg cholesterol
       978 mg sodium
        19 g carbohydrate
         4 g fiber
        14 g protein

Diabetic Exchanges: 2 lean meat, 1 starch.

Taco Twist Soup

Cream of Vegetable Soup

Clam Chowder

Chris Sheetz, Olmsted Falls, Ohio

PREP: 10 MIN. **COOK:** 35 MIN.

- 2 cups sliced fresh mushrooms
- 4 celery ribs with leaves, chopped
- 1 medium onion, chopped
- 2 tablespoons reduced-fat margarine
- 2 cans (10-3/4 ounces *each*) reduced-fat reduced-sodium condensed cream of mushroom soup, undiluted
- 1 bottle (8 ounces) clam juice
- 1/2 cup white wine *or* chicken broth
- 6 medium unpeeled red potatoes, cubed
- 1/2 teaspoon salt
- 1/4 teaspoon white pepper
- 3 cans (6-1/2 ounces *each*) minced clams, undrained

In a Dutch oven or soup kettle, saute the mushrooms, celery and onion in margarine until tender. In a bowl, whisk the soup, clam juice and wine or broth; stir into vegetable mixture. Add the potatoes, salt and pepper. Bring to a boil.

Reduce heat; cover and simmer for 25 minutes. Add clams; cover and simmer for 5-15 minutes or until potatoes are tender. **YIELD:** 10 SERVINGS.

Editor's Note: This recipe was tested with Parkay Light stick margarine.

Nutrition Facts: One serving (1 cup) equals:
- 202 calories
- 4 g fat (1 g saturated fat)
- 43 mg cholesterol
- 497 mg sodium
- 24 g carbohydrate
- 2 g fiber
- 17 g protein

Diabetic Exchanges: 2 very lean meat, 1-1/2 starch, 1/2 fat.

Cream of Vegetable Soup

Vicki Kamstra, Spokane, Washington

PREP: 25 MIN. **COOK:** 30 MIN. + COOLING

- 2 cups chopped sweet onions
- 1-1/2 cups chopped carrots
- 1 cup chopped celery
- 2 tablespoons canola oil
- 4 cups cubed peeled potatoes
- 1 large head cauliflower, broken into florets
- 3 cans (14-1/2 ounces *each*) reduced-sodium chicken broth *or* vegetable broth
- 2 teaspoons salt
- 2 teaspoons white pepper
- 1/2 cup half-and-half

Fresh basil

In a large kettle or Dutch oven, saute onions, carrots and celery in oil until onions are tender. Add potatoes and cauliflower; saute 5-6 minutes longer. Add the broth, salt and pepper. Bring to a boil. Reduce heat; cover and simmer for 10-12 minutes or until vegetables are tender. Let stand until cool.

In a food processor or blender, cover and process soup in batches until smooth. Return to pan. Stir in cream; heat through (do not boil). Garnish with fresh basil. **YIELD:** 11 SERVINGS.

Nutrition Facts: One serving (1 cup) equals:
- 132 calories
- 4 g fat (1 g saturated fat)
- 5 mg cholesterol
- 773 mg sodium
- 21 g carbohydrate
- 4 g fiber
- 5 g protein

Diabetic Exchanges: 1 starch, 1 vegetable, 1/2 fat.

Tart Cherry Soup

Neva Arthur, New Berlin, Wisconsin

PREP: 5 MIN. **COOK:** 15 MIN. + CHILLING

Tart Cherry Soup

2	cans (14-1/2 ounces *each*) water-packed pitted tart cherries
1/2	cup orange juice
1/2	cup sugar
2	tablespoons lime juice
1	teaspoon grated lime peel
1/2	teaspoon ground cinnamon
4	lime slices

Place the cherries in a blender or food processor; cover and process until finely chopped. Transfer to a saucepan; add the orange juice, sugar, lime juice, peel and cinnamon. Bring to a boil. Reduce heat; cover and simmer for 10 minutes. Refrigerate until chilled. Garnish with lime slices. **YIELD:** 4 SERVINGS.

Nutrition Facts: One serving (1 cup) equals:
198 calories
1 g fat (1 g saturated fat)
0 cholesterol
15 mg sodium
49 g carbohydrate
3 g fiber
2 g protein

Diabetic Exchanges: 1-1/2 starch, 1-1/2 fruit.

Lemon Lentil Soup

Jean Rawlings, Saskatoon, Saskatchewan

PREP: 10 MIN. **COOK:** 1 HOUR

1	cup chopped leeks (white portion only)
2	tablespoons canola oil
1	can (15 ounces) tomato puree
1	cup chopped celery
1	cup chopped carrots
1/4	cup chopped peeled parsnips
2	tablespoons dried basil
8	cups water
1-1/2	cups lentils, rinsed
2	bay leaves
1	tablespoon grated lemon peel
1-1/2	teaspoons salt
1	teaspoon dill weed
1/2	teaspoon pepper
2	to 3 tablespoons lemon juice

In a large saucepan, saute leeks in oil until tender. Add the tomato puree, celery, carrots, parsnips and basil; saute for 3-4 minutes. Add water; bring to a boil. Add lentils and bay leaves.

Reduce heat; cover and simmer for 30 minutes. Stir in lemon peel, salt, dill and pepper; simmer 30 minutes longer or until lentils are tender. Discard bay leaves. Stir in lemon juice. **YIELD:** 6 SERVINGS.

Nutrition Facts: One serving (1-1/2 cups) equals:
248 calories
5 g fat (1 g saturated fat)
0g cholesterol
637 mg sodium
39 g carbohydrate
14 g fiber
14 g protein

Diabetic Exchanges: 2 vegetable, 1-1/2 starch, 1 very lean meat, 1 fat.

Sweet Pepper Chowder

Beverly Leveque, Fireside, British Columbia

PREP: 10 MIN. **COOK:** 40 MIN.

6	cups chicken broth
6	medium potatoes, peeled and shredded
4	medium carrots, shredded
4	celery ribs, diced
1	large onion, chopped
1	large green pepper, diced
1	large sweet red pepper, diced
1	small sweet yellow pepper, diced
1/2	cup all-purpose flour
1-1/2	teaspoons salt
1	teaspoon Italian seasoning
1/4	to 1/2 teaspoon pepper
1	cup water
4	cups 2% milk

In a Dutch oven or soup kettle, combine the broth, potatoes, carrots, celery and onion; bring to a boil. Reduce heat; cover and simmer for 20 minutes. Add the peppers; return to a boil. Reduce heat; cover and simmer for 10-15 minutes or until vegetables are tender.

In a bowl, combine the flour, salt, Italian seasoning, pepper and water until blended. Stir into the vegetable mixture. Bring to a boil; cook and stir for 2 minutes or until thickened. Reduce heat. Stir in milk; heat through (do not boil). **YIELD:** 20 SERVINGS.

Nutrition Facts: One serving (1 cup) equals:
92 calories
1 g fat (1 g saturated fat)
4 mg cholesterol
500 mg sodium
18 g carbohydrate
2 g fiber
5 g protein

Diabetic Exchanges: 2 vegetable, 1/2 starch.

Campfire Bean 'n' Ham Soup

Tom Greaves, Carrollton, Illinois

PREP: 15 MIN. + STANDING **GRILL:** 1-1/2 HOURS

1	pound dried navy beans
2	small onions

- 8 cups water
- 4 cups cubed fully cooked lean ham (1-1/2 pounds)
- 2 smoked ham hocks
- 2 cups chopped celery
- 1 cup chopped carrots
- 1/2 teaspoon dried basil
- 1/2 teaspoon pepper

Place beans in an ovenproof Dutch oven; add enough water to cover by 2 in. Bring to a boil; boil for 2 minutes. Remove from the heat; cover and let stand for 1 hour. Chop one onion; slice the second onion and separate into rings.

Drain and rinse beans, discarding liquid. Return beans to the pan. Add onions and remaining ingredients. Cover pan and place on the grill rack over indirect medium heat. Cover grill; cook for 1 hour or until beans are almost tender. Uncover the Dutch oven; cover grill and cook 30 minutes longer or until beans are tender. Discard ham hocks. **YIELD:** 12 SERVINGS (3 QUARTS).

Nutrition Facts: One serving (1 cup) equals:
- 293 calories
- 9 g fat (3 g saturated fat)
- 43 mg cholesterol
- 692 mg sodium
- 26 g carbohydrate
- 7 g fiber
- 27 g protein

Diabetic Exchanges: 3 lean meat, 1-1/2 starch, 1 vegetable.

Fresh Pumpkin Soup

Fresh Pumpkin Soup

low fat

Jane Shapton, Portland, Oregon

PREP: 50 MIN.   **COOK:** 8 HOURS

- 8 cups chopped fresh pumpkin (about 3 pounds)
- 4 cups chicken broth

Campfire Bean 'n' Ham Soup

- 3 small tart apples, peeled and chopped
- 1 medium onion, chopped
- 2 tablespoons lemon juice
- 2 teaspoons minced fresh gingerroot
- 2 garlic cloves, minced
- 1/2 teaspoon salt

TOASTED PUMPKIN SEEDS:

- 1/2 cup fresh pumpkin seeds
- 1 teaspoon vegetable oil
- 1/8 teaspoon salt

In a 5-qt. slow cooker, combine the first eight ingredients. Cover and cook on low for 8-10 hours or until pumpkin and apples are tender.

Meanwhile, toss pumpkin seeds with oil and salt. Spread into an ungreased 15-in. x 10-in. x 1-in. baking pan. Bake at 250° for 45-50 minutes or until golden brown. Set aside.

Cool soup slightly. In a food processor or blender, cover and process soup in batches until smooth. Transfer to a large saucepan; heat through. Garnish with toasted pumpkin seeds. **YIELD:** 9 SERVINGS (ABOUT 2 QUARTS).

Nutrition Facts: One serving (1 cup) equals:
- 102 calories
- 2 g fat (1 g saturated fat)
- 0 cholesterol
- 567 mg sodium
- 22 g carbohydrate
- 3 g fiber
- 3 g protein

Diabetic Exchanges: 1 starch, 1/2 fruit.

Roasted Pepper Potato Soup

Hollie Powell, St. Louis, Missouri

PREP: 30 MIN.   **COOK:** 15 MIN.

- 2   medium onions, chopped
- 2   tablespoons canola oil
- 1   jar (7-1/4 ounces) roasted red peppers, undrained, chopped
- 1   can (4 ounces) chopped green chilies, drained
- 2   teaspoons ground cumin
- 1   teaspoon salt
- 1   teaspoon ground coriander
- 3   cups diced peeled potatoes
- 3   cups vegetable broth
- 2   tablespoons minced fresh cilantro
- 1   tablespoon lemon juice
- 1/2 cup reduced-fat cream cheese, cubed

In a large saucepan, saute onions in oil until tender. Stir in the roasted peppers, chilies, cumin, salt and coriander. Cook and stir for 2 minutes. Stir in potatoes and broth; bring to a boil.

Reduce heat; cover and simmer for 10-15 minutes or until potatoes are tender. Stir in cilantro and lemon juice. Cool slightly.

In a food processor or blender, cover and process the cream cheese and half of the soup until smooth. Return all to pan and heat through. **YIELD:** 6 SERVINGS.

Nutrition Facts: One serving (1 cup) equals:
- 204   calories
- 9 g   fat (3 g saturated fat)
- 11 mg cholesterol
- 1,154 mg sodium
- 26 g carbohydrate
- 4 g   fiber
- 6 g   protein

Diabetic Exchanges: 2 vegetable, 1-1/2 fat, 1 starch.

Cheddar Potato Chowder

Ellie Rausch, Goodsoil, Saskatchewan

PREP: 20 MIN.   **COOK:** 20 MIN.

- 2   cups water
- 2   cups diced unpeeled red potatoes
- 1   cup diced carrot
- 1/2 cup diced celery
- 1/4 cup chopped onion
- 1   teaspoon salt
- 1/4 teaspoon pepper
- 1/4 cup all-purpose flour
- 2   cups 2% milk
- 2   cups (8 ounces) shredded reduced-fat cheddar cheese
- 1   cup cubed fully cooked lean ham

In a Dutch oven, combine the first seven ingredients. Bring to a boil. Reduce heat; cover and simmer for 10-12 minutes or until vegetables are tender.

Meanwhile, place flour in a large saucepan; gradually whisk in milk. Bring to a boil over medium heat; cook and stir for 2 minutes or until thickened. Remove from the heat. Add cheese; stir until melted. Stir the ham and the cheese sauce into undrained vegetables until combined. **YIELD:** 7 SERVINGS.

Nutrition Facts: One serving (1 cup) equals:
- 212   calories
- 9 g   fat (5 g saturated fat)
- 29 mg cholesterol
- 847 mg sodium
- 18 g carbohydrate
- 2 g   fiber
- 16 g protein

Diabetic Exchanges: 1 starch, 1 lean meat, 1 fat, 1/2 fat-free milk.

Cheddar Potato Chowder

Wintertime Beef Soup

Carol Tupper, Joplin, Missouri

PREP: 10 MIN.   **COOK:** 55 MIN.

- 1   pound lean ground beef
- 4   celery ribs, coarsely chopped
- 1   medium onion, coarsely chopped

Wintertime Beef Soup

1 medium green pepper, coarsely chopped
1 garlic clove, minced
2 cups water
2 cups reduced-sodium tomato juice
1 can (14-1/2 ounces) diced tomatoes, undrained
1 can (8 ounces) tomato sauce
2 teaspoons reduced-sodium beef bouillon granules
2 teaspoons chili powder
1/2 teaspoon salt
2 cans (16 ounces *each*) kidney beans, rinsed and drained
2 cups coarsely chopped cabbage

In a large saucepan or Dutch oven, cook the beef, celery, onion, green pepper and garlic over medium heat until meat is no longer pink; drain. Stir in the water, tomato juice, tomatoes, tomato sauce, bouillon, chili powder and salt. Bring to a boil.

Reduce heat; cover and simmer for 30 minutes. Stir in kidney beans; return to a boil. Stir in cabbage. Reduce heat; cover and cook 12 minutes longer or until cabbage is tender. **YIELD:** 8 SERVINGS.

Nutrition Facts: One serving (1-2/3 cups) equals:
238 calories
4 g fat (2 g saturated fat)
28 mg cholesterol
703 mg sodium
30 g carbohydrate
8 g fiber
20 g protein

Diabetic Exchanges: 2 lean meat, 2 vegetable, 1 starch.

Spicy Kielbasa Soup

Carol Custer, Clifton Park, New York

PREP: 15 MIN. **COOK:** 8 HOURS

1/2 pound reduced-fat smoked turkey kielbasa, sliced
1 medium onion, chopped
1 medium green pepper, chopped
1 celery rib with leaves, thinly sliced
4 garlic cloves, minced
2 cans (14-1/2 ounces *each*) reduced-sodium chicken broth
1 can (15-1/2 ounces) great northern beans, rinsed and drained
1 can (14-1/2 ounces) stewed tomatoes, cut up
1 small zucchini, sliced
1 medium carrot, shredded
1 tablespoon dried parsley flakes
1/4 teaspoon crushed red pepper flakes
1/4 teaspoon pepper

In a nonstick skillet, cook kielbasa over medium heat until lightly browned. Add the onion, green pepper, celery and garlic. Cook and stir for 5 minutes or until vegetable are tender.

Transfer to a slow cooker. Stir in the remaining ingredients. Cover and cook on low for 8-9 hours. **YIELD:** 5 SERVINGS.

Nutrition Facts:
One serving (1-1/2 cups) equals:
194 calories
2 g fat (trace saturated fat)
16 mg cholesterol
1,187 mg sodium
32 g carbohydrate
7 g fiber
14 g protein

Diabetic Exchanges: 3 vegetable, 2 very lean meat, 1 starch.

Spicy Kielbasa Soup

French Sweet Onion Soup

Marion Lowery, Medford, Oregon

PREP: 25 MIN. **COOK:** 1 HOUR

- 1 tablespoon butter
- 1 tablespoon olive oil
- 5 large sweet onions, sliced
- 2 cans (14-1/2 ounces *each*) reduced-sodium beef broth
- 1-2/3 cups water
- 1-1/4 cups apple cider *or* juice
- 1 bay leaf
- 1/2 teaspoon dried thyme
- 1/4 teaspoon salt
- 1/4 teaspoon pepper
- 7 slices French bread (1/2 inch thick)
- 3/4 cup grated reduced-fat Swiss cheese
- 1/4 cup grated Parmesan cheese

In a Dutch oven or large kettle, melt butter. Add oil and onions. Cover and cook over low heat until onions are soft, about 30 minutes, stirring occasionally. Stir in the broth, water, cider or juice, bay leaf, thyme, salt and pepper. Bring to a boil; reduce heat.

Cover and simmer for 20 minutes. Discard bay leaf.

Meanwhile, arrange bread on a broiler pan; broil until each side is golden brown. Ladle soup into individual ovenproof soup bowls. Float a slice of bread in each bowl and sprinkle with Swiss and Parmesan cheeses. Broil until cheese is melted and bubbly. Serve immediately. **YIELD:** 7 SERVINGS.

Nutrition Facts: One serving (1-1/4 cups soup with 1 slice of cheese-topped bread) equals:
- 256 calories
- 9 g fat (4 g saturated fat)
- 16 mg cholesterol
- 483 mg sodium
- 35 g carbohydrate
- 4 g fiber
- 10 g protein

Diabetic Exchanges: 3 vegetable, 1 starch, 1 lean meat, 1 fat, 1/2 fruit.

Brown Rice Turkey Soup

Bobby Langley, Rocky Mount, North Carolina

PREP/TOTAL TIME: 30 MIN.

- 1 cup diced sweet red pepper
- 1/2 cup chopped onion
- 1/2 cup sliced celery
- 2 garlic cloves, minced
- 2 tablespoons butter
- 3 cans (14-1/2 ounces *each*) reduced-sodium chicken broth
- 3/4 cup white wine *or* additional reduced-sodium chicken broth
- 1 teaspoon dried thyme
- 1/4 teaspoon pepper
- 2 cups cubed cooked turkey breast
- 1 cup instant brown rice
- 1/4 cup sliced green onions

In a Dutch oven, saute the red pepper, onion, celery and garlic in butter for 5-7 minutes or until vegetables are tender. Add the broth, wine or additional broth, thyme and pepper. Bring to a boil.

Reduce heat; cover and simmer for 5 minutes. Stir in turkey and rice. Bring to a boil; simmer, uncovered, for 5 minutes or until rice is tender. Garnish with green onions. **YIELD:** 5 SERVINGS.

Nutrition Facts:
One serving (1-1/2 cups) equals:
- 259 calories
- 8 g fat (4 g saturated fat)
- 55 mg cholesterol
- 766 mg sodium
- 20 g carbohydrate
- 2 g fiber
- 22 g protein

Diabetic Exchanges: 3 lean meat, 1 starch, 1 vegetable.

Brown Rice Turkey Soup

Meatless Chili

Eve Visser, South Bend, Indiana

PREP/TOTAL TIME: 30 MIN.

- 1   can (15-1/2 ounces) hot chili beans
- 1   can (15 ounces) black beans, rinsed and drained
- 1   can (14-1/2 ounces) Mexican stewed tomatoes
- 1   cup frozen corn, thawed
- 1/2 cup chunky salsa
- 1/2 cup coarsely chopped green pepper
- 1/2 cup coarsely chopped sweet red pepper
- 1   tablespoon ground cumin
- 2   teaspoons chili powder
- 4   tablespoons fat-free sour cream
- 4   tablespoons shredded reduced-fat cheddar cheese

In a large saucepan, combine the first nine ingredients. Bring to a boil. Reduce heat; cover and simmer for 15 minutes or until vegetables are crisp-tender. Top each serving with sour cream and cheese. **YIELD:** 4 SERVINGS.

Nutrition Facts:
One serving (1-1/2 cups) equals:
- 318 calories
- 3 g fat (2 g saturated fat)
- 8 mg cholesterol
- 1,148 mg sodium
- 56 g carbohydrate
- 14 g fiber
- 16 g protein

Meatless Chili

Italian Wedding Soup

Paula Sullivan, Barker, New York

PREP: 35 MIN.   **COOK:** 20 MIN.

- 1   egg, lightly beaten
- 1   tablespoon dry bread crumbs
- 1   tablespoon dried parsley flakes
- 1   tablespoon plus 1/4 cup grated Parmesan cheese, *divided*
- 1/2 teaspoon onion powder
- 1/2 teaspoon salt, *divided*
- 1/8 teaspoon plus 1/4 teaspoon pepper, *divided*
- 1/2 pound lean ground beef
- 1/4 cup uncooked orzo pasta *or* acini di pepe pasta
- 1   medium onion, finely chopped
- 3   celery ribs, chopped
- 2   garlic cloves, minced
- 1   tablespoon olive oil
- 4   cans (14-1/2 ounces *each*) reduced-sodium chicken broth
- 1   can (16 ounces) kidney beans, rinsed and drained
- 4   cups chopped fresh spinach

In a large bowl, combine the egg, bread crumbs, parsley, 1 tablespoon Parmesan cheese, onion powder, 1/4 teaspoon salt and 1/8 teaspoon pepper. Crumble beef over mixture and mix well. Shape into 42 meatballs.

Place in a 15-in. x 10-in. x 1-in. baking pan coated with nonstick cooking spray. Bake at 350° for 8-10 minutes or until juices run clear; drain.

Cook pasta according to package directions; drain. In a large saucepan or soup kettle, saute the onion, celery and garlic in oil until tender. Stir in the broth, beans and spinach. Stir in pasta, meatballs and remaining salt and pepper. Cook until spinach is tender and meatballs are heated through. Garnish with remaining Parmesan cheese. **YIELD:** 7 SERVINGS.

Nutrition Facts: One serving (1-1/3 cups) equals:
- 205 calories
- 6 g fat (2 g saturated fat)
- 49 mg cholesterol
- 1,024 mg sodium
- 20 g carbohydrate
- 4 g fiber
- 17 g protein

Diabetic Exchanges: 2 lean meat, 1 starch, 1 vegetable.

Chipotle Turkey Chili

Christie Ladd, Mechanicsburg, Pennsylvania

PREP: 25 MIN.   **COOK:** 1-1/2 HOURS

1	can (7 ounces) chipotle peppers in adobo sauce
1-1/4	pounds lean ground turkey
3	medium carrots, chopped
1	medium green pepper, chopped
1/2	cup chopped onion
4	garlic cloves, minced
1	can (28 ounces) crushed tomatoes
1	can (14-1/2 ounces) reduced-sodium chicken broth
1	can (8 ounces) tomato sauce
1-1/2	teaspoons dried oregano
1-1/2	teaspoons dried basil
1	teaspoon chili powder
1/2	teaspoon ground cumin
1	can (16 ounces) kidney beans, rinsed and drained
1	can (15 ounces) garbanzo beans *or* chickpeas, rinsed and drained

Drain chipotle peppers; set aside 2 tablespoons adobo sauce. Seed and chop three peppers; set aside. (Save remaining peppers and sauce for another use.)

In a large Dutch oven or soup kettle coated with nonstick cooking spray, cook the turkey, carrots, green pepper, onion, garlic and reserved peppers over medium heat until meat is no longer pink; drain if necessary. Stir in the tomatoes, broth, tomato sauce, oregano, basil, chili powder, cumin and reserved adobo sauce. Bring to a boil. Reduce heat; cover and simmer for 1 hour.

Stir in the beans. Cover and simmer for 15-20 minutes or until heated through. **YIELD:** 8 SERVINGS.

Editor's Note: When cutting or seeding hot peppers, use rubber or plastic gloves to protect your hands. Avoid touching your face.

Nutrition Facts: One serving (1 cup) equals:
- 293 calories
- 8 g fat (2 g saturated fat)
- 56 mg cholesterol
- 844 mg sodium
- 35 g carbohydrate
- 9 g fiber
- 22 g protein

Diabetic Exchanges: 3 lean meat, 3 vegetable, 1 starch.

Chipotle Turkey Chili

Cheesy Ham 'n' Potato Soup

Taste of Home Test Kitchen
Greendale, Wisconsin

PREP/TOTAL TIME: 30 MIN.

2-1/4	cups cubed potatoes
1-1/2	cups water
1-1/2	cups cubed fully cooked lean ham
1	large onion, chopped
2	teaspoons canola oil
1/4	cup nonfat dry milk powder
3	tablespoons all-purpose flour
1/4	teaspoon pepper
3	cups fat-free milk
1-1/2	cups (6 ounces) finely shredded reduced-fat cheddar cheese
1	cup frozen broccoli florets, thawed and chopped

In a saucepan, bring potatoes and water to a boil. Cover and cook for 10-15 minutes or until tender. Drain, reserving 1 cup cooking liquid. In a blender or food processor, cover and process reserved liquid and 1/4 cup cooked potatoes until smooth; set aside. Set remaining potatoes aside.

In a large saucepan, saute ham and onion in oil until onion is tender. In a bowl, combine milk powder, flour, pepper, milk and processed potato mixture until smooth. Stir into ham and onion. Bring to a boil; cook and

Cheesy Ham 'n' Potato Soup

stir for 2 minutes or until thickened.

Reduce heat to low. Add the cheese, broccoli and reserved potatoes; cook and stir over low heat until cheese is melted and heated through. Serve immediately. **YIELD:** 7 SERVINGS.

Nutrition Facts: One serving (1 cup) equals:
228 calories
8 g fat (4 g saturated fat)
36 mg cholesterol
616 mg sodium
21 g carbohydrate
1 g fiber
18 g protein

Diabetic Exchanges: 2 lean meat, 1 starch, 1/2 fat-free milk.

Sixteen-Bean Soup

Laura Prokash, Algoma, Wisconsin

PREP: 10 MIN. + STANDING   **COOK:** 2-3/4 HOURS

1 package (12 ounces) 16-bean soup mix
1 large onion, chopped
2 garlic cloves, minced
1 teaspoon salt
1 teaspoon chili powder
1/4 teaspoon pepper
1/8 teaspoon hot pepper sauce
1 bay leaf
2 quarts water
1 can (14-1/2 ounces) stewed tomatoes
1 tablespoon lemon juice

Set seasoning packet from beans aside. Place beans in a Dutch oven or soup kettle; add

water to cover by 2 in. Bring to a boil; boil for 2 minutes. Remove from the heat; cover and let stand for 1 hour. Drain and rinse beans, discarding liquid.

Return beans to the pan. Add contents of bean seasoning packet, onion, garlic, salt, chili powder, pepper, hot pepper sauce, bay leaf and water. Bring to a boil.

Reduce heat; cover and simmer for 2-1/2 to 3 hours or until beans are tender. Add tomatoes and lemon juice. Simmer, uncovered, until heated through. Discard bay leaf before serving. **YIELD:** 10 SERVINGS (2-1/2 QUARTS).

Nutrition Facts: One serving (1 cup) equals:
79 calories
trace fat (trace saturated fat)
0 cholesterol
746 mg sodium
22 g carbohydrate
11 g fiber
7 g protein

Diabetic Exchange: 1 starch.

Rich Onion Beef Soup

Nina Hall, Spokane, Washington

PREP: 5 MIN.   **COOK:** 30 MIN.

2 cups thinly sliced onions
1 tablespoon butter
2 cups cubed cooked lean beef
2 cans (14-1/2 ounces *each*) beef broth
3 tablespoons all-purpose flour
1/2 teaspoon ground mustard
1/2 teaspoon sugar
1/2 cup dry red wine *or* additional beef broth
1 teaspoon browning sauce

In a large saucepan, cook onions in butter over medium-low heat for 15-20 minutes or until tender and golden brown, stirring occasionally. Add beef and broth. Bring to a boil. Reduce heat; cover and simmer for 10 minutes.

In a small bowl, combine the flour, mustard and sugar; stir in wine or additional broth and browning sauce until smooth. Stir into soup. Bring to a boil; cook and stir for 1-2 minutes or until slightly thickened. **YIELD:** 5 SERVINGS.

Nutrition Facts: One serving (1 cup) equals:
165 calories
6 g fat (3 g saturated fat)
43 mg cholesterol
631 mg sodium
9 g carbohydrate
1 g fiber
16 g protein

Diabetic Exchanges: 2 lean meat, 1/2 starch, 1/2 fat.

Rich Onion Beef Soup

Satisfying Salads.

Need a standout side dish for a special main course, a tangy take-along for the neighborhood barbecue or an appetizing addition to your lunchtime lineup? Look no further than these garden-fresh, good-for-you salads!

Honey Lime Fruit Toss

Honey Lime Fruit Toss `low fat` `low sodium` `meat less`

Angela Oelschlaeger, Tonganozie, Kansas

PREP/TOTAL TIME: 10 MIN.

- 1 can (20 ounces) unsweetened pineapple chunks
- 1 can (11 ounces) mandarin oranges, drained
- 2 cups sliced fresh strawberries
- 2 medium firm bananas cut into 1/4-inch slices
- 2 kiwifruit, peeled, halved and sliced
- 2 tablespoons lime juice
- 1 tablespoon honey
- 1/4 teaspoon grated lime peel

Drain pineapple, reserving 1/4 cup juice; set juice aside. In a bowl, combine the pineapple, mandarin oranges, strawberries, bananas and kiwi.

In a small bowl, combine the lime juice, honey, lime peel and reserved pineapple juice. Pour over fruit; gently toss to coat. YIELD: 6 SERVINGS.

Nutrition Facts: One serving (3/4 cup) equals:
- 133 calories
- 1 g fat (1 g saturated fat)
- 0 cholesterol
- 7 mg sodium
- 33 g carbohydrate
- 4 g fiber
- 1 g protein

Diabetic Exchange: 2 fruit.

Citrus Tossed Salad `low fat` `low sodium` `meat less`

Marge Werner, Broken Arrow, Oklahoma

PREP: 10 MIN. + CHILLING

- 1 teaspoon cornstarch
- 1/4 cup orange juice
- 1/4 cup unsweetened grapefruit juice
- 2 tablespoons cider vinegar
- 2 tablespoons orange marmalade
- 1 teaspoon Dijon mustard
- 1/2 teaspoon grated orange peel
- 1/8 teaspoon garlic powder
- 1/8 teaspoon onion powder
- 8 cups torn leaf lettuce
- 1 medium grapefruit, peeled and sectioned
- 1 medium navel orange, peeled and sectioned

In a saucepan, combine cornstarch and orange juice until smooth. Stir in the grapefruit juice, vinegar, marmalade, mustard, orange peel, garlic powder and onion powder. Bring to a boil; cook and stir for 2 minutes or until thickened.

Remove from the heat; refrigerate until chilled. Divide lettuce and fruit among four salad plates; drizzle with dressing. YIELD: 4 SERVINGS.

Nutrition Facts: One serving (2 cups) equals:
- 98 calories
- 1 g fat (trace saturated fat)
- 0 cholesterol
- 48 mg sodium
- 24 g carbohydrate
- 4 g fiber
- 3 g protein

Diabetic Exchanges: 1 vegetable, 1 fruit.

Cannellini Bean Salad `meat less`

Dorothy Majewski, Vienna, Virginia

PREP: 15 MIN. + CHILLING

- 2 cans (15 ounces *each*) cannellini *or* white kidney beans, rinsed and drained
- 3 celery ribs with leaves, sliced
- 3/4 cup chopped red onion
- 1/2 cup chopped sweet red pepper
- 1/2 cup minced fresh parsley
- 1/4 cup chopped green onions
- 2 tablespoons olive oil
- 2 tablespoons balsamic vinegar
- 1/2 teaspoon salt
- 1/4 teaspoon pepper

In a large bowl, toss the beans, celery, red onion, red pepper, parsley and green onions. In a small bowl, combine the oil, vinegar, salt and pepper. Pour over salad and toss to coat. Cover and refrigerate for 1 hour or until chilled. YIELD: 7 SERVINGS.

Nutrition Facts: One serving (3/4 cup) equals:
- 145 calories
- 4 g fat (1 g saturated fat)
- 0 cholesterol
- 440 mg sodium
- 21 g carbohydrate
- 6 g fiber
- 5 g protein

Diabetic Exchanges: 1 starch, 1 vegetable, 1 fat.

Mediterranean Medley Salad

Merwyn Garbini, Tucson, Arizona

PREP: 10 MIN. + CHILLING

- 2 cups cooked brown rice
- 1 can (6 ounces) light water-packed tuna, drained and flaked
- 1/2 cup sliced ripe olives
- 1/2 cup sliced celery
- 1/2 cup frozen peas, thawed
- 1 medium tomato, diced
- 1/2 cup chopped green pepper
- 1/4 cup thinly sliced radishes
- 1/4 cup sliced green onions
- 1/4 cup grated carrots

LEMON-HERB SALAD DRESSING:

- 2 tablespoons olive oil
- 2 tablespoons water
- 2 tablespoons lemon juice
- 1 tablespoon Italian seasoning
- 1 teaspoon sugar
- 1/2 teaspoon salt
- 1 garlic clove, minced
- 1/4 teaspoon lemon-pepper seasoning

In a large bowl, combine the first 10 ingredients. In a jar with a tight-fitting lid, combine the salad dressing ingredients; shake well. Pour over salad and toss to coat. Cover and refrigerate for at least 1 hour. **YIELD:** 4 SERVINGS.

Nutrition Facts: One serving (1-1/2 cups) equals:
- 284 calories
- 11 g fat (2 g saturated fat)
- 18 mg cholesterol
- 669 mg sodium
- 33 g carbohydrate
- 5 g fiber
- 14 g protein

Diabetic Exchanges: 2 very lean meat, 1-1/2 starch, 1-1/2 fat, 1 vegetable.

Mediterranean Medley Salad

Colorful Pepper Salad

Colorful Pepper Salad

Christa Boylston, Shelby, North Carolina

PREP/TOTAL TIME: 20 MIN.

- 3 *each* large green, sweet red and sweet yellow peppers, thinly sliced
- 18 cherry tomatoes, halved

DRESSING:

- 1/4 cup finely chopped red onion
- 3 tablespoons cider vinegar
- 3 tablespoons olive oil
- 3 tablespoons honey
- 1 tablespoon Dijon mustard
- 1/4 teaspoon salt
- 1/4 teaspoon garlic powder
- 1/4 teaspoon celery seed
- 1/4 teaspoon pepper
- 1/8 teaspoon crushed red pepper flakes, optional

In a large bowl, combine peppers and tomatoes. In a jar with a tight-fitting lid, combine the dressing ingredients; shake well. Pour over vegetables and toss to coat. **YIELD:** 16 SERVINGS.

Nutrition Facts: One serving (3/4 cup) equals:
- 71 calories
- 3 g fat (0 saturated fat)
- 0 cholesterol
- 54 mg sodium
- 11 g carbohydrate
- 2 g fiber
- 1 g protein

Diabetic Exchanges: 2 vegetable, 1/2 fat.

Tabbouleh

Wanda Watson, Irving, Texas

PREP: 40 MIN. + CHILLING

- 1 cup bulgur
- 2 cups boiling water
- 3 tablespoons lemon juice
- 2 tablespoons olive oil
- 2 tablespoons sliced green onions (tops only)
- 1 tablespoon minced fresh parsley
- 1 teaspoon salt
- 1 teaspoon minced fresh mint
- 1 medium tomato, seeded and diced
- 6 romaine leaves

Place bulgur in a bowl; stir in water. Cover and let stand for 30 minutes or until liquid is absorbed. Drain and squeeze dry. Stir in the lemon juice, oil, onions, parsley, salt and mint. Cover and refrigerate for 1 hour. Just before serving, stir in tomato. Serve in a lettuce-lined bowl. **YIELD:** 6 SERVINGS.

Nutrition Facts: One serving (3/4 cup) equals:
- 129 calories
- 5 g fat (1 g saturated fat)
- 0 cholesterol
- 399 mg sodium
- 20 g carbohydrate
- 5 g fiber
- 3 g protein

Diabetic Exchanges: 1 starch, 1 fat.

Tabbouleh

Summer Fruit 'n' Pasta Salad

Donna Williams, Las Vegas, Nevada

PREP/TOTAL TIME: 20 MIN. + CHILLING

- 8 ounces uncooked elbow macaroni
- 3/4 cup fat-free plain yogurt
- 3/4 cup reduced-fat mayonnaise
- 4 teaspoons snipped fresh dill
- 1/4 teaspoon salt
- Dash hot pepper sauce
- 2 medium tart green apples, chopped
- 2 medium red apples, chopped
- 1-1/2 cups seedless grapes
- 2 celery ribs, thinly sliced
- 1 can (15 ounces) mandarin oranges, drained
- 2 medium firm bananas cut into 1/4-inch slices
- 1/2 cup chopped walnuts

Cook pasta according to package directions. Rinse with cold water and drain. In a bowl, combine the yogurt, mayonnaise, dill, salt and hot pepper sauce.

In a large serving bowl, combine the pasta, apples, grapes, celery and mandarin oranges. Gently stir in 1 cup yogurt mixture.

Cover and refrigerate salad and remaining yogurt mixture for 2-3 hours. Just before serving, stir in bananas, walnuts and remaining yogurt mixture. **YIELD:** 14 SERVINGS.

Nutrition Facts: One serving (1 cup) equals:
- 199 calories
- 8 g fat (1 g saturated fat)
- 5 mg cholesterol
- 160 mg sodium
- 31 g carbohydrate
- 3 g fiber
- 4 g protein

Diabetic Exchanges: 1 starch, 1 fruit, 1 fat.

Broccoli Tortellini Salad

Tiffany Anderson-Taylor, Gulfport, Florida

PREP: 25 MIN. + CHILLING

- 4 cups broccoli florets
- 2 packages (9 ounces *each*) refrigerated cheese tortellini
- 1/2 cup finely chopped red onion
- 1/4 cup raisins
- 1/2 cup reduced-fat mayonnaise
- Sugar substitute equivalent to 3 tablespoons sugar
- 1 tablespoon cider vinegar
- 5 slices bacon, cooked and crumbled
- 1/4 cup unsalted sunflower kernels

Broccoli Tortellini Salad

In a large saucepan, cook broccoli in 6 cups boiling water for 2 minutes. Drain and immediately rinse in cold water. In the same saucepan, cook tortellini according to package directions. Drain and immediately rinse in cold water.

In a large bowl, combine the red onion, raisins, broccoli and tortellini. Combine the mayonnaise, sugar substitute and vinegar. Pour over tortellini mixture; toss to coat. Refrigerate for at least 1 hour. Just before serving, stir in bacon and sunflower kernels. **YIELD:** 12 SERVINGS.

Editor's Note: This recipe was tested with Splenda No Calorie Sweetener.

Nutrition Facts: One serving (2/3 cup) equals:
- 217 calories
- 10 g fat (3 g saturated fat)
- 24 mg cholesterol
- 287 mg sodium
- 25 g carbohydrate
- 2 g fiber
- 8 g protein

Diabetic Exchanges: 1-1/2 starch, 1 lean meat, 1 fat.

Spicy Crunchy Veggies

low carb | meat less

Grady Jones, Midland, Texas

PREP: 15 MIN. + CHILLING

- 2 cups fresh broccoli florets
- 2 ounces reduced-fat Monterey Jack cheese, cut into small cubes
- 1/3 cup finely chopped red onion
- 1/4 cup fresh cauliflowerets
- 1/4 cup julienned carrot
- 2 tablespoons finely chopped sweet red pepper
- 1 small jalapeno pepper, seeded and chopped
- 2 tablespoons fat-free plain yogurt
- 2 tablespoons reduced-fat mayonnaise
- 1/2 teaspoon salt-free spicy seasoning blend
- 1/8 teaspoon salt
- 1 tablespoon slivered almonds, toasted

In a large bowl, combine the first seven ingredients. In a small bowl, combine the yogurt, mayonnaise, seasoning blend and salt. Stir into vegetable mixture. Cover and refrigerate for at least 1 hour. Just before serving, sprinkle with almonds. **YIELD:** 4 SERVINGS.

Editor's Note: When cutting or seeding hot peppers, use rubber or plastic gloves to protect your hands. Avoid touching your face.

Nutrition Facts: One serving (3/4 cup) equals:
- 87 calories
- 5 g fat (2 g saturated fat)
- 12 mg cholesterol
- 281 mg sodium
- 7 g carbohydrate
- 2 g fiber
- 6 g protein

Diabetic Exchanges: 1 vegetable, 1 fat.

Spicy Crunchy Veggies

Grapefruit Shrimp Salad

Mock Caesar Salad

low carb | meat less

Sue Yaeger, Boone, Iowa

PREP/TOTAL TIME: 10 MIN.

- 1/3 cup fat-free plain yogurt
- 1/4 cup reduced-fat mayonnaise
- 1 tablespoon red wine vinegar
- 2 teaspoons Dijon mustard
- 1 teaspoon Worcestershire sauce
- 1/4 teaspoon garlic powder
- 1/8 teaspoon pepper
- 6 cups torn romaine
- 1/2 cup fat-free salad croutons
- 2 tablespoons shredded Parmesan cheese

In a small bowl, whisk together the first seven ingredients. In a salad bowl, combine the romaine, croutons and cheese. Drizzle with dressing; toss to coat. **YIELD:** 5 SERVINGS.

Nutrition Facts: One serving (1-1/4 cups) equals:
- 90 calories
- 5 g fat (1 g saturated fat)
- 7 mg cholesterol
- 299 mg sodium
- 9 g carbohydrate
- 1 g fiber
- 4 g protein

Diabetic Exchanges: 1 fat, 1/2 starch.

Grapefruit Shrimp Salad

low carb

Joanne Beaupre, Manchester, Connecticut

PREP/TOTAL TIME: 15 MIN.

- 1 head Bibb or Boston lettuce
- 1 large grapefruit, peeled and sectioned
- 1 medium ripe avocado, peeled and thinly sliced
- 1 pound cooked medium shrimp, peeled and deveined

CITRUS VINAIGRETTE:

- 2 tablespoons orange juice
- 2 tablespoons red wine vinegar
- 1 tablespoon olive oil
- 2 teaspoons Dijon mustard
- 1/4 teaspoon salt

Place lettuce on four serving plates. Arrange grapefruit, avocado and shrimp over lettuce. In a bowl, whisk together vinaigrette ingredients. Drizzle over each salad. **YIELD:** 4 SERVINGS.

Nutrition Facts: One serving (3/4 cup) equals:
- 266 calories
- 12 g fat (2 g saturated fat)
- 221 mg cholesterol
- 445 mg sodium
- 14 g carbohydrate
- 4 g fiber
- 26 g protein

Diabetic Exchanges: 3 very lean meat, 2 fat, 1 vegetable, 1/2 fruit.

Pineapple Salad

low fat | low sodium | low carb | meat less

Vickie Madrigal, Shreveport, Louisiana

PREP: 15 MIN. + COOLING

- 1 can (8 ounces) unsweetened pineapple slices
- 1 tablespoon olive oil
- 1 tablespoon honey
- 1-1/2 teaspoons cider vinegar
- 1-1/2 teaspoons reduced-sodium soy sauce
- 6 cups torn romaine
- 1/2 cup thinly sliced red onion

Drain pineapple, reserving juice. Cut slices in half; set aside. In a jar with a tight-fitting lid, combine the oil, honey, vinegar, soy sauce and reserved pineapple juice; shake well. Refrigerate for at least 30 minutes.

Combine the romaine, onion slices and pineapple slices in a serving dish. Drizzle with dressing; toss to coat. **YIELD:** 6 SERVINGS.

Nutrition Facts: One serving (1 cup) equals:
- 64 calories
- 2 g fat (1 g saturated fat)
- 0 cholesterol
- 59 mg sodium
- 11 g carbohydrate
- 1 g fiber
- 1 g protein

Diabetic Exchanges: 1 vegetable, 1/2 fruit.

Garlic Green And Wax Beans

low fat | low carb | meat less

Marilou Robinson, Portland, Oregon

PREP: 5 MIN.   COOK: 10 MIN. + CHILLING

1-1/2   pounds fresh green beans
1-1/2   pounds fresh wax beans
   7   garlic cloves, minced, *divided*
1/4   cup reduced-fat sour cream
1/4   cup fat-free milk
   1   teaspoon white wine vinegar
   1   teaspoon olive oil
1/2   teaspoon salt
1/8   teaspoon pepper
   1   cup shredded part-skim mozzarella cheese
Minced fresh parsley

Place beans and 6 garlic cloves in a steamer basket. Place in a large saucepan over 1 in. of water; bring to a boil. Cover and steam for 8-10 minutes or until beans are crisp-tender. Transfer to a large bowl; set aside.

In a small bowl, combine the sour cream, milk and vinegar; let stand for 1 minute. Whisk in the oil, salt, pepper and remaining garlic. Pour over beans and toss. Cover and refrigerate for at least 2 hours. Just before serving, sprinkle with cheese and parsley. YIELD: 12 SERVINGS.

Nutrition Facts: One serving (3/4 cup) equals:
           76 calories
            2 g fat (1 g saturated fat)
            7 mg cholesterol
          157 mg sodium
            9 g carbohydrate
            4 g fiber
            5 g protein

Diabetic Exchanges: 2 vegetable, 1/2 fat.

BLT Bow Tie Pasta Salad

BLT Bow Tie Pasta Salad

low sodium | low carb

Jennifer Madsen, Rexburg, Idaho

PREP/TOTAL TIME: 25 MIN.

2-1/2   cups uncooked bow tie pasta
   6   cups torn romaine
1-1/2   cups cubed cooked chicken breast
   1   medium tomato, diced
   4   bacon strips, cooked and crumbled
1/3   cup reduced-fat mayonnaise
1/4   cup water
   1   tablespoon barbecue sauce
1-1/2   teaspoons white vinegar
1/4   teaspoon pepper

Cook pasta according to package directions. Drain and rinse under cold water. In a large serving bowl, combine the pasta, romaine, chicken, tomato and bacon.

In a small bowl, whisk together the mayonnaise, water, barbecue sauce, vinegar and pepper. Pour over pasta mixture; toss to coat evenly. Serve immediately. YIELD: 11 SERVINGS.

Nutrition Facts: One serving (1 cup) equals:
          134 calories
            5 g fat (1 g saturated fat)
           21 mg cholesterol
          125 mg sodium
           14 g carbohydrate
            1 g fiber
            9 g protein

Diabetic Exchanges: 1 starch, 1 lean meat.

Garlic Green and Wax Beans

Roasted Pear Salad

Taste of Home Test Kitchen
Greendale, Wisconsin

PREP: 15 MIN. **BAKE:** 15 MIN. + COOLING

2	firm ripe pears, halved and cored
4	teaspoons olive oil, *divided*
2	tablespoons cider vinegar
1	teaspoon water
1	teaspoon honey
1/4	teaspoon salt
1/8	teaspoon white pepper
1	package (10 ounces) mixed baby salad greens
1	cup watercress sprigs
1/4	cup chopped hazelnuts, toasted
1/4	cup dried cranberries

In a bowl, toss pears with 1 teaspoon oil. Place in a 15-in. x 10-in. x 1-in. baking pan coated with nonstick cooking spray. Bake at 400° for 10 minutes. Turn pears over; bake 5-7 minutes longer or until golden and tender.

When cool enough to handle, peel pears. Thinly slice two pear halves lengthwise and set aside. Place remaining pear halves in a food processor or blender. Add the vinegar, water, honey, salt and white pepper; cover and process until smooth. While processing, slowly add remaining oil.

In a large bowl, toss the salad greens, watercress, nuts and cranberries. Arrange pear slices on top; drizzle with dressing. **YIELD:** 4 SERVINGS.

Nutrition Facts: One serving (1 cup) equals:
- 174 calories
- 9 g fat (1 g saturated fat)
- 0 cholesterol
- 178 mg sodium
- 24 g carbohydrate
- 5 g fiber
- 3 g protein

Diabetic Exchanges: 2 fat, 1 vegetable, 1 fruit.

Cheddar-Apple Turkey Salad

Luci Knepper, Salem, Ohio

PREP: 20 MIN. + CHILLING

1	package (3 ounces) ramen noodles
1-1/2	cups cubed red apples
1-1/4	cups cubed cooked turkey breast
1/2	cup reduced-fat cheddar cheese
1/2	cup frozen peas, thawed
1/4	cup sliced green onion
1/4	cup chopped sweet red pepper
1/2	cup fat-free poppy seed salad dressing
2	tablespoons reduced-fat sour cream
1/4	teaspoon salt

Remove seasoning packet from ramen noodles and discard or save for another use. Prepare noodles according to package directions. Drain and rinse in cold water.

In a bowl, combine the noodles, apples, turkey, cheese, peas, green onions and red pepper. In a small bowl, combine the dressing, sour cream and salt. Stir into noodle mixture. Cover and refrigerate for at least 1 hour. **YIELD:** 4 SERVINGS.

Nutrition Facts: One serving (1-1/4 cups) equals:
- 259 calories
- 8 g fat (5 g saturated fat)
- 24 mg cholesterol
- 456 mg sodium
- 35 g carbohydrate
- 3 g fiber
- 11 g protein

Diabetic Exchanges: 2 starch, 1 lean meat, 1/2 fruit, 1/2 fat.

Cheddar-Apple Turkey Salad

Calico Cranberry Couscous Salad

Rosemarie Matheus, Germantown, Wisconsin

PREP/TOTAL TIME: 20 MIN.

1	cup water
3/4	cup uncooked couscous
1/2	cup dried cranberries

Calico Cranberry Couscous Salad

1/2 cup chopped celery

1/2 cup shredded carrot

1/4 cup chopped green onions

1/4 cup slivered almonds, toasted

DRESSING:

3 tablespoons red wine vinegar

1 tablespoon olive oil

1 tablespoon Dijon mustard

1/4 teaspoon salt

1/4 teaspoon pepper

In a small saucepan, bring water to a boil. Stir in couscous; cover and remove from the heat. Let stand for 5 minutes. Fluff with a fork; cool.

In a serving bowl, combine the couscous, cranberries, celery, carrot, onions and almonds.

In a jar with a tight-fitting lid, combine the dressing ingredients; shake well. Pour over salad and toss to coat. Serve at room temperature or chilled. **YIELD:** 6 SERVINGS.

Nutrition Facts: One serving (1/2 cup) equals:
- 171 calories
- 5 g fat (1 g saturated fat)
- 0 cholesterol
- 176 mg sodium
- 29 g carbohydrate
- 3 g fiber
- 5 g protein

Diabetic Exchanges: 1-1/2 starch, 1 fat, 1/2 fruit.

Berry Nectarine Salad

Mindee Myers, Lincoln, Nebraska

PREP: 15 MIN. + CHILLING

4 medium unpeeled nectarines, sliced

1/4 cup sugar

1/2 teaspoon ground ginger

1 teaspoon lemon juice

2 cups fresh raspberries

1 cup fresh blueberries

3 ounces reduced-fat cream cheese

Place nectarines in a large bowl. Combine sugar and ginger; sprinkle over nectarines and gently stir to evenly coat. Drizzle with lemon juice. Cover and refrigerate for 1 hour, stirring once.

Drain and reserve liquid. Gently stir raspberries and blueberries into nectarines. In a small mixing bowl, beat cream cheese until smooth. Gradually beat in reserved liquid. Spoon over fruit; serve immediately. **YIELD:** 8 SERVINGS.

Nutrition Facts: One serving (3/4 cup) equals:
- 117 calories
- 2 g fat (1 g saturated fat)
- 6 mg cholesterol
- 33 mg sodium
- 23 g carbohydrate
- 4 g fiber
- 2 g protein

Diabetic Exchanges: 1-1/2 fruit, 1/2 fat.

Berry Nectarine Salad

Smoky Thousand Island Salad Dressing

Betty McConoughey, Loves Park, Illinois

PREP/TOTAL TIME: 5 MIN.

- 1/2 cup reduced-fat mayonnaise
- 2 tablespoons sweet pickle relish
- 2 tablespoons ketchup
- 1 tablespoon hickory barbecue sauce
- 1 teaspoon prepared horseradish
- 1 teaspoon prepared mustard
- 1 teaspoon Liquid Smoke, optional

In a small bowl, combine the first six ingredients; add Liquid Smoke if desired and stir until well-blended. Store, uncovered, in the refrigerator. **YIELD:** 14 TABLESPOONS.

Nutrition Facts:
One serving (2 tablespoons) equals:
- 56 calories
- 3 g fat (1 g saturated fat)
- 5 mg cholesterol
- 278 mg sodium
- 6 g carbohydrate
- 1 g fiber
- 1 g protein

Diabetic Exchanges: 1/2 starch, 1/2 fat.

Smoky Thousand Island Salad Dressing

Asian Linguine Salad

Pat Hilmer, Oshkosh, Wisconsin

PREP: 35 MIN. COOK: 10 MIN. + CHILLING

- 8 ounces uncooked linguine
- 1/3 cup reduced-sodium soy sauce
- 1/4 cup water
- 2 tablespoons lemon juice
- 1-1/2 teaspoons sesame oil
- 2 medium carrots, julienned
- 1/2 medium sweet red pepper, julienned
- 1-1/2 teaspoons olive oil, *divided*
- 1/2 cup fresh snow peas
- 1 garlic clove, minced
- 1 small zucchini, julienned
- 1/2 cup canned bean sprouts
- 1 green onion, julienned

Cook linguine according to package directions; drain and place in a large serving bowl. In a small bowl, whisk the soy sauce, water, lemon juice and sesame oil. Refrigerate 1/4 cup for dressing. Pour remaining mixture over hot linguine; toss to coat evenly.

In a large nonstick skillet or wok coated with nonstick cooking spray, stir-fry carrots and red pepper in 3/4 teaspoon olive oil for 2 minutes. Add snow peas and garlic; stir-fry 2 minutes longer. Add to linguine.

Stir-fry the zucchini, bean sprouts and onion in remaining olive oil for 2 minutes;

add to linguine mixture. Cover and refrigerate for at least 2 hours. Just before serving, add dressing and toss to coat. **YIELD:** 8 SERVINGS.

Nutrition Facts: One serving (3/4 cup) equals:
- 141 calories
- 2 g fat (trace saturated fat)
- 0 cholesterol
- 415 mg sodium
- 25 g carbohydrate
- 2 g fiber
- 5 g protein

Diabetic Exchanges: 1-1/2 starch, 1/2 fat.

Herb Vegetable Orzo Salad

Taste of Home Test Kitchen
Greendale, Wisconsin

PREP/TOTAL TIME: 25 MIN.

- 1 cup uncooked orzo pasta
- 2 cups frozen corn, thawed
- 1/2 cup chopped sweet red pepper
- 1/2 cup grape *or* cherry tomatoes
- 1/2 cup pitted Greek olives, halved
- 1/4 cup chopped sweet onion
- 1/4 cup minced fresh basil *or* 4 teaspoons dried basil
- 2 tablespoons minced fresh parsley
- 3 tablespoons olive oil
- 2 tablespoons balsamic vinegar
- 1/4 teaspoon salt
- 1/4 teaspoon pepper

Cook pasta according to package directions; drain and rinse in cold water. Place in a large serving bowl; add the corn, red pepper, tomatoes, olives, onion, basil and parsley.

In a jar with a tight-fitting lid, combine the oil, vinegar, salt and pepper; shake well. Pour over salad and toss to coat. **YIELD:** 8 SERVINGS.

Nutrition Facts: One serving (3/4 cup) equals:
- 192 calories
- 7 g fat (1 g saturated fat)
- 0 cholesterol
- 157 mg sodium
- 29 g carbohydrate
- 2 g fiber
- 5 g protein

Diabetic Exchanges: 2 starch, 1 fat.

Chicken Salad With Crispy Wontons

Kylea Rorabaugh, Kansas City, Missouri

PREP/TOTAL TIME: 30 MIN.

- 10 wonton wrappers, cut into 1/4-inch strips
- 1/4 cup cider vinegar
- 3 tablespoons canola oil

3/4 teaspoon sesame oil

2 tablespoons sugar

3/4 teaspoon salt

1/4 teaspoon pepper

5 cups torn romaine

3 cups cubed cooked chicken breast

1 medium sweet red pepper, cut into 1/4-inch strips

1 medium sweet yellow pepper, cut into 1/4-inch strips

1/2 cup halved grape tomatoes

Lightly spritz both sides of wonton strips with nonstick cooking spray; place on a baking sheet. Broil 4-6 in. from the heat for 2-3 minutes or until golden brown. Turn strips over; broil 2-3 minutes longer or until golden brown. Remove to wire racks to cool.

For dressing, in a small bowl, whisk the vinegar, canola oil, sesame oil, sugar, salt and pepper; set aside. In a large bowl, combine the romaine, chicken, peppers and tomatoes. Just before serving, drizzle with dressing and toss to coat. Top with wonton strips. **YIELD:** 10 SERVINGS.

Nutrition Facts: One serving (1 cup) equals:
149 calories
6 g fat (1 g saturated fat)
33 mg cholesterol
253 mg sodium
10 g carbohydrate
1 g fiber
14 g protein

Diabetic Exchanges: 2 very lean meat, 1 fat, 1/2 starch.

Three-Step Taco Salad

Phyllis Schmalz, Kansas City, Kansas

PREP/TOTAL TIME: 20 MIN.

1 pound lean ground beef

3/4 cup water

Chicken Salad with Crispy Wontons

Three-Step Taco Salad

1 envelope reduced-sodium taco seasoning

4 cups baked tortilla chips, broken

8 cups shredded lettuce, *divided*

1 can (16 ounces) kidney beans, rinsed and drained

2 medium tomatoes, seeded and chopped, *divided*

1 can (2-1/4 ounces) sliced ripe olives, drained

1 cup (4 ounces) shredded reduced-fat cheddar cheese, *divided*

2/3 cup fat-free sour cream

2/3 cup salsa

In a nonstick skillet, cook beef over medium heat until no longer pink; drain. Add water and taco seasoning; bring to a boil. Reduce heat; simmer, uncovered, for 5 minutes, stirring occasionally.

In a large bowl, layer tortilla chips, 7 cups lettuce, beans, half of tomatoes, olives, half of cheese and meat mixture. Top with remaining tomatoes, cheese and lettuce. In a small bowl, combine sour cream and salsa. Serve with salad. **YIELD:** 10 SERVINGS.

Nutrition Facts: One serving (1-1/2 cups with 2 tablespoons sour cream mixture) equals:
239 calories
7 g fat (3 g saturated fat)
38 mg cholesterol
591 mg sodium
27 g carbohydrate
4 g fiber
17 g protein

Diabetic Exchanges: 2 lean meat, 1-1/2 starch, 1 vegetable.

Shrimp Linguine Salad

Eileen Herr, Indianapolis, Indiana

PREP: 15 MIN. + CHILLING

- 8 ounces uncooked linguine, broken in half
- 1 pound cooked medium shrimp, peeled and deveined
- 3 cups fresh broccoli florets
- 1 can (14 ounces) water-packed artichoke hearts, rinsed, drained and chopped
- 1/2 pound fresh mushrooms, sliced
- 12 cherry tomatoes, halved
- 3/4 cup shredded carrots
- 1/2 cup sliced green onions
- 1/3 cup olive oil
- 1/3 cup reduced-sodium soy sauce
- 1 tablespoon lemon juice
- 1 garlic clove, minced
- 1/2 teaspoon hot pepper sauce
- 2 tablespoons sesame seeds, toasted

Cook linguine according to package directions; drain and rinse in cold water. Place in a bowl; add the shrimp, broccoli, artichokes, mushrooms, tomatoes, carrots and onions.

In a jar with a tight-fitting lid, combine the oil, soy sauce, lemon juice, garlic and hot pepper sauce; shake well. Pour over salad and toss to coat. Cover and refrigerate for at least 1 hour. Just before serving, sprinkle with sesame seeds. **YIELD:** 9 SERVINGS.

Nutrition Facts: One serving (1-1/3 cup) equals:
- 286 calories
- 10 g fat (1 g saturated fat)
- 77 mg cholesterol
- 721 mg sodium
- 31 g carbohydrate
- 5 g fiber
- 18 g protein

Diabetic Exchanges: 2 vegetable, 1-1/2 starch, 1-1/2 fat, 1 lean meat.

Hold-the-Oil French Dressing

Ruth Koberna, Brecksville, Ohio

PREP/TOTAL TIME: 10 MIN.

- 1 can (10-3/4 ounces) reduced-fat reduced-sodium condensed tomato soup, undiluted
- 1/3 cup sugar
- 1/3 cup cider vinegar
- 1 tablespoon Worcestershire sauce
- 1 tablespoon grated onion
- 1 teaspoon salt
- 1/2 teaspoon ground mustard
- 1 garlic clove, minced
- 1/2 teaspoon paprika
- 1/4 teaspoon pepper

Salad greens and vegetables of your choice

In a bowl, whisk the first 10 ingredients until blended. Serve with a tossed salad. Refrigerate leftover dressing.
YIELD: 14 SERVINGS (1-3/4 CUPS).

Nutrition Facts:
One serving (2 tablespoons) equals:
- 38 calories
- trace fat (trace saturated fat)
- 0 cholesterol
- 260 mg sodium
- 9 g carbohydrate
- trace fiber
- trace protein

Diabetic Exchange: 1/2 starch.

Tangy Four-Bean Salad

Sharon Cain, Revelstoke, British Columbia

PREP: 20 MIN. + CHILLING

- 1 can (16 ounces) kidney beans, rinsed and drained
- 1 can (15 ounces) garbanzo beans *or* chickpeas, rinsed and drained
- 1 can (14-1/2 ounces) cut green beans, drained
- 1 can (14-1/2 ounces) cut wax beans, drained
- 1 cup sliced fresh mushrooms
- 1 cup chopped green pepper
- 1 cup chopped onion

Shrimp Linguine Salad

Tangy Four-Bean Salad

DRESSING:

- 1/2 cup cider vinegar
- 1/3 cup sugar
- 1/4 cup canola oil
- 1 teaspoon celery seed
- 1/2 teaspoon pepper
- 1/4 teaspoon salt
- 1/8 teaspoon dried basil
- 1/8 teaspoon dried oregano

In a large bowl, combine the beans, mushrooms, green pepper and onion. In a jar with a tight-fitting lid, combine the dressing ingredients; shake well.

Pour dressing over bean mixture and stir to coat. Cover and refrigerate for at least 4 hours. Serve with a slotted spoon. **YIELD:** 12 SERVINGS.

Nutrition Facts: One serving (3/4 cup) equals:
- 162 calories
- 6 g fat (trace saturated fat)
- 0 cholesterol
- 366 mg sodium
- 24 g carbohydrate
- 5 g fiber
- 5 g protein

Diabetic Exchanges: 1 starch, 1 vegetable, 1 fat.

Curried Chicken Tossed Salad

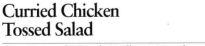

Irene Tetreault, South Hadley, Massachusetts

PREP/TOTAL TIME: 30 MIN.

- 2 cups water
- 2 cups cut fresh asparagus (1-inch pieces)
- 1/2 cup julienned carrot (2-inch strips)
- 4 cups mixed salad greens
- 2 cups coarsely chopped spinach
- 2 cups cubed cooked chicken breast
- 5 tablespoons fat-free mayonnaise
- 2 tablespoons olive oil
- 2 tablespoons fat-free milk
- 1 tablespoon lemon juice
- 1 teaspoon thinly sliced green onion
- 1 teaspoon honey
- 3/4 teaspoon dried basil
- 3/4 teaspoon curry powder
- 1/4 teaspoon salt
- 1/8 teaspoon pepper

In a small nonstick skillet, bring water to boil. Add asparagus; cover and boil for 1 minute. Add carrots; cover and boil 1-1/2 to 2 minutes longer. Drain and immediately place asparagus and carrots in ice water. Drain and pat dry.

In a large bowl, combine the salad greens, spinach, chicken and blanched vegetables. In a small bowl, whisk together the remaining ingredients. Serve with salad. **YIELD:** 4 SERVINGS.

Nutrition Facts: One serving (2 cups) equals:
- 236 calories
- 10 g fat (2 g saturated fat)
- 62 mg cholesterol
- 378 mg sodium
- 12 g carbohydrate
- 4 g fiber
- 25 g protein

Diabetic Exchanges: 3 lean meat, 1 vegetable, 1/2 starch.

Curried Chicken Tossed Salad

Antipasto Tossed Salad

Amy Bauman, Modesto, California

PREP: 20 MIN. + CHILLING

1-3/4   cups thinly sliced halved zucchini
1-1/2   cups cauliflowerets
1/4   cup thinly sliced green onions
1   cup reduced-fat Italian salad dressing
1   tablespoon lemon juice
12   cups torn romaine
2   medium tomatoes, cut into wedges
4   large fresh mushrooms, thinly sliced
4   ounces sliced turkey salami, julienned
4   ounces reduced-fat provolone cheese, julienned
1   can (2-1/4 ounces) sliced ripe olives, drained
1   cup fat-free Italian croutons
1/4   cup shredded Parmesan cheese

In a bowl, combine the zucchini, cauliflower and onions. Combine the salad dressing and lemon juice; pour over vegetables and toss to coat. Cover and refrigerate for at least 4 hours.

Just before serving, combine the romaine, tomatoes, mushrooms, salami, provolone and olives in a serving bowl. Add marinated vegetables; toss to coat. Top with croutons and Parmesan cheese. YIELD: 16 SERVINGS.

Nutrition Facts: One serving (1 cup) equals:
86   calories
5 g   fat (2 g saturated fat)
12 mg   cholesterol
329 mg   sodium
7 g   carbohydrate
1 g   fiber
6 g   protein

Diabetic Exchanges: 1/2 starch, 1/2 lean meat, 1/2 fat.

Nectarine Arugula Salad

Christine Laba, Arlington, Virginia

PREP/TOTAL TIME: 20 MIN.

4   cups fresh arugula or baby spinach
4   cups torn Bibb or Boston lettuce
3   medium nectarines, sliced
2   tablespoons pine nuts, toasted
2   tablespoons crumbled blue cheese
2   tablespoons raspberry vinegar
2   teaspoons sugar
1   teaspoon Dijon mustard
1/8   teaspoon salt
Dash pepper
3   tablespoons olive oil

In a large salad bowl, combine the first five ingredients. In a small bowl, whisk the vinegar, sugar, mustard, salt and pepper until

blended. Gradually whisk in oil until dressing thickens. Drizzle over salad; toss to coat. YIELD: 8 SERVINGS.

Nutrition Facts: One serving (1 cup) equals:
101   calories
7 g   fat (1 g saturated fat)
2 mg   cholesterol
86 mg   sodium
9 g   carbohydrate
1 g   fiber
2 g   protein

Diabetic Exchanges: 1-1/2 fat, 1/2 starch.

Marinated Salad

Susan Branch, Kalamazoo, Michigan

PREP: 10 MIN. + CHILLING

3-1/4   cups fresh whole kernel corn, cooked and drained
2   cups cherry tomatoes, halved
1-1/2   cups cooked rigatoni or large tube pasta
1   medium zucchini, halved lengthwise and thinly sliced
1/2   cup pitted ripe olives
1/3   cup tarragon vinegar
2   tablespoons olive oil
1-1/2   teaspoons dill weed
1   teaspoon salt
1/2   teaspoon ground mustard
1/4   teaspoon garlic powder
1/4   teaspoon pepper

In a large bowl, combine the corn, tomatoes, rigatoni, zucchini and olives.

In a small bowl, whisk together the vinegar, oil, dill, salt, mustard, garlic powder and pepper. Pour over corn mixture; toss to coat. Cover and refrigerate for at least 2 hours. YIELD: 7 SERVINGS.

Nutrition Facts: One serving (1 cup) equals:
166   calories
6 g   fat (1 g saturated fat)
0   cholesterol
429 mg   sodium
28 g   carbohydrate
4 g   fiber
4 g   protein

Diabetic Exchanges: 1-1/2 starch, 1 vegetable, 1 fat.

Cucumber Couscous Salad

Evelyn Lewis, Independence, Missouri

PREP: 25 MIN. + CHILLING

1-1/4   cups water
1   cup uncooked couscous
2   medium cucumbers, peeled, quartered lengthwise and sliced
1   cup chopped sweet red pepper

Antipasto Tossed Salad

1/4 cup thinly sliced green onions
1/2 cup buttermilk
1/4 cup reduced-fat plain yogurt
2 tablespoons minced fresh dill
2 tablespoons white vinegar
1 tablespoon olive oil
1/2 teaspoon salt
1/4 teaspoon pepper

In a saucepan, bring water to a boil. Stir in couscous. Remove from the heat; cover and let stand for 5 minutes. Fluff with a fork. Cool to room temperature.

In a large bowl, combine the couscous, cucumber, red pepper and onions. Whisk together the buttermilk, yogurt, dill, vinegar, oil, salt and pepper. Pour over couscous mixture. Cover and refrigerate for at least 1 hour. **YIELD:** 8 SERVINGS.

Nutrition Facts: One serving (2/3 cup) equals:
- 126 calories
- 2 g fat (trace saturated fat)
- 1 mg cholesterol
- 172 mg sodium
- 22 g carbohydrate
- 2 g fiber
- 5 g protein

Diabetic Exchanges: 1 starch, 1 vegetable, 1/2 fat.

Crab Coleslaw Medley

low carb

Edith Frost, Mountain View, California

PREP/TOTAL TIME: 15 MIN.

1 package (16 ounces) coleslaw mix
6 cups torn romaine
3/4 cup finely chopped onion
1 package (8 ounces) imitation crabmeat, chopped
1/3 cup canola oil

Crab Coleslaw Medley

Cucumber Couscous Salad

3 tablespoons cider vinegar
2 tablespoons sugar
1 teaspoon salt
1/2 teaspoon pepper
1 package (3 ounces) chicken ramen noodles
2 tablespoons slivered almonds, toasted
2 tablespoons sesame seeds, toasted

In a large bowl, combine the coleslaw mix, romaine, onion and crab. In a jar with a tight-fitting lid, combine the oil, vinegar, sugar, salt, pepper and contents of seasoning packet from noodles; shake well.

Break noodles into small pieces. Sprinkle noodles, almonds and sesame seeds over salad; mix well. Drizzle with dressing and toss to coat. Serve immediately. **YIELD:** 12 SERVINGS.

Nutrition Facts: One serving (1 cup) equals:
- 149 calories
- 8 g fat (1 g saturated fat)
- 4 mg cholesterol
- 527 mg sodium
- 15 g carbohydrate
- 3 g fiber
- 5 g protein

Diabetic Exchanges: 1 starch, 1 vegetable, 1 fat.

New Waldorf Salad

Marie Engwall, Willmar, Minnesota

PREP/TOTAL TIME: 20 MIN.

- 1 medium unpeeled red apple, chopped
- 1 medium unpeeled green apple, chopped
- 1 medium unpeeled pear, chopped
- 1/2 cup green grapes
- 1/4 cup raisins
- 1/4 cup slivered almonds, toasted
- 1 carton (6 ounces) reduced-fat lemon yogurt
- 2 teaspoons lemon juice
- 2 teaspoons orange juice
- 2 teaspoons honey
- 1 teaspoon grated orange peel

Lettuce leaves, optional

In a large bowl, combine the apples, pear, grapes, raisins and almonds. In a small bowl, combine the yogurt, lemon and orange juices, honey and orange peel; pour over fruit mixture and stir to coat. Serve immediately in lettuce-lined bowls if desired. **YIELD:** 4 SERVINGS.

Nutrition Facts: One serving (1 cup) equals:
- 193 calories
- 5 g fat (1 g saturated fat)
- 2 mg cholesterol
- 33 mg sodium
- 35 g carbohydrate
- 4 g fiber
- 5 g protein

Diabetic Exchanges: 2 fruit, 1/2 fat-free milk, 1/2 fat.

New Waldorf Salad

Chili-Cumin Bean Salad

Michelle Smith, Running Springs, California

PREP: 10 MIN. + CHILLING

- 4 cups chopped tomatoes
- 1 can (15-1/2 ounces) hominy, rinsed and drained
- 1 can (15 ounces) black beans, rinsed and drained
- 1 can (15 ounces) pinto beans, rinsed and drained
- 1-1/2 cups chopped red onion
- 1 cup minced fresh cilantro
- 1/4 cup lime juice
- 3 tablespoons olive oil
- 2-1/2 teaspoons chili powder
- 2-1/2 teaspoons ground cumin
- 1 teaspoon pepper
- 1/2 teaspoon salt

In a large bowl, combine the tomatoes, hominy, beans, onion and cilantro. In a jar with a tight-fitting lid, combine the remaining ingredients; shake well. Pour over salad and toss to coat. Refrigerate for at least 2 hours before serving. **YIELD:** 12 SERVINGS.

Nutrition Facts: One serving (3/4 cup) equals:
- 140 calories
- 5 g fat (1 g saturated fat)
- 0 cholesterol
- 413 mg sodium
- 21 g carbohydrate
- 6 g fiber
- 5 g protein

Diabetic Exchanges: 1-1/2 starch, 1 fat.

Vegetarian Taco Salad

Susan LeBrun, Sulphur, Louisiana

PREP/TOTAL TIME: 25 MIN.

- 4 whole wheat tortillas (8 inches)
- 6 cups shredded romaine
- 1/2 cup canned pinto beans, rinsed and drained
- 1 small tomato, chopped
- 1/4 cup shredded reduced-fat cheddar cheese
- 1/4 cup chopped green onions
- 2 tablespoons sliced ripe olives, drained

Sliced jalapeno peppers, optional

DRESSING:

- 1/2 cup fat-free sour cream
- 2 tablespoons prepared fat-free ranch salad dressing
- 1 teaspoon taco seasoning
- 1/4 teaspoon hot pepper sauce, optional

Place four 10-oz. custard cups upside down in a shallow baking pan; set aside. Place the tortillas in a single layer on ungreased

Vegetarian Taco Salad

baking sheets. Bake at 425° for 1 minute. Place a tortilla over each custard cup, pinching sides to form a bowl shape. Bake for 7-8 minutes or until crisp. Remove tortillas from cups to cool on wire racks.

In a large bowl, combine the romaine, beans, tomato, cheese, onions, olives and jalapenos if desired. In a small bowl, whisk the dressing ingredients; pour over salad and toss to coat. Serve in tortilla bowls.
YIELD: 4 SERVINGS.

Nutrition Facts: One serving (1 each) equals:
194 calories
3 g fat (1 g saturated fat)
10 mg cholesterol
489 mg sodium
38 g carbohydrate
5 g fiber
10 g protein

Diabetic Exchange: 2-1/2 starch.

Herbed Tuna Salad

Rebecca Schweizer, Chesapeake, Virginia

PREP/TOTAL TIME: 15 MIN.

- 1 can (6 ounces) light water-packed tuna, drained and flaked
- 2 tablespoons finely chopped red onion
- 1 teaspoon minced fresh parsley
- 1-1/2 teaspoons dill weed
- 1/8 teaspoon garlic salt
- 1/8 teaspoon dried thyme
- 1/8 teaspoon pepper
- Pinch cayenne pepper
- 2 tablespoons fat-free mayonnaise
- 1 tablespoon reduced-fat sour cream
- 3 cups spring mix salad greens
- 1 medium tomato, cut into wedges

In a small bowl, combine the first eight ingredients. Combine the mayonnaise and sour cream; stir into the tuna mixture.

Divide the salad greens between two plates. Top with tuna mixture and tomato wedges. **YIELD:** 2 SERVINGS.

Nutrition Facts: One serving (1 each) equals:
170 calories
2 g fat (1 g saturated fat)
30 mg cholesterol
452 mg sodium
14 g carbohydrate
4 g fiber
25 g protein

Diabetic Exchanges: 3 very lean meat, 2 vegetable.

Herbed Tuna Salad

Zippy Chicken Coleslaw

Broil 3-4 in. from the heat for 5-6 minutes on each side or until juices run clear. When chicken is cool enough to handle, shred with two forks; cool completely.

Set aside seasoning packet from ramen noodles. Break noodles into small pieces; place in a large bowl. Add the cabbage, broccoli coleslaw, onions, sesame seeds, almonds and chicken.

In a jar with a tight-fitting lid, combine the dressing ingredients. Add the contents of seasoning packet; shake well. Pour over coleslaw and toss to coat. **YIELD:** 9 SERVINGS.

Nutrition Facts: One serving (2/3 cup) equals:
- 132 calories
- 5 g fat (1 g saturated fat)
- 14 mg cholesterol
- 405 mg sodium
- 15 g carbohydrate
- 2 g fiber
- 8 g protein

Diabetic Exchanges: 1 starch, 1 very lean meat, 1/2 fat.

Zippy Chicken Coleslaw

`low carb`

Kathy Egan, Oceanside, California

PREP: 40 MIN. **COOK:** 10 MIN.

- 1 tablespoon paprika
- 1/2 teaspoon dried thyme
- 1/4 teaspoon sugar
- 1/4 teaspoon salt
- 1/4 teaspoon onion powder
- 1/4 teaspoon garlic powder
- 1/4 teaspoon pepper
- 1/8 teaspoon cayenne pepper
- 1/2 pound boneless skinless chicken breast
- 1 package (3 ounces) hot and spicy ramen noodles
- 4 cups shredded cabbage
- 2 cups broccoli coleslaw mix
- 3 green onions, chopped
- 2 tablespoons sesame seeds, toasted
- 2 tablespoons sliced almonds, toasted

DRESSING:
- 3 tablespoons sugar
- 2 tablespoons reduced-sodium soy sauce
- 4-1/2 teaspoons cider vinegar
- 2-1/4 teaspoons water
- 2-1/4 teaspoons canola oil
- 1/8 teaspoon pepper

In a small bowl, combine the first eight ingredients; rub over both sides of chicken.

Grilled Corn Salad

`low fat` `meat less`

Patty Cook, West Palm Beach, Florida

PREP: 30 MIN. + MARINATING

- 1 bottle (16 ounces) fat-free Italian salad dressing
- 1 to 2 tablespoons minced fresh rosemary *or* 1 to 2 teaspoons dried rosemary, crushed
- 7 medium ears sweet corn, husks removed
- 7 plum tomatoes, sliced
- 7 cups torn fresh spinach

Coat grill rack with nonstick cooking spray before starting the grill. In a large resealable plastic bag, combine the dressing and rosemary; add corn. Seal bag and turn to coat; remove corn from marinade. Seal bag and refrigerate marinade.

Grill corn, covered, over medium heat for 15-18 minutes or until tender, turning occasionally. Return corn to the marinade; add tomatoes. Seal bag and turn to coat; refrigerate for at least 4 hours or overnight.

Drain corn and tomatoes, reserving marinade. Cut corn off the cob. Arrange spinach on salad plates; top with tomatoes and corn. Drizzle with reserved marinade. **YIELD:** 7 SERVINGS.

Nutrition Facts: One serving (1 cup) equals:
- 141 calories
- 2 g fat (trace saturated fat)
- 2 mg cholesterol
- 873 mg sodium
- 29 g carbohydrate
- 5 g fiber
- 5 g protein

Diabetic Exchanges: 1-1/2 starch, 1 vegetable.

Roasted Asparagus Salad

low carb | meat less

Virginia Anthony, Jacksonville, Florida

PREP/TOTAL TIME: 20 MIN.

- 1 pound fresh asparagus, trimmed and cut into 1-inch pieces
- 1/2 teaspoon olive oil

DRESSING:
- 1/2 cup orange juice
- 2 tablespoons olive oil
- 2 tablespoons orange marmalade
- 1 tablespoon lime juice
- 1/2 teaspoon salt

Dash ground ginger *or* 1/2 teaspoon minced fresh gingerroot
- 7 cups torn mixed salad greens
- 3 tablespoons sunflower kernels, toasted

Place asparagus in a 13-in. x 9-in. x 2-in. baking dish. Drizzle with oil. Bake, uncovered, at 400° for 10 minutes or until crisp-tender. Cool.

For dressing, combine the orange juice, oil, marmalade, lime juice, salt and ginger in a jar with a tight-fitting lid; shake well. Refrigerate.

To serve, place the greens in a salad bowl or on individual plates; top with asparagus. Drizzle with dressing and sprinkle with sunflower kernels. YIELD: 6 SERVINGS.

Nutrition Facts: One serving (1-1/4 cups) equals:
- 124 calories
- 7 g fat (1 g saturated fat)
- 0 cholesterol
- 224 mg sodium
- 14 g carbohydrate
- 4 g fiber
- 4 g protein

Diabetic Exchanges: 1 vegetable, 1/2 starch, 1/2 fat.

Roasted Asparagus Salad

Zesty Potato Salad

Zesty Potato Salad

low fat | meat less

Raquel Haggard, Edmond, Oklahoma

PREP: 25 MIN. + CHILLING

- 2 pound red potatoes, cubed
- 3/4 cup fat-free mayonnaise
- 1/3 cup reduced-fat sour cream
- 1/3 cup minced fresh cilantro
- 1 can (4 ounces) chopped green chilies
- 3 green onions, finely chopped
- 1 tablespoon lemon juice
- 1 teaspoon chili powder
- 1/2 teaspoon salt
- 1/4 teaspoon pepper

Dash garlic powder

Place potatoes in a saucepan and cover with water. Bring to a boil. Reduce heat; cover and cook for 15 minutes or just until tender. Drain and rinse with cold water.

In a small bowl, combine the remaining ingredients. Place potatoes in a large bowl. Add dressing and toss to coat. Cover and refrigerate for 2 hours or until chilled. YIELD: 6 SERVINGS.

Nutrition Facts: One serving (3/4 cup) equals:
- 162 calories
- 2 g fat (1 g saturated fat)
- 7 mg cholesterol
- 693 mg sodium
- 32 g carbohydrate
- 4 g fiber
- 4 g protein

Diabetic Exchange: 2 starch.

Emerald Fruit Salad

Beth Scholke, Barrington, Illinois

PREP/TOTAL TIME: 15 MIN.

- 3 medium tart green apples, cubed
- 2 cups cubed honeydew
- 2 cups halved green grapes
- 3 kiwifruit, peeled, sliced and quartered
- 1 cup (8 ounces) reduced-fat plain yogurt
- 3 tablespoons confectioners' sugar
- 3 tablespoons orange juice
- 1/2 teaspoon grated orange peel

In a large bowl, combine the fruit. In a small bowl, combine the yogurt, sugar, orange juice and peel. Spoon over fruit; serve immediately. **YIELD:** 7 SERVINGS.

Nutrition Facts: One serving (1 cup) equals:
- 136 calories
- 1 g fat (trace saturated fat)
- 2 mg cholesterol
- 31 mg sodium
- 32 g carbohydrate
- 3 g fiber
- 3 g protein

Diabetic Exchange: 2 fruit.

Emerald Fruit Salad

Green Pepper Tomato Salad

Lili Hill, Athens, Georgia

PREP/TOTAL TIME: 15 MIN. + CHILLING

- 3 medium tomatoes, seeded and chopped
- 1 medium green pepper, chopped
- 1 celery rib, thinly sliced
- 1/2 cup chopped red onion
- 2 tablespoons cider vinegar
- 1 tablespoon sugar
- 1/2 teaspoon salt
- 1/8 teaspoon pepper

In a large bowl, combine the tomatoes, green pepper, celery and onion. In a small bowl, combine the vinegar, sugar, salt and pepper. Stir into tomato mixture. Cover and refrigerate for at least 2 hours, stirring several times. Serve with a slotted spoon. **YIELD:** 6 SERVINGS.

Nutrition Facts: One serving (3/4 cup) equals:
- 34 calories
- trace fat (trace saturated fat)
- 0 cholesterol
- 213 mg sodium
- 8 g carbohydrate
- 1 g fiber
- 1 g protein

Diabetic Exchange: 1 vegetable.

Cucumber Fennel Salad

Taste of Home Test Kitchen
Greendale, Wisconsin

PREP/TOTAL TIME: 20 MIN.

- 3 large cucumbers, sliced
- 1 medium sweet onion, thinly sliced
- 1 small fennel bulb, thinly sliced
- 3 tablespoons lemon juice
- 3 tablespoons olive oil
- 3/4 teaspoon dill weed
- 1/2 teaspoon salt
- 1/4 teaspoon pepper
- 1/4 teaspoon grated lemon peel

In a large bowl, combine the cucumber, onion and fennel. In a jar with a tight-fitting lid, combine the remaining ingredients; shake well. Pour over cucumber mixture and toss to coat. Refrigerate until chilled. **YIELD:** 8 SERVINGS.

Nutrition Facts: One serving (1 cup) equals:
- 80 calories
- 5 g fat (1 g saturated fat)
- 0 cholesterol
- 165 mg sodium
- 8 g carbohydrate
- 2 g fiber
- 1 g protein

Diabetic Exchanges: 1 vegetable, 1 fat.

Italian Market Salad

Italian Market Salad `low carb`

Karen Schmidt, Plymouth, Wisconsin

PREP: 25 MIN. + CHILLING

- 2 cups cooked brown rice, cooled
- 2 cups (8 ounces) shredded part-skim mozzarella cheese
- 4 plum tomatoes, seeded and chopped
- 1/2 medium green pepper, julienned
- 4 ounces sliced turkey pepperoni, quartered
- 1/2 cup diced fully cooked turkey ham
- 4 green onions, sliced
- 1 can (2-1/4 ounces) sliced ripe olives, drained
- 1/2 cup reduced-fat Italian salad dressing

In a large bowl, combine the first eight ingredients. Pour dressing over salad; toss to coat. Cover and refrigerate for 2 hours or until chilled. **YIELD:** 9 SERVINGS.

Nutrition Facts: One serving (3/4 cup) equals:
- 199 calories
- 9 g fat (3 g saturated fat)
- 36 mg cholesterol
- 612 mg sodium
- 15 g carbohydrate
- 2 g fiber
- 13 g protein

Diabetic Exchanges: 2 lean meat, 1 starch, 1/2 fat.

Creamy Lime Potato Salad `meat less`

Angela Accorinti, Okeana, Ohio

PREP/TOTAL TIME: 30 MIN.

- 4 cups cubed red potatoes
- 1/3 cup reduced-fat mayonnaise
- 1/4 cup reduced-fat sour cream
- 2 tablespoons lime juice
- 1 tablespoon minced fresh thyme *or* 1 teaspoon dried thyme
- 1/2 teaspoon grated lime peel
- 1/2 teaspoon salt
- 1/2 teaspoon pepper

Place potatoes in a saucepan and cover with water. Bring to a boil. Reduce heat; cover and cook for 13-18 minutes or until potatoes are tender. Drain. Cool potatoes for 10 minutes.

Meanwhile, in a bowl, combine the mayonnaise, sour cream, lime juice, thyme, lime peel, salt and pepper. Pour over potatoes; toss gently to coat. Serve warm or chilled. **YIELD:** 5 SERVINGS.

Nutrition Facts: One serving (3/4 cup) equals:
- 158 calories
- 6 g fat (2 g saturated fat)
- 10 mg cholesterol
- 376 mg sodium
- 22 g carbohydrate
- 2 g fiber
- 3 g protein

Diabetic Exchanges: 1-1/2 starch, 1 fat.

Creamy Lime Potato Salad

End-of-Summer Tomato Salad

End-of-Summer Tomato Salad

Carol Birkemeier, Nashville, Indiana

PREP: 15 MIN. + CHILLING

- 8 small tomatoes (2 pounds), sliced
- 1/2 cup chopped ripe olives
- 2 tablespoons olive oil
- 1 tablespoon white wine vinegar
- 4 teaspoons Dijon mustard
- 2 teaspoons sugar
- 2 garlic cloves, minced
- 1 teaspoon salt
- 1/2 teaspoon pepper
- Leaf lettuce, optional
- 1/4 cup minced fresh parsley
- 1/4 cup chopped green onions

Arrange tomatoes in a 13-in. x 9-in. x 2-in. dish; sprinkle with olives. In a jar with a tight-fitting lid, combine the oil, vinegar, mustard, sugar, garlic, salt and pepper; shake well. Pour over tomatoes and olives.

Cover and refrigerate overnight, turning tomatoes and olives occasionally. Serve on lettuce if desired. Sprinkle with parsley and onions. **YIELD:** 6 SERVINGS.

Nutrition Facts: One serving (1 cup) equals:
- 98 calories
- 7 g fat (1 g saturated fat)
- 0 cholesterol
- 589 mg sodium
- 10 g carbohydrate
- 2 g fiber
- 2 g protein

Diabetic Exchanges: 2 vegetable, 1 fat.

Classic Macaroni Salad

Dorothy Bayes, Sardis, Ohio

PREP/TOTAL TIME: 30 MIN.

- 2 cups uncooked elbow macaroni
- 1 cup fat-free mayonnaise
- 2 tablespoons sweet pickle relish
- Sugar substitute equivalent to 2 teaspoons sugar
- 3/4 teaspoon ground mustard
- 1/4 teaspoon salt
- 1/8 teaspoon pepper
- 1/2 cup chopped celery
- 1/3 cup chopped carrot
- 1/4 cup chopped onion
- 1 hard-cooked egg, sliced
- Dash paprika

Cook macaroni according to package directions; drain and rinse with cold water. Cool completely.

For dressing, in a small bowl, combine the mayonnaise, pickle relish, sugar substitute, mustard, salt and pepper. In a large bowl, combine the macaroni, celery, carrot and onion. Add dressing and toss gently to coat. Refrigerate until serving. Garnish with egg and paprika. **YIELD:** 8 SERVINGS.

Editor's Note: This recipe was tested with Splenda No Calorie Sweetener.

Nutrition Facts: One serving (3/4 cup) equals:
- 111 calories
- 2 g fat (trace saturated fat)
- 30 mg cholesterol
- 362 mg sodium
- 20 g carbohydrate
- 2 g fiber
- 4 g protein

Diabetic Exchange: 1-1/2 starch.

Tortellini Bean Salad

Lenore Adams, Dayton, Ohio

PREP: 20 MIN. + CHILLING

- 1 package (10 ounces) refrigerated spinach tortellini
- 2 cups broccoli florets
- 1/2 large red onion, thinly sliced
- 1 cup canned garbanzo beans or chickpeas, rinsed and drained
- 1 cup canned red kidney beans, rinsed and drained
- 1 cup canned white kidney beans or cannellini beans, rinsed and drained
- 1 can (6 ounces) pitted ripe olives, drained
- 1 bottle (8 ounces) fat-free creamy Italian salad dressing
- 1/4 cup shredded Parmesan cheese,
- 1 teaspoon dried oregano
- 24 cherry tomatoes, halved

Prepare tortellini according to package directions; drain and place in a serving bowl. Add broccoli, onion, beans and olives. Combine the salad dressing, 2 tablespoons Parmesan cheese and oregano; pour over salad and toss gently.

Cover and refrigerate for at least 8 hours. Just before serving, stir in tomatoes and sprinkle with remaining Parmesan. **YIELD:** 9 SERVINGS.

Nutrition Facts: One serving (1 cup) equals:
    218 calories
      6 g fat (2 g saturated fat)
    44 mg cholesterol
  758 mg sodium
    31 g carbohydrate
     7 g fiber
    10 g protein

Diabetic Exchanges: 2 starch, 1 lean meat.

Lemon Artichoke Romaine Salad

Kathleen Law, Pullman, Washington

PREP/TOTAL TIME: 10 MIN.

- 10 cups torn romaine
- 4 plum tomatoes, sliced
- 1 can (14 ounces) water-packed artichoke hearts, rinsed, drained and quartered
- 1 can (2-1/4 ounces) sliced ripe olives, drained
- 3 tablespoons water
- 3 tablespoons lemon juice
- 3 tablespoons olive oil
- 2 garlic cloves, minced
- 1 teaspoon salt
- 1 teaspoon coarsely ground pepper
- 1/3 cup shredded Parmesan cheese

In a bowl, combine the first four ingredients. Combine water, lemon juice, oil, garlic, salt and pepper. Pour over salad; toss to coat. Sprinkle with cheese. **YIELD:** 8 SERVINGS.

Nutrition Facts: One serving (1-1/2 cups) equals:
  114 calories
    7 g fat (1 g saturated fat)
    2 mg cholesterol
 730 mg sodium
   10 g carbohydrate
    4 g fiber
    5 g protein

Diabetic Exchanges: 2 vegetable, 1 fat.

Peachy Fruit Salad

Lori Daniels, Beverly, West Virginia

PREP/TOTAL TIME: 10 MIN.

- 2 medium fresh peaches, peeled and sliced
- 1 medium red apple, chopped
- 1 cup halved seedless red grapes
- 1 medium ripe mango, peeled and sliced
- 1 medium firm banana, sliced
- 1-1/2 cups apple pie filling

In a large bowl, combine the fruit. Add pie filling and toss to coat. Refrigerate until serving. **YIELD:** 8 SERVINGS.

Nutrition Facts: One serving (3/4 cup) equals:
  103 calories
     trace fat (trace saturated fat)
    0 cholesterol
   6 mg sodium
  26 g carbohydrate
    2 g fiber
    1 g protein

Diabetic Exchange: 2 fruit.

Peachy Fruit Salad

Tortellini Bean Salad

Sensational Sides.

For the perfect partners to any meal, start with these accompaniments! From fresh vegetables and pleasing pastas and potatoes to simmering sautes and comforting casseroles and bakes, you'll discover healthy options to round out any meal.

Asparagus Mushroom Casserole

Asparagus Mushroom Casserole

M. Kay Lacey, Apache Junction, Arizona

PREP: 10 MIN. BAKE: 35 MIN.

- 4 cups sliced fresh mushrooms
- 1 cup chopped onion
- 4 tablespoons butter, *divided*
- 2 tablespoons all-purpose flour
- 1 teaspoon chicken bouillon granules
- 1/2 teaspoon salt
- 1/8 teaspoon ground nutmeg
- 1/8 teaspoon pepper
- 1 cup 2% milk
- 1 package (12 ounces) frozen cut asparagus, thawed and drained
- 1/4 cup diced pimientos
- 1-1/2 teaspoons lemon juice
- 3/4 cup soft bread crumbs

In a nonstick skillet, cook mushrooms and onion in 3 tablespoons butter until tender. Remove vegetables with a slotted spoon and set aside. Stir the flour, bouillon, salt, nutmeg and pepper into drippings until smooth. Gradually add milk. Bring to a boil; cook and stir for 2 minutes or until thickened. Stir in asparagus, pimientos, lemon juice and the mushroom mixture.

Pour into a 1-1/2-qt. baking dish coated with nonstick cooking spray. Melt remaining butter; toss with bread crumbs. Sprinkle over top. Bake, uncovered, at 350° for 35-40 minutes or until heated through. **YIELD:** 6 SERVINGS.

Nutrition Facts: One serving (1 cup) equals:
- 162 calories
- 9 g fat (5 g saturated fat)
- 24 mg cholesterol
- 532 mg sodium
- 16 g carbohydrate
- 2 g fiber
- 6 g protein

Diabetic Exchanges: 1 starch, 1 fat, 1/2 lean meat.

East Indian Split Pea Pilaf

Marilyn Rodriquez, Fairbanks, Alaska

PREP: 35 MIN. COOK: 30 MIN.

- 2/3 cup dried yellow split peas
- 4-3/4 cups water, *divided*
- 1 bay leaf
- 3 tablespoons canola oil
- 1 large onion, chopped
- 1/2 to 1 teaspoon ground cinnamon
- 3/4 teaspoon ground cumin
- 1/2 teaspoon salt
- 1/4 teaspoon ground cloves
- 1/4 teaspoon ground turmeric
- 1-1/2 cups uncooked long grain rice
- 2-1/2 cups chicken broth

In a large saucepan, combine peas and 4 cups water. Bring to a boil. Reduce heat; simmer, uncovered, for 30-35 minutes or until tender. Drain and keep warm.

In a large nonstick skillet, cook the bay leaf in oil until golden, about 3 minutes. Add onion; saute until tender. Stir in the seasonings; saute for 30 seconds. Add the rice; cook and stir for 3 minutes. Stir in broth and remaining water. Bring to a boil. Reduce heat; cover and simmer for 20-25 minutes or until rice is tender. Add peas; heat through. Discard bay leaf. **YIELD:** 6 SERVINGS.

Nutrition Facts: One serving (1 cup) equals:
- 214 calories
- 7 g fat (1 g saturated fat)
- 0 cholesterol
- 572 mg sodium
- 30 g carbohydrate
- 1 g fiber
- 8 g protein

Diabetic Exchanges: 2 starch, 1 fat.

Spinach Cheddar Squares `low carb` `meat less`

Elaine Anderson, Aliquippa, Pennsylvania

PREP: 15 MIN. BAKE: 40 MIN. + STANDING

- 1 tablespoon dry bread crumbs
- 3/4 cup shredded reduced-fat cheddar cheese, *divided*
- 1 package (10 ounces) frozen chopped spinach, thawed and squeezed dry
- 1/4 cup finely chopped sweet red pepper
- 1-1/2 cups egg substitute
- 3/4 cup fat-free milk
- 2 tablespoons grated Parmesan cheese
- 1/2 teaspoon dried minced onion
- 1/2 teaspoon salt
- 1/4 teaspoon garlic powder
- 1/4 teaspoon pepper

Sprinkle bread crumbs evenly into an 8-in. square baking dish coated with nonstick cooking spray. Top with 1/2 cup cheese, spinach and red pepper. In a small bowl, combine the remaining ingredients; pour over the top.

Bake, uncovered, at 350° for 35 minutes. Sprinkle with remaining cheese. Bake 2-3 minutes longer or until a knife inserted near the center comes out clean. Let stand for 15 minutes before cutting. **YIELD:** 4 SERVINGS.

Nutrition Facts: One serving (1 piece) equals:

- 219 calories
- 10 g fat (6 g saturated fat)
- 31 mg cholesterol
- 596 mg sodium
- 9 g carbohydrate
- 2 g fiber
- 26 g protein

Diabetic Exchanges: 3 lean meat, 1 vegetable, 1/2 starch.

Unfried Refried Beans

`low fat` `meat less`

Michele Martinez, Albany, New York

PREP: 20 MIN. + STANDING **COOK:** 2 HOURS

- 8 ounces dried pinto beans, sorted and rinsed
- 2 quarts water
- 2 tablespoons chili powder
- 2 garlic cloves, slightly crushed
- 2 teaspoons ground cumin, *divided*
- 1 teaspoon pepper
- 1 teaspoon salt, *divided*
- 1/8 to 1/4 teaspoon crushed red pepper flakes

Tostada shells, optional

Toppings of your choice, optional

Spinach Cheddar Squares

Unfried Refried Beans

Place beans in a soup kettle or Dutch oven; add water to cover by 2 in. Bring to a boil; boil for 2 minutes. Remove from the heat; cover and let stand for 1 hour. Drain and rinse beans, discarding liquid.

Return beans to Dutch oven; add the 2 quarts water. Add the chili powder, garlic, 1-3/4 teaspoons cumin, pepper, 3/4 teaspoon salt and pepper flakes. Bring to a boil. Reduce heat; cover and simmer for 2-3 hours or until beans are tender.

Drain beans, reserving 3/4 cup liquid. Place bean mixture in a bowl; coarsely mash. Gradually stir in reserved cooking liquid until mixture reaches desired consistency. Stir in the remaining cumin and salt. Serve on tostada shells with toppings of your choice if desired. **YIELD:** 5 SERVINGS.

Nutrition Facts: One serving (1/2 cup) equals:

- 165 calories
- 1 g fat (1 g saturated fat)
- 0 cholesterol
- 505 mg sodium
- 31 g carbohydrate
- 11 g fiber
- 10 g protein

Diabetic Exchanges: 1-1/2 starch, 1 very lean meat.

Monterey Jack Corn Bake

Donna Nortman, Camillus, New York

PREP: 10 MIN. **BAKE:** 30 MIN.

- 1 egg
- 2 egg whites
- 1-1/2 cups (12 ounces) reduced-fat sour cream
- 2-3/4 cups fresh *or* frozen corn, thawed
- 1/2 cup soft bread crumbs
- 2 ounces Monterey Jack cheese, diced
- 1/2 teaspoon salt
- 1/8 teaspoon pepper
- 1/2 cup shredded reduced-fat cheddar cheese

In a large bowl, combine the egg, egg whites and sour cream. Add the corn, bread crumbs, Monterey Jack cheese, salt and pepper; mix well.

Pour into a shallow 1-1/2-qt. baking dish coated with nonstick cooking spray. Bake, uncovered, at 350° for 30-40 minutes or until a knife inserted near the center comes out clean. Sprinkle with cheddar cheese; cover and let stand 5 minutes before serving. **YIELD:** 6 SERVINGS.

Nutrition Facts: One serving (2/3 cup) equals:
- 225 calories
- 11 g fat (7 g saturated fat)
- 70 mg cholesterol
- 409 mg sodium
- 20 g carbohydrate
- 2 g fiber
- 13 g protein

Diabetic Exchanges: 2 fat, 1 starch, 1 lean meat.

Monterey Jack Corn Bake

Parmesan Potato Wedges

Beth Ask, Ulster, Pennsylvania

PREP: 10 MIN. **BAKE:** 30 MIN.

- 4 large baking potatoes (2 pounds)
- 1/4 cup grated Parmesan cheese
- 1 teaspoon garlic salt
- 1/2 teaspoon garlic powder
- 1/2 teaspoon dried oregano
- 1/2 teaspoon paprika

Line a baking sheet with heavy-duty foil. Cut each potato into eight wedges; place on foil. Coat with nonstick cooking spray. Sprinkle with Parmesan cheese and seasonings. Bake at 400° for 30 minutes or until tender. **YIELD:** 8 SERVINGS.

Nutrition Facts: One serving (4 wedges) equals:
- 129 calories
- trace fat (trace saturated fat)
- 1 mg cholesterol
- 249 mg sodium
- 29 g carbohydrate
- 3 g fiber
- 3 g protein

Diabetic Exchange: 1-1/2 starch.

Roasted Vegetable Ziti Bake

Helen Carpenter, Albuquerque, New Mexico

PREP: 40 MIN. **BAKE:** 40 MIN.

- 1 pound eggplant, peeled and cut into 1-inch cubes
- 1 large red onion, cut into 1-inch pieces
- 2 medium sweet yellow peppers, cut into 1-inch pieces
- 1 tablespoon olive oil
- 1/2 teaspoon salt

SAUCE:
- 1-1/2 cups chopped onions
- 2 teaspoons olive oil
- 6 garlic cloves, minced
- 1/2 teaspoon crushed red pepper flakes
- 1/2 teaspoon fennel seed, crushed
- 1 can (28 ounces) crushed tomatoes
- 1 can (14-1/2 ounces) diced tomatoes, undrained
- 1/4 cup minced fresh parsley
- 1-1/4 teaspoons salt
- 1/2 teaspoon pepper
- 1/4 teaspoon sugar
- 1/8 teaspoon dried thyme
- 1 package (16 ounces) ziti *or* other small tube pasta
- 4 cups chopped fresh spinach
- 1 cup (4 ounces) shredded part-skim mozzarella cheese

In a 15-in. x 10-in. x 1-in. baking pan coated with nonstick cooking spray,

Roasted Vegetable Ziti Bake

combine the eggplant, red onion and yellow peppers. Drizzle with oil; sprinkle with salt. Bake, uncovered, at 400° for 35-45 minutes or until edges of peppers begin to brown, stirring every 10 minutes.

Meanwhile, in a saucepan, saute onions in oil until tender. Add garlic, red pepper flakes and fennel; cook and stir for 1 minute. Add the tomatoes, parsley, salt, pepper, sugar and thyme. Bring to a boil. Reduce heat; simmer, uncovered, for 15 minutes. Cook pasta according to package directions; drain.

In two greased 2-qt. baking dishes, spread 1/2 cup sauce each. In each dish, layer a fourth of the pasta, a fourth of the roasted vegetables and 1/2 cup sauce. Top with 2 cups spinach and 1/2 cup sauce. Top with remaining roasted vegetables, pasta and sauce.

Cover and bake at 350° for 30 minutes. Uncover; sprinkle with cheese. Bake 10-15 minutes longer or until heated through and cheese is melted. **YIELD:** 12 SERVINGS.

Nutrition Facts: One serving (1 cup) equals:
- 230 calories
- 5 g fat (1 g saturated fat)
- 5 mg cholesterol
- 497 mg sodium
- 40 g carbohydrate
- 4 g fiber
- 10 g protein

Diabetic Exchanges: 2 starch, 2 vegetable, 1 fat.

Parsley Pesto Spaghetti

Jeannette Simec, Ottawa, Illinois

PREP/TOTAL TIME: 20 MIN.

- 3 tablespoons olive oil
- 1 cup packed fresh parsley leaves
- 1 teaspoon *each* dried basil, oregano and marjoram
- 1 teaspoon salt
- 1/2 teaspoon garlic powder
- 1/2 teaspoon pepper
- 12 ounces uncooked spaghetti
- 1/4 cup chopped walnuts, toasted
- 1/4 cup shredded Parmesan cheese

For pesto, combine the oil, parsley and seasonings in a blender or food processor; cover and process until blended. Cook spaghetti according to package directions; drain. Transfer to a serving bowl; add walnuts, Parmesan cheese and pesto. Toss to coat; serve immediately. **YIELD:** 6 SERVINGS.

Nutrition Facts: One serving (1 cup) equals:
- 328 calories
- 12 g fat (2 g saturated fat)
- 3 mg cholesterol
- 479 mg sodium
- 44 g carbohydrate
- 2 g fiber
- 10 g protein

Diabetic Exchanges: 3 starch, 2 fat.

Parsley Pesto Spaghetti

Gingered Squash Saute

Lemon Carrots And Rutabaga

Bernice Larsen, Gretna, Nebraska

PREP/TOTAL TIME: 25 MIN.

   4   medium carrots, cut into 3-inch julienne strips (about 2 cups)
   1   small rutabaga (10 ounces), peeled and cut into 3-inch julienne strips (about 2 cups)
 1/2   cup water
   2   tablespoons butter
   1   tablespoon brown sugar
   1   tablespoon lemon juice
 1/2   teaspoon grated lemon peel
 1/4   teaspoon dill weed

In a large saucepan, combine the carrots, rutabaga and water. Bring to a boil. Reduce heat to medium; cover and cook for 13-15 minutes. Meanwhile, in a small saucepan, combine the remaining ingredients; cook, uncovered, over medium heat for 2-3 minutes or until butter is melted.

   Drain vegetables; add butter mixture. Cook for 3-4 minutes or until vegetables are glazed, stirring occasionally. **YIELD:** 5 SERVINGS.

Nutrition Facts: One serving (3/4 cup) equals:
       93 calories
        5 g fat (3 g saturated fat)
     12 mg cholesterol
     77 mg sodium
       13 g carbohydrate
        3 g fiber
        1 g protein

Diabetic Exchanges: 2 vegetable, 1 fat.

Gingered Squash Saute

Ruth Andrewson, Leavenworth, Washington

PREP/TOTAL TIME: 20 MIN.

   1   pound yellow summer squash
 1/2   pound small zucchini, sliced
   1   medium onion, thinly sliced
   1   medium green pepper, julienned
   4   teaspoons butter
   3   medium tomatoes, peeled and quartered
 3/4   teaspoon salt
 1/2   to 1 teaspoon ground ginger

Cut yellow squash in half lengthwise, then into 1/2-in. slices. In a large skillet, saute squash, zucchini, onion and green pepper for 3 minutes. Add tomatoes, salt and ginger. Cover and cook for 2-3 minutes or until heated through. **YIELD:** 9 SERVINGS.

Nutrition Facts: One serving (3/4 cup) equals:
       48 calories
        2 g fat (1 g saturated fat)
        5 mg cholesterol
     219 mg sodium
        7 g carbohydrate
        2 g fiber
        2 g protein

Diabetic Exchanges: 1 vegetable, 1/2 fat.

Potato Spinach Pie

Lola Kauffmann, Goshen, Indiana

PREP: 10 MIN.   BAKE: 45 MIN.

   3   cups coarsely shredded peeled potatoes
   2   tablespoons olive oil, *divided*
   1   teaspoon salt, *divided*
 1/3   cup chopped onion
   1   package (10 ounces) frozen chopped spinach, thawed and squeezed dry
   1   cup (4 ounces) shredded reduced-fat Swiss cheese
 1/2   cup fat-free evaporated milk
   2   eggs, lightly beaten
   2   egg whites, lightly beaten
 1/2   to 1 teaspoon dried oregano
 1/4   teaspoon ground nutmeg

In a bowl, combine the potatoes, 4 teaspoons oil and 1/2 teaspoon salt. Press onto the bottom and up the sides of a 9-in. pie plate coated with nonstick cooking spray. Bake at 425° for 20-25 minutes or until crust is lightly browned. Cool on a wire rack. Reduce temperature to 350°.

In a nonstick skillet, saute onion in remaining oil until tender. In a bowl, combine the spinach, Swiss cheese, milk, eggs, egg whites, oregano, nutmeg, onion and remaining salt. Pour into crust.

Bake for 25-30 minutes or until top begins to brown and a knife inserted near the center comes out clean. Let stand for 10 minutes before cutting. **YIELD:** 6 SERVINGS.

Nutrition Facts: One serving (1 piece) equals:
    251 calories
    12 g fat (4 g saturated fat)
    84 mg cholesterol
    555 mg sodium
    24 g carbohydrate
    3 g fiber
    14 g protein

Diabetic Exchanges: 2 lean meat, 1-1/2 starch, 1 fat.

Penne with Veggies 'n' Black Beans

meat less

Vickie Spoerle, Carmel, Indiana

PREP/TOTAL TIME: 20 MIN.

- 10 ounces uncooked penne pasta
- 1 cup sliced zucchini
- 1 cup sliced carrots
- 1/2 cup sliced fresh mushrooms
- 1/2 cup julienned green *or* sweet red pepper
- 1 small onion, thinly sliced
- 1 garlic clove, minced
- 1 tablespoon *each* minced fresh basil, oregano and thyme *or* 1 teaspoon *each* dried basil, oregano and thyme
- 1/2 teaspoon salt
- 1/4 teaspoon pepper
- 2 tablespoons olive oil, *divided*
- 1 can (15 ounces) black beans, rinsed and drained
- 2/3 cup chopped seeded tomatoes
- 1/3 cup shredded Parmesan cheese
- 2 tablespoons minced fresh parsley

Cook pasta according to package directions. Meanwhile, in a large nonstick skillet, saute the zucchini, carrots, mushrooms, green pepper, onion, garlic and seasonings in 1 tablespoon oil until crisp-tender. Stir in the beans.

Drain pasta; add to vegetable mixture. Add tomatoes and remaining olive oil; toss gently. Sprinkle with Parmesan cheese and parsley. **YIELD:** 6 SERVINGS.

Nutrition Facts: One serving (1-1/3 cups) equals:
    315 calories
    8 g fat (2 g saturated fat)
    3 mg cholesterol
    502 mg sodium
    50 g carbohydrate
    7 g fiber
    13 g protein

Diabetic Exchanges: 3 starch, 1 vegetable, 1 fat.

Penne with Veggies 'n' Black Beans

Potato Spinach Pie

Citrus Veggie Stir-Fry

Dorothy Swanson, Affton, Missouri

PREP: 10 MIN. **COOK:** 15 MIN.

- 1 tablespoon cornstarch
- 1 cup orange juice
- 2 tablespoons balsamic vinegar
- 2 garlic cloves, minced
- 1 teaspoon grated orange peel
- 1/2 teaspoon ground ginger
- 1/8 teaspoon hot pepper sauce
- 1 cup sliced carrots
- 1 cup julienned sweet red pepper
- 1 cup julienned green pepper
- 1 tablespoon canola oil
- 1 cup sliced fresh mushrooms
- 2 cups fresh *or* frozen snow peas
- 1/2 cup sliced green onions
- 1/3 cup salted cashews
- 4 cups hot cooked rice

In a bowl, combine the first seven ingredients until blended; set aside. In a large nonstick skillet or wok, stir-fry carrots and peppers in oil for 5 minutes. Add mushrooms and snow peas; stir-fry for 6 minutes. Add green onions; stir-fry for 3 minutes or until the vegetables are crisp-tender.

Stir orange juice mixture and add to pan. Bring to a boil; cook and stir for 2 minutes or until thickened. Stir in cashews. Serve with rice. **YIELD:** 4 SERVINGS.

Nutrition Facts: One serving (1 cup vegetable mixture with 1 cup rice) equals:
- 400 calories
- 10 g fat (1 g saturated fat)
- 0 cholesterol
- 97 mg sodium
- 71 g carbohydrate
- 5 g fiber
- 9 g protein

Diabetic Exchanges: 4 starch, 2 vegetable, 1/2 fat.

Carrot Lentil Casserole

Stacey Krawczyk, Champaign, Illinois

PREP: 10 MIN. **BAKE:** 1 HOUR

- 1 large onion, chopped
- 1 cup finely chopped carrots
- 3/4 cup dried lentils, rinsed
- 3/4 cup uncooked brown rice
- 3/4 cup shredded reduced-fat cheddar cheese
- 1/2 cup chopped green pepper
- 1/2 teaspoon *each* dried thyme, basil and oregano
- 1/4 teaspoon salt
- 1/4 teaspoon rubbed sage
- 1/4 teaspoon garlic powder
- 1 can (14-1/2 ounces) chicken broth
- 1 can (14-1/2 ounces) diced tomatoes, undrained

In a 3-qt. baking dish coated with nonstick cooking spray, combine the onion, carrots, lentils, rice, cheese, green pepper and seasonings. Stir in broth and tomatoes. Cover and bake at 350° for 1-1/4 to 1-3/4 hours or until the liquid is absorbed and lentils and rice are tender. **YIELD:** 6 SERVINGS.

Nutrition Facts: One serving (1 cup) equals:
- 239 calories
- 4 g fat (2 g saturated fat)
- 8 mg cholesterol
- 557 mg sodium
- 41 g carbohydrate
- 8 g fiber
- 14 g protein

Diabetic Exchanges: 2 starch, 1 lean meat, 1 vegetable.

Stuffed Zucchini Boats

Billie Moss, Walnut Creek, California

PREP: 20 MIN. **BAKE:** 20 MIN.

- 4 medium zucchini
- 1 egg
- 1 cup chopped fresh spinach

Citrus Veggie Stir-Fry

Stuffed Zucchini Boats

3/4 cups dry bread crumbs
1/2 cup tomato sauce
1/3 cup grated Parmesan cheese
1/3 cup finely chopped onion
1 garlic clove, minced
1/4 teaspoon salt
1/8 teaspoon pepper
1 can (14-1/2 ounces) diced tomatoes, drained and finely chopped
1 cup (4 ounces) shredded reduced-fat Swiss cheese

Trim ends of zucchini; place in a steamer basket. In a saucepan, bring 1 in. of water to a boil; add basket. Cover and steam for 5 minutes. When zucchini is cool enough to handle, cut in half lengthwise; scoop out pulp, leaving a 1/4-in. shell. Set pulp aside.

In a bowl, beat the egg; add spinach, bread crumbs, tomato sauce, Parmesan cheese, onion, garlic, salt, pepper and zucchini pulp. Spoon into zucchini shells.

Place in an ungreased 13-in. x 9-in. x 2-in. baking dish. Bake, uncovered, at 350° for 20 minutes. Top each with tomatoes and Swiss cheese. Bake 5-10 minutes longer or until cheese is melted. **YIELD:** 8 SERVINGS.

Nutrition Facts: One serving (1 zucchini boat) equals:

148 calories
6 g fat (3 g saturated fat)
40 mg cholesterol
429 mg sodium
15 g carbohydrate
3 g fiber
10 g protein

Diabetic Exchanges: 2 vegetable, 1-1/2 lean meat, 1/2 fat.

Cajun Buttered Corn

Anne-Lise Botting, Duluth, Georgia

PREP/TOTAL TIME: 20 MIN.

8 medium ears sweet corn
2 tablespoons butter
1/4 teaspoon chili powder
1/4 teaspoon coarsely ground pepper
1/8 teaspoon garlic powder
1/8 teaspoon cayenne pepper
1 teaspoon cornstarch
1/4 cup reduced-sodium chicken *or* vegetable broth

In a large kettle, bring 3 qts. of water to a boil; add corn. Return to a boil; cook for 3-5 minutes or until tender.

Meanwhile, in a small saucepan, melt butter. Stir in the chili powder, pepper, garlic powder and cayenne; cook and stir for 1 minute. Combine cornstarch and broth until smooth; gradually whisk into butter mixture. Bring to a boil; cook and stir for 1-2 minutes or until slightly thickened. Drain corn; serve with seasoned butter. **YIELD:** 8 SERVINGS.

Nutrition Facts: One serving (1 ear of corn with 1-1/2 teaspoons seasoned butter) equals:

105 calories
4 g fat (2 g saturated fat)
8 mg cholesterol
63 mg sodium
18 g carbohydrate
2 g fiber
3 g protein

Diabetic Exchanges: 1 starch, 1/2 fat.

Cajun Buttered Corn

Three-Cheese Potato Souffle

Three-Cheese Potato Souffle `meatless`

Kathy Kittell, Lenexa, Kansas

PREP: 15 MIN.   **BAKE:** 40 MIN.

- 4 cups mashed potatoes (without added milk *or* butter)
- 1 cup fat-free milk
- 1 cup (4 ounces) shredded reduced-fat cheddar cheese
- 2/3 cup shredded reduced-fat Swiss cheese
- 1/3 cup shredded Parmesan cheese
- 1/3 cup chopped green onions
- 1 small onion, chopped
- 1-1/4 teaspoons salt
- 1/4 teaspoon pepper
- 4 eggs, *separated*

In a large bowl, combine the potatoes, milk, cheeses, onions, salt and pepper. Beat egg yolks; stir into potato mixture. In a small mixing bowl, beat egg whites until stiff peaks form; gently fold into potato mixture.

Transfer to a 2-qt. souffle dish coated with nonstick cooking spray. Bake, uncovered, at 375° for 40-45 minutes or until golden. Serve immediately. **YIELD:** 12 SERVINGS.

Nutrition Facts: One serving (1/2 cup) equals:
- 153 calories
- 5 g fat (3 g saturated fat)
- 83 mg cholesterol
- 442 mg sodium
- 16 g carbohydrate
- 1 g fiber
- 11 g protein

Diabetic Exchanges: 1 starch, 1 lean meat, 1/2 fat.

Vegetable Fried Rice `low fat` `meatless`

Taste of Home Test Kitchen
Greendale, Wisconsin

PREP/TOTAL TIME: 20 MIN.

- 1/4 cup finely chopped onion
- 2 teaspoons canola oil
- 2 teaspoons minced fresh gingerroot
- 2 garlic cloves, minced
- 3 tablespoons reduced-sodium teriyaki sauce
- 2 tablespoons lime juice
- 1 teaspoon brown sugar
- 1/4 teaspoon salt
- 1/4 teaspoon hot pepper sauce
- 3 cups cold cooked rice
- 2 cups frozen mixed vegetables, thawed

In a nonstick skillet, saute onion in oil until tender. Add ginger and garlic; saute 1 minute longer. Add the teriyaki sauce, lime juice, brown sugar, salt and hot pepper sauce; bring to a boil. Reduce heat; cook and stir for 2 minutes. Add rice and mixed vegeta-

bles; cook and stir over medium heat until vegetables are tender. **YIELD:** 6 SERVINGS.

Nutrition Facts: One serving (3/4 cup) equals:
- 169 calories
- 2 g fat (trace saturated fat)
- 0 cholesterol
- 286 mg sodium
- 34 g carbohydrate
- 3 g fiber
- 5 g protein

Diabetic Exchanges: 2 vegetable, 1-1/2 starch.

Baked Mushrooms `low fat` `low sodium` `low carb` `meatless`

Patty Kile, Plymouth Meeting, Pennsylvania

PREP: 15 MIN.   **BAKE:** 25 MIN.

- 1 pound whole fresh mushrooms
- 1 celery rib, chopped
- 2 green onions, thinly sliced
- 1 tablespoon butter
- 1/2 cup white wine *or* chicken broth
- 1/8 teaspoon salt
- 1/8 teaspoon pepper

Place mushrooms in an 8-in. square baking dish coated with nonstick cooking spray. In a nonstick skillet, saute celery and onions in butter until tender. Stir in the wine or broth, salt and pepper; heat through. Pour over mushrooms. Bake, uncovered, at 350° for 25-30 minutes or until mushrooms are tender, stirring several times. **YIELD:** 6 SERVINGS.

Nutrition Facts: One serving (1/2 cup) equals:
- 52 calories
- 2 g fat (1 g saturated fat)
- 5 mg cholesterol
- 79 mg sodium
- 4 g carbohydrate
- 1 g fiber
- 2 g protein

Diabetic Exchanges: 1 vegetable, 1/2 fat.

Baked Garlic Sweet Potatoes `meatless`

Michelle Bishop, Peru, Indiana

PREP: 5 MIN.   **BAKE:** 40 MIN.

- 1 tablespoon olive oil
- 4 garlic cloves
- 1 teaspoon chopped fresh rosemary *or* 1/4 teaspoon dried rosemary, crushed
- 1/2 teaspoon salt
- 1-1/2 pounds sweet potatoes, peeled and cut into 3/4-inch chunks
- 1/4 cup reduced-sodium chicken broth *or* vegetable broth

In a large bowl, combine oil, garlic, rosemary and salt; add sweet potatoes and toss to coat. Transfer to a 13-in. x 9-in. x 2-in. baking dish coated with nonstick cooking spray.

Bake, uncovered at 350° for 30 minutes. Add broth; bake 10-15 minutes longer or until potatoes are tender, stirring occasionally. **YIELD:** 4 SERVINGS.

Nutrition Facts: One serving (3/4 cup) equals:
142 calories
4 g fat (trace saturated fat)
0 cholesterol
343 mg sodium
26 g carbohydrate
3 g fiber
2 g protein

Diabetic Exchanges: 1-1/2 starch, 1/2 fat.

Jambalaya

Betty May, Topeka, Kansas

PREP: 5 MIN.   **COOK:** 30 MIN.

1/2 pound boneless skinless chicken breasts, cut into 1-inch pieces
1 large onion, chopped
3/4 cup chopped green pepper
1 celery rib, chopped
2 jalapeno peppers, seeded and finely chopped
2 garlic cloves, minced
1 tablespoon canola oil
2 cans (14-1/2 ounces *each*) diced tomatoes, undrained
1/2 cup water
1 teaspoon dried thyme

Jambalaya

1/2 teaspoon salt
1/4 teaspoon pepper
1/8 to 1/4 teaspoon cayenne pepper
1 pound uncooked medium shrimp, peeled and deveined
2 cups cooked long grain rice

In a large Dutch oven or saucepan, saute the chicken, onion, green pepper, celery, jalapenos and garlic in oil until chicken is no longer pink. Add the tomatoes, water, thyme, salt, pepper and cayenne; bring to a boil. Reduce heat; cover and simmer for 15 minutes. Add shrimp; simmer 6-8 minutes longer or until shrimp turn pink. Stir in rice. **YIELD:** 6 SERVINGS.

Editor's Note: When cutting or seeding hot peppers, use rubber or plastic gloves to protect your hands. Avoid touching your face.

Nutrition Facts: One serving (1-1/2 cups) equals:
229 calories
4 g fat (1 g saturated fat)
112 mg cholesterol
502 mg sodium
27 g carbohydrate
4 g fiber
21 g protein

Diabetic Exchanges: 3 very lean meat, 2 vegetable, 1 starch, 1/2 fat.

Baked Garlic Sweet Potatoes

Cranberry Hazelnut Dressing

Virginia Anthony, Jacksonville, Florida

PREP: 20 MIN. **BAKE:** 45 MIN.

- 1/2 cup dried cranberries
- 1/4 cup orange juice
- 1-1/4 cups *each* chopped celery and onions
- 1 tablespoon canola oil
- 1 teaspoon poultry seasoning
- 1/2 pound reduced-fat pork sausage
- 4-1/2 cups seasoned stuffing croutons
- 2 cups chopped peeled apples
- 1 cup cooked wild rice
- 1/2 cup chopped hazelnuts *or* pecans, toasted
- 1/2 cup minced fresh parsley
- 1-1/4 cups reduced-sodium chicken broth
- 1 teaspoon salt
- 1/2 teaspoon pepper

In a saucepan, bring cranberries and juice to a boil. Remove from the heat; cover and set aside. In a nonstick skillet, saute celery and onions in oil. Stir in poultry seasoning. Place in a bowl.

In the same skillet, cook sausage over medium heat until no longer pink; drain and add to bowl. Add stuffing croutons, apples, rice, nuts, parsley and reserved cranberry mixture; toss to combine. Drizzle with broth. Sprinkle with salt and pepper; toss.

Place in a 13-in. x 9-in. x 2-in. baking dish coated with nonstick cooking spray. Cover; bake at 325° for 35 minutes. Uncover; bake 10-15 minutes or until lightly browned. **YIELD:** 12 SERVINGS.

Nutrition Facts: One serving (1 cup) equals:
- 212 calories
- 8 g fat (2 g saturated fat)
- 13 mg cholesterol
- 657 mg sodium
- 27 g carbohydrate
- 3 g fiber
- 7 g protein

Diabetic Exchanges: 1 starch, 1 lean meat, 1 fat, 1/2 fruit.

Cranberry Hazelnut Dressing

Whipped Cauliflower `low carb` `meat less`

Taste of Home Test Kitchen
Greendale, Wisconsin

PREP/TOTAL TIME: 20 MIN.

- 1 medium head cauliflower, cut into florets
- 1/4 cup fat-free milk
- 2 tablespoons canola oil
- 1/4 teaspoon salt
- 1/8 teaspoon white pepper

Place cauliflower in a steamer basket; place in a saucepan over 1 in. of water. Bring to a boil; cover and steam for 8-10 minutes or until tender. Cool slightly.

Place the milk and oil in a blender or food processor. Add the cauliflower, salt and pepper; cover and process until blended. Transfer to a bowl. Serve immediately. **YIELD:** 4 SERVINGS.

Nutrition Facts: One serving (1/2 cup) equals:
- 105 calories
- 7 g fat (1 g saturated fat)
- 1 mg cholesterol
- 199 mg sodium
- 8 g carbohydrate
- 4 g fiber
- 3 g protein

Diabetic Exchanges: 1-1/2 fat, 1 vegetable.

Garlic Brussels Sprouts `low fat` `low carb`

Myra Innes, Auburn, Kansas

PREP/TOTAL TIME: 30 MIN.

- 1-1/2 pounds fresh brussels sprouts
- 4 garlic cloves, chopped
- 3 teaspoons butter, *divided*
- 2 teaspoons olive oil
- 1/2 cup reduced-sodium chicken broth
- 1/4 teaspoon salt
- 1/8 teaspoon pepper

Cut an X in the core end of each brussels sprout; set aside. In a large saucepan, saute garlic in 1 teaspoon butter and oil for 2-3 minutes or until golden brown. Add sprouts; toss to coat. Add the broth, salt and

Couscous with Grilled Vegetables

1/2 cup chopped green onions
4-1/2 teaspoons lemon juice
2-1/4 teaspoons minced fresh thyme *or*
      1/2 teaspoon dried thyme

Spritz vegetables with nonstick cooking spray; sprinkle with 1/4 teaspoon salt and 1/4 teaspoon pepper. Coat grill rack with nonstick cooking spray before preparing the grill for indirect heat. Arrange vegetables on grill over the side for indirect heat. Grill, covered, over medium indirect heat for 4-5 minutes on each side or until tender. Let stand until cool enough to handle.

In a saucepan, bring broth to a boil. Stir in couscous. Remove from the heat; cover and let stand for 5 minutes or until liquid is absorbed. Cut grilled vegetables into 1/2-in. pieces. Fluff couscous with a fork. Add vegetables, green onions, lemon juice, thyme and remaining salt and pepper; toss until combined. **YIELD:** 8 SERVINGS.

Nutrition Facts: One serving (1 cup) equals:
 163 calories
   trace fat (trace saturated fat)
  0 cholesterol
 384 mg sodium
  34 g carbohydrate
  4 g fiber
  7 g protein

Diabetic Exchanges: 2 starch, 1 vegetable.

pepper; cover and cook for 12-14 minutes or until sprouts are tender. Drain; add the remaining butter and toss until melted.
YIELD: 6 SERVINGS.

Nutrition Facts: One serving (2/3 cup) equals:
 83 calories
  3 g fat (1 g saturated fat)
  5 mg cholesterol
 198 mg sodium
  11 g carbohydrate
  4 g fiber
  4 g protein

Diabetic Exchanges: 2 vegetable, 1/2 fat.

Couscous with Grilled Vegetables

`low fat` `meat less`

Kathy Herrala, Martinez, California

PREP: 15 MIN.   **COOK:** 15 MIN. + COOLING

2 small zucchini, quartered lengthwise
1/2 medium eggplant, sliced widthwise 1/2 inch thick
1 medium sweet red pepper, quartered
1 small onion, sliced 1/2 inch thick
3/4 teaspoon salt, *divided*
1/2 teaspoon pepper, *divided*
2 cups reduced-sodium chicken *or* vegetable broth
1 package (10 ounces) couscous

Lemon Pecan Pilaf

Cindie Ekstrand, Duarte, California

PREP/TOTAL TIME: 30 MIN.

5 cups chicken broth
2-1/2 cups uncooked long grain rice
2 tablespoons butter
1/2 cup pecan halves
3 tablespoons lemon juice
1 teaspoon grated lemon peel
1/4 cup minced fresh parsley

In a saucepan, bring broth to a boil. Stir in rice; return to a boil. Reduce heat; cover and simmer for 20-25 minutes or until the rice is tender.

Meanwhile, melt butter in a nonstick skillet. Add the pecans; saute until golden. Stir in the lemon juice and peel. Pour over rice and stir to coat. Sprinkle with parsley.
YIELD: 10 SERVINGS.

Nutrition Facts: One serving (3/4 cup) equals:
 247 calories
  8 g fat (2 g saturated fat)
  6 mg cholesterol
 527 mg sodium
  39 g carbohydrate
  1 g fiber
  5 g protein

Diabetic Exchanges: 2-1/2 starch, 1 fat.

Lemon Pecan Pilaf

Sweet Carrots

Sweet Carrots

Taste of Home Test Kitchen
Greendale, Wisconsin

PREP/TOTAL TIME: 15 MIN.

- 1-1/2 cups baby carrots
- 2 teaspoons brown sugar
- 1 teaspoon butter
- 1 teaspoon white wine vinegar
- 1/8 teaspoon salt
- 1 teaspoon minced chives

Place carrots in a steamer basket. Place in a saucepan over 1 in. of water; bring to a boil. Cover and steam for 5-8 minutes or until tender. Transfer carrots to a bowl. Add the brown sugar, butter, vinegar and salt; toss until butter is melted and carrots are coated. Sprinkle with chives. **YIELD:** 2 SERVINGS.

Nutrition Facts: One serving (3/4 cup) equals:
- 76 calories
- 2 g fat (1 g saturated fat)
- 5 mg cholesterol
- 202 mg sodium
- 14 g carbohydrate
- 3 g fiber
- 1 g protein

Diabetic Exchanges: 2 vegetable, 1/2 fruit.

Sweet Potato Pear Bake

Miriam Lavella, Kersey, Pennsylvania

PREP: 10 MIN.   **COOK:** 25 MIN.

- 3 medium sweet potatoes
- 1/4 cup packed brown sugar
- 1-1/2 teaspoons cornstarch
- 1/4 cup orange juice
- 3 tablespoons pear juice
- 4-1/2 teaspoons butter, cubed
- 1/8 teaspoon salt
- 2 tablespoons raisins
- 2 tablespoons golden raisins
- 3 medium firm pears, peeled and cut into 1/4-inch slices

Pierce sweet potatoes and place on a microwave-safe plate. Microwave, uncovered, on high for 13-15 minutes or until tender. Cool. Peel and cut into 1/4-in. slices; set aside.

In a large microwave-safe bowl, combine the brown sugar and cornstarch. Stir in the orange juice and pear juice until smooth. Stir in butter and salt. Microwave, uncovered, on high for 1-1/2 to 2 minutes, stirring every 30 seconds, or until mixture is thickened and bubbly. Stir in raisins.

In an 8-in. square microwave-safe dish coated with nonstick cooking spray, layer half of the sweet potatoes, pears and sauce. Repeat layers. Cover and microwave on high for 8-10 minutes or until pears are tender. Let stand for 5 minutes before serving. **YIELD:** 8 SERVINGS.

Editor's Note: This recipe was tested in a 1,100-watt microwave.

Nutrition Facts: One serving equals:
- 148 calories
- 2 g fat (1 g saturated fat)
- 6 mg cholesterol
- 66 mg sodium
- 32 g carbohydrate
- 3 g fiber
- 1 g protein

Diabetic Exchanges: 1 starch, 1 fruit.

Brown Sugar Baked Beans

Debra Hogenson, Brewster, Minnesota

PREP: 1 HOUR 10 MIN. + STANDING
BAKE: 25 MIN.

- 1-2/3 cups dried pinto beans
- 1 medium onion, chopped
- 1 cup chunky salsa
- 1/2 cup packed brown sugar
- 1/2 teaspoon garlic powder
- 1/2 teaspoon ground cumin
- 1/4 teaspoon dried oregano
- 1/8 to 1/4 teaspoon cayenne pepper

Place beans in a Dutch oven or soup kettle; add water to cover by 2 in. Bring to a boil; boil for 2 minutes. Remove from the heat; cover and let stand for 1 hour.

Drain and rinse beans; discard liquid. Return beans to Dutch oven; add onion and enough water to cover by 2 in. Bring to a boil. Reduce heat; cover and simmer for 60-70 minutes or until the beans are tender.

Drain beans and place in an ungreased 2-qt. baking dish. Add the remaining ingredients. Cover and bake at 350° for 25 minutes or until heated through. **YIELD:** 8 SERVINGS.

Nutrition Facts: One serving (1/2 cup) equals:
- 207 calories
- 1 g fat (trace saturated fat)
- 0 cholesterol
- 150 mg sodium
- 42 g carbohydrate
- 10 g fiber
- 9 g protein

Diabetic Exchange: 2-1/2 starch.

Three-Grain Pilaf

Mary Knudson, Bermuda Dunes, California

PREP: 5 MIN.   **COOK:** 50 MIN.

- 1 large onion, chopped
- 1 garlic clove, minced
- 2 tablespoons olive oil

Creamy Macaroni 'n' Cheese

2/3 cup shredded carrot
1/3 cup uncooked brown rice
1/3 cup uncooked medium pearl barley
1/3 cup uncooked bulgur
2 cups vegetable *or* reduced-sodium chicken broth
1/4 cup sherry, optional
1 teaspoon minced fresh oregano *or* 1/4 teaspoon dried oregano
1 teaspoon minced fresh basil *or* 1/4 teaspoon dried basil
1/2 teaspoon salt
1/4 teaspoon pepper
1/3 cup minced fresh parsley
1/3 cup sliced almonds, toasted

In a large nonstick skillet, saute onion and garlic in oil for 2 minutes. Add carrot; saute for 2 minutes or until the vegetables are crisp-tender. Stir in the rice, barley and bulgur; saute for 4 minutes or until grains are lightly browned. Gradually add broth and sherry if desired. Bring to a boil.

Reduce heat; stir in oregano, basil, salt and pepper. Cover and simmer for 40-45 minutes or until grains are tender and the liquid is absorbed. Stir in parsley and sprinkle with almonds. **YIELD:** 5 SERVINGS.

Editor's Note: Look for bulgur in the cereal, rice or organic food aisle of your grocery store.

Nutrition Facts: One serving (3/4 cup) equals:
238 calories
9 g fat (1 g saturated fat)
0 cholesterol
498 mg sodium
33 g carbohydrate
6 g fiber
7 g protein

Diabetic Exchanges: 2 starch, 1-1/2 fat.

Three-Grain Pilaf

Creamy Macaroni 'n' Cheese

Dawn Royer, Albany, Oregon

PREP/TOTAL TIME: 30 MIN.

1/3 cup finely chopped onion
3-1/2 cups cooked elbow macaroni
1-3/4 cups shredded reduced-fat cheddar cheese
2 tablespoons minced fresh parsley
1/2 cup fat-free evaporated milk
1-3/4 cups 2% cottage cheese
1 teaspoon Dijon mustard
1/2 teaspoon salt
1/4 teaspoon pepper

In a microwave-safe bowl, cover and microwave onion on high for 2 minutes or until tender; drain. Add the macaroni, cheddar cheese and parsley.

In a blender or food processor, combine the milk, cottage cheese, mustard, salt and pepper; cover and process until smooth. Stir into macaroni mixture.

Pour into a 1-1/2-qt. baking dish coated with nonstick cooking spray. Bake, uncovered, at 350° for 20-25 minutes or until lightly browned. **YIELD:** 8 SERVINGS.

Nutrition Facts: One serving (2/3 cup) equals:
229 calories
6 g fat (4 g saturated fat)
19 mg cholesterol
491 mg sodium
24 g carbohydrate
1 g fiber
20 g protein

Diabetic Exchanges: 2 lean meat, 1-1/2 starch.

Basil-Parmesan Angel Hair

Barbara Dorsett, San Diego, California

PREP/TOTAL TIME: 30 MIN.

- 1 package (16 ounces) angel hair pasta
- 2 tablespoons olive oil
- 1 can (12 ounces) fat-free evaporated milk
- 2/3 cup shredded Parmesan cheese
- 1/2 cup thinly sliced green onions
- 1/4 cup minced fresh basil
- 1 teaspoon grated lemon peel
- 1/2 teaspoon salt
- 1/2 teaspoon garlic powder
- 1/4 teaspoon pepper
- Additional fresh basil
- 12 lemon slices

Cook pasta according to package directions. Drain and return to the pan. Add oil; toss to coat. Add the milk, Parmesan cheese, onions, basil, lemon peel, salt, garlic powder and pepper. Cook and stir over medium heat until heated through. Sprinkle with additional basil. Serve with lemon. **YIELD:** 12 SERVINGS.

Nutrition Facts: One serving (2/3 cup) equals:
- 203 calories
- 5 g fat (1 g saturated fat)
- 5 mg cholesterol
- 219 mg sodium
- 32 g carbohydrate
- 2 g fiber
- 9 g protein

Diabetic Exchanges: 1-1/2 starch, 1 fat, 1/2 fat-free milk.

Basil-Parmesan Angel Hair

Seasoned Brown Rice

Betsy Larimer, Somerset, Pennsylvania

PREP: 5 MIN. **COOK:** 35 MIN.

- 1-1/3 cups water
- 2/3 cup long grain brown rice
- 1 tablespoon reduced-sodium soy sauce
- 1/2 teaspoon dried basil
- 1/4 to 1/2 teaspoon ground ginger
- 1/8 teaspoon cayenne pepper

In a small saucepan, bring water and rice to a boil. Reduce heat; cover and simmer for 35-45 minutes or until water is absorbed and rice is tender. Stir in the remaining ingredients. **YIELD:** 4 SERVINGS.

Nutrition Facts: One serving (1/2 cup) equals:
- 118 calories
- 1 g fat (trace saturated fat)
- 0 cholesterol
- 157 mg sodium
- 24 g carbohydrate
- 2 g fiber
- 3 g protein

Diabetic Exchange: 1-1/2 starch.

Ratatouille Pasta

Carol Dodds, Aurora, Ontario

PREP: 10 MIN. + STANDING **COOK:** 15 MIN.

- 2 cups diced peeled eggplant
- 2 cups sliced zucchini
- 1/2 teaspoon salt
- 1-1/3 cups uncooked spiral pasta
- 1 cup sliced onion
- 1 tablespoon olive oil
- 1 can (14-1/2 ounces) diced tomatoes, undrained
- 2 tablespoons tomato paste
- 1 teaspoon dried oregano
- 1/2 teaspoon garlic powder
- 1/2 teaspoon dried basil
- Dash pepper
- 1 cup (4 ounces) shredded part-skim mozzarella cheese

Place eggplant and zucchini in a colander over a plate; sprinkle with salt and toss. Let stand for 30 minutes; rinse and drain well.

Cook pasta according to package directions. Meanwhile, in a large nonstick skillet, saute the eggplant, zucchini and onion in oil until tender. Add the tomatoes, tomato paste, oregano, garlic powder, basil and pepper. Bring to a boil. Reduce heat; cook, uncovered, over medium-low heat for 3 minutes, stirring occasionally.

Drain pasta; place on an ovenproof platter. Top with vegetable mixture. Sprinkle with mozzarella cheese. Broil 4-6 in. from

Ratatouille Pasta

the heat until cheese is melted. **YIELD:** 3 SERVINGS.

Nutrition Facts: One serving (1 cup sauce with 2/3 cup pasta) equals:

    344 calories
    12 g fat (5 g saturated fat)
  22 mg cholesterol
835 mg sodium
    45 g carbohydrate
     7 g fiber
    17 g protein

Diabetic Exchanges: 3 vegetable, 2 starch, 1 lean meat, 1 fat.

Broccoli Mashed Potatoes

Jim Hadley, Charlotte, North Carolina

PREP/TOTAL TIME: 30 MIN.

1-1/2 pounds small unpeeled red potatoes, cubed
    2 fresh broccoli spears
1-2/3 cups chopped onions
  1/3 cup reduced-fat sour cream
    1 teaspoon salt
  1/4 teaspoon pepper

Place potatoes in a large saucepan and cover with water; bring to a boil. Reduce heat; cover and cook for 10 minutes. Remove broccoli florets from stems. Peel stems and cut into 1/4-in. slices; cut slices in half. Add florets and stems to potatoes. Cook 10-12

minutes longer or until potatoes and broccoli are tender; drain.

In a nonstick skillet coated with nonstick cooking spray, cook onions until tender. Drain potato mixture. Add onions, sour cream, salt and pepper; mash. Serve warm. **YIELD:** 6 SERVINGS.

Nutrition Facts: One serving (2/3 cup) equals:

    119 calories
    1 g fat (1 g saturated fat)
   4 mg cholesterol
413 mg sodium
    23 g carbohydrate
     3 g fiber
     4 g protein

Diabetic Exchange: 1-1/2 starch.

Sage Polenta

Taste of Home Test Kitchen
Greendale, Wisconsin

PREP: 20 MIN. + CHILLING   **COOK:** 25 MIN.

1/2 cup chopped onion
1/2 cup chopped sweet red pepper
  1 garlic clove, minced
  1 teaspoon butter
  3 cups water
  1 cup fat-free milk
  1 cup cornmeal
1/4 cup grated Parmesan cheese
  2 tablespoons minced fresh sage
3/4 teaspoon salt
1/4 teaspoon pepper
  2 teaspoons canola oil

In a large nonstick saucepan, saute the onion, red pepper and garlic in butter until tender. Stir in water and milk; bring to a boil over medium heat. Gradually whisk in cornmeal, whisking constantly to prevent lumping. Reduce heat; cover and simmer for 8-10 minutes or until cornmeal is tender.

Stir in the Parmesan cheese, sage, salt and pepper. Spread into a 13-in. x 9-in. x 2-in. pan coated with nonstick cooking spray. Cover and refrigerate for 30-45 minutes or until firm.

Cut into 12 squares. In a large nonstick skillet, cook polenta in batches in oil over medium-high heat for 3-4 minutes on each side or until lightly browned. Serve warm. **YIELD:** 6 SERVINGS.

Nutrition Facts: One serving (2 squares) equals:

    143 calories
    4 g fat (1 g saturated fat)
   5 mg cholesterol
386 mg sodium
    22 g carbohydrate
     2 g fiber
     5 g protein

Diabetic Exchanges: 1-1/2 starch, 1/2 fat.

Sage Polenta

Pasta Shells with Herbs

Vegetable Lo Mein

Sara Tatham, Plymouth, New Hampshire

PREP/TOTAL TIME: 25 MIN.

      6 ounces uncooked linguine
      1 teaspoon cornstarch
      1 teaspoon vegetable bouillon granules
    1/2 cup water
    1/4 cup reduced-sodium soy sauce
    1/2 pound fresh mushrooms, quartered
      2 tablespoons canola oil, *divided*
    1/2 pound fresh snow peas
      8 green onions, sliced
      4 celery ribs with leaves, sliced
      1 large sweet red pepper, thinly sliced
      1 can (14 ounces) bean sprouts, rinsed and
         drained

Cook pasta according to package directions; drain and set aside. In a small bowl, combine the cornstarch and bouillon granules; stir in the water and soy sauce and set aside.

   In a nonstick skillet, stir-fry mushrooms in 1 tablespoon oil for 3 minutes or until tender; remove and keep warm. In same pan, heat remaining oil. Add remaining vegetables; stir-fry for 5 minutes or until crisp-tender. Stir soy sauce mixture; add to pan. Bring to a boil; cook and stir for 2 minutes or until thickened. Add pasta and mushrooms. Heat through. **YIELD:** 4 SERVINGS.

Nutrition Facts: One serving (1-1/2 cups) equals:
       327 calories
         8 g fat (1 g saturated fat)
         1 mg cholesterol
     1,081 mg sodium
        50 g carbohydrate
         7 g fiber
        12 g protein

Diabetic Exchanges: 3 vegetable, 2 starch, 1-1/2 fat.

Pasta Shells with Herbs

Marilyn Pozzo, Fruitvale, British Columbia

PREP/TOTAL TIME: 20 MIN.

     12 ounces uncooked medium pasta shells
      1 medium sweet red pepper, julienned
      2 garlic cloves, minced
      2 tablespoons butter
      2 tablespoons olive oil
    1/2 cup minced fresh parsley
    1/2 cup 2% milk
    1/3 cup chopped fresh tarragon, basil, thyme
         or oregano *or* 1 tablespoon dried tarragon,
         basil, thyme *or* oregano
      1 teaspoon salt
    1/8 teaspoon pepper

Cook pasta according to package directions. In a large nonstick skillet, saute the red pepper and garlic in butter and oil until tender. Drain pasta; add to pepper mixture. Add remaining ingredients; toss to combine. Serve immediately. **YIELD:** 6 SERVINGS.

Nutrition Facts: One serving (1 cup) equals:
       308 calories
        10 g fat (3 g saturated fat)
        12 mg cholesterol
       448 mg sodium
        46 g carbohydrate
         2 g fiber
         9 g protein

Diabetic Exchanges: 3 starch, 1-1/2 fat.

Lemon-Maple Butternut Squash

Barbara Ballast, Grand Rapids, Michigan

PREP: 10 MIN.   **BAKE:** 50 MIN.

      1 large butternut squash (2-1/2 pounds),
         halved lengthwise and seeded
    1/4 cup water
    1/4 cup maple syrup
      1 tablespoon butter, melted
      1 tablespoon lemon juice
    1/2 teaspoon grated lemon peel

Place squash cut side down in an ungreased 13-in. x 9-in. x 2-in. baking dish. Add water. Cover and bake at 350° for 50-60 minutes or until tender. Scoop out the squash and place in a mixing bowl. Add the syrup, butter, lemon juice and peel; beat until smooth. **YIELD:** 4 SERVINGS.

Nutrition Facts: One serving (3/4 cup) equals:
         186 calories
           3 g fat (2 g saturated fat)
         8 mg cholesterol
       41 mg sodium
         42 g carbohydrate
           8 g fiber
           2 g protein

Diabetic Exchanges: 2-1/2 starch, 1/2 fat.

Asparagus Linguine

Carolyn DiPasquale
Middletown, Rhode Island

PREP/TOTAL TIME: 25 MIN.

    6   ounces uncooked linguine
    1   small onion, chopped
    2   garlic cloves, minced
    1   tablespoon olive oil
    2   teaspoons butter
  1/2   pound fresh asparagus, trimmed and cut into 1/2-inch pieces
    2   tablespoons white wine *or* chicken broth
    2   tablespoons grated Parmesan cheese
    1   tablespoon lemon juice
  1/4   teaspoon salt
  1/8   teaspoon pepper

Cook linguine according to package directions. Meanwhile, in a nonstick skillet, saute the onion and garlic in oil and butter until tender. Add asparagus; cook and stir for 2 minutes or until crisp-tender. Add wine or broth; cook and stir for 1-2 minutes or until liquid is reduced. Remove from the heat.

Drain linguine; add to asparagus mixture. Add remaining ingredients; toss to coat.

Lemon-Maple Butternut Squash

Asparagus Linguine

Serve immediately. **YIELD:** 4 SERVINGS.

Nutrition Facts: One serving (1 cup) equals:
         245 calories
           7 g fat (2 g saturated fat)
         7 mg cholesterol
     217 mg sodium
         36 g carbohydrate
           3 g fiber
           8 g protein

Diabetic Exchanges: 2 starch, 1 vegetable, 1 fat.

Baby Carrots With Curry Sauce

Pat Patty, Spring, Texas

PREP/TOTAL TIME: 25 MIN.

    1   package (16 ounces) baby carrots
  1/4   cup reduced-fat mayonnaise
    2   tablespoons fat-free sour cream
    1   teaspoon lemon juice
    1   teaspoon fat-free milk
    1   teaspoon honey
  1/2   to 1 teaspoon curry powder
  1/4   teaspoon salt

Place carrots in a steamer basket over 1 in. of boiling water in a saucepan. Cover and steam for 12-14 minutes or until crisp-tender. Meanwhile, combine the remaining ingredients in a small saucepan; cook and stir over medium-low heat until heated through (do not boil). Drain carrots; add sauce and toss to coat. **YIELD:** 4 SERVINGS.

Nutrition Facts: One serving (3/4 cup) equals:
         110 calories
           6 g fat (1 g saturated fat)
         5 mg cholesterol
     313 mg sodium
         14 g carbohydrate
           2 g fiber
           2 g protein

Diabetic Exchanges: 1 starch, 1 vegetable.

Sesame Green Beans 'n' Water Chestnuts

low carb | meat less

Dot Christiansen, Bettendorf, Iowa

PREP/TOTAL TIME: 30 MIN.

1-1/4 pounds fresh green beans (about 5 cups), trimmed
   1 can (8 ounces) sliced water chestnuts, drained
   1 cup sliced fresh mushrooms
   2 garlic cloves, minced
   2 teaspoons canola oil
   2 teaspoons sesame oil
   2 tablespoons water
   4 teaspoons reduced-sodium soy sauce
   2 teaspoons sugar
 1/4 teaspoon pepper
 1/8 teaspoon salt
   2 teaspoons sesame seeds, toasted

In a nonstick skillet, saute the beans, water chestnuts, mushrooms and garlic in canola oil and sesame oil for 5-6 minutes or until almost tender. Add the water, soy sauce, sugar, pepper and salt. Reduce heat; cover and simmer for 10-12 minutes or until beans are tender. Sprinkle with sesame seeds. **YIELD:** 6 SERVINGS.

Nutrition Facts: One serving (3/4 cup) equals:
   87 calories
    4 g fat (1 g saturated fat)
    0 cholesterol
 189 mg sodium
  12 g carbohydrate
    4 g fiber
    3 g protein

Diabetic Exchanges: 2 vegetable, 1/2 fat.

Sesame Green Beans 'n' Water Chestnuts

Zesty Rice 'n' Bean Casserole

meat less

Daphne Blandford
Gander, Newfoundland and Labrador

PREP: 35 MIN. **BAKE:** 15 MIN.

   2 medium green peppers, chopped
1-1/2 cups sliced fresh mushrooms
   1 medium onion, chopped
   2 garlic cloves, minced
 1/2 cup water
   1 teaspoon canola oil
   1 can (28 ounces) diced tomatoes, undrained
   1 can (16 ounces) kidney beans, rinsed and drained
 3/4 cup uncooked long grain rice
   2 teaspoons ground cumin
   1 teaspoon chili powder
 1/4 teaspoon cayenne pepper
   1 cup (4 ounces) shredded part-skim mozzarella cheese, *divided*

In a large nonstick skillet, saute the green peppers, mushrooms, onion and garlic in water and oil until onion is tender. Add the tomatoes, beans, rice and seasonings. Bring to a boil. Reduce heat; cover and simmer for 25 minutes or until rice is tender and most of the liquid is absorbed. Remove from the heat; stir in 1/2 cup cheese.

Transfer to a 2-1/2-qt. baking dish coated with nonstick cooking spray. Sprinkle with remaining cheese. Bake, uncovered, at 350° for 15-20 minutes or until cheese is melted. **YIELD:** 8 SERVINGS.

Nutrition Facts: One serving (1 cup) equals:
 195 calories
   7 g fat (2 g saturated fat)
   8 mg cholesterol
392 mg sodium
  33 g carbohydrate
   7 g fiber
  10 g protein

Diabetic Exchanges: 1-1/2 starch, 1 lean meat, 1 vegetable.

Snappy Peas And Carrots

low fat | low sodium | low carb | meat less

Taste of Home Test Kitchen
Greendale, Wisconsin

PREP/TOTAL TIME: 15 MIN.

   3 quarts water
1-1/4 pounds baby carrots
   1 pound fresh *or* frozen sugar snap peas
1-1/2 teaspoons canola oil
   2 garlic cloves, minced
   2 tablespoons reduced-sodium chicken broth *or* vegetable broth
   1 teaspoon dried mint

Apple-Spice Acorn Squash

1/4 teaspoon salt

1/4 teaspoon grated lemon peel

1/8 teaspoon pepper

In a Dutch oven, bring water to a boil. Add carrots; cover and boil for 4 minutes. Add peas; cover and boil 1 minute longer. Drain and pat dry. In a large nonstick skillet, saute vegetables in oil for 3 minutes. Add garlic; saute for 1 minute. Stir in the remaining ingredients; saute until heated through. **YIELD:** 8 SERVINGS.

Nutrition Facts: One serving (3/4 cup) equals:
69 calories
1 g fat (trace saturated fat)
0 cholesterol
125 mg sodium
11 g carbohydrate
4 g fiber
2 g protein

Diabetic Exchange: 2 vegetable.

Apple-Spice Acorn Squash

low sodium | meat less

Joann Fell, Fostoria, Ohio

PREP/TOTAL TIME: 30 MIN.

1 medium acorn squash

1 medium tart apple, chopped

1/4 cup golden raisins

1/8 teaspoon ground cinnamon

1/8 teaspoon ground nutmeg

2 teaspoons butter

Cut squash in half; discard seeds. Place squash cut side down in a microwave-safe baking dish. Add 1/2 in. of water. Microwave, uncovered, on high for 10-13 minutes or until almost tender; drain.

Combine the apple, raisins, cinnamon and nutmeg; spoon into squash cavities. Dot with butter. Microwave, uncovered, on high for 6-8 minutes or until squash and apples are tender. Let stand for 5 minutes before serving. **YIELD:** 2 SERVINGS.

Editor's Note: This recipe was tested in a 1,100-watt microwave.

Nutrition Facts: One serving (1 filled squash half) equals:
207 calories
4 g fat (2 g saturated fat)
10 mg cholesterol
47 mg sodium
45 g carbohydrate
5 g fiber
2 g protein

Diabetic Exchanges: 1-1/2 starch, 1-1/2 fruit, 1 fat.

Linguine with Fresh Tomatoes

meat less

Susan Jones, Downers Grove, Illinois

PREP/TOTAL TIME: 15 MIN.

8 ounces uncooked linguine

3 medium tomatoes, chopped

6 green onions, sliced

1/2 cup grated Parmesan cheese

1/4 cup minced fresh basil *or* 4 teaspoons dried basil

2 garlic cloves, minced

1 teaspoon salt

1/2 teaspoon pepper

3 tablespoons butter

Cook pasta according to package directions. Meanwhile, in a large serving bowl, combine the tomatoes, onions, Parmesan cheese, basil, garlic, salt and pepper. Drain pasta and toss with butter. Add to tomato mixture; toss to coat. **YIELD:** 6 SERVINGS.

Nutrition Facts: One serving (1 cup) equals:
211 calories
9 g fat (5 g saturated fat)
22 mg cholesterol
680 mg sodium
26 g carbohydrate
2 g fiber
8 g protein

Diabetic Exchanges: 2 fat, 1-1/2 starch.

Linguine with Fresh Tomatoes

Italian Broccoli Cheese Bake

Italian Broccoli Cheese Bake

meat less

Rachel Greenawalt Keller, Roanoke, Virginia

PREP: 25 MIN.   **BAKE:** 25 MIN.

- 1-1/2 pounds fresh broccoli spears, cut into 1/4-inch slices
- 1/4 teaspoon salt
- 2 cups (16 ounces) 1% small-curd cottage cheese
- 2 egg whites
- 1/4 cup grated Parmesan cheese
- 3 tablespoons all-purpose flour
- 1/2 teaspoon Italian seasoning
- 3/4 cup meatless spaghetti sauce
- 1 cup (4 ounces) shredded part-skim mozzarella cheese

In a large saucepan, bring 8 cups water to a boil. Add broccoli and salt; cover and boil for 5 minutes. Drain and pat dry. In a blender, combine the cottage cheese, egg whites, Parmesan cheese, flour and Italian seasoning; cover and process until smooth.

Place half of the broccoli in an 11-in. x 7-in. x 2-in. baking dish coated with nonstick cooking spray; top with half of the cottage cheese mixture. Repeat layers. Spoon spaghetti sauce over the top; sprinkle with mozzarella cheese. Bake, uncovered, at 375° for 25-30 minutes or until bubbly. Let stand for 5 minutes before serving. **YIELD:** 4 SERVINGS.

Nutrition Facts: One serving equals:
- 266 calories
- 9 g fat (5 g saturated fat)
- 32 mg cholesterol
- 977 mg sodium
- 22 g carbohydrate
- 4 g fiber
- 27 g protein

Diabetic Exchanges: 3 lean meat, 2 vegetable, 1/2 starch.

Mashed Winter Vegetables

low fat *meat less*

Kathy Lynch, Aloha, Oregon

PREP: 20 MIN.   **COOK:** 45 MIN.

- 1 large rutabaga, peeled and cut into 3/4-inch cubes
- 3 medium turnips, peeled and cut into 3/4-inch cubes
- 2 medium parsnips, peeled and cut into 1/2-inch slices
- 2 medium carrots, cut into 1/2-inch slices
- 1/4 cup fat-free milk
- 2 tablespoons butter
- 1-1/4 teaspoons salt
- 1/2 teaspoon pepper
- 1/2 teaspoon sugar

Place the rutabaga, turnips, parsnips and carrots in a large saucepan; cover with water. Bring to a boil. Reduce heat; cover and simmer for 40 minutes or until tender. Drain and place the vegetables in a large bowl; mash. Add the milk, butter, salt, pepper and sugar; stir until blended. **YIELD:** 10 SERVINGS.

Nutrition Facts: One serving (2/3 cup) equals:
- 89 calories
- 3 g fat (1 g saturated fat)
- 6 mg cholesterol
- 362 mg sodium
- 16 g carbohydrate
- 4 g fiber
- 2 g protein

Diabetic Exchanges: 1 starch, 1/2 fat.

Classic Green Bean Casserole

low fat *low carb* *meat less*

Taste of Home Test Kitchen
Greendale, Wisconsin

PREP: 20 MIN.   **BAKE:** 25 MIN. + STANDING

- 1 package (16 ounces) frozen cut green beans
- 1 medium onion, chopped
- 1 garlic clove, minced
- 1 teaspoon butter
- 1/2 pound fresh mushrooms, chopped
- 1 can (12 ounces) fat-free evaporated milk
- 1/4 cup all-purpose flour
- 1/2 cup fat-free milk
- 1 teaspoon reduced-sodium soy sauce

1/2   teaspoon salt
1/4   teaspoon poultry seasoning
1/8 to 1/4 teaspoon pepper
TOPPING:
2   cups sliced onions
1   teaspoon butter
1/2   cup soft bread crumbs

Place beans in a microwave-safe dish. Cover and cook on high for 7-9 minutes or until tender; drain.

In a nonstick skillet, cook onion and garlic in butter over medium heat until tender, about 4 minutes. Add mushrooms; cook until softened. Reduce heat to medium-low; gradually stir in evaporated milk. Combine flour and milk until smooth; stir into mushroom mixture. Add the soy sauce, salt, poultry seasoning and pepper. Bring to a boil; cook and stir for 2 minutes or until thickened. Stir in beans. Transfer to a 2-qt. baking dish coated with nonstick cooking spray. Bake, uncovered, at 375° for 15 minutes.

For topping, in a large nonstick skillet, cook onions in butter over medium-low heat until golden brown. Add the bread crumbs; cook until dry and golden brown. Sprinkle over casserole. Bake 7-10 minutes longer or until heated through and topping is browned. Let stand for 10 minutes before serving. **YIELD:** 12 SERVINGS.

Nutrition Facts: One serving (1/2 cup) equals:
86   calories
1 g   fat (1 g saturated fat)
3 mg   cholesterol
200 mg   sodium
15 g   carbohydrate
2 g   fiber
5 g   protein

Diabetic Exchanges: 2 vegetable, 1/2 fat-free milk.

Pasta with Roasted Red Pepper Sauce

Antoinette Ronzio
North Providence, Rhode Island

PREP/TOTAL TIME: 30 MIN.

1   can (14-1/2 ounces) Italian stewed tomatoes, undrained
1   jar (7 ounces) roasted red peppers, drained
1   teaspoon sugar
1/2   teaspoon ground cumin
1/4   teaspoon salt
1/4   teaspoon dried oregano
1/4   teaspoon cayenne pepper
1/4   teaspoon red wine vinegar
1   small onion, chopped
2   garlic cloves, minced
1   tablespoon olive oil

Hot cooked pasta

In a blender, combine the first eight ingredients; cover and process until smooth. In a large nonstick skillet, saute onion and garlic in oil until tender. Stir in pepper mixture. Bring to a boil. Reduce heat; simmer, uncovered, for 10 minutes, stirring frequently. Serve sauce over pasta. **YIELD:** 5 SERVINGS.

Nutrition Facts: One serving (1/2 cup sauce, calculated without pasta) equals:
73   calories
5 g   fat (trace saturated fat)
0   cholesterol
681 mg   sodium
8 g   carbohydrate
1 g   fiber
1 g   protein

Diabetic Exchanges: 1 vegetable, 1 fat.

Pasta with Roasted
Red Pepper Sauce

Classic Green Bean Casserole

Bountiful Breads.

Balance your meal plan with the goodness of grains and this delectable assortment of crusty breads, flaky rolls, mouth-watering muffins and more! From savory to sweet, these bread-basket basics are best fresh from the oven.

Apple Gingerbread

Apple Gingerbread

low fat

Pam Blockey, Bozeman, Montana

PREP: 15 MIN. **BAKE:** 30 MIN.

- 2/3 cup sugar
- 1/3 cup unsweetened applesauce
- 1 egg
- 3 tablespoons molasses
- 1 cup all-purpose flour
- 1/2 cup whole wheat flour
- 2 teaspoons ground ginger
- 1 teaspoon baking powder
- 1 teaspoon baking soda
- 1 teaspoon ground cinnamon
- 1/4 teaspoon ground nutmeg
- 1/8 teaspoon ground allspice
- 1/2 cup reduced-fat plain yogurt
- 1-1/2 cups chopped peeled Granny Smith *or* other tart apples (about 1 medium)
- 1 cup plus 2 tablespoons reduced-fat whipped topping

In a mixing bowl, combine the sugar, applesauce, egg and molasses; mix well. Combine the flours, ginger, baking powder, baking soda and spices; add to the molasses mixture alternately with yogurt, beating just until combined. Fold in the apples.

Pour into an 8-in. square baking dish coated with nonstick cooking spray. Bake at 350° for 30-35 minutes or until a toothpick inserted near the center comes out clean. Cool on a wire rack. Cut into squares; dollop with whipped topping. **YIELD:** 9 SERVINGS.

Nutrition Facts: One serving (1 piece with 2 tablespoons whipped topping) equals:
- 203 calories
- 2 g fat (1 g saturated fat)
- 24 mg cholesterol
- 186 mg sodium
- 42 g carbohydrate
- 2 g fiber
- 4 g protein

Diabetic Exchanges: 2 starch, 1 fruit.

> **All recipes** in this chapter are designated meatless. You will find them indexed under this category beginning on page 336.

Blueberry Corn Muffins

Genevieve Fairchild, Chester, Iowa

PREP: 15 MIN. **BAKE:** 20 MIN. + COOLING

- 1/4 cup butter, softened
- 1/4 cup sugar
- 1/4 cup packed brown sugar
- 1 egg
- 1 cup all-purpose flour
- 1/2 cup cornmeal
- 2 teaspoons baking powder
- 1/4 teaspoon salt
- 1/4 teaspoon ground nutmeg
- 1/2 cup 2% milk
- 1 cup fresh *or* frozen blueberries

In a mixing bowl, cream butter and sugars. Add egg; mix well. Combine the flour, cornmeal, baking powder, salt and nutmeg; add to creamed mixture alternately with milk just until moistened. Fold in blueberries.

Coat muffin cups with nonstick cooking spray or use paper liners; fill two-thirds full with batter. Bake at 400° for 18-22 minutes or until a toothpick comes out clean. Cool for 5 minutes before removing from pan to a wire rack. **YIELD:** 1 DOZEN.

Editor's Note: If using frozen blueberries, do not thaw before adding to batter.

Nutrition Facts: One serving (1 muffin) equals:
- 146 calories
- 5 g fat (3 g saturated fat)
- 29 mg cholesterol
- 141 mg sodium
- 23 g carbohydrate
- 1 g fiber
- 3 g protein

Diabetic Exchanges: 1 starch, 1 fruit.

Cheesy Biscuit Triangles

Suzette Jones, Tulsa, Oklahoma

PREP: 25 MIN. **BAKE:** 15 MIN.

- 2 cups all-purpose flour
- 3 teaspoons baking powder
- 1/2 teaspoon salt
- 1/2 teaspoon dried oregano, *divided*
- 1/2 teaspoon dried basil, *divided*
- 2 egg whites
- 1 egg
- 1 cup (4 ounces) crumbled feta cheese
- 1/2 cup reduced-fat ricotta cheese
- 1/3 cup buttermilk
- 1/4 cup reduced-fat sour cream

In a bowl, combine the flour, baking powder, salt, 1/4 teaspoon oregano and 1/4 teaspoon basil. Set one egg white aside.

In a bowl, combine the egg, cheeses, buttermilk, sour cream and remaining egg white; mix well. Stir into the dry ingredients just until moistened.

On a lightly floured surface, roll dough into a 12-in. x 9-in. rectangle. Cut into twelve 3-in. squares; cut each diagonally in half. Place triangles on baking sheets coated with nonstick cooking spray. Beat reserved egg white; brush over tops. Sprinkle with remaining oregano and basil. Bake at 425° for 12-15 minutes or until golden brown. **YIELD:** 2 DOZEN.

Nutrition Facts: One serving (2 triangles) equals:
- 128 calories
- 4 g fat (3 g saturated fat)
- 32 mg cholesterol
- 360 mg sodium
- 17 g carbohydrate
- 1 g fiber
- 6 g protein

Diabetic Exchanges: 1 starch, 1 fat.

Fruit-Filled Windmill Rolls

`low sodium`

Taste of Home Test Kitchen
Greendale, Wisconsin

PREP: 30 MIN. + RISING   **BAKE:** 15 MIN.

- 3 to 3-1/2 cups all-purpose flour
- 1/3 cup plus 2 tablespoons sugar, *divided*
- 1 package (1/4 ounce) quick-rise yeast
- 1/2 teaspoon salt
- 1/2 cup fat-free milk
- 1/3 cup butter, softened
- 1/4 cup water
- 1 egg
- 1 egg white
- 1 tablespoon orange juice
- 1/2 teaspoon ground cinnamon

TOPPING:
- 1 egg white

Fruit-Filled Windmill Rolls

- 1 tablespoon water
- 2 teaspoons sugar
- 1/2 cup 100% apricot and cherry spreadable fruit

In a large mixing bowl, combine 2 cups flour, 1/3 cup sugar, yeast and salt. In a small saucepan, heat the milk, butter and water to 120°-130°. Add to dry ingredients; beat until moistened. Add egg and egg white; beat on medium speed for 2 minutes. Stir in enough remaining flour to form a soft dough. Turn onto a lightly floured surface. Cover and let rest for 10 minutes.

Roll into a 12-in. square. Brush orange juice over dough. Combine cinnamon and remaining sugar; sprinkle over dough. Cut into sixteen 3-in. squares.

To form windmills, diagonally cut dough from each corner to within 3/4 in. of the center. Fold every other point toward the center, overlapping pieces. Place 3 in. apart on baking sheets coated with nonstick cooking spray. Cover and let rise in a warm place until doubled, about 40 minutes.

Press center firmly to seal. Beat egg white and water; brush over windmills. Sprinkle with sugar. Bake at 350° for 13-17 minutes or until golden brown. Remove from pans to wire rack to cool slightly. Spoon spreadable fruit into center of windmills. Serve warm. **YIELD:** 16 ROLLS.

Nutrition Facts: One serving (1 roll) equals:
- 196 calories
- 4 g fat (2 g saturated fat)
- 24 mg cholesterol
- 128 mg sodium
- 35 g carbohydrate
- 1 g fiber
- 4 g protein

Diabetic Exchanges: 2 starch, 1/2 fruit, 1/2 fat.

Blueberry Cheese Danish

Taste of Home Test Kitchen
Greendale, Wisconsin

PREP: 20 MIN. + CHILLING **BAKE:** 20 MIN.

- 3/4 cup 1% cottage cheese
- 1/3 cup sugar
- 1/3 cup 1% milk
- 1/4 cup canola oil
- 1 teaspoon vanilla extract
- 2 cups all-purpose flour
- 2 teaspoons baking powder
- 1/2 teaspoon salt

FILLING:
- 4 ounces reduced-fat cream cheese
- 1/4 cup sugar
- 1 egg, *separated*
- 1 teaspoon grated lemon peel
- 1 teaspoon vanilla extract
- 1 cup fresh *or* frozen blueberries
- 1 tablespoon water

GLAZE:
- 1/2 cup confectioners' sugar
- 2 teaspoons lemon juice

In a blender or food processor, cover and process cottage cheese until smooth. Add sugar, milk, oil and vanilla; process until smooth. Combine the flour, baking powder and salt; add to cheese mixture. Process just until dough forms a ball (dough will be sticky). Turn onto a floured surface; knead 4-5 times. Place in a bowl; cover and refrigerate for 30 minutes.

In a mixing bowl, beat cream cheese and sugar until smooth. Add egg yolk, lemon peel and vanilla; mix well. Turn dough onto a 17-in. x 13-in. piece of parchment paper. Roll into a 16-in. x 12-in. rectangle. Transfer with paper to a baking sheet. Spread cream cheese mixture lengthwise in a 3-1/2-in.-wide strip down center of dough; sprinkle with blueberries. On each long side, cut 1-in.-wide strips about 3-3/4 in. into center. Fold alternating strips at an angle across berries. Pinch ends to seal and tuck under. Beat egg white and water; brush over dough.

Bake at 400° for 20-22 minutes or until golden brown. Remove to a wire rack. Combine glaze ingredients; drizzle over warm pastry. Refrigerate leftovers. **YIELD:** 10 SERVINGS.

Editor's Note: If using frozen blueberries, do not thaw before adding to batter.

Nutrition Facts: One serving (1 slice) equals:
- 260 calories
- 8 g fat (1 g saturated fat)
- 30 mg cholesterol
- 339 mg sodium
- 41 g carbohydrate
- 1 g fiber
- 7 g protein

Diabetic Exchanges: 2 starch, 1 fruit, 1 fat.

Blueberry Cheese Danish

Honey Bagels

Taste of Home Test Kitchen
Greendale, Wisconsin

PREP: 1 HOUR + STANDING **BAKE:** 20 MIN.

- 1 tablespoon active dry yeast
- 1-1/4 cups warm water (110° to 115°)
- 3 tablespoons canola oil
- 3 tablespoons sugar
- 3 tablespoons plus 1/4 cup honey, *divided*
- 1 teaspoon brown sugar
- 2 teaspoons salt
- 1 egg
- 4 to 5 cups bread flour
- 2 tablespoons dried minced onion
- 2 tablespoons sesame seeds
- 2 tablespoons poppy seeds

In a large mixing bowl, dissolve yeast in warm water. Add the oil, sugar, 3 table-spoons honey, brown sugar, salt and egg; mix well. Stir in enough flour to form a soft dough.

Turn onto a floured surface; knead until a smooth, firm dough forms, about 8-10

Honey Bagels

minutes. Cover and let rest for 10 minutes.

Shape into 12 pieces; roll each piece into a 10-in. rope. Form bagels by overlapping the ends; pinch to seal. Place on a lightly floured surface. Cover and let rest for 20 minutes.

In a large saucepan or Dutch oven, bring 8 cups water and remaining honey to a boil. Drop bagels, one at a time, into boiling water. Cook bagels for 45 seconds; turn and cook 45 seconds longer. Remove bagels with a slotted spoon; drain and sprinkle with onion, and sesame and poppy seeds.

Place bagels 2 in. apart on baking sheets lined with parchment paper. Bake at 425° for 12 minutes. Turn and bake 5 minutes longer or until golden brown. **YIELD:** 1 DOZEN.

Nutrition Facts: One serving (1 bagel) equals:
- 243 calories
- 4 g fat (trace saturated fat)
- 18 mg cholesterol
- 398 mg sodium
- 44 g carbohydrate
- 1 g fiber
- 7 g protein

Diabetic Exchanges: 2-1/2 starch, 1 fat.

Dill Bread

low fat

Corky Huffsmith, Salem, Oregon

PREP: 10 MIN. + RISING
BAKE: 35 MIN. + COOLING

- 1 package (1/4 ounce) active dry yeast
- 1/4 cup warm water (110° to 115°)
- 1 cup small-curd 2% cottage cheese
- 1/4 cup snipped fresh dill *or* 4 teaspoons dill weed
- 1 tablespoon butter, melted
- 1-1/2 teaspoons salt
- 1 teaspoon sugar
- 1 teaspoon dill seed
- 1 egg, beaten
- 2-1/4 to 2-3/4 cups all-purpose flour

In a mixing bowl, dissolve yeast in warm water. Heat cottage cheese to 110°-115°; add to yeast mixture. Add the fresh dill, butter, salt, sugar, dill seed, egg and 1 cup flour; beat well. Stir in enough remaining flour to form a soft dough. Do not knead. Cover and let rise in a warm place until doubled, about 1 hour.

Punch dough down. Turn onto a lightly floured surface; shape into a 6-in. circle. Transfer to a 9-in. round baking pan coated with nonstick cooking spray. Cover and let rise until doubled, about 45 minutes.

Bake at 350° for 35-40 minutes or until bread sounds hollow when tapped. Remove from pan to a wire rack to cool. Cut into wedges before serving. **YIELD:** 12 SERVINGS.

Nutrition Facts: One serving (1 piece) equals:
- 118 calories
- 2 g fat (1 g saturated fat)
- 22 mg cholesterol
- 385 mg sodium
- 19 g carbohydrate
- 1 g fiber
- 6 g protein

Diabetic Exchanges: 1 starch, 1/2 fat.

Dill Bread

Apricot Breakfast Rolls

style; pinch seam to seal. Cut into 12 pieces; place in a 13-in. x 9-in. x 2-in. baking dish coated with nonstick cooking spray. Cover and let rise until doubled, about 30 minutes.

Bake at 350° for 30-35 minutes or until lightly browned. Cool on a wire rack for 30 minutes. For glaze, in a bowl, combine confectioners' sugar, cold milk and remaining fruit spread. Drizzle over rolls. **YIELD:** 1 DOZEN.

Nutrition Facts: One serving (1 roll) equals:
271 calories
1 g fat (trace saturated fat)
1 mg cholesterol
225 mg sodium
60 g carbohydrate
2 g fiber
7 g protein

Apricot Breakfast Rolls

low fat

Connie Knudtson, Joplin, Missouri

PREP: 30 MIN. + RISING
BAKE: 30 MIN. + COOLING

1 package (1/4 ounce) active dry yeast
1/2 cup warm water (110° to 115°)
2 cups warm fat-free milk (110° to 115°)
1 teaspoon salt
1 cup whole wheat flour
3-1/2 to 4-1/2 cups all-purpose flour
1 jar (14-1/2 ounces) apricot spreadable fruit, *divided*
1/2 teaspoon ground cinnamon
GLAZE:
1 cup confectioners' sugar
1/2 teaspoon cold fat-free milk

In a mixing bowl, dissolve yeast in warm water. Stir in warm milk, salt, whole wheat flour and 3 cups all-purpose flour; beat until smooth. Stir in enough remaining all-purpose flour to form a soft dough. Turn onto a floured surface; knead until smooth and elastic, about 6-8 minutes. Place in a bowl coated with nonstick cooking spray, turning once to coat top. Cover and let rise in a warm place until doubled, about 1-1/4 hours.

Punch dough down. Turn onto a floured surface; knead 8 times. Cover and let rest for 5 minutes. Roll into an 18-in. square. Spread 1 cup fruit spread to within 1/2 in. of edges; sprinkle with cinnamon. Roll up jelly-roll

Caramel Apple Bread

Valerie Long, Oklahoma City, Oklahoma

PREP: 30 MIN. **BAKE:** 45 MIN. + COOLING

1 cup fat-free plain yogurt
3/4 cup sugar
2 eggs
2 teaspoons vanilla extract
2 cups all-purpose flour
2 teaspoons baking powder
1/2 teaspoon baking soda
1/2 teaspoon salt
1-1/2 cups chopped peeled tart apples
3/4 cup chopped pecans
1/4 cup packed brown sugar
2 tablespoons butter
1 tablespoon fat-free milk

In a large mixing bowl, beat the yogurt, sugar, eggs and vanilla. Combine the flour, baking powder, baking soda and salt; add to yogurt mixture and beat until just combined. Fold in apples and pecans.

Pour into a 9-in. x 5-in. x 3-in. loaf pan coated with nonstick cooking spray. Bake at 350° for 45-55 minutes or until a toothpick inserted near the center comes out clean. Cool for 10 minutes before removing from pan to a wire rack.

In a small saucepan, bring the brown sugar, butter and milk to a boil, stirring constantly. Cover and cook for 1 minute. Cool slightly. Spread over cooled bread. Let stand for 15 minutes. **YIELD:** 1 LOAF (12 SLICES).

Nutrition Facts: One serving (1 slice) equals:
239 calories
8 g fat (2 g saturated fat)
41 mg cholesterol
232 mg sodium
38 g carbohydrate
2 g fiber
5 g protein

Cheesy Onion Quick Bread `low carb`

Davonna Henderson, Bountiful, Utah

PREP: 15 MIN. **BAKE:** 20 MIN. + COOLING

- 1 medium onion, chopped
- 1 teaspoon olive oil
- 1-1/2 cups reduced-fat biscuit/baking mix
- 1 egg, lightly beaten
- 1/2 cup fat-free milk
- 1 cup (4 ounces) shredded reduced-fat cheddar cheese, *divided*
- 2 teaspoons poppy seeds
- 1 tablespoon butter

In a small nonstick skillet, saute onion in oil until tender; set aside. Place biscuit mix in a bowl. Combine egg and milk; mix well. Stir into the biscuit mix just until moistened. Stir in the onion mixture, 1/2 cup cheese and poppy seeds.

Transfer to an 8-in. x 4-in. x 2-in. loaf pan coated with nonstick cooking spray. Sprinkle with the remaining cheese. Drizzle with butter. Bake at 400° for 20-25 minutes or until a toothpick inserted near the center comes out clean and loaf is golden brown. Cool for 10 minutes before removing from pan to a wire rack. Store in the refrigerator. **YIELD:** 1 LOAF.

Nutrition Facts: One serving (1 slice) equals:
- 115 calories
- 5 g fat (2 g saturated fat)
- 27 mg cholesterol
- 275 mg sodium
- 12 g carbohydrate
- 1 g fiber
- 5 g protein

Diabetic Exchanges: 1 starch, 1 fat.

Cheesy Onion Quick Bread

Chocolate Chip Banana Muffins

Chocolate Chip Banana Muffins

Lauren Heyn, Oak Creek, Wisconsin

PREP: 15 MIN. **BAKE:** 20 MIN.

- 3/4 cup all-purpose flour
- 3/4 cup whole wheat flour
- 1/2 cup wheat bran
- 1/2 cup packed brown sugar
- 1 teaspoon baking powder
- 3/4 teaspoon baking soda
- 1/2 teaspoon salt
- 2 eggs, lightly beaten
- 1/4 cup fat-free milk
- 1-1/3 cups mashed ripe bananas (2 to 3 medium)
- 1/3 cup unsweetened applesauce
- 1 teaspoon vanilla extract
- 1/2 cup miniature chocolate chips
- 1/3 cup chopped pecans

In a large bowl, combine the first seven ingredients. In another bowl, combine the eggs and milk; stir in the bananas, apple-sauce and vanilla. Stir into dry ingredients just until moistened. Stir in chocolate chips.

Coat muffin cups with nonstick cooking spray or use paper liners; fill three-fourths full with batter. Sprinkle with pecans. Bake at 375° for 18-22 minutes or until a tooth-pick comes out clean. Cool for 5 minutes before removing from pan to a wire rack. **YIELD:** 1 DOZEN.

Nutrition Facts: One serving (1 muffin) equals:
- 191 calories
- 6 g fat (2 g saturated fat)
- 36 mg cholesterol
- 236 mg sodium
- 33 g carbohydrate
- 4 g fiber
- 4 g protein

Diabetic Exchanges: 2 starch, 1/2 fat.

Cinnamon Loaf

Dorothy Bateman, Carver, Massachusetts

PREP: 20 MIN.   BAKE: 45 MIN. + COOLING

- 1/4 cup butter, softened
- 1 cup plus 2 tablespoons sugar, *divided*
- 2 eggs
- 1 teaspoon vanilla extract
- 2 cups all-purpose flour
- 1 teaspoon baking powder
- 1/2 teaspoon baking soda
- 1/2 teaspoon salt
- 1 cup buttermilk
- 1 teaspoon ground cinnamon

In a large mixing bowl, beat butter until light and fluffy, about 1 minute. Gradually beat in 1 cup sugar. Add eggs, one at a time, beating well after each addition. Stir in vanilla. Combine the flour, baking powder, baking soda and salt. Add to creamed mixture alternately with buttermilk just until mixed.

Transfer half of the mixture to a 9-in. x 5-in. x 3-in. loaf pan coated with nonstick cooking spray. Combine cinnamon and remaining sugar. Sprinkle three-fourths of mixture over batter. Top with remaining butter and sprinkle with remaining cinnamon mixture.

Bake at 350° for 45-50 minutes or until a toothpick inserted near the center comes out clean. Cool for 10 minutes before removing from pan to a wire rack to cool completely.
YIELD: 14 SERVINGS.

Nutrition Facts: One serving (1 slice) equals:
- 173 calories
- 4 g fat (2 g saturated fat)
- 40 mg cholesterol
- 225 mg sodium
- 30 g carbohydrate
- 1 g fiber
- 3 g protein

Diabetic Exchanges: 2 starch, 1/2 fat.

Cran-Apple Tea Ring

Nellie Grimes, Jacksonville, Texas

PREP: 45 MIN. + RISING
BAKE: 20 MIN. + COOLING

- 1 package (1/4 ounce) active dry yeast
- 1/4 cup warm water (110° to 115°)
- 1/2 cup warm fat-free milk (110° to 115°)
- 1 egg
- 2 tablespoons butter, softened
- 1 tablespoon grated orange peel
- 1 teaspoon salt
- 3 tablespoons plus 1/2 cup sugar, *divided*
- 2-3/4 to 3-1/4 cups all-purpose flour
- 1 cup thinly sliced peeled apple
- 1 cup dried cranberries
- 1/2 cup chopped walnuts, toasted
- 1-1/2 teaspoons ground cinnamon
- 1 egg white
- 1 tablespoon water
- 1/2 cup confectioners' sugar
- 1 tablespoon orange juice

In a large mixing bowl, dissolve yeast in warm water. Add milk, egg, butter, orange peel, salt, 3 tablespoons sugar and 1 cup flour; beat until smooth. Stir in enough remaining flour to form a soft dough.

Turn onto a floured surface; knead until smooth and elastic, about 6-8 minutes. Place in a bowl coated with nonstick cooking spray; turn once to coat top. Cover and let rise in a warm place for 1 hour.

In a bowl, toss the apple, cranberries, walnuts, cinnamon and remaining sugar; set aside. Punch dough down; turn onto a lightly floured surface. Roll into a 20-in. x 10-in. rectangle. Combine egg white and water; chill 3 tablespoons. Brush remaining mixture over dough. Spoon fruit mixture to within 1 in. of edges. Roll up tightly jelly-roll style, starting with a long side; seal ends.

Place seam side down in a 15-in. x 10-in. x 1-in. baking pan coated with nonstick

Cinnamon Loaf

Cran-Apple Tea Ring

cooking spray; pinch ends to form a ring. With scissors, cut from outside edge two-thirds of the way toward center of ring at 1-in. intervals. Separate strips slightly; twist so filling shows. Cover and let rise until doubled, about 40 minutes.

Brush with reserved egg white mixture. Bake at 375° for 20-25 minutes or until golden brown (cover with foil during the last 10 minutes). Remove to a wire rack to cool. Combine confectioners' sugar and orange juice; drizzle over ring. **YIELD:** 16 SERVINGS.

Nutrition Facts: One serving (1 piece) equals:
200 calories
4 g fat (1 g saturated fat)
17 mg cholesterol
174 mg sodium
37 g carbohydrate
2 g fiber
4 g protein

Diabetic Exchanges: 2 starch, 1 fat, 1/2 fruit.

Herbed Swirl Bread

`low fat`

Laura Dennison, Pensacola, Florida

PREP: 30 MIN. + RISING   **BAKE:** 40 MIN.

3 packages (1/4 ounce *each*) active dry yeast
2-1/2 cups warm water (110° to 115°), *divided*
1 teaspoon sugar
3-1/4 cups whole wheat flour
1 tablespoon salt
2-3/4 to 3-1/2 cups bread flour
6 green onions, finely chopped
1 garlic clove, minced
1 cup minced fresh parsley
2 tablespoons minced fresh rosemary
1 tablespoon *each* minced fresh basil and oregano
1 teaspoon minced fresh thyme
1/4 teaspoon pepper
2 tablespoons butter
1 egg, beaten

In a large mixing bowl, dissolve yeast in 3/4 cup warm water. Add sugar; let stand for 5 minutes. Add the whole wheat flour, salt and remaining water; beat until smooth. Stir in enough bread flour to form a soft dough (dough will be sticky).

Turn onto a floured surface; knead until smooth and elastic, about 6-8 minutes. Place in a bowl coated with nonstick cooking spray; turn once to coat top. Cover and let rise in a warm place until doubled, about 1 hour. In a nonstick skillet, saute onions, garlic, herbs and pepper in butter until tender. Set aside.

Punch dough down and turn onto a floured surface; divide in half. Roll each piece into a 14-in. x 9-in. rectangle. Brush with some of the egg; refrigerate rest of egg. Spread herb mixture over dough to within 1/2 in. of edges. Roll up jelly-roll style, starting with a short side; pinch seams to seal and tuck ends under. Place seam side down in two 9-in. x 5-in. x 3-in. loaf pans coated with nonstick cooking spray. Cover; let rise until doubled, about 45 minutes.

Brush with reserved egg. Bake at 375° for 40-50 minutes or until bread sounds hollow when tapped. Remove from pans to wire racks. **YIELD:** 2 LOAVES (12 SLICES EACH).

Herbed Swirl Bread

Nutrition Facts: One serving (1 slice) equals:
134 calories
2 g fat (1 g saturated fat)
11 mg cholesterol
309 mg sodium
25 g carbohydrate
3 g fiber
5 g protein

Diabetic Exchange: 1-1/2 starch.

Cranberry Breakfast Pretzels

Cranberry Breakfast Pretzels

Nicki Woods, Springfield, Missouri

PREP: 25 MIN. + RISING   **BAKE:** 15 MIN.

- 3/4 cup dried cranberries
- 1/3 cup unsweetened applesauce
- 2 tablespoons sugar, *divided*
- 1 package (1/4 ounce) active dry yeast
- 1 cup warm milk (110° to 115°)
- 3 tablespoons canola oil
- 1-1/2 teaspoons salt
- 3-1/2 to 4 cups all-purpose flour
- 2 quarts water

TOPPING:

- 1 egg white, beaten
- 1/2 teaspoon ground cinnamon
- 1 tablespoon sugar
- Honey *or* cream cheese, optional

In a food processor or blender, place the dried cranberries, applesauce and 1 tablespoon sugar; cover and process until finely chopped. Set aside. In a mixing bowl, dissolve yeast in warm milk. Add the remaining sugar; let stand for 5 minutes. Add the cranberry mixture, oil, salt and enough flour to form a soft dough. Turn onto a lightly floured surface; knead until smooth and elastic, about 6-8 minutes. Place in a bowl coated with nonstick cooking spray, turning once to coat the top. Cover and let rise in a warm place until doubled, about 1-1/2 hours.

Punch dough down. Turn onto a floured surface. Divide dough into 15 balls. Roll each ball into a 14-in. rope and form into a pretzel shape.

In a large saucepan, bring water to a boil. Drop pretzels, one at a time, into water; boil for 10 seconds on each side. Remove with a slotted spoon; drain on paper towels.

Place pretzels on baking sheets coated with nonstick cooking spray. Cover and let rise in a warm place until puffy, about 25 minutes. Brush with egg white. Combine cinnamon and sugar; sprinkle over tops. Bake at 375° for 12-14 minutes or until golden brown. Serve with honey or cream cheese if desired. **YIELD:** 15 SERVINGS.

Nutrition Facts: One serving (1 pretzel) equals:
- 170 calories
- 3 g fat (1 g saturated fat)
- 1 mg cholesterol
- 248 mg sodium
- 31 g carbohydrate
- 1 g fiber
- 4 g protein

Diabetic Exchange: 2 starch.

Lentil Bread

Mike Buescher, Ft. Wayne, Indiana

PREP: 1 HOUR 40 MIN. + RISING   **BAKE:** 35 MIN.

- 3/4 cup lentils, rinsed
- 1-1/2 cups water
- 4-1/2 teaspoons finely chopped onion
- 1 garlic clove, minced
- 2 packages (1/4 ounce *each*) active dry yeast
- 1 cup warm water (110° to 115°)
- 1-1/2 cups warm fat-free milk (110° to 115°)
- 1/4 cup olive oil
- 1/4 cup sugar
- 1 tablespoon grated Parmesan cheese
- 1 tablespoon salt
- 1 cup whole wheat flour
- 6 to 7 cups bread flour

In a saucepan, combine the lentils, water, onion and garlic; bring to a boil. Reduce heat; cover and simmer for about 30 minutes or until lentils are tender. Cool slightly. Transfer mixture to a blender or food processor; cover and process until smooth. Cool to 110°-115°.

In a mixing bowl, dissolve yeast in warm water. Add the milk, lentil mixture, oil, sugar, Parmesan cheese, salt, whole wheat flour and 3 cups bread flour. Beat until smooth. Stir in enough remaining bread flour to form a soft dough. Turn onto a floured surface; knead until smooth and elastic, about 6-8 minutes. Place in a bowl coated with nonstick cooking spray, turning once to coat top. Cover and let rise in a warm place until doubled, about 1 hour.

Punch dough down. Turn onto a lightly floured surface. Divide into thirds; shape into loaves. Place in three greased 9-in. x 5-in. x 3-in. loaf pans. Cover and let rise until doubled, about 30-40 minutes. Bake at 375° for 35-45 minutes or until golden brown. Remove from pans to wire racks to cool. **YIELD:** 3 LOAVES (12 SLICES EACH).

Nutrition Facts: One serving (1 slice) equals:
- 118 calories
- 2 g fat (trace saturated fat)
- trace cholesterol
- 205 mg sodium
- 22 g carbohydrate
- 2 g fiber
- trace protein

Diabetic Exchange: 1-1/2 starch.

Herb Cheese Bread

Taste of Home Test Kitchen
Greendale, Wisconsin

PREP: 15 MIN.   **BAKE:** 20 MIN.

- 1/4 cup finely chopped green onions
- 2 garlic cloves, minced

1/3 cup reduced-fat margarine
1/2 teaspoon ground cumin
1/4 teaspoon dried oregano
1/4 teaspoon dried thyme
1/8 teaspoon salt
1/8 teaspoon crushed red pepper flakes
1 loaf (1 pound) unsliced French bread, halved lengthwise
3/4 cup shredded reduced-fat cheddar cheese

In a small nonstick skillet, saute onions and garlic in margarine for 1-2 minutes. Stir in the seasonings. Brush over cut sides of French bread; sprinkle with cheese.

Wrap each piece of bread loosely in a large piece of heavy-duty foil; seal edges of foil. Bake at 400° for 20-25 minutes or until heated through and cheese is melted. Cut each piece into six slices. Serve warm. **YIELD:** 12 SERVINGS.

Nutrition Facts: One serving (1 slice) equals:
147 calories
5 g fat (2 g saturated fat)
5 mg cholesterol
339 mg sodium
20 g carbohydrate
1 g fiber
5 g protein

Diabetic Exchanges: 1-1/2 starch, 1 fat.

Vegetable Focaccia

Vegetable Focaccia

Michele Fairchok, Grove City, Ohio

PREP: 15 MIN. + RISING   **BAKE:** 15 MIN.

2 to 2-1/4 cups bread flour
1 package (1/4 ounce) quick-rise yeast
1 teaspoon salt
1 cup warm water (120° to 130°)
1 tablespoon olive oil

TOPPING:
3 plum tomatoes, chopped
5 medium fresh mushrooms, sliced

1/2 cup chopped green pepper
1/2 cup sliced ripe olives
1/4 cup chopped onion
3 tablespoons olive oil
2 teaspoons red wine vinegar
3/4 teaspoon salt
1/4 teaspoon garlic powder
1/4 teaspoon dried oregano
1/4 teaspoon pepper
2 teaspoons cornmeal

In a mixing bowl, combine 2 cups flour, yeast and salt. Add water and oil; beat until smooth. Stir in enough remaining flour to form a soft dough. Turn onto a floured surface; knead until smooth and elastic, about 4 minutes. Cover and let rest for 15 minutes. Meanwhile, in a bowl, combine the tomatoes, mushrooms, green pepper, olives, onion, oil, vinegar and seasonings.

Coat a 15-in. x 10-in. x 1-in. baking pan with nonstick cooking spray; sprinkle with cornmeal. Press dough into pan. Prick dough generously with a fork. Bake at 475° for 5 minutes or until lightly browned. Cover with vegetable mixture. Bake 8-10 minutes longer or until edges of crust are golden. **YIELD:** 12 SERVINGS.

Nutrition Facts: One serving (1 piece) equals:
121 calories
5 g fat (1 g saturated fat)
0 cholesterol
376 mg sodium
17 g carbohydrate
1 g fiber
3 g protein

Diabetic Exchanges: 1 starch, 1 fat.

Herb Cheese Bread

Apple Pie Coffee Cake

Sandra Castillo, Janesville, Wisconsin

PREP: 10 MIN. **BAKE:** 40 MIN. + COOLING

- 1 package (18-1/4 ounces) spice cake mix
- 1 can (21 ounces) apple pie filling
- 3 eggs
- 3/4 cup fat-free sour cream
- 1/4 cup water
- 2 tablespoons canola oil
- 1 teaspoon almond extract
- 2 tablespoons brown sugar
- 1-1/2 teaspoons ground cinnamon

GLAZE:
- 2/3 cup confectioners' sugar
- 2 teaspoons fat-free milk

Set aside 1 tablespoon cake mix. Set aside 1-1/2 cups pie filling. In a mixing bowl, combine eggs, sour cream, water, oil, extract and remaining cake mix and pie filling. Beat on medium speed for 2 minutes. Pour half into a 10-in. fluted tube pan coated with nonstick cooking spray.

Combine the brown sugar, cinnamon and reserved cake mix; sprinkle over batter. Spoon reserved pie filling over batter to within 3/4 in. of edges; top with remaining batter. Bake at 350° for 40-45 minutes or until a toothpick inserted near the center comes out clean. Cool for 10 minutes before removing from pan to a wire rack.

In a small bowl, combine glaze ingredients. drizzle over cooled cake. **YIELD:** 14 SERVINGS.

Nutrition Facts: One serving (1 piece) equals:
- 283 calories
- 8 g fat (2 g saturated fat)
- 46 mg cholesterol
- 296 mg sodium
- 49 g carbohydrate
- 2 g fiber
- 5 g protein

Diabetic Exchanges: 2 starch, 1-1/2 fat, 1 fruit.

Nutty Rosemary Bread

low sodium

Naomi Knobloch, Lester, Iowa

PREP: 30 MIN. + RISING **BAKE:** 35 MIN.

- 2 packages (1/4 ounce *each*) active dry yeast
- 2-1/2 cups warm water (110° to 115°), *divided*
- 3/4 cup whole wheat flour
- 1/4 cup canola oil
- 1/4 cup honey
- 3 tablespoons cornmeal
- 1 tablespoon dried rosemary, crushed
- 1 teaspoon salt
- 5 to 6 cups bread flour
- 1 cup chopped pecans
- 1 egg, beaten

In a large mixing bowl, dissolve yeast in 1/2 cup warm water. Add the whole wheat flour, oil, honey, cornmeal, rosemary, salt, 1 cup bread flour and remaining water. Beat until smooth. Stir in enough remaining bread flour to form a soft dough. Turn onto a floured surface; add pecans. Knead until smooth and elastic, about 6-8 minutes. Place in a bowl coated with nonstick cooking spray, turning once to coat top. Cover and let rise in a warm place until doubled, about 1 hour.

Punch dough down. Divide in half; shape into two loaves. Place in two 9-in. x 5-in. x 3-in. loaf pans coated with nonstick cooking spray. Cover and let rise until doubled, about 30 minutes.

Brush egg over loaves. Bake at 350° for 35-40 minutes or until bread sounds hollow when tapped. Remove from pans to wire racks. **YIELD:** 2 LOAVES (16 SLICES EACH).

Nutrition Facts: One serving (1 slice) equals:
- 150 calories
- 5 g fat (trace saturated fat)
- 7 mg cholesterol
- 76 mg sodium
- 23 g carbohydrate
- 1 g fiber
- 4 g protein

Diabetic Exchanges: 1-1/2 starch, 1 fat.

Apple Pie Coffee Cake

Nutty Rosemary Bread

Raspberry Streusel Muffins

Kristin Stank, Indianapolis, Indiana

PREP: 25 MIN. **BAKE:** 20 MIN.

1-1/2 cups all-purpose flour
1/4 cup sugar
1/4 cup packed brown sugar
2 teaspoons baking powder
1 teaspoon ground cinnamon
1/4 teaspoon salt
1 egg, lightly beaten
1/2 cup plus 2 tablespoons fat-free milk
2 tablespoons butter, melted
1-1/4 cups fresh *or* frozen raspberries
1 teaspoon grated lemon peel
TOPPING:
1/4 cup chopped pecans
1/4 cup packed brown sugar
2 tablespoons all-purpose flour
1 teaspoon ground cinnamon
1 teaspoon grated lemon peel
1 tablespoon butter, melted
GLAZE:
1/4 cup confectioners' sugar
1-1/2 teaspoons lemon juice

In a large bowl, combine the first six ingredients. Combine egg, milk and butter; stir into dry ingredients until just moistened. Fold in raspberries and lemon peel. Coat muffin cups with nonstick cooking spray or use

paper liners; fill three-fourths full with batter.

Combine topping ingredients; sprinkle about 1 tablespoon over each muffin. Bake at 350° for 18-22 minutes or until a toothpick comes out clean. Cool for 5 minutes before removing from pan to a wire rack. Combine glaze ingredients; drizzle over warm muffins. **YIELD:** 1 DOZEN.

Editor's Note: If using frozen raspberries, do not thaw before adding to batter.

Nutrition Facts: One serving (1 muffin) equals:
181 calories
5 g fat (2 g saturated fat)
26 mg cholesterol
133 mg sodium
31 g carbohydrate
2 g fiber
3 g protein

Diabetic Exchanges: 2 starch, 1 fat.

Whole Wheat Pumpkin Nut Bread

Jean-Marie Hirsch, East Rochester, New York

PREP: 15 MIN. **BAKE:** 60 MIN. + COOLING

1 cup whole wheat flour
1 cup sugar
2/3 cup all-purpose flour
1 teaspoon baking soda
1 teaspoon ground cinnamon
1/2 teaspoon baking powder
1/2 teaspoon salt
1/2 teaspoon ground cloves
1 cup canned pumpkin
1/2 cup egg substitute
1/3 cup water
1/4 cup canola oil
1/2 cup chopped walnuts

In a bowl, combine the first eight ingredients. In another bowl, combine the pumpkin, egg substitute, water and oil; mix well. Stir into dry ingredients just until moistened. Fold in walnuts.

Spoon into a 9-in. x 5-in. x 3-in. baking pan coated with nonstick cooking spray. Bake at 350° for 60-65 minutes or until a toothpick inserted near the center comes out clean. Cool for 15 minutes before removing from pan to a wire rack. **YIELD:** 1 LOAF (12 SLICES).

Nutrition Facts: One serving (1 slice) equals:
208 calories
8 g fat (1 g saturated fat)
1 mg cholesterol
239 mg sodium
31 g carbohydrate
3 g fiber
5 g protein

Diabetic Exchanges: 2 starch, 1 fat.

Whole Wheat Pumpkin Nut Bread

Banana Nut Bread

Banana Nut Bread

Taste of Home Test Kitchen
Greendale, Wisconsin

PREP: 15 MIN. **BAKE:** 60 MIN.

      2 tablespoons butter, softened
    3/4 cup sugar
      1 egg
      1 egg white
      2 cups mashed ripe bananas (about
         4 medium)
    1/4 cup unsweetened applesauce
    1/4 cup honey
      1 teaspoon vanilla *or* rum extract
  1-1/3 cups all-purpose flour
    2/3 cup whole wheat flour
      1 teaspoon baking soda
    1/2 teaspoon salt
    1/4 cup chopped pecans

In a mixing bowl, beat butter and sugar for 2 minutes or until crumbly. Add egg, then egg white, beating well after each addition. Beat on high speed until light and fluffy. Stir in the bananas, applesauce, honey and extract. Combine the flours, baking soda and salt; stir into banana mixture just until moistened.

Pour into a 9-in. x 5-in. x 3-in. loaf pan coated with nonstick cooking spray. Sprinkle with nuts. Bake at 325° for 60-65 minutes or until a toothpick inserted near the center comes out clean. Cool for 10 minutes before removing from pan to a wire rack. **YIELD:** 1 LOAF (10 SLICES).

Nutrition Facts: One serving (1 slice) equals:
      266 calories
        6 g fat (2 g saturated fat)
       27 mg cholesterol
      280 mg sodium
       52 g carbohydrate
        3 g fiber
        4 g protein

Diabetic Exchanges: 2-1/2 starch, 1 fruit, 1 fat.

Spinach Herb Twists

`low fat` `low carb`

Amy Estes, Wichita, Kansas

PREP: 35 MIN. + RISING **BAKE:** 15 MIN.

      5 cups packed torn fresh spinach
      2 green onions, sliced
      1 garlic clove, minced
      5 tablespoons butter, *divided*
    1/4 cup grated Parmesan cheese
    1/2 teaspoon dried basil
    1/2 teaspoon dried oregano
      1 package (16 ounces) hot roll mix
      1 cup warm water (120° to 130°)
      1 egg

Place spinach in a steamer basket; place in a saucepan over 1 in. of water. Bring to a boil; cover and steam for 2-3 minutes or until limp. Drain well and set aside. In a small skillet, saute onions and garlic in 1 tablespoon butter until tender; transfer to a bowl. Stir in the Parmesan cheese, basil, oregano and spinach; set aside.

In a large bowl, stir the hot roll mix, warm water, egg and 2 tablespoons butter until dough pulls away from sides of bowl. Turn onto a lightly floured surface; knead until smooth and elastic, about 5 minutes. Cover and let rest for 5 minutes.

Divide dough in half. Roll each portion into a 12-in. x 10-in. rectangle. Melt the remaining butter; brush over dough. Spread spinach mixture over dough to within 1/4 in. of edges. Fold each rectangle in half lengthwise; pinch seams to seal. Cut each rectangle into twelve 1-in.-wide strips.

Twist strips and place on baking sheets coated with nonstick cooking spray. Cover and let rise in a warm place until doubled, about 25 minutes. Bake at 375° for 12-16 minutes or until golden brown. Serve warm. Refrigerate leftovers. **YIELD:** 2 DOZEN.

Nutrition Facts: One serving (1 twist) equals:
       90 calories
        3 g fat (2 g saturated fat)
       16 mg cholesterol
      156 mg sodium
       12 g carbohydrate
        1 g fiber
        2 g protein

Diabetic Exchanges: 1 starch, 1/2 fat.

Raisin Cinnamon Rolls

`low fat`

Carolyn Wolbers, Loveland, Ohio

PREP: 1 HOUR + RISING **BAKE:** 20 MIN.

      2 medium potatoes, peeled and diced
      1 package (1/4 ounce) active dry yeast
    1/2 teaspoon plus 1/4 cup sugar, *divided*
    1/2 cup evaporated fat-free milk
    1/4 cup honey
      3 tablespoons canola oil
      1 teaspoon salt
    1/2 teaspoon butter flavoring
      5 cups all-purpose flour
      2 egg whites, lightly beaten, *divided*
  1-1/4 cups packed brown sugar
    1/2 cup raisins
      2 teaspoons ground cinnamon
GLAZE:
  1-1/2 cups confectioners' sugar
      3 tablespoons fat-free milk
    1/2 teaspoon vanilla extract

In a saucepan, cook potatoes in 1-1/2 cups

water until very tender; drain, reserving 3/4 cup cooking liquid. Mash potatoes; set aside 1 cup (refrigerate any remaining potatoes for another use). Heat reserved cooking liquid to 110°-115° if necessary. In a mixing bowl, dissolve yeast in warm liquid. Add 1/2 teaspoon sugar; let stand for 5 minutes.

Add the milk, honey, oil, salt, butter flavoring, remaining sugar, 2 cups flour and reserved potatoes. Beat until smooth. Stir in enough remaining flour to form a soft dough. Turn onto a floured surface; knead until smooth and elastic, about 6-8 minutes. Place in a bowl coated with nonstick cooking spray, turning once to coat top. Cover and let rise in a warm place until doubled, about 1-1/2 hours.

Punch dough down. Turn onto a lightly floured surface; roll into an 18-in. x 13-in. rectangle. Brush with some of the egg whites. Combine brown sugar, raisins and cinnamon; sprinkle over dough to within 1 in. of edges. Roll up jelly-roll style, starting with a long side; pinch seam to seal. Cut into 18 slices. Place cut side down in two 9-in. square baking pans coated with nonstick cooking spray. Brush with remaining egg white. Cover and let rise until doubled, about 30 minutes.

Bake at 350° for 20-25 minutes or until golden brown. Cool on a wire rack. Combine glaze ingredients; drizzle over rolls. **YIELD:** 18 ROLLS.

Nutrition Facts: One serving (1 roll) equals:
- 288 calories
- 2 g fat (trace saturated fat)
- trace cholesterol
- 184 mg sodium
- 64 g carbohydrate
- 1 g fiber
- 5 g protein

Lemon-Blueberry Oat Muffins

Jamie Brown, Walden, Colorado

PREP: 15 MIN. **BAKE:** 20 MIN.

- 1 cup quick-cooking oats
- 1 cup all-purpose flour

Raisin Cinnamon Rolls

Lemon-Blueberry Oat Muffins

- 1/2 cup sugar
- 3 teaspoons baking powder
- 1/4 teaspoon salt
- 1 egg
- 1 egg white
- 1 cup fat-free milk
- 2 tablespoons butter, melted
- 1 teaspoon grated lemon peel
- 1 teaspoon vanilla extract
- 1 cup fresh *or* frozen blueberries

TOPPING:
- 1/2 cup quick-cooking oats
- 2 tablespoons brown sugar
- 1 tablespoon butter, softened

In a bowl, combine the first five ingredients. In another bowl, combine the egg, egg white, milk, butter, lemon peel and vanilla; mix well. Add to dry ingredients just until moistened. Fold in berries. Coat muffin cups with nonstick cooking spray or use paper liners; fill two-thirds full with batter. Combine topping ingredients; sprinkle over batter. Bake at 400° for 20-22 minutes or until top is lightly browned and springs back when lightly touched. Cool 5 minutes; remove to a wire rack. **YIELD:** 1 DOZEN.

Editor's Note: If using frozen blueberries, do not thaw before adding to batter.

Nutrition Facts: One serving (1 muffin) equals:
- 166 calories
- 4 g fat (2 g saturated fat)
- 26 mg cholesterol
- 158 mg sodium
- 28 g carbohydrate
- 2 g fiber
- 4 g protein

Diabetic Exchanges: 1-1/2 starch, 1 fat.

Teddy Bear Paws

Hollyce Swan, Spokane, Washington

PREP: 50 MIN. + RISING
BAKE: 10 MIN. + COOLING

  1 cup finely chopped fresh *or* frozen
     cranberries
Sugar substitute equivalent to 3/4 cup sugar
1-1/2 teaspoons grated orange peel
  2 packages (1/4 ounce *each*) active dry yeast
1/2 cup warm water (110° to 115°)
1/2 cup warm fat-free milk (110° to 115°)
1/2 cup sugar
  2 eggs
1/4 cup butter, softened
  1 teaspoon salt
3-1/2 to 4 cups all-purpose flour
1/4 cup slivered almonds, toasted
ICING:
  2 tablespoons butter, softened
  1 cup confectioners' sugar
1/8 teaspoon almond extract
  1 to 2 tablespoons fat-free milk

In a large saucepan, bring the cranberries, sugar substitute and orange peel to a boil. Reduce heat to medium; cook and stir for 5 minutes or until thickened. Cool.

In a large mixing bowl, dissolve yeast in warm water. Add milk, sugar, eggs, butter, salt and 2 cups flour; beat until smooth. Stir in enough remaining flour to form a soft dough. Turn onto a lightly floured surface; knead until smooth and elastic, about 6-8 minutes. Place in a bowl coated with

nonstick cooking spray, turning once to coat top. Cover and let rise in a warm place until doubled, about 1 hour.

Punch dough down. Turn onto a lightly floured surface; cover and let rest for 10 minutes. Roll into a 16-in. x 12-in. rectangle. Cut in half, forming two 16-in. x 6-in. strips. Spread cranberry filling down the center of each strip to within 1 in. of long edge. Fold lengthwise over filling and pinch seam to seal. Cut each strip into eight pieces. With a kitchen scissors, cut each piece two times from pinched seam to about 1 in. from folded side. Push an almond into the end of each section for bear claws.

Place 2 in. apart on baking sheets coated with nonstick cooking spray. Curve folded side slightly to separate strips and allow filling to show. Cover and let rise in a warm place until doubled, about 30 minutes. Bake at 375° for 10-14 minutes or until golden brown. Remove from pans to wire racks to cool. Combine icing ingredients; spread over rolls. **YIELD:** 16 ROLLS.

Editor's Note: This recipe was tested with Splenda No Calorie Sweetener.

Nutrition Facts: One serving (1 roll) equals:
    223 calories
      6 g fat (3 g saturated fat)
   38 mg cholesterol
  204 mg sodium
     38 g carbohydrate
      1 g fiber
      5 g protein

Diabetic Exchanges: 2-1/2 starch, 1 fat.

Maple Walnut Banana Bread

Amy Hawk, Seabrook, New Jersey

PREP: 10 MIN. **BAKE:** 50 MIN. + COOLING

1-3/4 cups all-purpose flour
1/3 cup sugar
1/3 cup packed brown sugar
  2 teaspoons baking powder
1/2 teaspoon baking soda
1/4 teaspoons salt
  2 eggs
  1 cup mashed ripe banana (2 to 3 medium)
  3 tablespoons butter, melted
  2 tablespoons fat-free milk
1/4 teaspoon maple flavoring
1/4 cup chopped walnuts

In a bowl, combine the first six ingredients. Combine the eggs, banana, butter, milk and flavoring; mix well. Stir into dry ingredients just until moistened. Spoon into an 8-in. x 4-in. x 2-in. loaf pan coated with nonstick cooking spray. Sprinkle with walnuts.

Bake at 350° for 50-55 minutes or until a toothpick inserted near the center comes out

Maple Walnut Banana Bread

cinnamon, baking soda, baking powder and salt. Drain apples, reserving juice. In another bowl, beat the egg, oil and reserved juice. Stir into the dry ingredients just until blended. Fold in zucchini and apples until moistened.

Pour into an 8-in. x 4-in. x 2-in. loaf pan coated with nonstick cooking spray. Combine topping ingredients; sprinkle over top. Bake at 350° for 50-55 minutes or until a toothpick inserted near the center comes out clean. Cool for 10 minutes before removing from pan to a wire rack. **YIELD:** 1 LOAF (12 SLICES).

Nutrition Facts: One serving (1 slice) equals:
- 193 calories
- 4 g fat (2 g saturated fat)
- 23 mg cholesterol
- 139 mg sodium
- 37 g carbohydrate
- 1 g fiber
- 3 g protein

Diabetic Exchanges: 1-1/2 starch, 1 fruit, 1 fat.

Apple Zucchini Loaf

clean. Cool for 10 minutes before removing from pan to a wire rack. **YIELD:** 1 LOAF.

Nutrition Facts: One serving (1 slice) equals:
- 197 calories
- 6 g fat (2 g saturated fat)
- 43 mg cholesterol
- 184 mg sodium
- 34 g carbohydrate
- 1 g fiber
- 4 g protein

Diabetic Exchanges: 1-1/2 starch, 1 fat, 1/2 fruit.

Apple Zucchini Loaf

low sodium

JoAnn Lee, Accord, New York

PREP: 15 MIN. BAKE: 50 MIN. + COOLING

- 1-1/2 cups all-purpose flour
- 1 cup sugar
- 1 teaspoon ground cinnamon
- 1/2 teaspoon baking soda
- 1/4 teaspoon baking powder
- 1/4 teaspoon salt
- 1 jar (4-1/2 ounces) diced apple baby food
- 1 egg
- 1 tablespoon canola oil
- 1 cup finely shredded zucchini

TOPPING:
- 1/4 cup quick-cooking oats
- 1/4 cup flaked coconut
- 1/4 cup packed brown sugar
- 2 tablespoons butter, melted

Dash ground cinnamon

In a large bowl, combine the flour, sugar,

Multigrain Muffins

low sodium

Peggy Corcoran, Apex, North Carolina

PREP/TOTAL TIME: 25 MIN.

- 1/2 cup all-purpose flour
- 1/2 cup cornmeal
- 1/2 cup quick-cooking oats
- 1/4 cup whole wheat flour
- 1/4 cup packed brown sugar
- 3 tablespoons toasted wheat germ
- 2 teaspoons baking powder
- 1/4 teaspoon salt
- 1 egg, lightly beaten
- 1 cup fat-free milk
- 1/4 cup canola oil
- 1/4 cup chopped walnuts
- 1/4 cup raisins

In a bowl, combine the first eight ingredients. In another bowl, combine the egg, milk and oil; stir into dry ingredients just until moistened. Fold in walnuts and raisins.

Coat muffin cups with nonstick cooking spray or use paper liners; fill two-thirds full with batter. Bake at 375° for 15-18 minutes or until a toothpick comes out clean. Cool for 5 minutes before removing from pan to a wire rack. **YIELD:** 1 DOZEN.

Nutrition Facts: One serving (1 muffin) equals:
- 166 calories
- 7 g fat (1 g saturated fat)
- 18 mg cholesterol
- 107 mg sodium
- 22 g carbohydrate
- 2 g fiber
- 4 g protein

Diabetic Exchanges: 1-1/2 starch, 1 fat.

Multigrain Muffins

Roasted Garlic Bread

remaining flour to form a soft dough. Turn onto a lightly floured surface; knead until smooth and elastic, about 6-8 minutes. Place in a bowl coated with nonstick cooking spray, turning once to coat top. Cover and let rise in a warm place until doubled, about 45 minutes. Meanwhile, add the sage, marjoram and rosemary to the reserved roasted garlic.

Punch dough down. Turn onto a lightly floured surface; divide in half. Roll each portion into a 10-in. x 8-in. rectangle. Spread garlic mixture to within 1/2 in. of edges. Sprinkle with Parmesan cheese. Roll up jelly-roll style, starting with a long side; pinch seam and ends to seal.

Coat a baking sheet with nonstick cooking spray. Place loaves seam side down on pan; tuck ends under. With a sharp knife, make several slashes across the top of each loaf. Cover and let rise until doubled, about 30 minutes. Bake at 375° for 20-25 minutes or until golden brown. Remove to wire racks; brush with butter. **YIELD:** 2 LOAVES (10 SLICES EACH).

Nutrition Facts: One serving (1 slice) equals:
    84 calories
    1 g fat (1 g saturated fat)
    2 mg cholesterol
  136 mg sodium
   15 g carbohydrate
    1 g fiber
    2 g protein

Diabetic Exchange: 1 starch.

Roasted Garlic Bread

Barb Alexander, Princeton, New Jersey

PREP: 45 MIN. + RISING **BAKE:** 20 MIN.

  2 medium whole garlic bulbs
  2 teaspoons olive oil
  1 package (1/4 ounce) active dry yeast
  1 cup warm water (110° to 115°)
  1 tablespoon sugar
  1 teaspoon salt
2-1/2 to 3 cups all-purpose flour
  2 tablespoons minced fresh sage *or* 2 teaspoons rubbed sage
  2 teaspoons minced fresh marjoram *or* 3/4 teaspoon dried marjoram
  1 teaspoon minced fresh rosemary *or* 1/2 teaspoon dried rosemary, crushed
  2 tablespoons grated Parmesan cheese
  1 tablespoon butter, melted

Remove papery outer skin from garlic (do not peel or separate cloves). Cut top off garlic bulbs; brush with oil. Wrap each bulb in heavy-duty foil. Bake at 425° for 30-35 minutes or until softened. Cool for 10-15 minutes. Squeeze softened garlic into a small bowl; set aside.

In a large mixing bowl, dissolve yeast in warm water. Add the sugar, salt and 1 cup flour; beat until smooth. Stir in enough

Nutty Whole Wheat Bread

Rosadene Herold, Lakeville, Indiana

PREP: 15 MIN. + RISING **BAKE:** 25 MIN.

2-1/4 cups all-purpose flour
1-1/4 cups whole wheat flour
 3/4 cup finely chopped walnuts
  2 tablespoons brown sugar
  1 package (1/4 ounce) quick-rise yeast
  1 teaspoon salt
  1 cup water
 1/3 cup reduced-fat plain yogurt
  2 tablespoons butter

In a mixing bowl, combine 1 cup all-purpose flour, whole wheat flour, walnuts, brown sugar, yeast and salt. In a saucepan, heat the water, yogurt and butter to 120°-130°. Add to dry ingredients; beat until smooth. Stir in enough remaining all-purpose flour to form a soft dough. Turn onto a floured surface; knead until smooth and elastic, about 4 minutes (do not let rise).

Shape dough into a ball; place on a baking sheet coated with nonstick cooking spray. Cover and let rest in a warm place for 20 minutes. Bake at 400° for 25-30 minutes or until golden brown. Remove from pan to cool on a wire rack. **YIELD:** 1 LOAF (16 SLICES).

Nutrition Facts: One serving (1 slice) equals:
156 calories
6 g fat (1 g saturated fat)
4 mg cholesterol
167 mg sodium
23 g carbohydrate
2 g fiber
4 g protein

Diabetic Exchanges: 1-1/2 starch, 1/2 fat.

Orange Marmalade Sweet Rolls

low fat

Lacey Griffin, Fredonia, Pennsylvania

PREP: 15 MIN. + RISING **BAKE:** 15 MIN.

1 loaf (1 pound) frozen bread dough, thawed
1/3 cup 100% orange marmalade spreadable fruit
2 tablespoons raisins
1/3 cup confectioners' sugar
1/2 teaspoon grated orange peel
2 teaspoons orange juice

On a floured surface, roll dough into a 12-in. x 8-in. rectangle; brush with spreadable fruit. Sprinkle with raisins. Roll up jelly-roll style, starting with a long side; pinch seam to seal.

Cut into 12 slices. Place cut side down in muffin cups coated with nonstick cooking spray. Cover and let rise until doubled, about 45 minutes.

Bake at 350° for 15-20 minutes or until golden brown. Immediately invert onto serving plates. Combine the confectioners'

Orange Marmalade Sweet Rolls

Raisin Wheat Bread

sugar, orange peel and orange juice; drizzle over warm rolls. **YIELD:** 12 SERVINGS.

Nutrition Facts: One serving (1 roll) equals:
140 calories
2 g fat (trace saturated fat)
0 cholesteroL
211 mg sodium
28 g carbohydrate
1 g fiber
4 g protein

Diabetic Exchange: 2 starch.

Raisin Wheat Bread

Lorraine Darocha, Mountain City, Tennessee

PREP: 10 MIN. **BAKE:** 3 HOURS

1-1/4 cups plus 1 tablespoon water (70° to 80°)
2 tablespoons olive oil
2 tablespoons honey
2 tablespoons molasses
1-1/2 teaspoons salt
1/3 cup unsalted sunflower kernels
2/3 cup raisins
2 cups whole wheat flour
1-1/3 cups bread flour
2-1/2 teaspoons active dry yeast

In bread machine pan, place all ingredients in order suggested by manufacturer. Select wheat bread setting. Choose crust color and loaf size if available. Bake according to bread machine directions (check dough after 5 minutes of mixing; add 1 to 2 tablespoons of water or flour if needed). **YIELD:** 1 LOAF (16 SLICES).

Nutrition Facts: One serving (1 slice) equals:
164 calories
4 g fat (trace saturated fat)
0 cholesterol
223 mg sodium
29 g carbohydrate
3 g fiber
5 g protein

Diabetic Exchanges: 2 starch, 1/2 fat.

Cinnamon Breadsticks

low fat **low sodium** **low carb**

Carol Birkemeier, Nashville, Indiana

PREP: 20 MIN. + RISING **BAKE:** 10 MIN.

- 1 package (16 ounces) hot roll mix
- 1 cup warm water (120° to 130°)
- 2 tablespoons canola oil
- 1 egg white, lightly beaten
- 1/2 cup sugar
- 1-1/2 teaspoons ground cinnamon

Refrigerated butter-flavored spray

In a bowl, combine roll mix and contents of yeast package. Add the water, oil and egg white; beat until smooth. Turn dough onto a lightly floured surface; knead until smooth and elastic, about 5 minutes. Cover and let rest for 10 minutes.

Roll into a 16-in. x 12-in. rectangle. Cut widthwise into sixteen 1-in. strips. Cut strips in half widthwise, forming 32 strips. Twist each strip 5-6 times; place on a baking sheet coated with nonstick cooking spray.

Combine sugar and cinnamon. Spray dough sticks generously with refrigerated butter-flavored spray; sprinkle with cinnamon-sugar. Cover and let rise in a warm place until doubled, about 25 minutes. Bake at 375° for 10-12 minutes or until golden brown. Serve warm. **YIELD:** 32 BREADSTICKS.

Nutrition Facts: One serving (1 breadstick) equals:

- 72 calories
- 1 g fat (trace saturated fat)
- 0 cholesterol
- 96 mg sodium
- 13 g carbohydrate
  - trace fiber
- 2 g protein

Diabetic Exchange: 1 starch.

Oatmeal Molasses Bread

low fat **low sodium**

Lyla Franklin, Phoenix, Arizona

PREP: 30 MIN. + RISING **BAKE:** 40 MIN.

- 2 cups boiling water
- 1 cup quick-cooking oats
- 1 package (1/4 ounce) active dry yeast
- 1/2 cup warm water (110° to 115°)
- 1/2 cup molasses
- 1 tablespoon canola oil
- 1 teaspoon salt
- 6 to 6-1/2 cups all-purpose flour
- 1 teaspoon butter, melted

In a bowl, pour boiling water over oats. Let stand until mixture cools to 110°-115°, stirring occasionally. In a mixing bowl, dissolve yeast in warm water. Add the molasses, oil, salt, oat mixture and 3 cups flour; beat until smooth. Stir in enough remaining flour to form a soft dough. Turn onto a floured surface; knead until smooth and elastic, about 6-8 minutes. Place in a bowl coated with nonstick cooking spray, turning once to coat top. Cover and let rise in a warm place until doubled, about 1-1/2 hours.

Punch dough down. Turn onto a lightly floured surface; divide in half. Shape into loaves. Place in two 9-in. x 5-in. x 3-in. loaf pans coated with nonstick cooking spray. Cover and let rise until doubled, about 1 hour.

Bake at 350° for 40-45 minutes or until golden brown. Remove from pans to cool on wire racks. Brush with melted butter. **YIELD:** 2 LOAVES (16 SLICES EACH).

Nutrition Facts: One serving (1 slice) equals:

- 114 calories
- 1 g fat (trace saturated fat)
  - trace cholesterol
- 77 mg sodium
- 23 g carbohydrate
- 1 g fiber
- 3 g protein

Diabetic Exchange: 1-1/2 starch.

Cinnamon Breadsticks

Cranberry Pecan Scones

Cranberry Pecan Scones

Sandy Ferrario, Ione, California

PREP: 20 MIN. BAKE: 20 MIN.

- 2 cups all-purpose flour
- 1/2 cup sugar
- 1 teaspoon baking powder
- 1/2 teaspoon salt
- 1/4 teaspoon baking soda
- 1/4 cup cold butter
- 1 egg
- 6 tablespoons orange juice
- 1 teaspoon vanilla extract
- 1/2 teaspoon grated orange peel
- 1/2 cup chopped fresh *or* frozen cranberries, thawed
- 3 tablespoons chopped pecans, toasted
- 1 egg white
- 1/2 teaspoon water

In a large bowl, combine the flour, sugar, baking powder, salt and baking soda; cut in butter until mixture resembles coarse crumbs. Beat the egg, orange juice, vanilla and orange peel. Add to flour mixture along with cranberries and pecans; stir just until moistened.

Pat dough into a 6-1/2-in. circle on a baking sheet coated with nonstick cooking spray. Combine egg white and water; brush over dough. Cut into eight wedges (do not separate). Bake at 400° for 20-25 minutes or until golden brown. Cool on a wire rack. YIELD: 8 SERVINGS.

Nutrition Facts: One serving (1 scone) equals:
    250 calories
    9 g fat (4 g saturated fat)
    42 mg cholesterol
    321 mg sodium
    38 g carbohydrate
    2 g fiber
    5 g protein

Diabetic Exchanges: 2 starch, 1-1/2 fat, 1/2 fruit.

Raspberry Lemon Loaf

Carol Dodds, Aurora, Ontario

PREP: 15 MIN. BAKE: 60 MIN. + COOLING

- 1-3/4 cups all-purpose flour
- 1/2 cup sugar
- 1 teaspoon baking powder
- 1/2 teaspoon baking soda
- 1/2 teaspoon salt
- 1 egg
- 2 egg whites
- 1 cup reduced-fat lemon yogurt
- 1/4 cup canola oil
- 2 teaspoons grated lemon peel
- 1 cup fresh raspberries

In a large bowl, combine the first five ingredients. In another bowl, whisk together the egg, egg whites, yogurt, oil and lemon peel. Add to the dry ingredients just until moistened. Fold in the raspberries.

Transfer to an 8-in. x 4-in. x 3-in. loaf pan coated with nonstick cooking spray. Bake at 350° for 60-65 minutes or until a toothpick inserted near the center comes out clean. Cool for 10 minutes before removing from pan to a wire rack to cool completely. YIELD: 1 LOAF (12 SLICES).

Nutrition Facts: One serving (1 slice) equals:
    176 calories
    6 g fat (1 g saturated fat)
    50 mg cholesterol
    218 mg sodium
    26 g carbohydrate
    1 g fiber
    4 g protein

Diabetic Exchanges: 1-1/2 starch, 1 fat.

Raspberry Lemon Loaf

Parmesan Basil Biscuits

Peanut Butter 'n' Jelly Muffins

Taste of Home Test Kitchen
Greendale, Wisconsin

PREP: 10 MIN. **BAKE:** 15 MIN. + COOLING

  2   cups all-purpose flour
  2   teaspoons baking powder
3/4   teaspoon baking soda
1/4   teaspoon salt
  2   eggs
3/4   cup apple juice concentrate
1/2   cup reduced-fat chunky peanut butter
1/4   cup fat-free milk
  3   tablespoons butter, melted
1/3   cup 100% strawberry spreadable fruit

In a large bowl, combine the flour, baking powder, baking soda and salt. Combine the eggs, apple juice concentrate, peanut butter, milk and butter; stir into dry ingredients just until moistened.

Coat 12 muffin cups with nonstick cooking spray. Spoon half of the batter into cups. Spoon about 1-1/4 teaspoons spreadable fruit into the center of each; top with remaining batter.

Bake at 350° for 15-20 minutes or until a toothpick comes out clean. Cool for 5 minutes before removing from pan to a wire rack to cool completely. **YIELD:** 1 DOZEN.

Nutrition Facts: One serving (1 muffin) equals:
        225   calories
          8 g   fat (3 g saturated fat)
      43 mg   cholesterol
    315 mg   sodium
        33 g   carbohydrate
          1 g   fiber
          6 g   protein

Diabetic Exchanges: 2 starch, 1-1/2 fat.

Parmesan Basil Biscuits

Taste of Home Test Kitchen
Greendale, Wisconsin

PREP: 20 MIN. **BAKE:** 20 MIN.

2-1/2   cups all-purpose flour
  1/4   cup shredded Parmesan cheese
    2   tablespoons minced fresh basil *or*
        2 teaspoons dried basil
2-1/2   teaspoons baking powder
  1/2   teaspoon baking soda
  1/2   teaspoon salt
  1/4   teaspoon pepper
    1   cup buttermilk
    3   tablespoons olive oil

In a large bowl, combine the flour, cheese, basil, baking powder, baking soda, salt and pepper; mix well. Add the buttermilk and oil; stir just until combined.

Turn onto a floured surface; gently knead three times. Roll dough to 1/2-in. thickness; cut with a floured 2-1/2-in. biscuit cutter. Place 1 in. apart on an ungreased baking sheet. Bake at 400° for 16-18 minutes or until lightly browned. Serve warm. **YIELD:** 1 DOZEN.

Nutrition Facts: One serving (1 biscuit) equals:
        129   calories
          4 g   fat (1 g saturated fat)
          2 mg   cholesterol
      301 mg   sodium
        19 g   carbohydrate
          1 g   fiber
          4 g   protein

Diabetic Exchanges: 1 starch, 1 fat.

Swedish Rye Loaves

`low fat`

Iola Egle, Bella Vista, Arkansas

PREP: 15 MIN. + RISING **BAKE:** 25 MIN.

1/4   cup old-fashioned oats
1/3   cup packed brown sugar
1/4   cup molasses
  5   tablespoons butter, *divided*
  2   teaspoons salt
  2   cups boiling water
  3   cups bread flour
  2   packages (1/4 ounce *each*) active dry yeast
  3   cups rye flour
  1   teaspoon caraway seeds

In a bowl, combine the oats, brown sugar, molasses, 4 tablespoons butter and salt; stir in boiling water. Let stand until mixture cools to 120°-130°, stirring occasionally. In a large mixing bowl, combine 2 cups bread flour and yeast. Add the molasses mixture just until moistened. Stir in rye flour and enough of the remaining bread flour to form a medium stiff dough. Turn onto a floured surface; knead until smooth and elastic, about 6-8 minutes. Place in a bowl coated with nonstick cooking spray, turning once to coat the top. Cover and let rise in a warm place until doubled, about 1 hour.

Punch down dough; cover and let rise in a warm place until doubled, about 30 minutes. Punch down dough. Turn onto a lightly floured surface; divide into three portions. Shape into loaves. Place on baking sheets coated with nonstick cooking spray. Cover and let rise until doubled, about 30 minutes. Bake at 375° for 25-30 minutes or until golden brown. Cool on wire racks. Melt remaining butter; brush over loaves and sprinkle with caraway seeds. Cool. **YIELD:** 3 LOAVES.

Nutrition Facts: One serving (1 slice) equals:
- 102 calories
- 2 g fat (1 g saturated fat)
- 4 mg cholesterol
- 149 mg sodium
- 19 g carbohydrate
- 2 g fiber
- 2 g protein

Diabetic Exchange: 1 starch.

Golden Oatmeal Bread

Taste of Home Test Kitchen
Greendale, Wisconsin

PREP: 15 MIN. BAKE: 50 MIN. + COOLING

- 1 cup all-purpose flour
- 3/4 cup plus 1 tablespoon quick-cooking oats, *divided*
- 1/2 cup whole wheat flour

Swedish Rye Loaves

Golden Oatmeal Bread

- 1/2 cup sugar
- 2 teaspoons baking powder
- 3/4 teaspoon baking soda
- 1/2 teaspoon ground cinnamon
- 3/4 cup unsweetened applesauce
- 1 egg
- 1-1/2 teaspoons vanilla extract
- 1/3 cup golden raisins
- 1/3 cup chopped pecans, toasted

In a large bowl, combine all-purpose flour, 3/4 cup oats, whole wheat flour, sugar, baking powder, baking soda and cinnamon. In another bowl, combine the applesauce, egg and vanilla; stir into dry ingredients just until moistened. Fold in raisins and pecans.

Pour into an 8-in. x 4-in. x 2-in. loaf pan coated with nonstick cooking spray. Sprinkle with remaining oats. Bake at 325° for 50-55 minutes or until a toothpick inserted near the center comes out clean. Cool for 10 minutes before removing from pan to wire rack. **YIELD:** 1 LOAF (10 SLICES).

Nutrition Facts: One serving (1 slice) equals:
- 188 calories
- 4 g fat (1 g saturated fat)
- 21 mg cholesterol
- 149 mg sodium
- 35 g carbohydrate
- 3 g fiber
- 4 g protein

Diabetic Exchanges: 2 starch, 1/2 fat.

Sunflower Wheat Rolls

into a ball. Place 2 in. apart on baking sheets coated with nonstick cooking spray. Cover and let rise in a warm place until doubled, about 45 minutes. Bake at 375° for 12 minutes or until golden brown. Remove from pans to cool on wire racks. **YIELD:** 20 ROLLS.

Editor's Note: If your bread machine has a time-delay feature, we recommend you do not use it for this recipe.

Nutrition Facts: One serving (1 roll) equals:
142 calories
5 g fat (1 g saturated fat)
11 mg cholesterol
122 mg sodium
22 g carbohydrate
2 g fiber
4 g protein

Diabetic Exchanges: 1 starch, 1 fat.

Honey Granola Bread

Erika Pimper, Brigham City, Utah

PREP: 30 MIN. + RISING   **BAKE:** 30 MIN.

3-1/2 cups all-purpose flour
2 packages (1/4 ounce *each*) active dry yeast
1 teaspoon salt
1-3/4 cups fat-free milk
1/2 cup plus 2 tablespoons honey
1/3 cup butter
2 eggs
2 cups whole wheat flour
1 cup reduced-fat granola without raisins
1 cup rye flour
1/2 cup cornmeal
1/2 cup quick-cooking oats
1/4 cup slivered almonds, toasted and chopped

In a large mixing bowl, combine 2 cups all-purpose flour, yeast and salt. In a saucepan, heat the milk, honey and butter to 120°-130°. Add to dry ingredients; beat just until moistened. Add eggs; beat until smooth. Stir in whole wheat flour and enough remaining all-purpose flour to form a soft dough (dough will be sticky). Stir in the granola, rye flour, cornmeal, oats and almonds.

Turn dough onto a floured surface; knead until smooth and elastic, about 6-8 minutes. Place in a bowl coated with nonstick cooking spray, turning once to coat top. Cover and let rise in a warm place until doubled, about 1 hour.

Punch dough down. Turn onto a floured surface. Divide in half; cover and let rest for 10 minutes. Shape each portion into a ball. Place on a greased baking sheet; flatten into 5-in. circles. Cover and let rise in a warm place until doubled, about 30 minutes. Bake at 375° for 20 minutes; cover with foil. Bake 10 minutes longer or until bread sounds

Sunflower Wheat Rolls

Roxann Field, Hutchinson, Minnesota

PREP: 30 MIN. + RISING   **BAKE:** 15 MIN.

1 cup water (70° to 80°)
1/4 cup canola oil
1/4 cup honey
1 egg
1 teaspoon salt
2-1/2 cups bread flour
1 cup whole wheat flour
1/4 cup toasted wheat germ
1/4 cup wheat bran
1/4 cup sunflower kernels
1 tablespoon poppy seeds
2-1/2 teaspoons active dry yeast

In bread machine pan, place all ingredients in the order suggested by manufacturer. Select dough setting (check dough after 5 minutes of mixing; add 1 to 2 tablespoons of water or flour if needed). When the cycle is completed, turn dough onto a lightly floured surface. Punch down; cover and let stand for 10 minutes.

Divide dough into 20 pieces; shape each

hollow when tapped. Remove to wire racks.
YIELD: 2 LOAVES (16 SLICES EACH).

Nutrition Facts: One serving (1 slice) equals:
- 165 calories
- 3 g fat (1 g saturated fat)
- 19 mg cholesterol
- 113 mg sodium
- 30 g carbohydrate
- 2 g fiber
- 5 g protein

Diabetic Exchanges: 2 starch, 1/2 fat.

Pumpkin Dinner Rolls

Toasted Walnut Bread

Linda Kees, Boise, Idaho

PREP: 15 MIN. **BAKE:** 50 MIN. + COOLING

- 1 cup all-purpose flour
- 1 cup whole wheat flour
- 1/3 cup sugar
- 3 teaspoons baking powder
- 1/2 teaspoon salt
- 1 egg, lightly beaten
- 1 cup fat-free milk
- 1/4 cup canola oil
- 1/2 teaspoon vanilla extract
- 1 cup coarsely chopped walnuts, toasted

In a large bowl, combine the flours, sugar, baking powder and salt. Combine the egg, milk, oil and vanilla. Stir into dry ingredients just until moistened. Fold in walnuts.

Transfer to an 8-in. x 4-in. x 2-in. loaf pan coated with nonstick cooking spray. Bake at 350° for 50-55 minutes or until a toothpick inserted near the center comes out clean. Cool for 10 minutes before removing from pan to a wire rack to cool completely. **YIELD:** 1 LOAF (12 SLICES).

Nutrition Facts: One serving (1 slice) equals:
- 202 calories
- 11 g fat (1 g saturated fat)
- 18 mg cholesterol
- 237 mg sodium
- 23 g carbohydrate
- 2 g fiber
- 5 g protein

Diabetic Exchanges: 2 fat, 1-1/2 starch.

Toasted Walnut Bread

Pumpkin Dinner Rolls

low fat

Connie Thomas, Jensen, Utah

PREP: 30 MIN. + RISING **BAKE:** 15 MIN.

- 2 teaspoons active dry yeast
- 1-1/2 cups warm water (110° to 115°)
- 1-1/4 cups canned pumpkin
- 1/2 cup butter, softened
- 1/3 cup sugar
- 2 eggs
- 2 teaspoons salt
- 2-1/2 cups whole wheat flour
- 4-1/2 to 5 cups all-purpose flour

In a large mixing bowl, dissolve yeast in warm water. Add the pumpkin, butter, sugar, eggs, salt and whole wheat flour; beat until smooth. Stir in enough all-purpose flour to form a soft dough. Turn onto a lightly floured surface; knead until smooth and elastic, about 6-8 minutes. Place in a bowl coated with nonstick cooking spray, turning once to coat top. Cover and let rise in a warm place until doubled, about 1 hour.

Punch dough down. Turn onto a lightly floured surface; divide into three portions. Roll each portion into a 12-in. circle; cut each circle into 12 wedges. Roll up wedges from the wide end and place pointed side down 2 in. apart on greased baking sheets. Curve ends to form crescents.

Cover and let rise until doubled, about 30 minutes. Bake at 400° for 12-15 minutes. Remove to wire racks. **YIELD:** 3 DOZEN.

Nutrition Facts: One serving (1 roll) equals:
- 134 calories
- 3 g fat (2 g saturated fat)
- 19 mg cholesterol
- 161 mg sodium
- 23 g carbohydrate
- 2 g fiber
- 4 g protein

Diabetic Exchanges: 1-1/2 starch, 1/2 fat.

Italian Pinwheel Rolls

`low fat`

Patricia Fitzgerald, Candor, New York

PREP: 35 MIN. + RISING **BAKE:** 25 MIN.

Italian Pinwheel Rolls

    1   package (1/4 ounce) active dry yeast
    1   cup warm water (110° to 115°)
1-1/2   teaspoons sugar
1-1/2   teaspoons butter, softened
    1   teaspoon salt
2-1/4   to 2-1/2 cups bread flour
FILLING:
    2   tablespoons butter, melted
  1/4   cup grated Parmesan cheese
    2   tablespoons minced fresh parsley
    6   garlic cloves, minced
    1   teaspoon dried oregano

In a large mixing bowl, dissolve yeast in warm water. Add the sugar, butter, salt and 1 cup flour; beat until smooth. Stir in enough remaining flour to form a soft dough.

Turn onto a floured surface; knead until smooth and elastic, about 6-8 minutes. Place in a bowl coated with nonstick cooking spray, turning once to coat top. Cover and let rise in a warm place until doubled, about 1 hour.

Punch dough down. Turn onto a lightly floured surface. Roll into a 12-in. x 10-in. rectangle. Brush with melted butter; sprinkle Parmesan cheese, parsley, garlic and oregano to within 1/2 in. of edges. Roll up jelly-roll style, starting with a long side; pinch seam to seal. Cut into 12 rolls.

Place rolls cut side up in a 13-in. x 9-in. x 2-in. baking pan coated with nonstick cooking spray. Cover and let rise until doubled, about 30 minutes. Bake at 350° for 25-30 minutes or until golden brown. Remove from pan to a wire rack. **YIELD:** 1 DOZEN.

Nutrition Facts: One serving (1 roll) equals:
        110 calories
          3 g fat (2 g saturated fat)
          8 mg cholesterol
        253 mg sodium
         18 g carbohydrate
          1 g fiber
          4 g protein

Diabetic Exchanges: 1 starch, 1/2 fat.

Sour Cream Blueberry Coffee Cake

Taste of Home Test Kitchen
Greendale, Wisconsin

PREP: 20 MIN. **BAKE:** 40 MIN. + COOLING

    2   cups all-purpose flour
  3/4   cup sugar
    1   teaspoon baking powder
  1/2   teaspoon salt
  1/4   teaspoon baking soda
    1   egg
    1   cup (8 ounces) reduced-fat sour cream
  1/4   cup unsweetened applesauce
    3   tablespoons canola oil
    1   teaspoon vanilla extract
1-1/2   cups fresh or frozen blueberries
TOPPING:
  1/4   cup packed brown sugar
  1/4   cup quick-cooking oats
  1/2   teaspoon ground cinnamon
    2   tablespoons cold butter

In a large bowl, combine the first five ingredients. In another bowl, combine the egg, sour cream, applesauce, oil and vanilla. Stir into dry ingredients just until moistened. Fold in blueberries. Pour into a 9-in. square baking pan coated with nonstick cooking spray.

For topping, in a bowl, combine the brown sugar, oats and cinnamon; cut in butter until mixture resembles coarse crumbs. Sprinkle over the batter. Bake at 350° for 40-45 minutes or until a toothpick inserted near the center comes out clean. Cool on a wire rack. **YIELD:** 12 SERVINGS.

Editor's Note: If using frozen blueberries, do not thaw before adding to batter.

Nutrition Facts: One serving (1 piece) equals:
        242 calories
          9 g fat (3 g saturated fat)
         31 mg cholesterol
        201 mg sodium
         38 g carbohydrate
          1 g fiber
          4 g protein

Diabetic Exchanges: 2-1/2 starch, 1-1/2 fat.

Cranberry Flax Muffins

Jennifer Wertz, Council Bluffs, Iowa

PREP/TOTAL TIME: 25 MIN.

1-1/2   cups bran flakes cereal
  3/4   cup all-purpose flour
  3/4   cup whole wheat flour
  1/2   cup ground flaxseed
  1/4   cup packed brown sugar
    2   teaspoons baking powder
    1   teaspoon ground cinnamon
  1/2   teaspoon baking soda
  1/4   teaspoon salt
    1   egg
    2   egg whites
    1   cup buttermilk
  1/2   cup honey
  1/4   cup canola oil

1-1/2 cups dried cranberries

2 tablespoons whole flaxseed

In a large bowl, combine the first nine ingredients. Whisk the egg, egg whites, buttermilk, honey and oil; stir into dry ingredients just until moistened. Stir in cranberries.

Coat muffin cups with nonstick cooking spray or use paper liners; fill two-thirds full. Sprinkle with whole flaxseed. Bake at 375° for 10-15 minutes or until a toothpick comes out clean. Cool for 5 minutes before removing to wire racks. **YIELD:** 1-1/2 DOZEN.

Nutrition Facts: One serving (1 muffin) equals:
- 183 calories
- 5 g fat (1 g saturated fat)
- 13 mg cholesterol
- 174 mg sodium
- 32 g carbohydrate
- 3 g fiber
- 4 g protein

Diabetic Exchanges: 2 starch, 1 fat.

Cardamom Braid

low sodium

Doris Lystila, Townsend, Massachusetts

PREP: 10 MIN. + RISING **BAKE:** 30 MIN.

1 cup warm fat-free milk (70° to 80°)

1/4 cup butter, softened

2 eggs, lightly beaten

3-3/4 cups bread flour

1/2 cup sugar

1 to 2 teaspoons ground cardamom

1/2 teaspoon salt

2-1/2 teaspoons active dry yeast

TOPPING:

1 egg

Cranberry Flax Muffins

2 tablespoons water

2 teaspoons sugar

1/4 cup sliced almonds

In bread machine pan, place the first eight ingredients in order suggested by manufacturer. Select dough setting (check dough after 5 minutes of mixing; add 1 to 2 tablespoons of water or flour if needed).

When cycle is completed, turn dough onto a lightly floured surface; divide into thirds. Shape each into a 20-in. rope. Place ropes on a parchment-lined baking sheet; braid. Pinch ends to seal and tuck under. Cover and let rise in a warm place until doubled, about 30 minutes.

In a small bowl, beat egg and water; brush over dough. Sprinkle with sugar and almonds. Bake at 350° for 30-35 minutes or until golden brown. Remove from pan to a wire rack to cool. **YIELD:** 1 LOAF.

Editor's Note: If your bread machine has a time-delay feature, we recommend you do not use it for this recipe.

Nutrition Facts: One serving (1 slice) equals:
- 141 calories
- 4 g fat (2 g saturated fat)
- 38 mg cholesterol
- 99 mg sodium
- 23 g carbohydrate
- 1 g fiber
- 5 g protein

Diabetic Exchanges: 1-1/2 starch, 1 fat.

Cardamom Braid

Dazzling Desserts.

Rich and rewarding, these sweet treats deliver all the satisfaction you want from a dessert with none of the guilt. So grab a fork and surrender to moist cakes, mile-high pies, chewy cookies and dozens of other decadent delights!

Apple Pockets

Apple Pockets

Sharon Martin, Terre Hill, Pennsylvania

PREP: 25 MIN. + RISING   **BAKE:** 15 MIN.

2-1/4   cups all-purpose flour, *divided*
   1   package (1/4 ounce) quick-rise yeast
   1   tablespoon sugar
 1/2   teaspoon salt
 2/3   cup water
 1/4   cup butter
FILLING:
   4   cups thinly sliced peeled Rome Beauty *or* other baking apples (2 to 3 medium)
 1/3   cup sugar
   2   tablespoons all-purpose flour
 1/2   teaspoon ground cinnamon
TOPPING:
 1/4   cup milk
   4   teaspoons sugar

In a mixing bowl, combine 1 cup flour, yeast, sugar and salt. In a saucepan, heat the water and butter to 120°-130°. Add to the dry ingredients; beat just until moistened. Stir in enough remaining flour to form a soft dough. Turn onto a floured surface; knead until smooth and elastic, about 6-8 minutes. Cover and let rest for 10 minutes.

Divide dough into four portions. Roll each portion into an 8-in. square. Cut into four 4-in. squares. Cut apple slices into thirds; toss with sugar, flour and cinnamon. Place 1/4 cup filling on each square; bring up the corners up over the filling and pinch to seal. Secure with a toothpick if needed. Place 3 in. apart on baking sheets coated with nonstick cooking spray. Cover and let rise in a warm place for 30 minutes.

Brush with milk; sprinkle with sugar. Bake at 375° for 12-14 minutes or until golden brown. Remove to wire racks. Discard toothpicks before serving. **YIELD:** 16 SERVINGS.

Nutrition Facts: One serving (1 pocket) equals:
     136   calories
       3 g   fat (2 g saturated fat)
      8 mg   cholesterol
   105 mg   sodium
     25 g   carbohydrate
      1 g   fiber
      2 g   protein

Diabetic Exchanges: 1 starch, 1/2 fruit, 1/2 fat.

Fruit-Filled Quesadillas

Cathy Yates, Cicero, New York

PREP/TOTAL TIME: 15 MIN.

   5   fresh apricots, halved
 1/4   cup apricot nectar
   2   teaspoons sugar, *divided*
 1/2   cup sliced fresh strawberries
 1/2   teaspoon ground cinnamon
   2   flour tortillas (8 inches)
Butter-flavored nonstick cooking spray
   2   cups reduced-fat vanilla ice cream
 1/4   cup fresh raspberries

In a nonstick skillet, cook and stir the apricots, nectar and 1 teaspoon sugar over low heat until apricots are tender, about 5 minutes. Stir in the strawberries; cover and remove from the heat. Combine cinnamon and remaining sugar; set aside.

In another nonstick skillet, cook one tortilla over low heat for 1-2 minutes on each side or until golden and crisp. Spritz one side with butter-flavored spray and sprinkle with half of the cinnamon-sugar. Repeat with remaining tortilla.

Place a tortilla sugared side down; spread with fruit mixture. Top with remaining tortilla sugared side up; cut into four wedges. Serve with ice cream and raspberries. **YIELD:** 4 SERVINGS.

Nutrition Facts: One serving (1 wedge with 1/2 cup of ice cream and 1 tablespoon of raspberries) equals:
     214   calories
       5 g   fat (2 g saturated fat)
      9 mg   cholesterol
   182 mg   sodium
     39 g   carbohydrate
      2 g   fiber
      6 g   protein

Diabetic Exchanges: 1-1/2 starch, 1 fruit, 1 fat.

Peach Angel Dessert

Marge Hubrich, St. Cloud, Minnesota

PREP: 20 MIN. + CHILLING

 3/4   cup sugar
   2   tablespoons cornstarch
   1   cup water
   2   tablespoons corn syrup
 1/4   cup peach, apricot *or* orange gelatin powder

- 1 loaf (10-1/2 ounces) angel food cake
- 1 package (8 ounces) reduced-fat cream cheese
- 2 tablespoons fat-free milk
- 2/3 cup confectioners' sugar
- 1 carton (8 ounces) frozen reduced-fat whipped topping, thawed
- 3 cups sliced peeled fresh *or* frozen peaches, thawed

In a small saucepan, combine sugar and cornstarch. Gradually whisk in water and corn syrup until smooth. Cook and stir until mixture comes to a boil. Cook for 1-2 minutes or until thickened. Remove from the heat; stir in gelatin until dissolved. Cool to room temperature, stirring several times.

Cut angel food cake into nine slices. Line an ungreased 13-in. x 9-in. x 2-in. dish with the slices. In a mixing bowl, beat cream cheese and milk until blended. Gradually beat in confectioners' sugar. Set aside 1/3 cup whipped topping for garnish. Fold remaining whipped topping into cream cheese mixture; spread over cake. Top with peaches. Pour gelatin mixture over peaches.

Cover and refrigerate for at least 4 hours. Cut into squares. Top each piece with about 1 teaspoon of reserved whipped topping. Refrigerate leftovers. **YIELD:** 15 SERVINGS.

Nutrition Facts: One serving (1 piece) equals:
- 215 calories
- 4 g fat (3 g saturated fat)
- 9 mg cholesterol
- 157 mg sodium
- 40 g carbohydrate
- 1 g fiber
- 3 g protein

Coconut Custard Pie

Eva Wright, Grant, Alabama

PREP: 25 MIN. + COOLING
BAKE: 40 MIN. + COOLING

- 1/2 cup flaked coconut
- 1 refrigerated pastry shell (9 inches)

Peach Angel Dessert

Coconut Custard Pie

- 4 eggs
- 1/2 teaspoon salt
- 1-3/4 cups fat-free milk
- Sugar substitute equivalent to 1/2 cup sugar
- 1-1/2 teaspoons coconut extract
- 1/2 teaspoon vanilla extract

Place coconut in an ungreased 9-in. pie plate. Bake at 350° for 4 minutes, stirring several times (coconut will not be fully toasted); set aside. Line unpricked pastry shell with a double thickness of heavy-duty foil. Bake at 450° for 8 minutes. Remove foil; bake 4-6 minutes longer. Cool.

In a mixing bowl, beat the eggs and salt for 5 minutes (mixture will be lemon-colored and slightly thickened). Add the milk, sugar substitute, coconut extract and vanilla. Transfer to crust (crust will be full).

Bake at 350° for 30 minutes. Sprinkle with coconut. Bake 8-10 minutes longer or until a knife inserted near the center comes out clean and coconut is lightly browned. Cool on a wire rack for 1 hour. Cover and refrigerate. **YIELD:** 8 SERVINGS.

Editor's Note: This recipe was tested with Splenda No Calorie Sweetener.

Nutrition Facts: One serving (1 piece) equals:
- 214 calories
- 12 g fat (6 g saturated fat)
- 112 mg cholesterol
- 322 mg sodium
- 20 g carbohydrate
- trace fiber
- 6 g protein

Diabetic Exchanges: 2 fat, 1-1/2 starch.

Molten Chocolate Cakes

Taste of Home Test Kitchen
Greendale, Wisconsin

PREP: 25 MIN **BAKE:** 10 MIN.

 1/3   cup butter, cubed
 1/3   cup baking cocoa
   3   squares (1 ounce *each*) semisweet
       chocolate, coarsely chopped
   3   eggs
   7   egg whites
   1   cup confectioners' sugar
 1/2   cup packed brown sugar
1-1/2 teaspoons vanilla extract
 1/3   cup all-purpose flour
 1/8   teaspoon salt

Place the butter, cocoa and chocolate in a microwave safe-bowl. Microwave, uncovered, at 50% power for 20 seconds; stir. Microwave at 50% power 20 seconds longer; stir until smooth. Add the eggs, egg whites, confectioners' sugar, brown sugar and vanilla; mix well. Stir in flour and salt until blended. Pour into seven 6-oz. custard cups coated with nonstick cooking spray.

Place custard cups on a baking sheet. Bake at 450° for 10-12 minutes or until a ther-mometer inserted near the center reads 160°. Remove from the oven and let stand for 1 minute. Run a knife around edge of custard cups; invert onto individual dessert plates. Serve immediately. **YIELD:** 7 SERVINGS.

Editor's Note: This recipe was tested in a 1,100-watt microwave.

Nutrition Facts: One serving (1 cake) equals:
        346   calories
         14 g fat (9 g saturated fat)
        114 mg cholesterol
        196 mg sodium
         47 g carbohydrate
          2 g fiber
          8 g protein

Apple Brown Betty

low fat

Dale Hartman, Coventry, Rhode Island

PREP: 15 MIN. **BAKE:** 55 MIN.

   6   cups sliced peeled Golden Delicious apple
Sugar substitute equivalent to 1/3 cup sugar
 1/4   teaspoon ground cinnamon
   2   slices reduced-calorie whole wheat bread
   2   tablespoons reduced-fat butter, melted
 1/2   cup orange juice
 1/3   cup fat-free whipped cream cheese
 1/2   cup reduced-fat whipped topping

Place apple slices in a bowl. Combine sugar substitute and cinnamon; sprinkle over apples and toss to coat evenly. Place bread in a food processor; cover and process until fine crumbs form. In a small bowl, combine bread crumbs and butter until blended.

Place half of apple mixture in an 8-in. square baking dish coated with nonstick cooking spray. Top with about 1/3 cup crumb mixture and remaining apple mixture. Pour orange juice over apples. Cover and bake at 350° for 30 minutes. Uncover; sprinkle with remaining crumb mixture. Bake 25-30 minutes longer or until apples are tender and crumb topping is golden brown.

In a mixing bowl, beat cream cheese until smooth. Beat in half of the whipped topping. Fold in remaining whipped topping. Serve with the betty. **YIELD:** 6 SERVINGS.

Editor's Note: This recipe was tested with Splenda No Calorie Sweetener.

Nutrition Facts: One serving with a rounded tablespoon of topping equals:
        134   calories
          3 g fat (2 g saturated fat)
          8 mg cholesterol
        142 mg sodium
         25 g carbohydrate
          2 g fiber
          3 g protein

Diabetic Exchanges: 1 fruit, 1/2 starch, 1/2 fat.

Molten Chocolate Cakes

Marbled Chocolate Cheesecake Bars

Marbled Chocolate Cheesecake Bars

Jean Komlos, Plymouth, Michigan

PREP: 20 MIN. **BAKE:** 20 MIN.

3/4 cup water
1/3 cup butter
1-1/2 squares (1-1/2 ounces) unsweetened chocolate
2 cups all-purpose flour
1-1/2 cups packed brown sugar
1 teaspoon baking soda
1/2 teaspoon salt
1 egg
1 egg white
1/2 cup reduced-fat sour cream

CREAM CHEESE MIXTURE:
1 package (8 ounces) reduced-fat cream cheese
1/3 cup sugar
1 egg white
1 tablespoon vanilla extract
1 cup (6 ounces) miniature semisweet chocolate chips

In a small saucepan, combine the water, butter and chocolate. Cook and stir over low heat until melted; stir until smooth. Cool.

In a large mixing bowl, combine the flour, brown sugar, baking soda and salt. Add egg, egg white and sour cream; beat on low speed just until combined. Stir in chocolate mixture until smooth. In another mixing bowl, beat cream cheese, sugar, egg white and vanilla; set aside.

Spread chocolate batter into a 15-in. x 10-in. x 1-in. baking pan coated with nonstick cooking spray. Drop the cream cheese mixture by tablespoonfuls over batter; cut through batter with a knife to swirl. Sprinkle with chocolate chips.

Bake at 375° for 20-25 minutes or until a toothpick inserted near the center comes out clean. Cool on a wire rack. **YIELD:** ABOUT 4 DOZEN.

Nutrition Facts: One serving (1 bar) equals:
95 calories
4 g fat (2 g saturated fat)
10 mg cholesterol
90 mg sodium
15 g carbohydrate
trace fiber
2 g protein

Diabetic Exchanges: 1 starch, 1/2 fat.

Cappuccino Mousse

Taste of Home Test Kitchen
Greendale, Wisconsin

PREP: 15 MIN. + CHILLING

1/2 teaspoon unflavored gelatin
1/4 cup fat-free milk
1-1/2 teaspoons baking cocoa
1/4 teaspoon instant coffee granules
1/3 cup fat-free coffee-flavored yogurt
2 tablespoons sugar
1/2 cup reduced-fat whipped topping

In a small saucepan, sprinkle gelatin over milk; let stand for 1 minute. Heat over low heat, stirring until gelatin is completely dissolved. Add cocoa and coffee; stir until dissolved. Transfer to a small mixing bowl; refrigerate until mixture begins to thicken.

Beat until light and fluffy. Combine yogurt and sugar; beat into gelatin mixture. Fold in whipped topping. Divide between two dessert dishes. Refrigerate until firm. **YIELD:** 2 SERVINGS.

Nutrition Facts: One serving (3/4 cup) equals:
125 calories
2 g fat (2 g saturated fat)
1 mg cholesterol
40 mg sodium
22 g carbohydrate
trace fiber
3 g protein

Diabetic Exchange: 1-1/2 starch.

Cappuccino Mousse

Chocolate Peanut Butter Pie

Chocolate Peanut Butter Pie

Judy Barrett, Oklahoma City, Oklahoma

PREP: 10 MIN. + CHILLING

PEANUT BUTTER LAYER:
- 1/3 cup nonfat dry milk powder
- 1-1/4 cups cold water
- 1 package (1 ounce) sugar-free instant vanilla pudding mix
- 1/2 cup reduced-fat chunky peanut butter
- 1 reduced-fat graham cracker crust (8 inches)

CHOCOLATE LAYER:
- 1/3 cup nonfat dry milk powder
- 1-1/4 cups cold water
- 1 package (1.4 ounces) sugar-free instant chocolate pudding mix
- 1 cup reduced-fat whipped topping
- 1/2 ounce semisweet chocolate, shaved into curls

For peanut butter layer, in a mixing bowl, beat milk powder and water on low speed for 20 seconds. Add vanilla pudding mix; beat on low for 1-1/2 minutes. Add peanut butter; beat on low for 30 seconds. Pour into crust.

For chocolate layer, in a mixing bowl, beat milk powder and water on low for 20 seconds. Add chocolate pudding mix; beat on low for 2 minutes. Carefully spread over peanut butter layer. Top with whipped topping and chocolate curls. Cover and refrigerate for at least 2 hours. **YIELD:** 8 SERVINGS.

Nutrition Facts: One serving (1 slice) equals:
- 257 calories
- 10 g fat (3 g saturated fat)
- 1 mg cholesterol
- 505 mg sodium
- 34 g carbohydrate
- 2 g fiber
- 8 g protein

Diabetic Exchanges: 2 starch, 2 fat.

Chock-full of Fruit Snackin' Cake

low sodium

Sami Taylor, Hermiston, Oregon

PREP: 15 MIN.   **BAKE:** 40 MIN. + COOLING

- 2 cups all-purpose flour
- 2 cups quick-cooking oats

Sugar substitute equivalent to 1-1/2 cups sugar
- 2-3/4 teaspoons baking powder
- 1/4 teaspoon baking soda
- 1/8 teaspoon salt
- 3 eggs
- 1 cup orange juice
- 1/3 cup canola oil
- 2 large carrots, shredded
- 2 medium apples, peeled and shredded
- 1 cup raisins
- 1 cup dried cranberries
- 1 cup chopped walnuts

In a large bowl, combine the first six ingredients. Whisk the eggs, orange juice and oil; stir into dry ingredients just until moistened. Fold in the remaining ingredients.

Pour into a 13-in. x 9-in. x 2-in. baking dish coated with nonstick cooking spray. Bake at 350° for 40-45 minutes or until a toothpick inserted near the center comes out clean. Cool on a wire rack. Cut into squares. **YIELD:** 18 SERVINGS.

Editor's Note: This recipe was tested with Splenda No Calorie Sweetener.

Nutrition Facts: One serving (1 piece) equals:
- 248 calories
- 10 g fat (1 g saturated fat)
- 35 mg cholesterol
- 84 mg sodium
- 36 g carbohydrate
- 3 g fiber
- 5 g protein

Diabetic Exchanges: 1-1/2 starch, 1-1/2 fat, 1 fruit.

Streuseled Zucchini Bundt Cake

Regina Stock, Topeka, Kansas

PREP: 25 MIN.   **BAKE:** 55 MIN. + COOLING

- 3 cups all-purpose flour
- 3/4 cup sugar
- 1-1/2 teaspoons baking powder
- 1 teaspoon baking soda
- 1/2 teaspoon salt
- 2 egg whites
- 1 egg
- 1-1/3 cups fat-free plain yogurt
- 1/3 cup canola oil
- 2 cups shredded zucchini, patted dry

4 teaspoons vanilla extract, *divided*
1 tablespoon dry bread crumbs
1/3 cup packed brown sugar
1/3 cup chopped walnuts
1/3 cup raisins
1 tablespoon ground cinnamon
1/2 teaspoon ground allspice
3/4 cup confectioners' sugar
2 to 3 teaspoons fat-free milk

In a large mixing bowl, combine the first five ingredients. In another bowl, beat the egg whites, egg, yogurt and oil until blended. Stir in zucchini and 3 teaspoons vanilla. Add to dry ingredients; mix well.

Coat a 10-in. fluted tube pan with nonstick cooking spray; sprinkle with bread crumbs. Pour a third of the batter into pan. Combine the brown sugar, walnuts, raisins, cinnamon and allspice; sprinkle half over batter. Top with another third of the batter. Sprinkle with remaining brown sugar mixture; top with remaining batter.

Bake at 350° for 55-65 minutes or until a toothpick comes out clean. Cool for 10 minutes before removing from pan to a wire rack to cool completely. In a small bowl, combine confectioners' sugar, milk and remaining vanilla; drizzle over cake. **YIELD:** 14 SERVINGS.

Nutrition Facts: One serving (1 piece) equals:
279 calories
8 g fat (1 g saturated fat)
16 mg cholesterol
233 mg sodium
48 g carbohydrate
2 g fiber
6 g protein

Streuseled Zucchini Bundt Cake

Chocolate Caramel Cheesecake

Chocolate Caramel Cheesecake

Tamara Trouten, Fort Wayne, Indiana

PREP: 35 MIN. **BAKE:** 30 MIN. + CHILLING

6 whole reduced-fat honey graham crackers, crushed
3 tablespoons butter, melted
25 caramels
1/4 cup fat-free evaporated milk
1/4 cup chopped pecans
2 packages (8 ounces *each*) reduced-fat cream cheese
1/3 cup sugar
2 eggs, lightly beaten
1/3 cup semisweet chocolate chips, melted and cooled

In a small bowl, combine graham cracker crumbs and butter. Press onto the bottom of a 9-in. springform pan coated with nonstick cooking spray. Place on a baking sheet. Bake at 350° for 5-10 minutes or until set. Cool on a wire rack.

In a small saucepan over low heat, stir caramels and milk until smooth. Pour over crust. Sprinkle with pecans. In a small mixing bowl, beat cream cheese and sugar until smooth. Add eggs; beat on low speed just until combined. Stir in melted chocolate. Pour over caramel layer. Place pan on a baking sheet.

Bake at 350° for 30-35 minutes or until center is almost set. Cool on a wire rack for 10 minutes. Carefully run a knife around edge of pan to loosen; cool 1 hour longer. Chill for 4 hours or overnight. Remove sides of pan. Refrigerate leftovers. **YIELD:** 12 SERVINGS.

Nutrition Facts: One serving (1 piece) equals:
284 calories
17 g fat (10 g saturated fat)
71 mg cholesterol
270 mg sodium
29 g carbohydrate
1 g fiber
7 g protein

Diabetic Exchanges: 3 fat, 2 starch.

Spice Bars

Brooke Pike, Durham, North Carolina

PREP: 20 MIN. **BAKE:** 20 MIN. + COOLING

- 6 tablespoons buttermilk
- 1/3 cup packed brown sugar
- 1/4 cup molasses
- 3 tablespoons butter, melted
- 1 egg
- 1 teaspoon vanilla extract
- 1-1/4 cups all-purpose flour
- 3/4 teaspoon ground cinnamon, *divided*
- 1-1/4 teaspoons Chinese five-spice powder
- 1/2 teaspoon baking powder
- 1/4 teaspoon baking soda
- 1/4 teaspoon salt
- 1/3 cup raisins
- 1 tablespoon confectioners' sugar

In a mixing bowl, combine the buttermilk, brown sugar, molasses, butter, egg and vanilla; mix well. Combine the flour, 1/2 teaspoon cinnamon, five-spice powder, baking powder, baking soda and salt; add to buttermilk mixture and beat until smooth. Stir in raisins.

Pour into a 9-in. square baking pan coated with nonstick cooking spray. Bake at 350° for 18-20 minutes or until a toothpick inserted near the center comes out clean. Cool on a wire rack. Combine confectioners' sugar and remaining cinnamon; sprinkle over bars. **YIELD:** 1 DOZEN.

Nutrition Facts: One serving (1 bar) equals:
- 139 calories
- 4 g fat (2 g saturated fat)
- 26 mg cholesterol
- 134 mg sodium
- 25 g carbohydrate
- 1 g fiber
- 2 g protein

Diabetic Exchanges: 1-1/2 starch, 1/2 fat.

Spice Bars

Rich Pumpkin Custard

Mary Alice Dick, Fort Wayne, Indiana

PREP: 20 MIN. **BAKE:** 35 MIN.

- 3 egg whites, lightly beaten
- 2/3 cup sugar
- 1 teaspoon ground cinnamon
- 1/2 teaspoon salt
- 1/2 teaspoon ground ginger
- 1/4 teaspoon ground nutmeg

Dash ground cloves

- 1 can (15 ounces) solid-pack pumpkin
- 1 teaspoon vanilla extract
- 1 can (12 ounces) fat-free evaporated milk

In a large mixing bowl, beat the egg whites, sugar, cinnamon, salt, ginger, nutmeg and cloves. Add pumpkin and vanilla; mix well. Gradually beat in milk. Pour into eight ungreased 6-oz. custard cups.

Place the cups in a 13-in. x 9-in. x 2-in. baking pan; add 1 in. of water to pan. Bake at 325° for 35-40 minutes or until a knife inserted near the center comes out clean. Serve warm or chilled. **YIELD:** 8 SERVINGS.

Nutrition Facts: One serving (1 custard) equals:
- 125 calories
- trace fat (trace saturated fat)
- 2 mg cholesterol
- 220 mg sodium
- 26 g carbohydrate
- 2 g fiber
- 5 g protein

Diabetic Exchange: 1-1/2 starch.

Chocolate Peanut Butter Cookies

Taste of Home Test Kitchen
Greendale, Wisconsin

PREP/TOTAL TIME: 25 MIN.

- 1 cup chunky peanut butter
- 1/4 cup canola oil

Chocolate Peanut Butter Cookies

3/4 cup packed brown sugar
1/2 cup sugar
2 eggs
1 tablespoon vanilla extract
1 cup all-purpose flour
1/3 cup baking cocoa
1 teaspoon baking soda
1/2 teaspoon salt
1/2 cup miniature chocolate chips

In a large mixing bowl, combine peanut butter and oil. Add brown sugar and sugar; mix well. Add eggs and vanilla; mix well. Combine the flour, cocoa, baking soda and salt. Add to peanut butter mixture; mix until blended (dough will be sticky). Stir in chocolate chips.

Drop by rounded teaspoonfuls 2 in. apart on ungreased baking sheets. Flatten slightly with a glass. Bake at 350° for 8-10 minutes or until set and tops are cracked. Cool for 2 minutes before removing to wire racks. **YIELD:** 4 DOZEN.

Nutrition Facts: One serving (1 cookie) equals:
86 calories
5 g fat (1 g saturated fat)
9 mg cholesterol
81 mg sodium
10 g carbohydrate
1 g fiber
2 g protein

Diabetic Exchanges: 1 starch, 1/2 fat.

Lime Honeydew Sorbet

Taste of Home Test Kitchen
Greendale, Wisconsin

PREP: 5 MIN. **FREEZE:** 30 MIN. + FREEZING

3 cups cubed honeydew
1/2 cup sugar
1/2 cup lime juice
1 tablespoon sweet white wine *or* water
2 teaspoons grated lime peel
2 to 3 drops green food coloring, optional

In a food processor or blender, combine honeydew and sugar; cover and process until sugar is dissolved. Add the remaining ingredients; cover and process until blended.

Freeze in an ice cream freezer according to manufacturer's directions. Spoon mixture into a freezer-safe container; cover and freeze in the refrigerator freezer 2-4 hours before serving. **YIELD:** 4 SERVINGS.

Nutrition Facts: One serving (3/4 cup) equals:
154 calories
trace fat (trace saturated fat)
0 cholesterol
14 mg sodium
40 g carbohydrate
1 g fiber
1 g protein

Diabetic Exchanges: 1-1/2 fruit, 1 starch.

Lime Honeydew Sorbet

Popover Apple Pie

Beki Kosydar-Krantz
Clarks Summit, Pennsylvania

PREP: 20 MIN. **BAKE:** 30 MIN.

Popover Apple Pie

- 3/4 cup all-purpose flour
- 1/2 teaspoon salt
-   2 eggs
-   2 egg whites
- 3/4 cup 1% milk
-   1 cup cold orange juice
-   1 package (.8 ounce) sugar-free cook-and-serve vanilla pudding mix
- 3/4 teaspoon apple pie spice
-   6 large peeled tart apples, sliced
- 1/2 cup dried cranberries
- 1/4 cup chopped walnuts
-   1 teaspoon confectioners' sugar

In a bowl, combine flour and salt. Combine the eggs, egg whites and milk; whisk into the dry ingredients just until blended. Pour into a 10-in. ovenproof skillet coated with butter-flavored nonstick cooking spray. Bake at 450° for 20 minutes. Reduce heat to 350° (do not open oven door). Bake 10-15 minutes longer or until deep golden brown (do not under-bake).

In a microwave-safe bowl, whisk the orange juice, pudding mix and apple pie spice. Stir in apples and cranberries. Cover and microwave on high for 5 minutes, stirring once. Cover and cook 3-4 minutes longer or until apples are tender, stirring once. Spoon hot apple mixture into crust. Sprinkle with walnuts. Dust with confectioners' sugar and serve immediately. **YIELD:** 8 SERVINGS.

Nutrition Facts: One serving (1 slice with 2/3 cup mixture) equals:
- 202 calories
-   4 g fat (1 g saturated fat)
- 55 mg cholesterol
- 307 mg sodium
- 37 g carbohydrate
-   3 g fiber
-   5 g protein

Diabetic Exchanges: 1-1/2 fruit, 1 starch, 1 fat.

Peanut Butter Pudding

Joyce Crouse, Chambersburg, Pennsylvania

PREP/TOTAL TIME: 15 MIN.

- 1-3/4 cups fat-free milk
-   2 tablespoons reduced-fat creamy peanut butter
-   1 package (1 ounce) sugar-free instant vanilla pudding mix
- 1/4 cup reduced-fat whipped topping
-   4 teaspoons chocolate syrup

In a bowl, whisk the milk and peanut butter until blended. Add pudding mix; whisk for 2 minutes or until slightly thickened. Spoon into dessert dishes. Refrigerate for at least 5 minutes or until set. Just before serving, dollop with whipped topping and drizzle with chocolate syrup. **YIELD:** 4 SERVINGS.

Nutrition Facts: One serving (1/2 cup with whipped topping) equals:
- 112 calories
-   3 g fat (1 g saturated fat)
-   2 mg cholesterol
- 186 mg sodium
- 14 g carbohydrate
-   1 g fiber
-   6 g protein

Diabetic Exchanges: 1/2 starch, 1/2 fat-free milk, 1/2 fat.

Classic Pumpkin Pie

Taste of Home Test Kitchen
Greendale, Wisconsin

PREP: 20 MIN. **BAKE:** 45 MIN. + COOLING

-   1 cup all-purpose flour
-   1 teaspoon sugar
- 1/4 teaspoon salt
-   3 tablespoons canola oil
-   1 tablespoon butter, melted
-   2 to 3 tablespoons cold water

FILLING:

-   1 egg
-   1 egg white
- 1/2 cup packed brown sugar
- 1/4 cup sugar
- 1/2 teaspoon salt
- 1/2 teaspoon ground cinnamon
- 1/8 teaspoon *each* ground allspice, nutmeg and cloves
-   1 can (15 ounces) solid-pack pumpkin
-   1 cup fat-free evaporated milk

In a small bowl, combine the flour, sugar and salt. Using a fork, stir in oil and butter until dough is crumbly. Gradually add enough water until dough holds together. Roll out between sheets of plastic wrap into an 11-in. circle. Freeze for 10 minutes.

Remove top sheet of plastic wrap; invert pastry into a 9-in. pie plate. Remove remaining plastic wrap. Trim and flute edges. Chill.

Roll pastry scraps to 1/8-in. thickness. Cut with a 1-in. leaf-shaped cookie cutter. Place on an ungreased baking sheet. Bake at 375° for 6-8 minutes or until edges are very lightly browned. Cool on a wire rack.

In a large mixing bowl, beat the egg, egg white, sugars, salt and spices until smooth. Beat in pumpkin. Gradually beat in milk.

Pour into pastry shell. Bake at 375° for 45-50 minutes or until a knife inserted near the center comes out clean. Cool on a wire rack. Garnish with leaf cutouts. Refrigerate leftovers. **YIELD:** 8 SERVINGS.

Nutrition Facts: One serving (1 piece) equals:

249	calories
8 g	fat (2 g saturated fat)
32 mg	cholesterol
295 mg	sodium
40 g	carbohydrate
3 g	fiber
6 g	protein

Diabetic Exchanges: 2-1/2 starch, 1 fat.

Cranberry Oat Yummies

low fat

Carol Birkemeier, Nashville, Indiana

PREP/TOTAL TIME: 30 MIN.

- 1/2 cup butter, melted
- 1/2 cup sugar
- 1 cup packed brown sugar
- 1 egg
- 1/4 cup egg substitute
- 2 tablespoons corn syrup
- 1-1/2 teaspoons vanilla extract
- 3 cups quick-cooking oats
- 1 cup all-purpose flour
- 1 teaspoon baking soda
- 1 teaspoon ground cinnamon
- 1/2 teaspoon baking powder
- 1/2 teaspoon salt
- 1/8 teaspoon ground nutmeg
- 1 cup dried cranberries

In a mixing bowl, cream butter and sugars. Add egg, egg substitute, corn syrup and

Cranberry Oat Yummies

vanilla; mix well. Combine the oats, flour, baking soda, cinnamon, baking powder, salt and nutmeg; gradually add to egg mixture. Stir in cranberries.

Drop by heaping tablespoonfuls 2 in. apart onto ungreased baking sheets. Bake at 375° for 8-10 minutes or until golden brown. Cool for 2 minutes before removing from pans to wire racks. **YIELD:** 3 DOZEN.

Nutrition Facts: One serving (1 cookie) equals:

109	calories
3 g	fat (2 g saturated fat)
13 mg	cholesterol
154 mg	sodium
19 g	carbohydrate
1 g	fiber
2 g	protein

Diabetic Exchanges: 1 starch, 1/2 fat.

Classic Pumpkin Pie

Granola Blondies

Janet Farley, Snellville, Georgia

PREP: 15 MIN. **BAKE:** 25 MIN.

- 1 egg
- 1 egg white
- 1-1/4 cups packed brown sugar
- 1/4 cup canola oil
- 1 cup all-purpose flour
- 1 teaspoon baking powder
- 1/2 teaspoon salt
- 2 cups reduced-fat granola with raisins
- 1 cup dried cranberries *or* cherries

In a mixing bowl, combine the egg, egg white, brown sugar and oil; mix well. Combine the flour, baking powder and salt; stir into sugar mixture just until blended. Stir in granola and cranberries (batter will be thick).

Spread into a 9-in. square baking pan coated with nonstick cooking spray. Bake at 350° for 25-30 minutes or until golden and set. Cool on a wire rack. Cut into bars. **YIELD:** 1 DOZEN.

Nutrition Facts: One serving (1 bar) equals:
- 256 calories
- 6 g fat (1 g saturated fat)
- 18 mg cholesterol
- 173 mg sodium
- 49 g carbohydrate
- 2 g fiber
- 3 g protein

Diabetic Exchanges: 3 starch, 1/2 fat.

Delicious Angel Food Dessert

Jessie Bradley, Bella Vista, Arkansas

PREP: 20 MIN. + CHILLING

- 2 cans (20 ounces *each*) unsweetened crushed pineapple, drained
- 4 medium firm bananas, sliced
- 1 loaf (10-1/2 ounces) angel food cake, cut into 1-inch cubes
- 3 cups cold fat-free milk
- 2 packages (1 ounce *each*) sugar-free instant vanilla pudding mix
- 1 carton (8 ounces) frozen reduced-fat whipped topping, thawed
- 1/3 cup chopped pecans, toasted

Place the pineapple in a bowl; gently fold in bananas. Place cake cubes in a 13-in. x 9-in. x 2-in. dish. Spoon fruit over cake.

In a bowl, whisk milk and pudding mixes for 2 minutes. Let stand for 2 minutes or until soft-set. Spread over fruit. Carefully spread whipped topping over pudding. Sprinkle with pecans. Cover and refrigerate for at least 2 hours before serving. **YIELD:** 15 SERVINGS.

Nutrition Facts: One serving (1 piece) equals:
- 210 calories
- 4 g fat (2 g saturated fat)
- 1 mg cholesterol
- 291 mg sodium
- 40 g carbohydrate
- 2 g fiber
- 4 g protein

Diabetic Exchanges: 1 starch, 1 fruit, 1/2 fat-free milk.

Granola Blondies

Tiramisu Parfaits

low fat

Nancy Granaman, Burlington, Iowa

PREP: 40 MIN. + CHILLING

- 4-1/2 teaspoons instant coffee granules
- 1/3 cup boiling water
- 2 cups cold fat-free milk
- 2 packages (1 ounce *each*) sugar-free instant vanilla pudding mix
- 4 ounces fat-free cream cheese
- 1 package (3 ounces) ladyfingers, split and cubed
- 2 cups fat-free whipped topping
- 2 tablespoons miniature chocolate chips
- 1 teaspoon baking cocoa

Dissolve coffee in boiling water; cool to room temperature. In a large bowl, whisk milk and pudding mixes for 2 minutes. In a large mixing bowl, beat cream cheese until smooth. Gradually fold in pudding.

Place ladyfinger cubes in a bowl; add coffee and toss to coat evenly. Let stand for 5 minutes. Divide half of the ladyfinger

Tiramisu Parfaits

cubes among six parfait glasses or serving dishes. Top with half of the pudding mixture, 1 cup whipped topping and 1 tablespoon chocolate chips. Repeat layers.

Cover and refrigerate for 8 hours or overnight. Just before serving, dust with cocoa. **YIELD:** 6 SERVINGS.

Nutrition Facts: One serving (1 parfait) equals:
- 189 calories
- 3 g fat (1 g saturated fat)
- 55 mg cholesterol
- 573 mg sodium
- 32 g carbohydrate
- 1 g fiber
- 7 g protein

Diabetic Exchange: 2 starch.

Frozen Mousse Brownie Sandwiches

Taste of Home Test Kitchen
Greendale, Wisconsin

PREP: 30 MIN. **BAKE:** 15 MIN. + FREEZING

- 1 package reduced-fat brownie mix (13-inch x 9-inch pan size)
- 2 cups cold fat-free milk
- 2 packages (1 ounce *each*) sugar-free instant vanilla pudding mix
- 3 tablespoons vanilla *or* white chips, melted and cooled
- 1/2 cup reduced-fat whipped topping

Line the bottom and sides of two 13-in. x 9-in. x 2-in. baking pans with parchment paper. Coat the paper with nonstick cooking spray. Prepare brownie mix according to package directions; divide batter evenly between the pans.

Bake at 350° for 15-18 minutes or until edges just begin to pull away from sides of pan and a toothpick inserted near the center comes out with moist crumbs. Cool on wire racks.

For mousse, in a bowl, whisk together the milk and pudding mixes for 2 minutes. Stir a small amount of the pudding into the melted chips, then return all to the pudding. Fold in whipped topping.

Cover two large cutting boards or inverted 15-in. x 10-in. x 1-in. baking pans with plastic wrap. Invert one pan of brownies onto prepared board or pan. Gently peel off the parchment paper. Spread the mousse to within 1/2 in. of edges. Carefully invert second brownie layer onto second board or pan. Gently peel off parchment paper, then place right side up over mousse filling.

Cover and freeze for about 4 hours or until the filling is firm. Remove from the freezer 10 minutes before cutting into sandwiches. Individually wrap leftover sandwiches; store in the freezer. **YIELD:** 15 SERVINGS.

Nutrition Facts: One serving (1 sandwich) equals:
- 206 calories
- 5 g fat (2 g saturated fat)
- 1 mg cholesterol
- 199 mg sodium
- 40 g carbohydrate
- 1 g fiber
- 4 g protein

Diabetic Exchange: 2-1/2 starch.

Frozen Mousse
Brownie Sandwiches

Lemon Cream Pie

Maria Dygert, Auburn, New York

PREP: 15 MIN. **BAKE:** 15 MIN. + CHILLING

Lemon Cream Pie

1-1/4 cups reduced-fat cinnamon graham
     crackers crumbs (about 14 squares)
1/4 cup reduced-fat margarine, melted
1 tablespoon plus 3/4 cup sugar, *divided*
5 tablespoons cornstarch
1/8 teaspoon salt
1 cup water
2/3 cup buttermilk
1/2 cup egg substitute
1/2 cup lemon juice
2 teaspoons grated lemon peel
2-1/2 cups reduced-fat whipped topping

In a small bowl, combine the graham cracker crumbs, margarine and 1 tablespoon sugar; mix well. Press onto the bottom and up the sides of a 9-in. pie plate coated with nonstick cooking spray. Bake at 350° for 8-10 minutes or until golden brown. Cool on a wire rack.

In a heavy saucepan, combine the cornstarch, salt and remaining sugar. Gradually stir in water and buttermilk until smooth. Bring to a boil; cook and stir for 2 minutes or until thickened. Remove from the heat. Stir a small amount of hot filling into egg substitute. Return all to pan, stirring constantly. Bring to a gentle boil; cook and stir for 2 minutes longer. Remove from the heat. Stir in lemon juice and peel. Pour into crust.

Cover and refrigerate for at least 4 hours. Just before serving, spread whipped topping over filling. **YIELD:** 8 SERVINGS.

Editor's Note: This recipe was tested with Blue Bonnet light stick margarine.

Nutrition Facts: One serving (1 piece) equals:
    252 calories
    6 g fat (3 g saturated fat)
    1 mg cholesterol
    227 mg sodium
    45 g carbohydrate
    1 g fiber
    3 g protein

Diabetic Exchanges: 3 starch, 1 fat.

Black Forest Ice Cream Pie

Beth Ask, Ulster, Pennsylvania

PREP: 20 MIN. + FREEZING

1 prepared chocolate crumb crust
    (9 inches)
3-1/2 cups reduced-fat vanilla ice cream
1 cup reduced-sugar cherry pie filling
2 whole chocolate graham crackers, broken
    into bite-size pieces
1 cup fat-free hot fudge ice cream topping,
    warmed

Fill crust with scoops of ice cream. Top with dollops of pie filling. Insert graham cracker pieces between scoops. Invert plastic cover from crust and place over pie.

Freeze for 2 hours or until firm. Remove from the freezer 15-20 minutes before serving. Drizzle with fudge topping. Cut into wedges. **YIELD:** 8 SERVINGS.

Nutrition Facts: One serving (1 piece) equals:
    306 calories
    7 g fat (2 g saturated fat)
    5 mg cholesterol
    194 mg sodium
    58 g carbohydrate
    5 g fiber
    5 g protein

Creme Brulee

`low fat`

Taste of Home Test Kitchen
Greendale, Wisconsin

PREP: 15 MIN. **BAKE:** 25 MIN.

2/3 cup sugar, *divided*
2 eggs
2 egg whites
1-1/2 cups 2% milk
1 teaspoon vanilla extract
1/8 teaspoon salt
3 tablespoons water

In a bowl, whisk together 1/3 cup sugar, eggs, egg whites, milk, vanilla and salt; pour into five 6-oz. custard cups. Place cups in a baking pan. Fill pan with boiling water to a depth of 1 in. Bake, uncovered, at 325° for 25-30 minutes or until a knife inserted near the center comes out clean. Remove from water bath. Cool for 10 minutes and refrigerate.

Before serving, in a heavy saucepan over medium heat, heat water and remaining sugar until sugar is melted. Do not stir. When sugar is melted, continue to cook until syrup is golden, about 5 minutes, swirling pan occasionally. With a spoon, quickly pour over custards, tilting cups to coat custard with syrup. Serve immediately. Refrigerate leftovers. **YIELD:** 5 SERVINGS.

Nutrition Facts: One serving (1 brulee) equals:
    183 calories
    3 g fat (2 g saturated fat)
    91 mg cholesterol
    150 mg sodium
    31 g carbohydrate
    0 fiber
    7 g protein

Diabetic Exchanges: 2 starch, 1 lean meat.

Cherry Coconut Bars

Taste of Home Test Kitchen
Greendale, Wisconsin

PREP: 15 MIN. **BAKE:** 35 MIN. + COOLING

- 3/4 cup all-purpose flour
- 3 tablespoons confectioners' sugar
- 3 tablespoons cold butter

FILLING:

- 1 egg
- 2 egg whites
- 1 cup sugar
- 1 teaspoon vanilla extract
- 1/4 cup all-purpose flour
- 1/2 teaspoon baking powder
- 1/4 teaspoon salt
- 1/2 cup quartered maraschino cherries
- 1/3 cup chopped walnuts
- 1/3 cup flaked coconut

In a food processor, place flour and confectioners' sugar; cover and process until blended. Add butter; cover and pulse 15 times or until mixture resembles fine crumbs. Press into a 9-in. square baking pan coated with nonstick cooking spray. Bake at 350° for 12-15 minutes or until lightly browned. Cool on a wire rack.

For filling, combine the egg, egg whites, sugar and vanilla in a bowl. Combine the flour, baking powder and salt; add the egg mixture. Stir in cherries, nuts and coconut. Spread over crust. Bake for 20-25 minutes or until firm. Cool on a wire rack. Cut into bars. Refrigerate leftovers. **YIELD:** 1 DOZEN.

Nutrition Facts: One serving (1 bar) equals:
- 194 calories
- 7 g fat (3 g saturated fat)
- 25 mg cholesterol
- 128 mg sodium
- 31 g carbohydrate
- 1 g fiber
- 3 g protein

Diabetic Exchanges: 2 starch, 1 fat.

Martha Washington Pies

Cherry Coconut Bars

Martha Washington Pies

Ginger Clark, Hinesville, Georgia

PREP: 30 MIN. **BAKE:** 25 MIN. + STANDING

- 4 egg whites
- 1/4 teaspoon cream of tartar
- 1 cup plus 1 tablespoon sugar, *divided*
- 1 cup finely chopped pecans
- 1/2 cup crushed saltines (about 12 crackers)
- 1 teaspoon vanilla extract
- 6 cups sliced fresh strawberries
- 2/3 cup reduced-fat whipped topping

In a large mixing bowl, beat egg whites and cream of tartar on medium speed until soft peaks form. Gradually beat in 1 cup sugar, 2 tablespoons at a time, on high until stiff glossy peaks form and sugar is dissolved. Fold in nuts, crackers and vanilla. Drop by rounded 1/3 cupfuls onto parchment-lined baking sheets. Shape into 3-1/2-in. rounds with the back of a spoon.

Bake at 300° for 25-30 minutes or until set. Turn oven off; leave in oven with door closed for 2 hours. Toss strawberries with the remaining sugar; spoon 2/3 cup into each shell. Dollop each with whipped topping. **YIELD:** 18 SERVINGS.

Nutrition Facts: One serving (1 pie) equals:
- 253 calories
- 11 g fat (2 g saturated fat)
- 0 cholesterol
- 78 mg sodium
- 38 g carbohydrate
- 4 g fiber
- 4 g protein

Cheesecake Phyllo Cups

low sodium low carb

Lorraine Chevalier, Merrimac, Massachusetts

PREP/TOTAL TIME: 25 MIN.

- 4 ounces reduced-fat cream cheese
- 1/2 cup reduced-fat sour cream

Sugar substitute equivalent to 2 tablespoons sugar

- 1 teaspoon vanilla extract
- 2 packages (2.1 ounces *each*) frozen miniature phyllo shells, thawed
- 1 can (11 ounces) mandarin oranges slices, drained
- 1 kiwifruit, peeled, sliced and cut into quarters

In a bowl, whisk together the cream cheese, sour cream, sugar substitute and vanilla until smooth. Pipe or spoon into phyllo shells. Top each with an orange segment and kiwi piece. Refrigerate until serving. **YIELD:** 1-1/2 DOZEN.

Editor's Note: This recipe was tested with Splenda Sugar Blend for Baking.

Nutrition Facts: One serving (3 filled phyllo cups) equals:

- 137 calories
- 7 g fat (3 g saturated fat)
- 15 mg cholesterol
- 83 mg sodium
- 13 g carbohydrate
- trace fiber
- 3 g protein

Diabetic Exchanges: 1 starch, 1 fat.

Cheesecake Phyllo Cups

Chocolate Mint Eclair Dessert

Renee Ratcliffe, Charlotte, North Carolina

PREP: 20 MIN. + CHILLING

- 23 whole chocolate graham crackers (5 inches x 2-1/2 inches)
- 3 cups cold fat-free milk
- 2 packages (3.3 to 3.4 ounces *each*) instant white chocolate *or* vanilla pudding mix
- 1/2 teaspoon mint *or* peppermint extract
- 3 to 4 drops green food coloring, optional
- 1 carton (8 ounces) frozen reduced-fat whipped topping, thawed

CHOCOLATE FROSTING:

- 1 tablespoon butter
- 2 tablespoons baking cocoa
- 2 tablespoons plus 1 teaspoon fat-free milk
- 1 teaspoon vanilla extract
- 1 cup confectioners' sugar

Coat a 13-in. x 9-in. x 2-in. dish with nonstick cooking spray. Break five whole graham crackers in half; line the bottom of pan with three half crackers and six whole crackers.

In a bowl, whisk milk and pudding mix for 2 minutes. Whisk in extract and food coloring if desired. Fold in whipped topping. Spread half over graham crackers. Top with a another layer of three half and six whole crackers. Top with remaining pudding mixture and graham crackers (save remaining half cracker for another use). Cover and refrigerate for 2 hours.

For frosting, melt butter in a saucepan. Stir in cocoa and milk until blended. Remove from the heat; stir in vanilla and confectioners' sugar. Spread over dessert. Cover and refrigerate overnight. **YIELD:** 15 SERVINGS.

Nutrition Facts: One serving (1 piece) equals:

- 244 calories
- 7 g fat (3 g saturated fat)
- 3 mg cholesterol
- 296 mg sodium
- 41 g carbohydrate
- 1 g fiber
- 4 g protein

Diabetic Exchanges: 2 starch, 1 fat, 1/2 fruit.

Lemon Poppy Seed Cake

Kristen Croke, Hanover, Massachusetts

PREP: 15 MIN. BAKE: 40 MIN.

- 6 tablespoons butter, softened
- 1-1/2 cups sugar, *divided*
- 1 tablespoon grated lemon peel
- 2 eggs
- 2 egg whites
- 2-1/2 cups cake flour

Lemon Poppy Seed Cake

2 tablespoons poppy seeds
1-1/2 teaspoons baking powder
1/2 teaspoon baking soda
1/2 teaspoon salt
1/4 teaspoon ground allspice
1-1/3 cups buttermilk
1/4 cup lemon juice

In a large mixing bowl, beat butter and 1-1/4 cups sugar until crumbly, about 2 minutes. Add lemon peel; mix well. Add eggs and egg whites, one at a time, beating well after each addition. Combine the flour, poppy seeds, baking powder, baking soda, salt and allspice. Add to the butter mixture alternately with buttermilk.

Transfer to a 10-in. tube pan heavily coated with nonstick cooking spray. Bake at 350° for 40-45 minutes or until a toothpick inserted near the center comes out clean. Cool in pan for 10 minutes. Carefully run a knife around the edge of pan and center tube to loosen. Remove to a wire rack.

Meanwhile, in a small saucepan, combine the lemon juice and remaining sugar. Cook and stir until mixture comes to a boil; cook and stir 1-2 minutes longer or until sugar is dissolved. Using a fork, poke holes in top of cake. Gradually pour hot syrup over cake. Cool completely. **YIELD:** 2 DOZEN SLICES.

Nutrition Facts: One serving (2 slices) equals:
266 calories
8 g fat (4 g saturated fat)
52 mg cholesterol
318 mg sodium
47 g carbohydrate
1 g fiber
5 g protein

Diabetic Exchanges: 3 starch, 1 fat.

Banana Split Dessert

Ann Jansen, Depere, Wisconsin

PREP: 25 MIN. + CHILLING

2 cups reduced-fat graham cracker crumbs (about 32 squares)
5 tablespoons reduced-fat margarine, melted
1 can (12 ounces) cold reduced-fat evaporated milk
1/4 cup cold fat-free milk
2 packages (1 ounce *each*) sugar-free instant vanilla pudding mix
2 medium firm bananas, sliced
1 can (20 ounces) unsweetened crushed pineapple, drained
1 carton (8 ounces) frozen reduced-fat whipped topping, thawed
3 tablespoons chopped walnuts
2 tablespoons chocolate syrup
5 maraschino cherries, quartered

Combine cracker crumbs and margarine; press onto the bottom of a 13-in. x 9-in. x 2-in. dish coated with nonstick cooking spray.

In a bowl, whisk the evaporated milk, fat-free milk and pudding mixes for 2 minutes or until slightly thickened. Spread pudding evenly over crust. Layer with bananas, pineapple and whipped topping. Sprinkle with nuts; drizzle with chocolate syrup. Top with cherries. Refrigerate for at least 1 hour before cutting. **YIELD:** 15 SERVINGS.

Editor's Note: This recipe was tested with Parkay Light stick margarine.

Nutrition Facts: One serving (1 piece) equals:
194 calories
6 g fat (3 g saturated fat)
4 mg cholesterol
312 mg sodium
33 g carbohydrate
1 g fiber
3 g protein

Diabetic Exchanges: 1 starch, 1 fruit, 1 fat.

Banana Split Dessert

Fruit Pizza

5-6 minutes or until golden brown. Cool on a wire rack.

In a saucepan, combine the water and pudding mix until smooth. Bring to a boil over medium heat, stirring constantly. Whisk in gelatin; cook and stir 1 minute longer or until thickened. Remove from the heat and let cool.

In a small mixing bowl, beat cream cheese and sugar substitute until smooth; fold in whipped topping. Spread cream cheese mixture over crust to within 1/2 in. of edges. Spread gelatin mixture evenly over cream cheese mixture. Arrange fruit over top. Refrigerate for 1 hour or until chilled. Refrigerate leftovers. **YIELD:** 8 SERVINGS.

Editor's Note: This recipe was tested with Splenda No Calorie Sweetener.

Nutrition Facts: One serving (1 piece) equals:
212 calories
8 g fat (4 g saturated fat)
7 mg cholesterol
400 mg sodium
28 g carbohydrate
2 g fiber
6 g protein

Diabetic Exchanges: 1-1/2 starch, 1-1/2 fat, 1/2 fruit.

Raspberry Pie with Oat Crust

Ginny Arandas, Greensburg, Pennsylvania

PREP: 25 MIN. + CHILLING

3/4 cup all-purpose flour
1/2 cup quick-cooking oats
1/2 teaspoon salt
1/4 cup canola oil
3 to 4 tablespoons cold water

FILLING:

2 cups water
1 package (.8 ounces) sugar-free cook-and-serve vanilla pudding mix
1 package (.3 ounce) sugar-free raspberry gelatin
4 cups fresh raspberries

In a food processor, combine the flour, oats and salt. While processing, slowly drizzle in oil. Gradually add water until a ball forms. Roll out dough between two sheets of waxed paper. Remove top sheet of waxed paper; invert dough onto a 9-in. pie plate. Remove remaining waxed paper. Trim, seal and flute edges. Prick bottom of crust with a fork in several places. Bake at 400° for 10-12 minutes or until golden brown. Cool completely on a wire rack.

In a saucepan, heat water over medium heat. Whisk in pudding mix. Cook and stir for 5 minutes or until thickened and bubbly. Whisk in gelatin until completely dissolved. Remove from the heat; cool slightly. Fold in

Fruit Pizza

Julie Meyer, Madison, Wisconsin

PREP: 35 MIN. + CHILLING

1 sheet refrigerated pie pastry
1 cup water
1 package (.8 ounce) sugar-free cook-and-serve vanilla pudding mix
1 package (.3 ounce) sugar-free lemon gelatin
1 package (8 ounces) fat-free cream cheese, cubed

Sugar substitute equivalent to 2 tablespoons sugar

1/2 cup reduced-fat whipped topping
1-1/2 cups quartered fresh strawberries
1-1/2 cups sliced halved peeled kiwifruit
1 can (8 ounces) unsweetened pineapple chunks, drained

On a lightly floured surface, roll out pastry to a 12-in. circle. Transfer to a 14-in. pizza pan; prick with a fork. Bake at 450° for

raspberries. Spoon into crust. Chill for at least 3 hours or overnight. Refrigerate left-overs. **YIELD:** 8 SERVINGS.

Nutrition Facts: One serving (1 piece) equals:
      167 calories
        8 g fat (1 g saturated fat)
        0 cholesterol
    238 mg sodium
      22 g carbohydrate
        5 g fiber
        3 g protein

Diabetic Exchanges: 1-1/2 fat, 1 starch, 1/2 fruit.

Coconut-Cherry Cream Squares

low sodium

Taste of Home Test Kitchen
Greendale, Wisconsin

PREP: 30 MIN. + CHILLING

    3/4   cup all-purpose flour
    1/3   cup flaked coconut
      3   tablespoons brown sugar
      3   tablespoons cold reduced-fat butter
FILLING:
    1/3   cup all-purpose flour
    1/4   cup sugar
Sugar substitute equivalent to 1/4 cup sugar
    1/4   teaspoon salt
  2-1/2   cups fat-free milk
      2   eggs, lightly beaten
    1/2   cup flaked coconut

Raspberry Pie with Oat Crust

Coconut-Cherry Cream Squares

      2   teaspoons coconut extract
      1   can (20 ounces) reduced-sugar cherry pie filling

In a small bowl, combine the flour, coconut and brown sugar; cut in butter until crumbly. Press into a 9-in. square baking pan coated with nonstick cooking spray. Bake at 400° for 7-10 minutes or until lightly browned. Cool on a wire rack.

In a small saucepan, combine the flour, sugar, sugar substitute and salt. Stir in milk until smooth. Cook and stir over medium-high heat until thickened and bubbly. Reduce heat; cook and stir 2 minutes longer. Remove from the heat.

Stir a small amount of hot filling into eggs; return all to the pan, stirring constantly. Bring to a gentle boil; cook and stir 2 minutes longer. Remove from the heat. Gently stir in coconut and extract. Pour over crust. Refrigerate until set. Top with pie filling. Refrigerate for at least 2 hours before cutting. **YIELD:** 16 SERVINGS.

Editor's Note: This recipe was tested with Splenda No Calorie Sweetener.

Nutrition Facts: One serving (1 square) equals:
      142 calories
        4 g fat (3 g saturated fat)
      31 mg cholesterol
      95 mg sodium
      24 g carbohydrate
        1 g fiber
        3 g protein

Diabetic Exchanges: 1-1/2 starch, 1/2 fat.

German Chocolate Torte

Lois Maxwell, Alexandria, Louisiana

PREP: 20 MIN.   BAKE: 30 MIN. + COOLING

- 1 package (4 ounces) German sweet chocolate
- 1/2 cup water
- 2 cups sugar
- 3/4 cup baking fat replacement
- 1/4 cup canola oil
- 4 eggs, *separated*
- 2-1/4 cups all-purpose flour
- 1 teaspoon baking soda
- 1/2 teaspoon salt
- 1 cup buttermilk
- 1 teaspoon vanilla extract
- 1/4 teaspoon butter flavoring

FROSTING:
- 3 egg yolks
- 1 cup fat-free evaporated milk
- 1 cup sugar
- 1/2 cup marshmallow creme
- 1 teaspoon vanilla extract
- 1/4 teaspoon butter flavoring
- 1-1/3 cups flaked coconut
- 3/4 cup chopped pecans

In a microwave-safe bowl, combine chocolate and water. Microwave on high for 1-1/2 to 2 minutes or until chocolate is melted; stir until smooth. In a mixing bowl, combine sugar, baking fat replacement and oil. Add egg yolks, one at time, beating well after each. Add melted chocolate; beat well. Combine flour, baking soda and salt; add to chocolate mixture alternately with buttermilk. Stir in vanilla and butter flavoring. In another mixing bowl, beat egg whites until stiff peaks form; fold into batter.

Pour into three 9-in. round baking pans coated with nonstick cooking spray. Bake at 350° for 30 minutes or until a toothpick inserted near the center comes out clean. Cool for 10 minutes before removing from pans to wire racks to cool completely.

For frosting, combine egg yolks, milk, sugar and marshmallow creme in a saucepan. Cook and stir over medium heat until thickened, about 15 minutes. Remove from the heat; stir in vanilla and butter flavoring. Fold in coconut and pecans. Cool completely. Spread between layers and over top of cooled cake. **YIELD:** 16 SLICES.

Editor's Note: This recipe was tested with Smucker's Baking Healthy. Look for it in the baking aisle of your grocery store.

Nutrition Facts: One serving (1 slice) equals:
- 432 calories
- 14 g fat (4 g saturated fat)
- 94 mg cholesterol
- 233 mg sodium
- 73 g carbohydrate
- 1 g fiber
- 6 g protein

German Chocolate Torte

Double Chocolate Cupcakes

low fat

Linda Utter, Sidney, Montana

PREP: 20 MIN.   BAKE: 15 MIN. + COOLING

- 2 tablespoons butter, softened
- 3/4 cup sugar
- 1 egg
- 1 egg white
- 1/2 cup plus 2 tablespoons buttermilk
- 1/3 cup water
- 1 tablespoon white vinegar
- 1 teaspoon vanilla extract
- 1-1/2 cups all-purpose flour
- 1/4 cup baking cocoa
- 1 teaspoon baking soda
- 1/2 teaspoon salt
- 1/3 cup miniature semisweet chocolate chips

Double Chocolate Cupcakes

In a mixing bowl, cream butter and sugar. Add egg and egg white, one at a time, beating well after each addition. Beat on high speed until light and fluffy. Stir in buttermilk, water, vinegar and vanilla. Combine the flour, cocoa, baking soda and salt; add to batter just until moistened. Stir in chocolate chips.

Fill muffin cups coated with nonstick cooking spray three-fourths full. Bake at 375° for 15-18 minutes or until a toothpick comes out clean. Cool for 5 minutes before removing from pans to wire racks. **YIELD:** 14 CUPCAKES.

Nutrition Facts: One serving (1 cupcake) equals:

- 139 calories
- 2 g fat (1 g saturated fat)
- 1 mg cholesterol
- 221 mg sodium
- 29 g carbohydrate
- 1 g fiber
- 3 g protein

Diabetic Exchanges: 1-1/2 starch, 1/2 fat.

Nutty Chocolate Fudge `low sodium` `low carb`

A. J. Ristow, Tucson, Arizona

PREP: 25 MIN. + CHILLING

- 1 jar (7 ounces) marshmallow creme
- 2/3 cup fat-free evaporated milk
- 1/2 cup butter, cubed
- 2 teaspoons vanilla extract
- 3 cups (18 ounces) semisweet chocolate chips
- 2 cups chopped pecans *or* walnuts, toasted

Line a 9-in. square pan with foil and coat foil with nonstick cooking spray; set aside. In a large saucepan, combine the marshmallow creme, evaporated milk and butter. Cook and stir over medium heat until smooth. Bring to a boil; boil for 5 minutes, stirring constantly. Remove from the heat; add vanilla. Stir in chocolate chips until melted. Add pecans. Pour into prepared pan. Refrigerate for 2 hours or until firm.

Using foil, remove fudge from pan; carefully remove foil. Cut into 1-in. squares. Store in the refrigerator. **YIELD:** 2-2/3 POUNDS (81 PIECES).

Nutrition Facts: One serving (1 piece) equals:

- 70 calories
- 5 g fat (2 g saturated fat)
- 3 mg cholesterol
- 16 mg sodium
- 7 g carbohydrate
- 1 g fiber
- 1 g protein

Diabetic Exchanges: 1 fat, 1/2 starch.

Nutty Chocolate Fudge

Fresh Strawberry Pie

No-Fuss Rice Pudding

Sheila Wilde, Welling, Alberta

PREP: 20 MIN. + STANDING

- 1 cup cooked rice
- 1 egg white
- 1 cup fat-free milk
- 1/4 cup sugar
- 1/4 cup golden raisins
- Dash ground cinnamon
- Dash ground nutmeg

In a small microwave-safe bowl, combine rice and egg white. Stir in the milk, sugar and raisins. Microwave, uncovered, on high for 2 minutes; stir. Microwave at 50% power for 9 minutes, stirring every 2 minutes. Sprinkle with cinnamon and nutmeg. Cover and let stand for 15 minutes. **YIELD:** 2 SERVINGS.

Nutrition Facts: One serving (3/4 cup) equals:
- 306 calories
- trace fat (trace saturated fat)
- 3 mg cholesterol
- 99 mg sodium
- 68 g carbohydrate
- 2 g fiber
- 9 g protein

Fresh Strawberry Pie

Judy Watson, Newmarket, Ontario

PREP: 10 MIN. **COOK** 5 MIN. + COOLING

- 3 pints plus 1 cup fresh strawberries
- 1 pastry shell (9 inches), baked
- 2/3 cup sugar
- 1/2 cup water
- 2 tablespoons cornstarch

- 2 tablespoons cold water
- 2 to 3 drops red food coloring, optional
- 8 tablespoons reduced-fat whipped topping

Set aside 1 cup strawberries. Arrange remaining berries in pastry shell. With a fork, mash reserved 1 cup strawberries; set aside.

In a saucepan, combine sugar and water; cook and stir until sugar is dissolved. Add mashed strawberries and bring to a boil. Combine cornstarch and cold water until smooth. Gradually stir into strawberry mixture. Bring to a boil; cook and stir for 2 minutes or until thickened. Stir in food coloring if desired.

Cool for 15-20 minutes, stirring occasionally. Spoon over strawberries in crust. Refrigerate for at least 2 hours. Garnish with whipped topping. **YIELD:** 8 SERVINGS.

Nutrition Facts: One serving (1 piece) equals:
- 234 calories
- 8 g fat (4 g saturated fat)
- 5 mg cholesterol
- 101 mg sodium
- 40 g carbohydrate
- 3 g fiber
- 2 g protein

Diabetic Exchanges: 1-1/2 fruit, 1-1/2 fat, 1 starch.

Rhubarb Shortcake Dessert

Carol Jean Gallagher, Ukarumpa, EHP

PREP: 30 MIN. **BAKE:** 1 HOUR + COOLING

- 1-1/2 cups all-purpose flour
- 2 tablespoons sugar
- 1/2 cup cold butter

FILLING:
- 3 egg yolks
- 1/4 cup reduced-sugar orange marmalade
- 1-1/4 cups sugar
- 1/3 cup all-purpose flour
- 1/4 teaspoon salt
- 5 cups chopped fresh *or* frozen rhubarb, thawed
- 1 cup 2% milk
- 1 tablespoon grated orange peel

MERINGUE:
- 6 egg whites
- 2 teaspoons vanilla extract
- 1/4 teaspoon cream of tartar
- 3/4 cup sugar
- 1 tablespoon finely chopped walnuts

Combine flour and sugar; cut in butter until crumbly. Press into a 13-in. x 9-in. x 2-in. baking dish. Bake at 350° for 10-15 minutes or until lightly browned. Cool.

In a mixing bowl, beat egg yolks and orange marmalade; add sugar, flour and salt. Stir in the rhubarb, milk and orange peel; pour over crust. Bake at 350° for 35-40 minutes or until a knife inserted near the center comes out clean.

In a large mixing bowl, beat the egg whites, vanilla and cream of tartar on medium speed until soft peaks form. Gradually beat in the sugar, 1 tablespoon at a time, until stiff peaks form. Immediately spread over hot filling, sealing edges; sprinkle with nuts. Bake 12-15 minutes longer or until lightly browned. Cool for at least 1 hour before serving. Refrigerate leftovers. **YIELD:** 12 SERVINGS.

Editor's Note: If using frozen rhubarb, measure rhubarb while still frozen, then thaw completely. Drain in a colander, but do not press out liquid.

Nutrition Facts: One serving (1 piece) equals:
- 332 calories
- 10 g fat (5 g saturated fat)
- 75 mg cholesterol
- 168 mg sodium
- 56 g carbohydrate
- 2 g fiber
- 6 g protein

Miracle Baklava

Sue Klima, Northlake, Illinois

PREP: 1 HOUR 25 MIN. **BAKE:** 40 MIN.

- 1 package (12 ounces) vanilla wafers, crushed
- 2 tablespoons sugar
- 1 teaspoon ground cinnamon
- Refrigerated butter-flavored spray (about 4 ounces)
- 1 package frozen phyllo dough (14-inch x 9-inch sheet size), thawed

SYRUP:
- 1 cup sugar
- 1 cup water
- 1/2 cup honey

Rhubarb Shortcake Dessert

Miracle Baklava

- 1 teaspoon grated lemon peel
- 1 teaspoon vanilla extract

In a large bowl, combine the wafer crumbs, sugar and cinnamon; set aside. Spritz a 13-in. x 9-in. x 2-in. baking pan with butter-flavored spray. Unroll phyllo sheets. Place one sheet of phyllo in pan; spritz with butter-flavored spray and brush to coat evenly. Repeat seven times, spritzing and brushing each layer. Keep remaining phyllo dough covered with plastic wrap to avoid drying out.

Sprinkle 1/4 cup crumb mixture over phyllo in pan. Layer with two sheets of phyllo, spritzing and brushing with butter-flavored spray between each. Sprinkle with 1/4 cup crumb mixture; repeat 11 times. Top with one phyllo sheet; spritz and brush with butter-flavored spray. Repeat seven more times, spritzing and brushing each layer.

Cut into 15 squares; cut each square in half diagonally. Bake at 350° for 40-45 minutes or until golden brown.

Meanwhile, in a saucepan, bring the sugar, water, honey and lemon peel to a boil. Reduce heat; simmer, uncovered, for 20 minutes. Remove from the heat; stir in vanilla. Cool to lukewarm. Pour syrup over warm baklava. **YIELD:** 30 SERVINGS.

Editor's Note: This recipe was tested with I Can't Believe It's Not Butter Spray.

Nutrition Facts: One serving (1 piece) equals:
- 154 calories
- 4 g fat (1 g saturated fat)
- 1 mg cholesterol
- 154 mg sodium
- 30 g carbohydrate
- 1 g fiber
- 2 g protein

Diabetic Exchange: 2 starch.

Mixed Berry Shortcake

until lightly browned. Cool on a wire rack.

Cut shortcake into 3/4-in. cubes. In parfait glasses, alternate layers of shortcake, custard, sliced strawberries and blueberries. Garnish with halved strawberries and a dollop of whipped topping. **YIELD:** 8 SERVINGS.

Nutrition Facts: One serving (1 parfait) equals:
382 calories
12 g fat (6 g saturated fat)
77 mg cholesterol
290 mg sodium
66 g carbohydrate
5 g fiber
6 g protein

Strawberries with Crisp Wontons

low sodium

Taste of Home Test Kitchen
Greendale, Wisconsin

PREP/TOTAL TIME: 20 MIN.

4 wonton wrappers
1 tablespoon butter, melted
2 tablespoons plus 1 teaspoon sugar, *divided*
2 pints fresh strawberries, sliced
2 cups reduced-fat whipped topping
1/8 teaspoon Chinese five-spice powder

Brush both sides of wonton wrappers with melted butter. Place 2 tablespoons sugar in a shallow dish; press wontons into sugar to coat both sides. Cut each wonton in half diagonally.

Place on a baking sheet coated with nonstick cooking spray. Bake at 425° for 4-5 minutes or until golden brown. Turn and bake 2 minutes longer or until golden brown. Remove to wire racks to cool.

Toss strawberries with remaining sugar. Combine the whipped topping and five-spice powder. Divide the strawberries among four plates. Top each with whipped topping and two wonton pieces. **YIELD:** 4 SERVINGS.

Nutrition Facts: One serving equals:
200 calories
8 g fat (6 g saturated fat)
8 mg cholesterol
77 mg sodium
30 g carbohydrate
3 g fiber
2 g protein

Diabetic Exchanges: 1-1/2 fat, 1 starch, 1 fruit.

Mixed Berry Shortcake

Taste of Home Test Kitchen
Greendale, Wisconsin

PREP: 25 MIN. **BAKE:** 15 MIN.

1/2 cup plus 1/3 cup sugar, *divided*
3 tablespoons cornstarch
2-3/4 cups fat-free milk
2 egg yolks, lightly beaten
1 teaspoon vanilla extract
2 cups all-purpose flour
1 teaspoon baking powder
1/4 teaspoon baking soda
1/4 teaspoon salt
6 tablespoons cold butter
2/3 cup buttermilk
4 cups sliced fresh strawberries
4 cups fresh blueberries
8 whole strawberries, halved
1/2 cup reduced-fat whipped topping

In a heavy saucepan, combine 1/2 cup sugar and cornstarch. Stir in milk until blended. Bring to a boil over medium-low heat; cook and stir for 1-2 minutes or until thickened. Remove from the heat. Stir a small amount into egg yolks; return all to the pan, stirring constantly. Remove from the heat; stir in vanilla. Transfer to a bowl; press a piece of plastic wrap on top of custard. Refrigerate.

In a bowl, combine the flour, baking powder, baking soda, salt and remaining sugar. Cut in butter until mixture resembles coarse crumbs. Stir in buttermilk until a soft dough forms. Pat gently into a 9-in. square baking pan coated with nonstick cooking spray. Bake at 400° for 15-20 minutes or

Caramel Fudge Brownies

Priscilla Renfrow, Wilson, North Carolina

PREP: 15 MIN. **BAKE:** 30 MIN.

4 squares (1 ounce *each*) unsweetened chocolate

3 egg whites, lightly beaten
1 cup sugar
2 jars (2-1/2 ounces *each*) prune baby food
1 teaspoon vanilla extract
1/2 teaspoon salt
1/2 cup all-purpose flour
1/4 cup chopped walnuts
6 tablespoons fat-free caramel ice cream topping
9 tablespoons reduced fat-whipped topping

In a microwave or saucepan, melt chocolate; stir until smooth. In a bowl, combine the egg whites, sugar, melted chocolate, prunes, vanilla and salt; mix well. Stir in flour until just moistened.

Pour into an 8-in. square baking pan coated with nonstick cooking spray. Sprinkle with walnuts. Bake at 350° for 30-32 minutes or until the top springs back when lightly touched. Cool on a wire rack. Cut into squares; drizzle with caramel topping and dollop with whipped topping. **YIELD:** 9 SERVINGS.

Nutrition Facts: One serving (1 piece) equals:
251 calories
10 g fat (5 g saturated fat)
0 cholesterol
170 mg sodium
42 g carbohydrate
3 g fiber
4 g protein

Diabetic Exchanges: 2 starch, 2 fat, 1/2 fruit.

Raspberry Custard Tart

low sodium

Taste of Home Test Kitchen
Greendale, Wisconsin

PREP: 25 MIN. **COOK:** 15 MIN. + CHILLING

3 tablespoons reduced-fat butter
1/2 cup sugar
3/4 cup all-purpose flour

Caramel Fudge Brownies

Raspberry Custard Tart

1/4 cup finely chopped pecans, toasted
FILLING:
1/3 cup sugar
1/4 cup all-purpose flour
2-1/4 cups fat-free milk
1 egg yolk
1/4 teaspoon almond extract
1 jar (12 ounces) 100% seedless raspberry spreadable fruit
1-1/2 cups fresh raspberries

In a small mixing bowl, beat butter and sugar for 2 minutes or until crumbly. Beat in flour and nuts. Coat a 9-in. fluted tart pan with removable bottom with nonstick cooking spray. Press crumb mixture onto the bottom and up the sides of pan. Bake at 425° for 8-10 minutes or until lightly browned. Cool on a wire rack.

In a small saucepan, combine sugar and flour. Stir in milk until smooth. Cook and stir over medium-high heat until thickened and bubbly. Reduce heat; cook and stir 2 minutes longer. Remove from the heat. Stir a small amount of hot filling into egg yolk; return all to the pan, stirring constantly. Bring to a gentle boil; cook and stir 2 minutes longer. Remove from the heat; gently stir in extract. Pour over crust. Refrigerate until set.

In a small bowl, whisk fruit spread until smooth; spread over filling. Garnish with raspberries. **YIELD:** 12 SERVINGS.

Editor's Note: This recipe was tested with Land O' Lakes light stick butter.

Nutrition Facts: One serving (1 piece) equals:
210 calories
4 g fat (1 g saturated fat)
24 mg cholesterol
42 mg sodium
41 g carbohydrate
2 g fiber
3 g protein

Diabetic Exchanges: 1-1/2 starch, 1 fruit, 1/2 fat.

Chocolate Souffles

Chocolate Souffles

Jeannette Mango, Parkesburg, Pennsylvania

PREP: 30 MIN. + STANDING **BAKE:** 25 MIN.

low sodium

7 teaspoons plus 2/3 cup sugar, *divided*
1/2 cup packed brown sugar
1/3 cup cake flour
1/2 cup baking cocoa
2 teaspoons instant coffee granules
3/4 cup water
4 squares (1 ounce *each*) semisweet chocolate
3 egg yolks, beaten
6 egg whites
1/2 teaspoon cream of tartar
1 teaspoon confectioners' sugar

Spray seven 10-oz. souffle dishes with nonstick cooking spray. Sprinkle 1 teaspoon of sugar into each dish, tilting to coat the bottom and sides; set aside.

In a saucepan, combine 1/3 cup sugar, brown sugar, flour, cocoa and coffee granules. Stir in water until blended. Bring to a boil; cook and stir for 1 minute (mixture will be thick). Remove from the heat. Stir in chocolate until melted. Stir a small amount of hot filling into egg yolks; return all to the pan, stirring constantly. Cool to room temperature.

Let egg whites stand at room temperature for 30 minutes. In a mixing bowl, beat egg whites until foamy. Add cream of tartar; beat on medium speed until soft peaks form. Gradually add remaining sugar, 1 tablespoon at a time, beating on high until stiff peaks form. Gently fold a fourth of the egg white mixture into chocolate mixture; fold in remaining egg white mixture.

Spoon batter into prepared dishes. Bake at 325° for 25-35 minutes or until a toothpick inserted near the center comes out clean. Cool on wire racks. Dust with confectioners' sugar. Refrigerate leftovers. **YIELD:** 7 SERVINGS.

Nutrition Facts: One serving (1 souffle) equals:
313 calories
8 g fat (4 g saturated fat)
91 mg cholesterol
57 mg sodium
58 g carbohydrate
5 g fiber
7 g protein

Blackberry Frozen Yogurt

low fat *low sodium*

Rebecca Baird, Salt Lake City, Utah

PREP: 30 MIN. + FREEZING

5 cups fresh *or* frozen blackberries
1/3 cup water
2 tablespoons lemon juice
1 cup sugar
2 teaspoons vanilla extract
4 cups (32 ounces) fat-free frozen vanilla yogurt

In a food processor or blender, puree blackberries, water and lemon juice. Strain blackberries, reserving juice and pulp. Discard seeds. Return pureed blackberries to food processor; add sugar and vanilla. Cover and process until smooth.

In a bowl, combine yogurt and blackberry mixture; mix well. Freeze in an ice cream freezer according to manufacturer's instructions. Allow to ripen in ice cream freezer or firm up in your refrigerator freezer 2-4 hours before serving. **YIELD:** 8 SERVINGS.

Nutrition Facts: One serving (3/4 cup) equals:
248 calories
1 g fat (trace saturated fat)
2 mg cholesterol
78 mg sodium
57 g carbohydrate
5 g fiber
6 g protein

Banana Chocolate Cake

Taste of Home Test Kitchen
Greendale, Wisconsin

PREP: 15 MIN. **BAKE:** 25 MIN. + COOLING

Sugar substitute equivalent to 3/4 cup sugar
1/3 cup packed brown sugar
1/3 cup butter, softened
2 eggs
2 teaspoons vanilla extract
2 medium ripe bananas, mashed
1/2 cup water
1-1/3 cups all-purpose flour
1/2 cup nonfat dry milk powder
3 tablespoons baking cocoa
1 teaspoon baking powder
1/2 teaspoon baking soda
1/2 teaspoon salt
3/4 teaspoon confectioners' sugar

In a large mixing bowl, beat the sugar substitute, brown sugar and butter on medium speed for 3 minutes. Add eggs and vanilla; mix well. Add bananas and water; mix well. Combine the flour, milk powder, cocoa, baking powder, baking soda and salt; add to sugar mixture, beating just until blended.

Pour into a 9-in. square baking pan coated with nonstick cooking spray. Bake at 375° for 23-28 minutes or until a toothpick inserted near the center comes out clean and edges of cake are just starting to pull away from sides of pan. Cool on a wire rack. Dust with confectioners' sugar. **YIELD:** 12 SERVINGS.

Editor's Note: This recipe was tested with Splenda No Calorie Sweetener.

Nutrition Facts: One serving (1 piece) equals:
> 179 calories
> 6 g fat (3 g saturated fat)
> 50 mg cholesterol
> 276 mg sodium
> 26 g carbohydrate
> 1 g fiber
> 5 g protein

Diabetic Exchanges: 1-1/2 starch, 1 fat.

Crunchy Macaroons `low fat` `low sodium` `low carb`

Taste of Home Test Kitchen
Greendale, Wisconsin

PREP: 15 MIN. **BAKE:** 20 MIN.

1-1/2 cups crisp rice cereal
1-1/4 cups flaked coconut
2 egg whites
3 tablespoons sugar
1/8 teaspoon almond extract

In a small bowl, combine all ingredients. With damp fingers, shape into 1-1/2-in. mounds on parchment paper-lined baking sheets. Bake at 300° for 20-25 minutes or until edges are lightly browned. Remove from pans to wire racks to cool. **YIELD:** 2 DOZEN.

Nutrition Facts: One serving (2 cookies) equals:
> 76 calories
> 3 g fat (3 g saturated fat)
> 0 cholesterol
> 66 mg sodium
> 11 g carbohydrate
> trace fiber
> 1 g protein

Diabetic Exchanges: 1 fat, 1/2 starch.

Crunchy Macaroons

Guilt-Free Chocolate Cake

Guilt-Free Chocolate Cake `low fat`

Brenda Ruse, Truro, Nova Scotia

PREP: 10 MIN. **BAKE:** 35 MIN. + COOLING

1 package (18-1/4 ounces) devil's food cake mix
1/2 cup baking cocoa
2 egg whites
1 egg
1-1/3 cups water
1 cup reduced-fat plain yogurt
1-1/2 teaspoons confectioners' sugar

In a large mixing bowl, combine cake mix and cocoa. Combine the egg whites, egg, water and yogurt; add to dry ingredients and beat well. Pour into a 10-cup fluted tube pan coated with nonstick cooking spray.

Bake at 350° for 35-40 minutes or until a toothpick inserted near the center comes out clean. Cool for 10 minutes before removing from pan to a wire rack to cool completely. Sprinkle with confectioners' sugar. **YIELD:** 12 SERVINGS.

Nutrition Facts: One serving (1 piece) equals:
> 191 calories
> 3 g fat (1 g saturated fat)
> 19 mg cholesterol
> 399 mg sodium
> 40 g carbohydrate
> 2 g fiber
> 5 g protein

Diabetic Exchange: 2-1/2 starch.

Health Categories Index

Food Categories Index

Alphabetical Index